Druids, Celts, and Romans

The Founders of Europe

A Narrative History

by

James Francis Smith

Text copyright @ 2004 by James F. Smith
Illustrations copyright @ 2004 by Sean Judy

The printed Book with eight illustrations by Sean Judy entitled, "Celtic Invasion of Rome" is available through Xlibris.com.

All rights reserved. No part of this book may be reproduced or transmitted in any form or by any means, electronic or mechanical, including photocopying, recording, or by any information storage and retrieval system, without permission in writing from copyright owner.

This is a work of fiction. Names, characters, places and incidents either are the product of the author's imagination or are used fictitiously and any resemblance to any actual persons living or dead, events, or locales is entirely coincidental.

Dedication

I wish to thank my wife Betty for putting up with my moods and listening to the many conversations about the book that quickly became old with the telling. I am most grateful to my children Joseph and Mary Eileen who read, edited and offered refreshing advice to improve the quality of my tale. I am indebted to the very talented Sean Judy for the intricate detail of his illustrations. Special thanks go to Emil Mihelich and my sister, Ann Jahn, for their early on editing advice. I am furthermore beholden to Patrick Russell, Val Dumond, Donna Andersen and the Tacoma Writer's Roundtable for their candor, assistance and encouragement and my gratitude to John O'Brien for his last-minute corrections of my typing. My eternal gratitude goes to John Herold, computer specialist extraordinaire.

Chapter	Contents	Page #
	Author's Comments	5
	Characters	6
	Illustrations	7 - 10
1	Druids' Meeting	11
2	Conel's Vision	27
3	The Bard of Parisii	43
4	The Bonding of the Trio	58
5	The Druid School	66
6	Community Life	82
7	Munli's Prophecy	96
8	The Priming of a Warrior	106
9	The Arrival of Julia	121
10	Beltain Feast	133
11	Intrusion by the German	138
12	The Return of the Mercenary	148
13	Arrival of the Bard	159
14	Crossing the Alps	173
15	The Druid Priesthood	188
16	The Po Valley	200
17	All Roads Lead to Rome	213
18	The Betrayal	225
19	Retribution	243
20	Blood for Blood	258
21	A Slave in Rome	270
22	Etruscan Encounter	286
23	Roman Army Defeated	301
24	The Invasion of Rome	319
25	The Aftermath	334

Celts-The Founders of Europe.

Before the dawn of written history, horsemen from the steppes of Russia swept across the European continent. Following their adherence to Druid laws and their conversion by priests from the British Isles, the Celts overran a swath of Europe from the British Isles southeast to Turkey, which they ruled for a thousand years. In addition to bringing the horse and iron to the continent, the Celts invented steel, the spoke wheel with its iron tire, the iron plow, rotation of crops, the wheeled harvester, and fertilizer—all of which enabled European nomads to settle in communities. Many European cities were originally Celtic settlements, including London, Paris, Budapest, and Milan.

In 387 BCE, they crossed the Alps, defeated the Roman Army, and invaded the eternal city. This epic battle dramatically changed the course of history.

Many historians advocate that the Druids and Celts originated in Asia, and came to Europe joined at the hip. This author, however, believes that about 1,200 BCE, Celts from Asia formed as a people in Germany's Hartz Mountains. They originated in the British Islands, and crossed over to the continent, where they converted the Celts to their beliefs. Furthermore, his research indicates that the Druid religion evolved from the beliefs of those who built Ireland's passage graves, Stonehenge, et al.

The future is unknown, and the past can't be changed. However, one wonders how civilization would look if the Romans and Greeks had treated women with the deference the Celts showed them as leaders and warriors

Fictional Characters

    Munli – Master Druid of the Helvetii Tribe
    Conel – Chief of the Mayri Clan
    Meva – Wife of Conel
    Mick, Una, & Hugh – Triples born to Conel & Meva
    Ragenos – Conel's brother-in-law and Champion of the Mayri
    Danous – Bard of Parisii Tribe
    Tomas – Brother of Danous
    Turk – Trader for the Mayri Tribe
    Lucius – Roman Senator
    Vopiscus – Father of Julia
    Julia – Granddaughter of Lucius

Historical characters:

    Vercingetorix – General who led Celtic army in Gaul (France)
    Gaius Julius Caesar – Roman Emperor and invader of Gaul
    Lucius Cassius – Roman consul
    Drappes & Lucterius – Celtic generals
    Divico – Celtic chieftain
    Vulcan – Etruscan sculptor
    Arruns and Lucomo – Etruscan rivals
    Quintus and Ambustus Fabius – members of the Fabii family
    Elico – Celtic metalsmith in Rome
    Marcus Furius – Conqueror of the Etruscan city of Veii
    Quintus Sulpicious – Roman general
    Dhulack – Celtic chieftain of the Boii tribe
    Marcus Manlius – Defender of Rome's Capitoline Hill
    Cominus Pontius – Roman tribune

Druids, Celts, and Romans

Oppidum – Celtic Hillfort

Celtic Warriors with Spoke Wheel

Furthest expansion of Celtic influence

Warrior Neck Torque

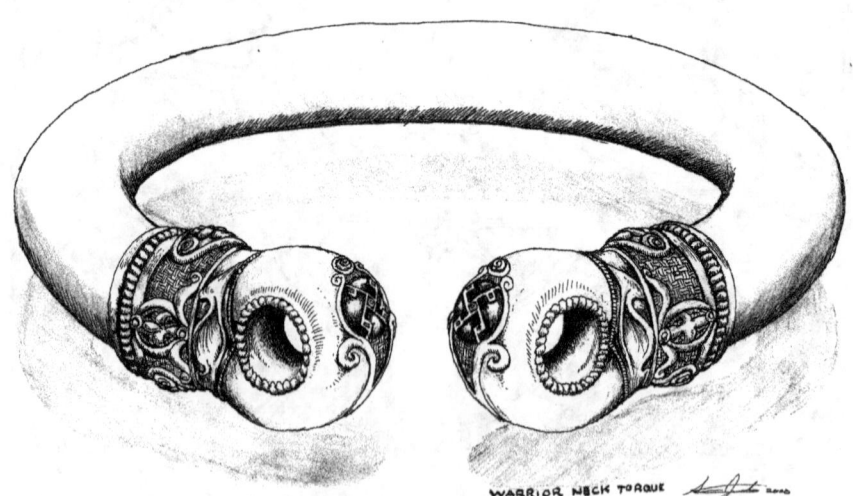

Druids, Celts, and Romans

Stonehenge 1800BCE

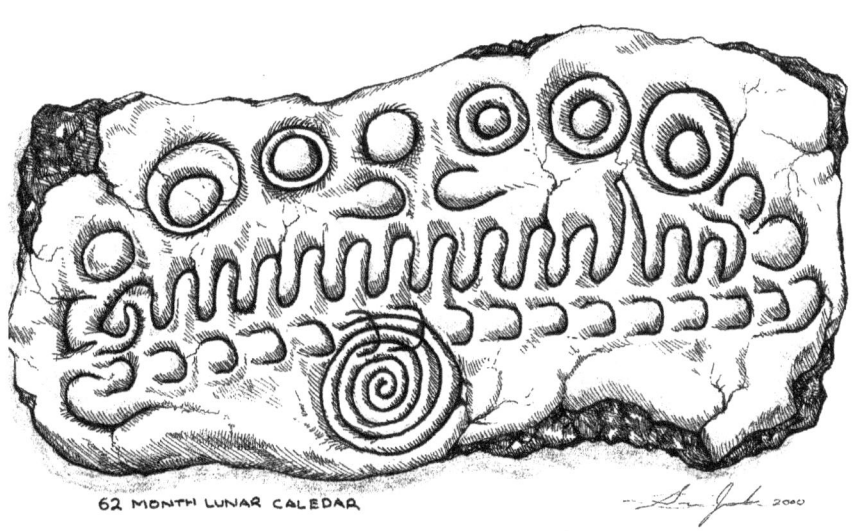

Lunar Calendar – Knowth, Ireland 3200BCE

Celtic Calendar, Coligny, France
100BCE

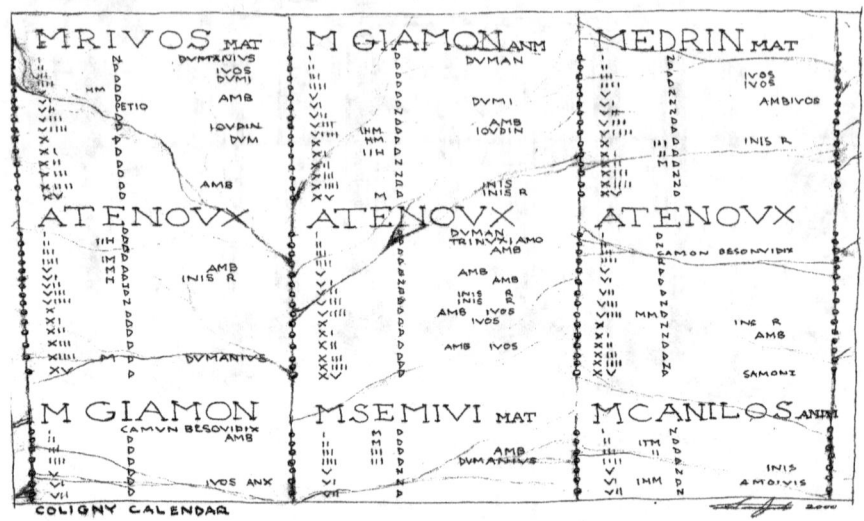

Passage Grave – New Grange, Ireland

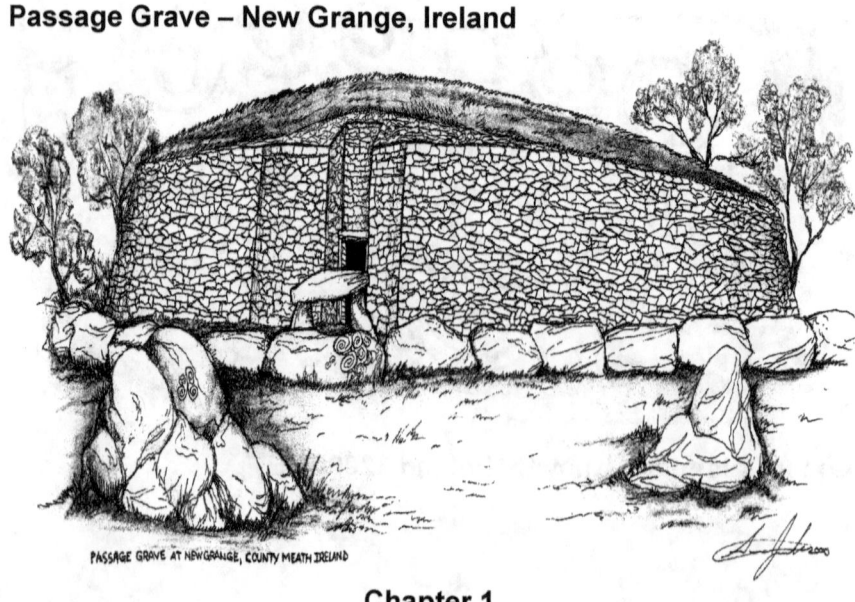

Chapter 1

Druids' Meeting

Helvetia (modern day Switzerland) circa 415 BC
For their final meeting, the brothers-in-law, Conel and Ragenos, arrived together. By the look on their faces, Master Druid Munli could tell the two intended to reject his request. He could not fault them if they did, but he had no alternative. He had to convince them to play their role. The greeting of old friends was cool, which made the hut seem colder yet. Munli stood and hugged each in turn, neither of whom returned the gesture with any warmth. Then he took their hands and bid them form a circle of three. Bowing his head, he intoned the blessing of the Goddess Sulis.

"May the patroness of our clan look down on us and bless the acts that must be done, no matter how evil they may seem."

Munli cinched up his trousers; and Conel twisted his mustache, while both watched Ragenos pound his meaty fist on the table and shout, "I won't do it!"

Reaching up and patting his tall friend on the shoulder, Munli begged him to listen, "I am not asking you to murder him outright. I am only asking you to be prepared to save my life. For if I were to die before completing my sacred charge, untold atrocities will most certainly occur. Take action only if you see, with your own eyes, that I am in mortal danger. That is all I ask."

"I won't do it," Ragenos repeated when the circle parted. He banged his massive fist on the table once more, this time making it jump. "I just won't do it! I can't imagine any circumstance where I would kill a Druid, especially in a nemeton, a sacred grove. It would be sacrilege and blasphemy."

Munli kept his silence for what seemed like an eternity, letting some of the tension dissipate; making sure his friend was prepared to hear what he had to say. Finally, he replied in a quiet voice forcing Ragenos to draw closer. "Ragenos, we have known each other since we were children. You and Conel are the most honorable men that I know. I would never ask you to do anything treacherous. I have knowledge, however, that shocking and horrible events are about to overtake the Celtic people. I cling to the hope that with your assistance, I can influence these future events that are only written in the stars and not yet cast into runes."

Standing off to one side, Conel maintained his poise and observed his short stocky friend. 'He's lost weight and his sense of humor,' the chief of the Mayri clan decided as he watched the Master Druid tighten his loose fitting trousers. 'Even though Munli has often gotten the three of us in trouble, he has never requested us to break a sacred law. Therefore, something of vital importance must be troubling him for he has never before asked a favor without an explanation.' "Why would you be in mortal danger from another Druid? Isn't it a grievous offense to kill anything on hallowed ground ... let alone a priest?" Conel asked, entering the conversation for the first time.

"Why would this Evos even consider trying to kill you?" Ragenos burst in before Munli could respond to Conel. "Is he evil?"

"I wouldn't categorize him as evil. He is hurtfully ambitious, which means he would put his prestige before the fate of the Celts. Even now, he plots against me, and such selfish acts would undermine our people's only hope. There will come a time when our very existence will be severely tested. If Evos were to prevail and become Master Druid, our people would perish. How I know this, I cannot reveal at this moment. I would confide in you if I could. Nothing in my life prepared me for the evil that I now face. Trust me!" he implored. "I am your friend, and I am in need. I will pray for your souls for the rest of eternity. The stakes are so great that I cannot bring myself to reveal them. You must do as I ask. I am your friend, and I am in need. Nay, our people are in need."

The session ended with seemingly little progress. As the Master Druid watched the broad backs of his friends exit, anxiety wracked his frame. Images and sounds from a session he tried to bury in his subconscious whirled past. His legs turned to jelly, and he gripped the table for support, as heart palpitations competed with gasping breaths while bowels weakened. He closed his eyes and willed the tightness in his chest to fade, the strength in his arms to return. Only then did he recall the parting words of the Goddess Sulis:

Triplets with exceptional talents to save the Celtic race will be born to a clan of your choosing. You, and you alone, must determine the clan, any deviation will forfeit my assurance of your people's survival. To seal this bargain, you, Druid Munli, must forsake any claim to save your soul.

With these words etched in his memory, Munli fainted. Awakening after the spell subsided, he prayed to the Goddess Sulis to make Ragenos agreeable to carry out the mission.

Meanwhile, the brothers-in-law rode home in silence, each dwelling on the request to violate all they considered holy. Agreeing to such a request would stain their immortal souls and perhaps doom them to be earthbound for all eternity—the fate a Celtic warrior considered worse than death.

Munli, alone in his small enclosure, could confide in no one. He had thought of bringing Conel into his confidence, but the timing was not yet right. First he needed to silence the revolt growing insidiously within the ranks of the very Druids of whom he was master. Much of his planning dealt with winning over his brother priests. The most envious and dangerous among his fellow Druids was his arch-rival, Evos. Munli grimaced, as he imagined the chaos his antagonist would spawn, 'Gaunt Evos, with his perpetual frown and his craving to be revered, could eradicate the priesthood all by himself. May the gods help us if he ever became the Master Druid.'

Finally after weeks of depression, followed by periods of resentment and spells of self-incrimination, Munli assumed the quiet desperation of a person on a mission doomed from the beginning. The loneliness and futility of the task dramatically changed his normally pleasant personality. Often when looking in his small bronze mirror, he wondered what ever became of that youthful scoundrel that used to smile back.

Sensing his anger, few entered his presence unbidden, and then rarely interrupted his thoughts even when asked. All who knew the rotund master watched as he wasted away. But none could assist because he refused to allow others to tend to him. Although he had not seen his rival for a considerable period of time, Munli knew that Evos, in particular, spread rumors of his impending demise. "Have you seen the condition of poor Munli?" he would ask of all he met. "I think it would be wise to plan for his replacement before we are caught unawares." As the word of Munli's deteriorating condition spread among the small Alpine Druid community associated with the Helvetii tribe, many of his enemies schemed to replace him. Ignoring the tempest that swirled around him, Munli prayed vigorously to his patroness, the Goddess Sulis, while he worked to achieve his initial goal of eliminating Evos. This would buy time to attain his unrevealed objective. Alone with his burden, Munli put his final design into place. He chose a location where the terrain enabled him to employ the deadly skills of his boyhood chum, Ragenos. He continued planning, knowing that if Ragenos did not play a role, the plan would fail. He believed, however, that Ragenos' natural curiosity would compel him to be present. And if present, his lifelong friendship would override any trepidation. Secondly, he devised a way to distract the attending Druids and to make certain that they could never learn of his objective. Each piece of the puzzle was meticulously thought-out and diligently carried through.

Shrine of the Goddess Sulis
The moment to depart for the assembly arrived. Munli was anxious, but as usual his fear diminished as the time for action drew near. Being from a minor clan, he had to surmount major obstacles to obtain his office. Lacking the physical stature of some colleagues and the silver tongue of others, he made up in intellect what he lacked in size.

As though mirroring his foul mood, a cold rain had saturated the earth. To confront the weather, Munli dressed in the woolen cloak of an ordinary traveler. He packed his gold-embroidered ceremonial cloak in lanolin-coated leather to prevent it from being soiled by the rain and the mud. In addition, he brought a gold neck torque to match his golden ear clasps. He would wear these adornments to impress the eminent gathering and to remind them that he was the master. His sinister plan would succeed only if he maintained an iron grip on the proceedings.

Ordinarily Munli arrived at tribal meetings on horseback as a sign of his high office, but these times were not ordinary times; therefore, the horses were tethered just inside the entrance to the dark forest. The threesome continued their trek on foot. Shortly after entering the woods, he bade his acolytes to immediately make camp under the protective branches of a giant evergreen. He placed a blanket on the soggy soil and built a small fire to brew water and herbs. "It will warm us while we wait for another," he said.

The noise of someone approaching warned the three, and they looked up as a fourth member joined the group. The acolytes gasped with astonishment when they recognized the vocation of the new arrival. Age lines crisscrossed his weather-beaten brow, and sunspots covered his withered hands. A wolf-skin framed the old man's haggard face with the soggy snout covering his forehead, giving him a look of demonic depravity. The two young assistants were terrified, but they dared not object to his presence for their master welcomed him and invited him to partake of the steaming brew.

"Is that the strongest you offer?" asked the new arrival in a menacing tone.

"That is the strongest drink you will imbibe until you have completed your mission," the master replied in a steely voice. Grunting in reply, the stranger accepted the mug that Munli offered. As soon as the newcomer had finished, the master stood and kicked dirt to extinguish the fire.

Munli lifted his pack and immediately departed the impromptu camp. His companions, who had no voice in any of the decisions that had been made, plodded along behind their leader through the muck of the forest trail. The stranger surprisingly kept pace at the end of the line. At times the mud covered their leather boots and sucked one foot down as they struggled to lift the other. The coolness of the night, augmented by the moisture-burdened leaves, chilled the party to the bone, as they made their way over the ridges of the dark and foreboding woodland that protected the Sulis grotto. Their leader held each branch to prevent the wet tree boughs from swinging into those following, but the water sprayed on them, nonetheless. Fortunately though sopping wet, their woolen cloaks retained their body heat to keep them alive.

All four travelers knew that only those who transact business with the gods would be in this holy place as the dark period of the year approached. Tonight even the wild animals seemed to take their leave. As he walked in the unearthly silence, Munli sensed the fear radiating from his companions. He sympathized, because he understood that even Druids could be terrified on a night like this. Munli, familiar with this forest since boyhood, more easily navigated the concealed trail than did his three companions, who tripped and slid as they followed in his wake. He purposely chose to avoid the more manageable main trail, because he did not wish to accidentally encounter any of the other attendees.

Munli's bone-weary acolytes blindly followed his lead, but neither ventured even a glance at the fourth member of their party. The two young assistants and the uncomfortable stranger held Munli's tracking skills in awe, and, typical of his calling, Munli did nothing to discourage this respect. During the past lunar month, this tracking ability had paid dividends when he met clandestinely with his friends, Conel and Ragenos.

The pungent smell of the familiar forest brought back memories of his boyhood, when he and his friends wandered these paths with impunity. On occasion, he and Conel had shared the thrill of spying on Druid ceremonies. Munli thought that one such occurrence may have been the root-cause of his calling to the priesthood. "The gods got their revenge for our youthful follies," he muttered as he smiled.

His thoughts returned to the forthcoming proceedings, the first in his role as Master Druid. The weight of his foreboding rode heavily in his stomach. Munli was particularly fretting about the Druids' reaction to the stranger, especially when they realized he was a Vate—a member of a sect that foretells the future from animal livers and entrails. Munli knew that conventional Druids, well versed in astronomy and astrology, relied on the stars to divine the influences of the gods on human affairs. In their minds, Vateism is superstition tainted by the evils of the otherworld.

Munli's plan involved the use of the number three and its multiples because of its magical significance among the Celts. To take advantage of this belief, the master had set the number of attendees at twenty-seven, the nine fold multiple of three. A gathering of such an auspicious number signifies a conclave of grave importance. As his fellow Druids counted the number in attendance, which he expected each to do, they would immediately realize the gravity of the event. Munli had invited by name those he wished to attend. He ordered each invitee to come alone without servants or assistants. Such a command would not sit lightly with the pampered priests, particularly with those who had reason to be suspicious. Smiling to himself, he wondered about Evos' response when he received the order. 'Was it fright or contempt?'

Stumbling through the wet underbrush, Munli continued reflecting upon his strategy. After deciding on the invitees, he had selected the meeting site with the utmost care, a sacred grove in which he was most comfortable. This nemeton, dedicated to the Goddess Sulis, was protected by the Mayri, the smallest clan in Alpine Helvetia but one of the most revered. The Mayri grotto contained the source of the cool spring water considered holy by Sulis, the goddess of fertility and dispenser of healing powers. In selecting this site, Munli signaled that he had the backing of this sympathetic deity. While his waterlogged traveling cloak slowed his progress, he silently prayed that his patroness would reward him with her favor and continued support. As the party slogged ahead, Munli envisioned the translucent water, bubbling from the earth that would bless the forthcoming event. The thought of the holy water brought to his mind another duty that he needed to perform. He decided that a blessing by water from the Sulis' spring would help to remove the guilt that his two friends would bear.

Munli silently brought his exhausted, shivering party to a halt on the lee side of the hill overlooking the sacred nemeton. Knowing that the warmth of the peat fire would hold the attention of the drenched priests, Munli cautioned his party to silence. He opened his pack and unraveled his gold embroidered cloak and dressed for the ceremony. After he was fully attired and had shown his traveling companions their positions, Munli strode past the tree line into the midst of the congregation. Obeying Munli's instructions, the Vate remained in the shadows just beyond the glow cast by the fire.

Recognizing the assembly's surprise, Munli knew he had gained the initial advantage by his unheralded appearance. Acknowledging warm nods from some and ignoring scowls from others, Munli assumed the position of honor. When he was seated on the platform reserved for the master, in an ancient language known only to ordained Druids, the haunting opening chant of the priesthood filled the raw night air:

Oh, God of the oak tree, we gather before you. Beseech your blessings, and promise our trust. We hold the lifeline of the Celts in our hands to protect the most ancient of lands. Join with us, as we worship, and counsel among us to preserve our priesthood, and all we hold dear.

Then, as if on cue, the night clouds dissipated, stars appeared, and most importantly, the rain ceased. Because of his forethought, Munli was the only one present wearing dry clothes. Though the others were soaked to the skin, excitement increased at the sight of the full moon. The fact that the meeting would finally begin generated a mixture of relief and anticipation. Evos, convinced that Munli had to resign as Master Druid, could hardly conceal his mirth. Most of those assembled shared Evos' opinion, though only his supporters shared his glee.

Spreading his arms, Munli called for silence, and remained motionless until he had gained their full attention. Finally, the master spoke. In a strong steady voice, he welcomed his fellow Druids to the Sulis grotto as though they were his equals. With a smile, he chided a Druid known for his preference of dry climate. "Hanalos, why didn't you bargain for better weather?" Munli asked, bringing forth a burst of laughter breaking the tension.

"Perhaps this may not be as ominous as I had thought," each murmured. Friend and foe alike waited for the master to make the fateful announcement about vacating his position. All took it to be a certainty, just as Evos had expected.

Now that Munli had managed to calm the assembled priests, he began his opening oration. "Druids of the first order, I welcome you to the grotto of Sulis. As a child, I dipped my hand in these blessed waters and asked for a sibling. The goddess never answered my hopeful, innocent plea, but I remained faithful. I ask you, the holders of the Celtic trust, to remain faithful despite what I am about to disclose. Over the past few months, I encountered many strange omens, which collectively have taken a toll on my health. I will describe these in some detail. But first, I must divulge the importance of these warnings to the future of our people." Curiosity beseeched attentiveness, and all remained silent.

Munli continued, "Already we Celts have expanded across this great landmass to the vast ocean in the west. Our people have settled along the great river we call the Danube, and we dominate the lands on both banks to its delta at the Black Sea, far to the east." Still believing the oratory was a build-up to his announcement that he would step aside, none stirred.

When he had captured the attention of his congregation, Munli withdrew a small vial from a secret pocket. Using sleight of hand to conceal his action, he cast the mixture of liquid tar and hallucinogenic herbs into the dying embers of the peat fire. The flame exploded and roared to life. Startled, the audience sensing that a declaration of great import was imminent sat in respectful silence. The long anticipated resignation, however, never came.

Instead, Munli averted the issue and changed the subject by turning their attention toward the German tribes held at bay on the northeast frontiers. All recognized and agreed with the potential danger. None of the assembled priests believed, however, that a horde of savages could match the might of the Celts. Then without preamble, he plunged into the topic he had been avoiding. Munli described how he was sucked into a dark abyss, where he stood alone as a representative of his people and faced the anger of the gods—a resentment which if left unappeased would lead to the destruction of the Celtic Empire. After rendering an account of the contrary reaction of each god present, he portrayed how only Sulis stood steadfast in her defense of the Celts and their Druid leaders.

Before the master finished relating his experience, a voice shouted, "Liar, liar." Thus, screamed Evos, a habitual user of the hallucinogenic drug now muting the minds of the others. "He lies. It is the raving of a lunatic," Evos howled as he recruited receptive Druids by his wrath. Driven by jealousy, Evos could not let Munli have the decided advantage of claiming a summons by the deities. "Have we not the force of the gods at our beck and call?" he asked the perplexed Druids. Smiling as he realized that he now had their attention, he raised his arms and screamed, "Munli lies!" Knowing that he had gained the initiative, he raged, using his anger as a tool, "Munli lies! He did not receive a summons from the gods," Evos repeated for emphasis. Stillness enveloped the waiting multitude each glancing to the next individual, but none willingly became involved for they knew such a dare could not go unanswered.

Anticipating this outburst, Munli was ready, and he challenged Evos to a duel by sorcery, knowing that his rival was not ready for such a contest. Just as two warriors fought to determine the champion, Druids battled with magic to resolve their supremacy. Using the shadow cast by the light of the peat fire and the confusion caused by the mind-altering drugs that he tossed into the fire, Munli called upon the last reserve of his shape-changing ability to convince his audience of the truth of his words.

Evos realized too late that Munli had baited him into a trap. Unprepared, he could not accept the challenge and maintained his silence, though it shamed him. He used his fury as a shield and awaited the chance that he knew would come.

When his rival withered under the dauntless stare of the master, Munli gazed across the crowd and offered the same challenge to everyone. "If none among you dare to match my powers, then I assume you agree that I should continue," mocked Munli. As he let the seed he planted concerning the German barbarians lie dormant, he led his listeners in another direction. He described an enemy of enormous military might, arising in the southern city of Rome with an army so powerful that they would rule the known world. He portrayed armor-clad soldiers by the thousands, following the standard of an eagle, marching in formation over the land of the Celts. "This is true. I swear because I have seen the vision."

Calling on the gods, Munli raised his arms toward the heavens, chanting as he moved. Suddenly, it seemed to the viewers that an enormous display of lightning appeared in coordination with his motion and snaked across the sky followed immediately by a roar of rolling thunder. The distraught body of Druids rotated as one toward the heavens, and at that moment, their uncertainty turned to alarm. For in the now cloudless sky, they saw etched in the stars the vision that Munli described. Even those unskilled in astrology could read the meaning when Munli pointed out the location of the planets. The heavens aligned in agreement with the prophecy of the Master Druid. None disputed the speaker, as he interpreted the clouds passing in front of the silvery moon, pointing out sign after sign, portent after portent. Evos attempted to fashion a response, but each time Munli would turn the crowd's attention to another formation. Timidity replaced anger as the assembly turned to their master for guidance. Meanwhile, Evos grew sullen as Munli's masterful performance captivated Druid after Druid.

Finally Munli moved on. "We cannot circumvent the will of the gods. Therefore we must appease them," he boldly proclaimed. A sickening feeling overcame the multitude when they realized that the Druids would have to surrender some of their supernatural power. Then Munli outlined the price of appeasement, "I have agreed to the following concession. The Druids would forsake their ability to shape-change," exclaimed Munli. "This means we retain our human form like all other men. Worse still, we would lose a measure of immortality because only by taking the shape of another being, such as a salmon or an eagle, could Druids increase their lifespan beyond that of mortal men."

"Why should we risk our powers of domination on the agreement of a madman?" an increasingly despondent Evos responded in a feeble effort to regain the upper hand. After seeing the signs in the heavens, most in attendance ignored his pleas and listened in dread to the master.

Disregarding Evos as though he did not exist, Munli continued. "As I departed the world of the gods, I recognized that civilization must be saved from this future disaster. For without our survival, humanity as we know it will cease to exist."

Munli's foretelling defeated Evos' last challenge to his authority. But Munli knew that he dare not mention the future destruction of the Druid priesthood, or the assembly would demand his blood. He kept this prediction in a secret place deep within his heart.

Without warning and with only a flourish of his gold embroidered cape—a signal to his acolytes—he ordered a rare white deer that had been previously drugged and secretly hidden in the deep forest be brought in front of the Druids. The apparition appeared as if from nowhere. Some time passed before anyone could recover from astonishment at the sight of the legendary albino. While they watched in awe, Munli petitioned for the favor of the gods. As he chanted, one of his acolytes cut a vein in the neck of the sluggish buck to allow the proud beast's blood mix with and cleanse the earth. The deer tumbled to the ground when the last of his life's essence flowed from him. All present prayed for the spirit of the magnificent animal.

While Munli continued the ritual, Evos tried to quietly rally his few remaining followers for one final attempt to diminish Munli's authority. "This is a trick," he whispered. "Munli has not told us all he knows. He plans to lead us toward destruction in order that he can gain ultimate power. He must be stopped."

Pretending not to notice the goings on of Evos and his followers, Munli commanded the acolytes to ritually prepare the beast. The unworldly animal was skinned before their eyes. Many among the multitude looked on with envy as they pictured themselves draped in the leather from the beautiful deer. While his acolytes worked at their grim task, Munli chanted over and over:

May this creature of virtue, die a death of proud honor, may its blood nourish our souls. May its entrails reveal an answer, which will ward off our pronounced fates.

The attentive priests received their third shock of this night. When their attention was focused on the deer, the wolf-clothed Vate came forth from the shadows. He announced his presence by blocking their view and kneeling before the partially skinned carcass. There, he withdrew his short sword; sliced open the belly of the beast, reached into the cavity, removed the entrails and spread them on the blood stained earth.

A roar of disgust arose among those present. Although consumed with their fear of the unknown, none dared prevent the Vate from using the beast's liver to read the future. He made numerous small cuts in the deer's bowel. With his hands and arms dripping with offal, he raised his voice to begin his own invocation to the gods:

Look down on an unworthy Vate, as he uses the gifts you provide. To cast aside the veil of tomorrow behind which, the unknown can hide.

After calling on the gods three times, the Vate dropped into a spell-induced trance. The Druids were appalled yet fascinated. They silently watched as the Vate rocked back and forth for many minutes. Awakening abruptly, he declared to his bewildered listeners, "A multiple birth must occur. Even twins will not appease the gods. The birth-children must number three. They must be born to a clan of the master's choosing!" He did not attempt to explain what this declaration meant, perhaps because he did not know.

The congregation had been waiting in silent trepidation mixed with controlled rage at the Vate. But upon hearing a pronouncement that defied the natural order, a cry of anguish went up from the multitude. "Such a thing is unheard of," shouted one.

"Impossible," whispered another. "Who among us has that kind of power," they asked a third. It was well known, even to novices, that the birthing of three children by one woman was impossible—a legend.

Munli, facing the fear of the assembly, attempted to take charge again. But before he could do so, there was movement in the crowd. Evos realized instantly that this was his last chance for he understood that controlling the triplets was key to controlling the Celts. Using his body as cover, he signaled a companion. The two rose from their places, withdrew belt knives and moved swiftly toward Munli. The master, catching the movement in his peripheral vision, kept his arms tightly at his sides. As the two approached him, Munli turned to face them as though to accept his fate.

With his arm posed for the killing stroke, Evos' steel blade flashed as it caught the light of the fire. In slow motion, he shuddered, tugged at the arrow lodged in his throat and crumpled to the ground. His companion swiftly perished in the same manner.

The stunned assembly remained rooted for none wanted to share the fate of those who were slain. Instead, they meekly looked around for the silent assassin, casting accusing glances at the two acolytes who accompanied Munli. However, the youths were unarmed and seemed as frightened as the others. Those who were in league with Evos felt particularly vulnerable and sat frozen in fear for their very lives.

To regain the initiative and to ensure that the assembly remained in shock, Munli took his sacramental knife from its sheath and abruptly cut out the tongues of the two slain Druids to silence them forever. Quickly he ordered that their bodies be stripped of all vestments and left in the forest for the carnivorous beasts, the customary sentence for any daring to violate the sanctity of a holy place. Fearing for their own lives, the two acolytes hurriedly carried out his command. Munli rejoiced for he knew his friends had come to his aid.

Arriving the evening before the meeting started, Conel and Ragenos had ample time to secretly position themselves. While the astounded congregation of Druids remained frozen in terror, the Mayri warriors maintained their silence, flexing and re-flexing their fingers in case additional arrows were called for. None were needed. Both arrows came from Ragenos' bow, for he was the superior archer; however, that did not relieve Conel of his guilt in the murder of priests. Though both were stiff from sitting stationary for a long period, neither moved a muscle for fear of revealing their hiding place in the limbs of the massive oak tree. Coated with black charcoal to blend in with the darkness, the concealed killers quietly prayed for their immortal souls.

With no reason to reveal his knowledge, Munli turned his attention to the distressed congregation and spoke over the murmuring of the participants. "For our prayers to be answered, we must forfeit the life of one here to offer up as a human sacrifice to the gods."

Dread gripped the heart of every Druid for each knew he or she could draw the burnt grain and forfeit his or her life. None dared protest against the power of the master, though the friends of Evos felt that they were most susceptible. 'Munli will surely get his revenge for my plotting against him,' was the common thought that flashed through the minds of those opposed to the Master Druid.

At a prearranged signal given by Munli, the second acolyte removed several branches of dry mistletoe from underneath his cloak and added them to the smoldering peat fire. Following Munli's blessing, a clay crock containing prepared dough was placed on the smoking parasitic shrub to begin the baking of sacrificial bread. When done, Munli broke the loaf into twenty-five bite-sized pieces. The morsel to designate the victim was returned to the fire to be blackened the color of coal. The Druids, in their flowing white robes and engulfed by the white smoke from the fire, circled the sacred site chanting an ancient prayer as they moved. The Vate slid in line between two aggravated Druids, causing a disruption in the orderly procession. Under cover of this distraction, one of the acolytes swiftly removed the blackened fragment and pressed the hot bread into Munli's hand. Each priest partook of the offering from the common pot. Some fingered the contents trying to detect the hardened piece.

When the Vate reached into the pot, an acolyte distracted him by pretending to stumble into him, while Munli slipped the burnt fragment into his hand. The Vate's eyes widened when he realized that Munli had betrayed him. He was about to cry out in protest when the first of the three sacrificial killing gestures silenced him forever. The master's acolytes efficiently delivered all the blows. The garrote, a rope with three-knots made of sinew from the slain deer, was tossed over his head, quickly strangling the Vate by constricting his air passages and then breaking his neck. The strangulation prevented him from feeling the second blow—a dagger plunged through his rib cage, or the third—an axe blow to his head.

Praying over the prostrate corpse, Munli felt an internal calm as the three killing deeds of human sacrifice were performed. The weak link in Munli's plans—the chance that the Vate would someday reveal his part—had been replaced by eternal silence. In one swift action, he had made certain that none would ever know the prediction of a triple-birth was preplanned. Nor did any of the living dare to lift a voice in protest for Munli had carried the day.

An acolyte slit the victim's jugular vein and collected blood in a sacred vessel from which all present drank. The lifeless body was cremated in the very peat fire that baked the bread, while Munli recited the rites of the dead and the gathering softly keened:

Lord of the otherworld accept our offering, clasp this one's soul to your bosom. Keep his spirit in your safe custody. When another needs to be replaced in our domain, Release our offering to return in human form in order that the cycle of Celtdom be complete.

The Druids circled until the cremation fire extinguished itself and darkness returned. Shrouded by the returning cloud cover, they departed while claps of thunder announced the coming of a winter storm. Many, who had arrived with a notion that a change in leadership was imminent, left with the realization that a change of a different sort had taken place. "Who would have thought that the young Master Druid had the courage to face Evos, let alone kill him?" a few of the braver priests whispered to each other. Only the two acolytes and the warriors hidden in the oak forest remained behind with Munli.

The Master Druid began preparing for his lonely vigil, while the acolytes dissected the carcass of the sacred white deer. Praying that he would be successful in his endeavors, a naked Munli crawled into the pelt and meditated for the remainder of the night. As he cuddled in the womb of the oozing corpse, Munli occasionally gagged at the smell of decay, but this did not stop him from continuing his plotting. A human sacrifice had been offered, and he knew the gods were pleased. He smiled at his good fortune. In his heart, he had written the names of the parents of the triplets, a decision he had made long ago. Now he only had to entice the Mayri chieftain to accept the burden. Inspired by his patroness, Munli decided that Conel would be drugged to experience a dream in which he would participate in a future catastrophe of the Celts. Praying silently, Munli began to lay additional plans. While he schemed, the acolytes dug a square pit into which they tossed the ashes of the cremated Vate and sat huddled together waiting for their master to emerge. When he arose, all three pulled the remains of the dead stag along the ground and pitched it into the pit, returning it to the bowel of the earth. Then they shoved covering dirt into the hole until it was again level with the surrounding soil.

As he returned to his hut through the sodden forest, Munli prayed first for his friends. Later he implored that the soul of the Vate be welcomed into the otherworld to be reincarnated. Munli never doubted that sooner or later the old Vate would have confessed his part in the deception. Therefore he had to die, but Munli still regretted the killing. The spirits of the two rebellious Druids were left to their fate, lacking prayers on their behalf.

The brothers-in-law, Conel and Ragenos, endured their uncomfortable hiding place until the departure of the Master Druid. Then in silence, they left the scene of their sin by a different route, still shocked by the necessity to slay priests in a sacred place.

On his ride back to the Mayri oppidum with guilt lying heavily on his spirit, Ragenos decided to leave his clan and follow the life of a mercenary. 'I would rather take my chances as a soldier of fortune than be involved Munli's schemes again.'

Mayri Oppidum

The news of Ragenos' decision was felt most heavily by his sister, Meva. The beautiful redhead sobbed inconsolably when he broke the news, and pleaded with him to give her a reason. The two had been tightly knit since childhood, and she became a warrior in order to be always by his side. The love shared between the siblings closely matched the love she now devoted to Conel, but the pending loss of her brother created a void in her spirit which would not be easily healed.

Custom demanded that a banquet be held to celebrate the departure of the warrior. In a depressed state, Ragenos began a farewell speech profusely praising the leaders of the Mayri clan.

Conel, nearly in tears, listened to the homage, but wasn't consoled. He could only think of his part in the act. 'If it weren't for me, Ragenos would have never become involved.' While he rolled this thought over and over in his mind, Ragenos praised him lavishly for his leadership skills. Finally, the two friends slowly hugged for the last time. In addition to leaving his loved ones, Ragenos regretted that he would not be available in case the Mayri needed his combat experience. "Conel, my friend, my brother, you must strengthen the oppidum until you have a warrior with the dexterity to take my place as the champion for the clan."

"I will think of you often, and I will miss your companionship and your counsel," Conel said. "Furthermore, I will heed your advice and see what can be done to strengthen our hill-fort."

The parting on the following day was as heartbreaking as any Meva had ever attended. 'Even losing my father was less painful than this separation from my brother.'

Meva and Conel were still visible on the ramparts, when Ragenos turned and gazed at his childhood home for the last time. Waving once more, he steeled himself not to look back again and turned his mount toward the road leading away from the home of the Mayri. As the trail approached a crossroads which led northwest, a small shape wearing a traveling cloak moved out from the brush and stood in his way. Even from a distance, he recognized the rotund figure of the Master Druid. If there were room on the trail, Ragenos would have steered his mount around the interference, but his former friend would not let him avoid the encounter. "May we talk?" Munli asked as he looked up at the tall, broad-shouldered warrior who towered over him.

"There is little to say. Conel and I did your bidding, and now we must live with the crime," Ragenos answered curtly.

"I know that you believe I used you to gain some type of prestige within the order. But I assure you that is not the case!"

"Then tell me why I had to kill Druids on sacred ground?"

"I would if I could, but I cannot. Someday, I will explain to Conel why it was necessary, but even then he will not be able to tell you. You were an instrument, like a sword. No one blames the sword, even if the killing is unjust. The gods will look at your deed in the same light."

"You have always been one with words, but your words do not lighten my heart."

"Please dismount and allow me to give you absolution for your deed. I have the purifying waters of the Sulis spring. Permit me to anoint you and keep you safe on your journey. I know you believe that you will never again visit your native oppidum or laugh in the company of Meva. I am here to tell you that is not the case. The day will come when the Mayri clan will need your services. When that time comes, you will feel it in your bones."

Ragenos dismounted, knelt and submitted to the Druid's blessing. Following the dispensation and without speaking a word, the warrior remounted and continued on his journey.

Chapter 2
Conel's Vision

Mayri Oppidum circa 410 BC
Conel, shouted for all to hear, "I'm going to be a father!" It was the most wonderful day of his life, and he knowingly indulged far too much. 'Surely Meva would forgive me this once,' he thought as he accepted congratulations from his friends and downed another dark ale. Thankfully, his spouse slept soundly, or pretended she slept when he entered their quarters. He lay on the animal skins, but the room would not stop spinning, a sure sign that he would suffer the next morning. Sleep came abruptly to the Mayri chief, during which a ghost-like Munli appeared and beckoned for him to follow, saying softly, "The only way you will really understand is to experience the future for yourself."

Southern Gaul circa 51 BC

'Where am I?' As this thought entered Conel's consciousness, he had a notion that somehow he had been hit on the head and his senses were scrambled. Such a sentiment made him sick to his stomach. Furthermore, he knew instinctively that he wasn't breathing the crisp mountain air of the Alps. At home, warm drizzle only fell in tepid weather, looking at the leafless trees, he knew that summer had long since departed.

He was even more surprised by the discipline displayed by the warriors around him. Just as he sensed the differences in the weather, he knew these unknown companions were warriors.

Before Conel could identify his whereabouts, an order came down from Mick, the young commander, to muzzle their mounts. Conel did as he was told, unaware at how efficiently he executed the maneuver. About forty gathered in the narrow draw between tree lined hills. The early morning drizzle slackened, and the soldiers rested amid the cold puddles accumulating under their feet. From his position at the rear of the formation, Conel could not see beyond a few paces. Coming from the entrance to the narrow vale, he heard shouts and what sounded like clashes of armed men, but his group did not stir. The young commander made his way to the rear, and whispered orders as he approached, "Do not forget our mission." The whisper sounded like a shout in the stillness of the confined space. Conel did not know where he was, let alone the mission.

"Those who are engaging the Roman guards are hot-tempered fools," Mick continued. "We will wait until the first squad has passed, and then we'll attack the supply train. Obtaining food is our purpose, not killing Romans. Keep that in mind! Await my command and maintain your silence." After repeating those few words, the young commander made his way back to the front.

Conel felt a thump on his arm and looked around at Ennos, a fellow warrior, without wondering how he knew the man's name. Ennos leaned forward and murmured in his ear, "Didn't I tell you we lucked out and got the best commander of the bunch? Those other simpletons are getting themselves killed for naught."

"Look after for my horse. I want to see what is going on," Conel said as he handed Ennos the reins and began to creep forward. When Conel neared a position where he could observe the fighting, he felt the edge of a blade against his throat. Turning slightly, he saw the commander at his right side. "If you make a move or sound, I will kill you," the young leader said with malice in hushed tones.

Conel nodded his assent and maintained his position as did Mick. From his vantage point behind a large bush, he observed squads of Roman soldiers, about two hundred men each, lined three deep and fighting a disciplined battle against the wildly charging Celts. Protected by body-length curved shields, the Romans flung javelins at the oncoming cavalry, killing many and maiming their horses. The mounted Celts ignored the spears. The first contact pushed the Roman line backward; however, the box-like formation held, and the patient legionnaires waited for an opportunity to use their short broadswords. The chain mail of the Celtic horsemen, which functioned well against a slashing attack, proved to be no match for the stabbing motion of the legionnaires. The shorter Romans closed ranks nullifying the erratic charge of the Celtic warriors. Victory was decided long before the first Celt fled the scene. The retreat was as disorganized as the attack, which ended when the well-rested Roman cavalry ran down the weary survivors.

"They will butcher every Celtic warrior along with every woman and every child who accompanied them. The Romans never rest until they have killed everyone involved in an attack to stifle discontent among those they conquer," the commander explained. "Now return to your post before I execute you for disobedience."

Conel quickly realized why the Celts, although their hot blood lusted to do battle, held their position. Even in his semi-dazed state, he sensed the power that the young commander possessed. 'Who is he? Why does his dialect and mannerisms seem so familiar?' Conel asked himself, as he waited with the others.

The sounds of metal clashing against metal, followed by dying men's screams in both Latin and Celtic, resounded down the rock sides of the cramped draw. The death shriek of a fallen horse shook Conel to the very fiber of his being. Horses were more precious than comrades, and the death of such magnificent beasts tore at the heartstrings of this horse lover. At long last, a Latin victory shout reached his ears followed by the sounds of celebration. After a time, the noise diminished, leaving only an eerie silence in its wake.

Conel could smell the sweat of those around him, which reeked of the pungent odor of defeat. Still, the warriors awaited their leader's command. After what seemed to be an eternity, the sound of motion increased. "Mount," the troopers whispered to each other. Then shouting a savage war cry, the young Mick led his men on a charge into the flank of the unprepared Roman column. Holding their body shields and swinging their long curved swords, the mounted Celts split into two lines as they sprang from concealment. Conel followed the group that charged the guards at the rear of the supply train. Like his companions, he maneuvered his steed around the multitude of bodies slain in the earlier battle. Drawing his sword from his scabbard and leaning on his horse's neck, he kicked with his heels to urge the animal forward.

The Romans relaxing in victory were astounded to find Celts charging them. Before they could form even the semblance of a fortified square, Mick's raiders were upon them and the slaughter began. Conel's first opponent had his head separated from his neck before he could recover from the surprise attack. Next, the Mayri chieftain's sword sliced through the shoulder armor of a Roman in full retreat, and left its wearer sprawled on the ground as Conel's mount leaped over him. After dispatching the astonished legionnaires, Conel and his cohorts captured the desired provisions needed for the siege that would certainly follow. Ox carts loaded with food were quickly and efficiently led into the narrow draw. When the last wagon made its way through the opening, Mick disguised their theft. He ordered the empty wagons to be filled with the bodies of the slain Romans. Then after facing the wagons in various directions, the tails of the animals were set afire. Screeching and bellowing, the oxen and mules raced across the broad valley, pulling their carts behind them. Conel leaped from his horse to help drag branches, cut from the surrounding trees, to cover the warrior's tracks and to disguise the opening. Mick's men hurried after their leader, as he made his way back up the draw.

After traveling over five leagues, the group camped beside a small stream flowing from hills that formed a barrier between them and the scouting parties of the Romans. Conel, who fought well at Ennos' side, needed the respite. After cleaning the dried blood from his sword and feeling grateful that the rain ceased, he lay on the rocky soil, closed his eyes and exhaled deeply. He listened to conversations taking place around the various campfires. Conel heard how Vercingetorix from the Arverni tribe, whose name means 'the High King who marched against the foe,' organized a confederation of tribes and almost defeated the Romans, using a scorched earth policy. Bile erupted in his stomach when a warrior told of how the Romans slaughtered one-quarter of the inhabitants of Avaricum, the Bituriges' capital, and enslaved the remainder. Soon after, Vercingetorix's forces at Gergovia, the chief town of the Arverni, put six legions to flight. Only the valiant rear guard action by Caesar's Tenth Legion prevented total annihilation of the Latin forces. Conel assumed that Caesar, another unfamiliar name, must be the enemy's general. Despair set in, when he heard that Vercingetorix withdrew to Alesia, only to be trapped there by the remnants of Caesar's army. Conel listened in awe as warrior after warrior described the Roman siege works. "One rampart stood forty-hands high and faced the town while a second enclosed the first," a Celt solemnly explained. "The guard on the second rampart faced outward to prevent an attack from the rear. These were not skimpy structures. They circled the town and contained the entire Roman army, including horses and supply wagons."

"What happened to our side?" asked one sitting on Conel's left.

"For a time, Vercingetorix matched the Roman general's construction efforts stride for stride. Whenever the Romans heightened their ramparts, Vercingetorix's engineers build up that section of the wall. Each side constructed towers and maintained a steady barrage of catapult shot."

"But what happened?" asked the young soldier.

"Our reinforcements could not break through the Roman fortifications, and Alesia was starved into submission. Vercingetorix surrendered and was taken to Rome in chains."

"Now we fight under Lucterius," a Celt announced. "He's a daring leader from the Cadurci tribe, who harassed the Romans to keep up the rebellion started by Vercingetorix."

Their squad leader, whom Conel found out was named 'Mick the Fifth' of the Helvetii tribe, had in the closing days of the Alesia siege, heroically brought his men through the Roman lines to safety. 'If he is from the Helvetii tribe, why haven't I heard of him?' "Why do they call our leader Mick the Fifth?" he asked Ennos.

"Mick is one of the fifth set of triplets born to the Mayri clan of the Helvetii tribe," Ennos answered. "Legend has it that the triplets are a gift from the gods and reappear whenever the Celtic empire is in danger."

Ennos' explanation made Conel's stomach churn and his head spin. He would have vomited, but his stomach held little substance. 'What has Munli done to me?' he wondered.

"Why does Mick fight so far from home?" the youth on Conel's left asked. "The Romans are no threat to the Helvetii."

"Now that's an interesting question," said a pleasant looking, small-framed Celt who joined the conversation. "I thought everyone knew the history of the Helvetii. They're the very tribe that got us into this mess for they drew Caesar north of the Alps. By the way, my name is Danous. I am the personal bard to Mick."

Conel shed his sick feeling by belching loudly. The weak spell was immediately replaced by a strong urge to challenge the pleasant bard, but he thought better of it and asked instead, "Tell us why you think the Helvetii are responsible?"

"Now don't take offense, big fellow," Danous replied with a grin as he noticed Conel's pallor. "I'm just having a little fun with you. I can tell by your accent that you are a Helvetii though your choice of words seems a bit out of date. Gather around, and I will explain how this man's tribe lies at the bottom of all our problems."

After that short introduction, Danous spent the better part of the next hour describing the esteemed place the Helvetii Tribe held in Celtic lore. "First and foremost, the Helvetii, or rather an off-shoot branch of theirs, the Volcae Tectosages, were the only Celtic army to destroy a Roman legion on Gaul's soil. About fifty years ago, a headstrong Roman consul named Lucius Cassius Longinus decided to make a name for himself by chasing Divico, a Celtic chieftain, and his followers into the Garone Valley. Thinking he had the advantage, the poor fellow led the Romans into the narrow vale only to find himself surrounded, when Divico brought his troops down from the hillsides and butchered poor Longinus' men. The Roman consul lost his life and fortunately didn't live to watch his troops show their servility by trudging in file under the yoke. And that's only the half of it." Danous strummed on his small lyre as he took a break to relieve himself and to get something to quench his thirst.

After he returned, he looked straight at the astounded Conel and said, "This big fellow here can probably fill you in on the details of the battle. In the meantime let me finish my tale. It seems that a greedy and ambitious Roman Consul named Gaius Julius Caesar of the Julian gen, haunted by the humiliating defeat of Longinus, saw his opportunity to extract revenge. As I hear, from those who claim to know, Caesar gained his consul post by borrowing a lot of money. He sat in his corrupt Rome and schemed to get the better of his two co-consuls, Gnaeus Magnus Pompeius better known as Pompey, and Marcus Licinius Crassus. Suddenly the perfect pretext to invade Gaul fell into Caesar's lap," Danous said while holding their attention with his tale.

"With pressure from Germans in the north and the Romans on the other side of the Alps, the Helvetti tribe had no space to expand. When their chieftain Orgetroix died, the tribal leaders decided to move. After planning for four years, four hundred thousand headed west across the continent to settle in Iberia. When Caesar heard of their plans, he crossed the Alps with his legions; came upon the Helvetii crossing the River Saône, caught them by surprise and cut the rear guard to bits," Danous halted to wet his parched throat.

"Of the original migrants, only one hundred thousand made it back to Helvetia. If you don't believe me, ask the big guy," Danous said once again pointing to Conel. "Judging from his scars, I'd say he took part in the battle. But I won't press it too much. He looks like he intends to take my head off." Before anyone could engage Conel in a conversation, Mick ordered his troops to get some rest.

Later that morning, their party arrived at a perimeter camp set up by Drappes and Lucterius. Looking around, Conel observed that the Celts, indeed, had accumulated a vast store of corn and other grains. He also noted that it was a cold camp with no fires allowed, which meant that the Celtic generals did not feel they had sufficient strength to withstand an attack.

"We must provide our brethren at Uxellodunum with sufficient supplies," Lucterius announced to the warriors that gathered around him. Then he continued, "It is my belief that Caesar will leave the field before the cold weather sets in and never return. We just have to be patient and wait him out." The general and his men filed down the trail that led through the woods to the oppidum. Mick's command lacked carts, so the horses served as pack animals to carry the greatest portion of the supplies, and the troops carried the remainder. After hours of marching, the exhausted party stopped to rest. Mick moved from one group to another, commanding them to silence. Perhaps because he was a Helvetii and not a Cadurci, the squad leader's order was ignored. The noise from the group carried over to enemy scouts, who quickly informed their leaders. Before dawn, while the weary Celts rested, the Romans attacked from the shelter of the woods. Though the Cadurci fought desperately, they were quickly isolated and then subdued by the well-trained Latins.

Mick, surprised as any by the enemy's stealth, rapidly ordered his forces to discard the supplies and mount their horses. The forces in the wake of their young leader cut their way through and raced to warn Drappes. When Mick arrived at Drappes' camp, he was shocked to find that the Celtic general had settled on a riverbank. The vultures and rodents chewing on the slaughtered bodies of the Celts proved the folly of such a strategy. "Won't they ever learn? The fools left safety on the high ground only to play to the strengths of the enemy. Now our food supply is in the hands of the Romans." All that remained of his company overheard Mick's anguished cry.

"What are we to do?" Ennos asked his leader.

"We will join those inside the oppidum and resist the invaders with all our might," Mick replied.

Cautioning his men to maintain their silence and discipline, he led the weary survivors toward Uxellodunum. After hiding most of the day in the woods behind the Roman lines, Mick's scouts reported that another legion, led by a General Fabius, was making its way into the Roman camp. Mick saw this as an opportunity for his men to pretend they were Germans and enter the camp as part of Fabius' army. At the right moment, they would dash across the barriers and join the encircled Celts.

For the first time, Conel felt a sense of elation. He and the others shouted in German, a language very similar to Celtic, while they swaggered proudly across the camp. Roman soldiers looked on in amusement as their barbarian allies blustered and bragged of their accomplishments. Conel soon realized that with his great height he resembled a German. Though the Celt's horses were smaller than those ridden by the Germans, no one seemed to notice. Several times, he turned to look into the eyes of his enemy to take their measure. 'These imbeciles aren't paying any attention. The conceited Romans did not believe the Celts could be intelligent enough to try such a maneuver.'

A river flowed swiftly through the valley and shielded all but three hundred feet of the mountain. Mick led his troop toward a tapering land connection. As he looked toward their destination, Conel was awe-struck by the natural fortifications of the oppidum. Uxellodunum, situated on a mountain surrounded by a deep valley, was protected on every side by a rock face. He could not see any weakness in the natural barriers of the oppidum; the rocks were impossible to scale, making Uxellodunum an impregnable fortress.

When the small party reached the causeway, Mick formed the unit in battle order. Conel turned once again to see if any would oppose them, but the Romans ceased their camp preparations, watched and wondered about the disguised Celts. When Mick gave the command to move out, the onlookers laughed at what they perceived to be a small force of Germans charging the barricaded enemy. Companies of Romans wagered among themselves about the outcome of the encounter. Mick hurriedly led his men across the narrow land bridge that separated the two forces. Within sight of the Celtic guards, the commander stopped and in Celtic demanded freedom to enter. "Open the gate!" he yelled. "Open the gate, you idiots. It is I, Mick the Mayri, with some stout-hearted help."

Only upon recognizing some of their fellow tribesmen did the defending Celts react. The barriers were quickly lowered, and Mick and his men gained admission. "I expected to fight my way in," Ennos declared.

"From the look of amusement on their faces, I think the Romans expected us to be entering a trap. I would love to see their bewilderment now," Conel replied.

After feeding his horse, Conel joined the all-night celebration as the story of deceiving the self-confident enemy was told and retold. With each telling, the feats became more heroic and the laughter intensified. Few within the stronghold held any fear of those surrounding them, and most believed it to be only a matter of time before a Celtic force, led by Lucterius and Drappes, would arrive to relieve them. Under the threat of a cruel death, none in Mick's party dared to reveal that the generals were not coming.

The following morning, Conel and Ennos spied on the Roman position from the upper rampart. For the first time, Conel saw the magnitude of their military might. As the two Celts watched, a force of thousands moved in a snake-like fashion. They approached the oppidum twenty abreast with their body length shields extending from below their eyes to just beneath their knees. Helmets strapped under their chins left only a narrow portion of their faces and ears unprotected. The soldiers wore heavy armor about the shoulders and neck to offset the slashing style of the Celtic horseman. The interior soldiers in the march extended their shields over the heads of those in front and those behind. The curved shields allowed an opening for the soldiers to see and made the protection almost absolute. To Conel, the force resembled a moving building. 'How are we expected to stop such an army?'

As he wondered what would come next, a pile of logs stored to repair breaks in the fortifications caught Conel's attention. "The Roman square reminds me of a moving wall. Why not attack it as one would any wall?" Conel pointed to the log pile and explained his plan to Mick.

Looking quizzically at the big Celt, Mick wondered, 'What is there about that man that seems so familiar?' Then without hesitation he ordered the men to follow Conel's orders.

The next day the Roman army attacked anew. When the train of armored shields neared, a cheer went up from those in the lead. They saw the large gates of the fort swing open, and stood their ground awaiting the charge on either foot or horse by their trapped opponents. Each legionnaire swelled with anticipation at an opportunity to face those madmen on equal terms. An avalanche of rock fell while their attention was diverted, then screaming Celts urged on by mighty war trumpets attacked with vengeance in their hearts. While the Romans fought off the initial charge, Conel led teams of warriors lugging sharpened timber. The massive Celts, four team members per log, threw themselves and their enormous wooden spears into the unsuspecting enemy and destroyed their now useless shields. The front line of the Roman army toppled under the weight of the charging Celts, and those behind scattered to regain their footing. Directed by Mick, mounted Celts raced from the oppidum and added their weight to the fray. As the Romans fled, the Celts carrying the logs quickly dropped them, drew their swords and joined in the slaughter. Mick blew the trumpet to retreat into the fort before the reckless Celts outran their protection. Picking up his massive log, though his arms ached from weariness, and ordering others to do likewise, Conel herded his fellow warriors back into the safety of the fort.

On the third evening following the successful foray, Mick and his attendant joined the group "Have you served under me before?" Mick queried Conel.

"Not that I can recall," came Conel's uncertain response.

"You seem very familiar," Mick the Fifth replied.

"Tell us more about the Germans," Conel asked.

Mick smiled and, beckoning his attendant to move closer to the fire said. "Some of you may not have met my constant companion and devoted admirer, Danous the Bard. He is the fifth in his line to bear that famous name, and he has been the bane of my life since I was a child," Mick continued affectionately. "Danous is one of the famous bards from the Parisii tribe. It has been our family's misfortune to have to put up with Parisii bards for hundreds of years. It seems that one of my ancestors made the mistake of allowing a bard of Parisii accompany him on his adventures, and we have been plagued by them ever since," Mick laughed. "Earn your keep my man, and tell them about the Germans and Romans."

Conel turned to study Mick's companion for the first time. The bard was slighter and smaller in stature than those around him. He was handsome, but his face lacked the large mustache of most Celts. Instead, he wore a small neatly trimmed mustache that outlined his upper lip. Though his mannerisms were almost feminine in nature, Conel felt an instant rapport with the little fellow. His ready smile at the ribbing from Mick made all relax while they awaited his description.

"The Germans are renowned horsemen and fierce fighters. They believe in absolute physical fitness as though it were a religion and have been known to kill those too weak to comply." He then took a sip from a cup of ale that never seemed to leave his side.

"Over the past several hundred years, the Celts have taught the Germans our ways and our language," Danous announced. "Today border tribes are so intermingled; it is difficult to distinguish Celts from Germans. Some German tribes have become Celtic in their habits, even to the names they bear; however, their blood has not mingled with ours. As often as not, the tribe's administrator is a Celt. Some, but I am not among them, believe the German race is related to the Celt." Following this narration, the bard took leave to replenish his container of ale.

"I am familiar with Germans. What tribe are these who oppose us?" asked a female whose name was unknown to Conel.

"These are merely mercenaries, who come from many different tribes." The bard responded when he returned. "As you are aware, the Roman is no horseman. Therefore, he hires others to provide a cavalry. Most of those we fight on horseback are Germans or Celts from distant lands, such as Iberia, which is to the southwest. These Celts from the other side of the Pyrenees Mountains have so intermarried with the native Iberian, that they are often called Celtiberian. Other Roman cavalry come from across the sea, south of the Latin lands, and are of a darker skin. Some, much to their dishonor, are Celts from Gaul who favor the Roman invader over their own kind." With this caustic comment a shout of rage resounded around the campfire.

"Tell us more about the Romans," Conel requested in a low voice that sounded almost like a plea.

"The Romans are part of a people called Latins, whom a millennium ago resided as a neighbor of our forefathers in the ancient homeland of the Celts, somewhere northeast of where we now stand. For reasons long forgotten, the Latin migrated south, crossed the Alps, passed through the land of the Etruscan, and settled. One of their outposts, originally established to keep the Etruscans at bay, is called Rome. It took hundreds of years before Rome became the capital and the Latins' center of power."

"How do you know so much about the Romans?" Conel asked.

"Because the advisor to the Julius Caesar is a Druid," Danous answered with a smile of complicity. He sipped once again then continued with his story. "After a great battle in which the Roman army was defeated, a large Celtic force invaded the city, but instead of destroying it, they were bought off with ransom. From that moment, the Romans considered the Celts their mortal enemy."

"There is no way they can enter our oppidum!" roared a Celt who had consumed too much ale.

"That is true," answered a somber Mick, adding to Danous' remarks. "They, however, outnumber our meager force by over a thirty to one. We barely have sufficient warriors to guard the perimeter. Only our natural defenses allow us any degree of comfort. Plus, we have an additional downside to consider. If the Romans can never get in, we can never get out. We are saved only if they lose patience and withdraw." With this grave comment, Mick and Danous took their leave.

As Mick observed, all was not secure. The Romans positioned their superior forces directly across from where the Celts descend to obtain well water that was fed by an underground stream. Hourly, Celts ran the gauntlet of the Roman arrow. Laden with water while attempting to return up the steep slope became all too precarious, and the toll, in men and women, was beginning to mount.

The pride of the Romans rose to a level unheralded when they learned, that their great General, Gaius Julius Caesar, was to join their ranks. Even Conel could sense the change in confidence as the activity across the way increased dramatically. Legionaries, who had previously lackadaisically trained, now drilled with a purpose. Ennos had told Conel about Caesar's legendary skill in motivating his men. Now, he had an opportunity to see for himself. After studying the site, Caesar ordered his legions to erect a walled terrace across from the source of the spring.

When the towers were finished, the wooden walls protected the Romans who rained arrows and missiles down on the charging Celts. In one of these assaults, Conel lost his good friend Ennos. But with the threat of their water supply being cut off, he had no time to mourn. His sleep gave way to isolated periods of rest for Mick drove his men to greater and greater acts of courage. This effort, however, was in vain. The terrace rose in height to over sixty feet, topped by a forty foot tower.

Caesar kept the Celts distracted by persistent frontal attacks, so they could not observe the activity behind the terrace. His troops dug tunnels to reach the spring's source and diverted the waters through man-made canals and rivulets. To the obvious pain of the besieged Celts, their water source magically dried up. Infants and old people were among the first to die. Many among the thirsty townspeople blamed the catastrophe on the desertion of their gods. Finally with hundreds dying on their feet, the tribal council sent messages of truce to Caesar.

The gates were thrown open. Conel watched as thousands of short, thick-legged, muscular men wearing bronze chain mail marched in formation behind the standard-bearers. Each carried a throwing spear in one hand and a leather-covered shield with metal studs in the other. Iron plated scabbards clinked as they marched with hatred gleaming in their eyes. "We'll get no mercy," Danous said as though nothing on earth frightened him.

Conel squatted with the other prisoners under the watchful eye of their German guards while the victorious Romans sacked the town and had their way with the women. Slavers wearing leather garments and carrying great horsewhips mingled with the soldiers. Treating the survivors as beasts of burden, the slavers went about their depraved work. The screaming of the chained captives being dragged away unnerved Conel.

Those who were deemed unfit were slain on the spot, and their bodies dumped into a great bonfire. Along with his companions, Conel was forced to rip down wooden huts to feed the fierce fire. The Romans showed no pity. They gave neither food nor water to the defeated warriors who inhaled the acrid smoke coming from the burning corpses. Too weary and thirsty to react, the overwhelmed Celts listened to the Roman leader's victory speech. It was soon apparent that the valiant defense rubbed raw the general's ego.

"I, Gaius Julius Caesar, have been too lenient with these ungrateful natives of Gaul. For far too long, they have avoided

Rome's rightful leadership. Rebellion after rebellion is too much for our worthy and brave troops to endure from barbarians such as these. I am well known for my clemency. Few would think me unjust and cruel if, for once, I were to order the punishment those who defy us justly deserve. Let this message go out to all those who would think to oppose the might of Rome." Then, Gaius Julius Caesar ordered that all who took up arms would lose their hands.

One by one, the heroic defenders of Uxellodunum were dragged before the mighty Caesar to have their hands severed. The great leader stood with his arms folded and watched while a few struggled and some screamed in agony. Others accepted the punishment with the stoic behavior often displayed by the Romans. When Mick was pushed down before the Roman general, he demanded his right as a warrior to have the deed accomplished by the steel of a Celtic blade. In his one act of mercy, Caesar granted the Celt's wish.

Dressed in his tattered tunic of bard blue, Danous dared to rise to his feet and speak for all the defenders of Uxellodunum. "You Julius Caesar, General of Rome, rank among the cruelest of men. Killing millions in your quest for power is an acceptable act of war, but cutting off a warrior's hands is tantamount to issuing a criminal's death sentence. A deformed warrior will surely die from either starvation or shame. For this terrible crime, I curse you to the depths of your soul. I predict that you will not have the honor to die a warrior's death. Instead, you will die by a shameful act of betrayal at the hands your friends. This I, Danous, Bard of Parisii, foretell." As he ended his stirring speech, Danous offered his hands to the Roman executioner. To show his disdain for the bard, Caesar came down and performed the despicable deed.

Conel could not remember whether he acted with courage or cowardice when his turn came, because everything became a blur. His one memory of the scene just before he held out his hands was the look of hatred on the face of Julius Caesar. Conel stared into the large black, deep-set, penetrating eyes of the general. He wondered how a small balding man with his thin, rugged face could command such allegiance from his troops.

Mayri Oppidum circa 410 BC
Upon awakening, Conel's head hurt like never before. He spent the morning throwing up everything that he had consumed the prior evening, and more. Meva showed no pity, an act that crushed Conel deeply for his pain came as a result of celebrating her

pregnancy. They accomplished little that day, and the Mayri chief retired early. As he began to doze, a sickening feeling descended upon him. In the confusing time between deep sleep and awakening, he remembered his participation in the siege of Uxellodunum. He abruptly sat up. 'Did I have a foretelling? Is that something that is still to come?' he wondered. 'Only Munli could have dammed my soul by forcing such an abomination upon me.' Conel's first instinctive reaction upon waking was to clasp his hands

Several mornings later when he awoke and looked upon his sleeping, pregnant wife, an image of Munli entered his thoughts. Then a sense of dread captured him, and a vision of legionnaires appeared before him. Determined to learn more about his future enemy, Conel silently left their hut and immediately sent for the merchant Turk. When Turk appeared, Conel asked, "What do you know about a people from the south called Romans?"

"I know that they come from a city called Rome and have conquered several of the surrounding tribes," Turk answered.

"How can I find out more about them?"

"Perhaps we can obtain information from the Etruscans. They are the people that trade wine for our iron."

"Why would they know about the Romans?" Conel asked.

"There is a mountain range that runs down the middle of the peninsula south of the Alps. The Etruscans occupy the territory west of these mountains between the Po Valley and the City of Rome. They are highly civilized people and enemies of Rome."

"Would they help us willingly?" Conel asked.

"Perhaps we can hire a scholar who will attend to your needs. Or else, we can purchase an Etruscan who speaks Celtic. Their language is difficult to understand, and one that I cannot speak."

"If you can't hire a scholar, then bring back a slave. Make certain that we can understand him. It is important that we learn as much as we can about Rome."

Months passed before joy reentered Conel's life when Meva gave birth not to one but to three sucklings. Gazing with love on his children, he could not help but notice the differences in each. The first born, a boy, had exceptional length and broad shoulders to carry his large head. The second birth provided the happy couple with a daughter. Her eyes opened almost as soon as she cleared the birth canal, and Conel looked into the deepest emerald green eyes he ever saw. The arrival of a third child astounded the women who were assisting with the birth. None had ever heard of such a wonder. Many warded themselves against evil by touching their face three times because they feared a supernatural occurrence. The last to be born was short and plump with broad shoulders.

Among all those present at the birthing, only Meva, though exhausted by the process, looked on the third child with love. "This one is going to be my Druid," she said as she nursed him for the first time. Pointing to the firstborn, Meva said, "This one, we shall call Mick, the female will be named Una, and the third, Hugh."

Conel felt sick in his stomach as he recalled his premonition about Mick the Fifth and the recurrent birth of triplets. "What ever possessed you to name him Mick?" he demanded to know.

"I think the name Mick embodies a fighting spirit. He just looks like a Mick, don't you think?"

Rome circa 410BC

A birthing event occurred in Rome at the same time as the birth of the Mayri triplets. "She's so scrawny and sickly," proclaimed Vopiscus Julius, as he looked upon his newborn daughter. "I think we should leave her by the roadside and let fate take its course."

"I doubt that he," his wife said, pointing to Vopiscus' father, "will allow that to happen. Everyday since she was born he has come into the room and cradled her in his arms."

"I know," answered her husband as he too glanced at Lucius Julius. "He wants to give her the family name and call her Julia. I would forbid it if I could, but he is the paterfamilias."

Lucius, aware of the tone of his son's remarks, looked gravely across the room and announced, "It is against the law to kill the firstborn, even if the child comes out a female." This edict quieted the rebellion that was smoldering in the breasts of the parents though they still held out hope until the day of the claiming. To be certain that the baby lived, Lucius brought in a wet nurse after learning that her mother refused to nurse her.

On the eighth day following the birth, Lucius, as was his right, picked up the child lying at his feet. Raising the baby girl for all to see, the paterfamilias of the Julian gens acknowledged that the child had all the rights and privileges of a Roman citizen. "I proclaim that this child shall be named Julia," he announced. After that simple pronouncement, Lucius made the appropriate sacrifice and purified the home of the Julius family. These rituals forever prevented Lucius grandchild from being an outcast.

Druids, Celts, and Romans

Ignored by her mother, Julia was raised by slaves who washed her, told her stories, sang cradlesongs and rocked her to sleep. Her only companions were pet doves, pigeons, geese, wax dolls and the slaves assigned to her care.

Chapter 3
The Bard of Parisii

Belga circa 408 BC
The Parisii youths emerged from the edge of the woods. Their stealth, after tethering their horses in the forest, seemed to be a blessing. They neither saw nor heard anyone guarding the Atrebate cattle. "Let us just cut out a few head from this end and be on our way," whispered one of the twenty.

"Why take just a few when for a little more effort we can steal many?" another asked in a harsh voice.

Tomas, the youngest rustler, maintained his silence. He left the covering of the trees and crept among the herd. Due to their inexperience, the youths became separated as they kept their heads below the great bodies of the beasts. As Tomas tried to drive a fair sized calf toward the woods, one of his friends screamed in terror. Off to their right, mounted warriors charged across the field. The youths ran for the protection of the forest. At that moment, one fell. Tomas turned to face the charging equestrians to gain time for his friend. That brave deed cost him his freedom. As the first Atrebate warrior passed, he grabbed Tomas by his hair and dragged him along as he disappeared over the hill.

Parisii Oppidum circa 405 BC
Danous stood watch over his father's corpse while a bard strummed cords on a delicate lyre. He felt shamed at the sparse funeral celebration, for his father had few friends and no money. Danous, an only child since the loss of Tomas, had never felt so alone in his entire life, nor so bitter after his recent failure before the review board of the bards.

'I should be the one playing the string instrument,' Danous thought as the music stirred his resentment. 'How much better I could praise my father if only the council had given me the opportunity. I could honor his warrior past, not the farmer he became. Thank the gods, I was able to obtain a burial that a former warrior deserved. I have no doubt that the tribal council still holds his protest about the cattle raid on the Belgae against him. They would not have tried to dishonor him if Tomas had come home a hero instead of being held captive. With the old man dead, poor Tomas will never be ransomed, and I will never become a bard. Eight years of studying wasted because a horse-drawn cart tumbled over poor Father and broke his skull. Oh God! Tomas, I miss you more than anything in life!' With these thoughts tugging at the youth's heart, he wept for his brother every bit as hard as he wept for his deceased father.

The nights before he appeared in front of the appeal board were sleepless ones. If he failed to convince the board of his talent, he knew that he would not become a singer of epic verse among the Parisii. Clutching his old damaged harp, he watched helplessly as three old fossils reviewed his accomplishments. Even though only in his teens, Danous knew that politics played a larger role than talent in the selection. He concealed his indignation under a cloak of remorse. "Surely in your heart you can find room for me?" Danous spoke as tears flowed down his cheeks. "I will work harder than ever to prove my worth."

His passionate plea went unheeded because the second son of a chief from a lesser clan received the nomination in Danous' stead. Upon hearing the selection, Danous could no longer hide his anger. His hands trembled as he strummed his lyre and composed an impromptu verse. With these few pathetic lines, Danous tried to make his replacement look like an unworthy fool:

> Three old men sat on a bench, pondering the evidence before them. The one with talent was brushed aside. The one with none was chosen.

"Hidden in the soul of this warrior race exists poets who seek eternal truth and desire to heal the physical earth. I believe Danous is just such a poet," said the venerable sage, head of the appeals review board when the young bard departed in rage. "Let us not remove his name from the list of the candidates. We may yet give him an opportunity to prove his worth."

A despondent Danous spent his lonely days wandering the inferior soil of his father's untended acreage. He knew, but no longer cared, that word of his banishment would spread, and he would be shunned throughout the Celtic world. His longing for his captive brother increased daily, consuming his every waking moment. The need to take action became paramount. 'I have to free Tomas or I will die,' he thought, as he wallowed in self-pity over his father's untimely death, his brother's enslavement and his own banishment from the bard's college.

One winter night while the snow lay on the ground, alone in the decrepit old farm shed, Danous settled on a scheme to free his brother. 'My love for him will overcome my inexperience,' he pledged. 'I will use what I learned in the school for poets to gain his release.'

Because he had no friends and few resources, Danous frittered away more than two months collecting the supplies he thought he would require. Praying that no one saw him, he stole away in the middle of the night, vowing never to set eyes on the Parisii tribe again. After covering a short distance, he mounted on an old plow horse, with his father's rusted iron sword secure at his side, and his battered harp tied to his back. In this manner, Danous began the long trek north to the land of the Belgae.

The training school for the bards had been only a short distance from his farm; therefore, Danous knew little about travel. He had never ventured beyond sight of the Parisii oppidum. His clothes were woven from the flax his father sowed, which proved unable to retain body heat when wet. Before long, the plow horse could no longer bear Danous' weight, so he led his only companion by the worn halter. He wandered aimlessly through the dense forest, often losing his way as each unmarked path crossed another similar path. Thankfully, he encountered few travelers in the dense woods, though unscrupulous strangers were not inclined to rob a person with so few possessions.

Thick foliage prevented the scant warmth of a winter sun to penetrate, making each day as miserable as the previous—the nights even worse. Night after night, a shivering Danous munched his rain-soaked bread. To add to his woes, he had miscalculated the supplies needed for himself and for his father's ancient horse. He assumed the animal would feed from the grass along the way, never realizing the thick forest prevented fodder from growing. After several weeks on the trail, a cold, drenched and starving Danous sat down where two paths crossed and waited for the gods to claim his wretched life.

He felt compassion for the faithful animal that carried his meager supplies, but he was too exhausted to end the horse's misery. He tethered it in hopes that its spirit would travel with him to the otherworld. Unaware that he chose a spot where runoff water collected, Danous lay in the ruts hollowed out by horse and wagon traffic. Unable to stray, the faithful plow horse stood guard over its master. As hypothermia overtook him, Danous spent his few remaining hours composing a song of praise in honor of his brother:

> Tomas, I love and admire you, for going on the cattle raid.
> A raid doomed to failure from the day the plans were made.
> The council had no business, sending lads on a senseless task to steal the Atrebate cattle, for which they were too proud to ask.
> Poorly armed, poorly led, you pushed on with good cheer.
> To the land of the vicious Belgae, your heart gripped with fear.
> Tomas, you stood your ground like a Celtic hero of old.
> Only when your comrades left you, did your courage fold.

Then unconsciousness overtook the youth and his spirit prepared to depart.

"There is something ahead blocking the path," cried the leader of the riders. The men of the front squadron drew their weapons and prepared for a surprise attack. Ragenos and his companions laughed as they encountered the body of Danous and his tethered old horse. "To think that a dead person can send shivers up our spines does not say much for our fighting courage," shouted one of the troop.

Ragenos was the first to dismount and turn over the body of young Danous as it lay in the mud of the cross-paths. The harp still secured to Danous' back was now plainly visible. "This lad is not yet dead," he shouted to his companions over the noise of the trotting horses. "Judging from the lute he carries, he may be a wandering singer. Let's build a fire and see if we can instill some life into these young bones."

"Stay if you wish," said one of the others. "We have a contract to deliver the Druids' gold. It is a commitment we dare not violate."

Ragenos, already condemned as a killer of Druids, dared not tempt the gods further. As the others pushed on, he lingered in indecision. Finally after a brief prayer, he chose to remain with the boy. The teachings of his childhood would never let him leave a bard to die alone. The squadron moved on and only Ragenos of the Mayri remained.

Druids, Celts, and Romans

In an attempt to save the youth, he applied all the medical knowledge that he had acquired during the past half-dozen years as a mercenary. Through the dark night, he added dry kindling to the fire and moistened the lad's parched lips with a damp cloth. Searching through his sparse belongings, he withdrew a woolen cloak and covered the boy. Even the two wolfhounds that accompanied the Mayri Celt were pressed into service. He ordered the dogs to lie on each side of the youth to share their warmth. The heat of the well-tended fire, in addition to the damp dog scent, kept many a hungry creature at bay. The few travelers made a wide berth when they noticed the weapons of the large bearded Celt. Unwilling to leave the sick youngster to hunt, Ragenos ate sparingly from his stock.

Hours passed before he could detect any noticeable improvement in his charge. On the second night of the first week, the young boy opened his eyes and looked into the face of his benefactor. "Water please," Danous said. "May I have some water?"

Lifting the thin face, Ragenos poured the precious liquid between the lad's parched lips. With his thirst satisfied, Danous returned to sleep, and slept soundly until the following morning.

Danous consumed solid food at the end of the fifth day. With the lad awake, Ragenos made short hunting forays to secure meat for their meals. Slowly, Danous returned to the land of the living. During this entire time, except for his first plea for water, neither of the two had spoken a word. Danous peeked from under his covers in awe at the dark-haired man who ministered to him. Though some from his tribe stood as large, a certain something about this person terrified Danous. Perhaps, it was the look of despondency in the stranger's eyes. Whatever it was, Danous lived in mortal fear. He tarried in silence for the soldier to harm him and steal his belongings, meager as they were.

After patiently waiting for a sound from the youth, Ragenos finally broke the silence. "I've never known a poet who lost his tongue. Can you speak at all?"

Thinking he had made the crossing to the otherworld, Danous offered his fidelity to the stranger. "I find myself in a strange new world, and I am afraid," he said meekly. "Look after me, and I will be your faithful servant for as long as we both occupy the otherworld."

The stranger smiled, and his beard parted, displaying his large white teeth. Then Ragenos laughed heartily as he made sense of the lad's strange comment. "We are not in the otherworld, and you have not died. By the looks of you, though, if the remainder of your life is as hard as the former, you may wish we were. I am Ragenos of the Mayri clan of the Helvetii tribe. I found you lying senseless on the path," he said while pointing to the horse, "with nothing for company except that sorry excuse for transportation."

Danous replied in a weak voice, "I am Danous of the Parisii tribe."

"I am glad to know what to call you. We will wait yet another week before rejoining my companions. That is if I can find a horse and some proper clothes for you."

When he considered the youth fit for travel, the two set off to catch up with Ragenos' comrades. He mounted Danous on his own packhorse and used the lad's old animal to carry the few supplies that remained. "We'll get you a better mount when the opportunity presents itself," Ragenos promised.

The weeks-old tracks of his companions churned the sodden path, making it easy for a person of Ragenos' skill to follow. When the trail exited the forest and crossed cleared meadows, the pair passed isolated farms where Ragenos bartered with the occupants to outfit the youth. Clothing the boy was more difficult than Ragenos imagined. The fact that he was small enough to wear children's clothes helped, but the problem lay elsewhere. The youth insisted on wearing cloth that matched the vibrant green and white plaid worn by his compatriot. "If I am to be your personal epic singer, then I should dress like you," Danous said as he turned down every offer of apparel.

Wayfarers with villainous intent often fled the trail and vanished into the surrounding countryside when the massive, well-armed warrior and his companion came into view. Merchants and other travelers, for their own protection, hurried to keep pace with the pair. As often as not, Danous obtained supplies by entertaining around a campfire. His talent was appreciated by all who listened, especially the females who were attracted to the teenaged musician. The young, and at times mature, women often reciprocated by offering delights of a different sort. While accepting one maid's sexual favors, Danous persuaded her to dye and weave him a cloak and trousers the equal of Ragenos'. Then he had to beg his patron to delay their travels until the garments were complete. Ragenos, who by this time had grown fond of the lad, shook his head and reluctantly agreed.

In his entire life, Danous had never been happier. He was warm and traveling with a friendly, though fierce-looking, companion. Ragenos proved to be a skilled hunter and provider. Ever on the alert for game, the pair ate well. It became a sort of ritual to tell their life histories at night when they huddled around the camp fire, cementing the friendship between the warrior and the troubadour. Danous would dream of Ragenos charging to the rescue of his brother, whom in his imagination was about to be hung. The memory of Tomas had faded while he was recovering, but it returned more forcefully as he regained his health.

Ragenos' tales of the mighty Mayri on the shores of Lake Lucerne enchanted the young minstrel. In his mind, he pictured the perfect setting on a large body of blue water teeming with fish, even though Danous had never eaten a fish. When Ragenos told a tale, he used all his faculties. At times, he would draw his sword, and demonstrate how he slashed an opponent. Danous was enthralled as he pictured his new friend thundering on horseback over the terrain. His mouth watered as Ragenos described great parties complete with platters of steaming hot food downed with tankards of ale. Danous dreamed of glory as his companion described wandering bards singing around the roaring fires of the Mayri.

As he listened to Ragenos describe his beautiful sister, Danous fell hopelessly in love with the image of Meva. Long after his companion had gone to sleep, he would stare into the dying embers of the fire and dream of winning the favor of such a noble lady. He fancied sitting at her feet, entertaining her with his music while he captivated her with his charm and wit. He imagined people from all over the world hearing of his talent and clamoring to visit. Danous dreamed of denying the jealous Parisii envoys entry into the oppidum of the marvelous Mayri. "You shunned me, and in turn I shun you," he pictured himself saying when he ordered the pathetic messengers back to their homeland.

For his part, Danous told of life among the Parisii and spoke with pride of a father trying to provide an existence on their infertile ground. He described his childhood, and how humiliating it felt to be the second son of a crippled warrior. "Second sons of poor farmers receive neither the land nor an inheritance upon their father's death. I possess neither the physical attributes of a warrior, nor the skill to forge metal. Because my father was no longer a warrior and I could play a lyre, I tried my hand at becoming a bard. I thanked my father in the only way I knew how. I prevented the dishonor of cremation by pleading with the council for a proper warrior's burial."

'This lad has spunk,' Ragenos thought to himself as he listened to the account of his lonesome companion. Danous' tale of mocking the review board brought a grim smile to the lips of Ragenos, while his poem describing how the Belgae captured his brother, brought tears to the Celt's eyes.

"I have left my home to fight for Tomas' freedom," Danous announced.

"You are untrained in the ways of warfare. How could you possibly expect to gain the release of your brother from the fierce Belgae?" Ragenos questioned aloud then to himself, 'Let alone survive on the paths in these troubled times, when even the Druids hire mercenaries to guard their gold. The gods must have left this immature youth in my care for a purpose.'

"I am a bard," Danous retorted. "I have already completed eight years of training. I am talented. Furthermore, I have a plan. I will sit outside the gates of the Belgae king's oppidum and tell all who pass that I am on a hunger strike to liberate my brother. I will starve until the king either frees Tomas, or sits opposite me and starves as well. The people will soon see that he is a cruel monarch and demand that he liberate my brother. If that doesn't work, I will compose satires."

Ragenos knew in his heart the power of a hunger strike, and admired the youth for his boldness. "The hunger strike may benefit you somewhat, because of a leader's fear of appearing guilty, but you are not a good candidate to try one."

"And why would that be?" asked the furious youth, who took Ragenos' comment to be a criticism about his talent as a troubadour.

"Just look at yourself. A king seeing such an undernourished specimen of a human would just laugh himself silly." As he had often done since the revival of the youth, Ragenos broke out in a fit of humor, imagining a hefty king sitting opposite this scrawny youth. "My friend, you are good for my humor. I have not laughed so much since I left the home of my sister, some seven years ago. I know what it means to miss someone you love. Since you appear to love your brother as much as I love my sister, I will help you secure his release."

Though Ragenos did not mention it, he saw some merit in the youth's plan. Next to satire, the formidable weapon of a bard was the hunger strike. When challenged, the Lord of the manor was expected to join in the strike. Whoever held their fast the longest was considered to be the winner. 'Maybe, just maybe, this bard is stubborn enough to outlive the king.' "Here, have another piece of meat," Ragenos said. "You will need more fat on your bones if you plan to outlast a well-fed lord. Do not expect me to join you in that part of your quest. I'm too accustomed to a good meal," Ragenos said, laughing once more.

With tears flowing down his cheeks, the young Danous thanked his newly acquired friend. "My promise to serve you in this world will be honored. I will proudly sing your praises, so in time; Ragenos of the Mayri will be the most honored warrior in all of Celtdom. I will follow you to the ends of the earth and tell everyone of your glory." This was an easy promise for Danous to make, since he vowed never to return to the Parisii.

Again Ragenos laughed as he fondly rubbed his young companion's hair. "You, my young friend, must wait until I do something of valor before you start to sing of it. Don't you think?"

After spending a month on the road, the twosome arrived at the camp of the Helvetii mercenaries where Ragenos and his youthful companion were heartily welcomed. Guarding the Druids' gold did not become the glorious adventure the group left home to find. Druid trade routes never left the land ruled by the Celts, and Celts, by their nature feared, the Druids. Because this inborn fear of stealing from the priests was further supplemented by mounted well-armed escorts, guarding the gold was nothing more than a dull routine. In a word, the guards were bored with their lot in life. Ragenos easily recruited the entire unit to assist in his effort to release the captured brother of the young singer. Danous was warmly accepted into the camaraderie because he provided them with an opportunity to participate in a glorious adventure. In addition, his nightly singing and storytelling proved to be highly entertaining to the weary soldiers. They demanded to hear tales of Celtic heroes, night after night, as they sat around the campfires. Each soldier reminisced about his youth and recalled similar tales told by the bards of his tribe. In honor of his friend Ragenos, Danous composed a song about the saving of a bard. The soldiers frequently requested it, to Ragenos' humiliation:

There came a brave warrior from the land of the Mayri,
who traveled afar from home in search of venture and glory.
On a bitter winter's eve, his quest took a turn for good
when he stumbled on a young bard, lying in a lonely wood.
A plow horse for company at death's door the youth lay
in search of his brother to bury him in the clay.
The warrior took pity on the boy just a bundle of skin and bone.
Leaving his brave companions, he stopped to claim him as his own.
In the world, there is none more faithful than the guard.
Two joined in one quest—the warrior and the bard.

Danous not only sung of Ragenos but he added to his luster by telling of the adventures of Ragenos' father, Ragelnos. With such a pedigree, the Mayri warrior and Danous were welcomed wherever they ventured. Game and water were plentiful, and the party of mercenaries obtained grain supplies from farmers by bartering on their talents. Most land dwellers welcomed the armed party and used them to settle disputes with their neighbors. As they ventured on, each member of the band shouldered his or her share of the responsibility. The most useful contribution by far came from the young singer because bards are always welcome.

Because of their numbers, the Helvetii party resembled marauders. To prevent unwanted trouble, Ragenos made the small army take circuitous routes around all oppida. Only Ragenos and Danous ventured into the strongholds to obtain information, while their companions made camp at a safe distance. No one feared a bard and his traveling companion. After the two entered a town and made themselves welcome, they sent for the remainder of the band. Frequently, the entire band joined in the festivities at an oppidum because the songs of Ragenos' fame traveled before them. Celts by their nature enjoyed merriment and used any excuse to hold a party. The stories and songs more than made up for the quantities of food and ale consumed. In this fashion, Ragenos and his band were content to ramble across the countryside in search of the Belgae.

Nervii Oppidum
As they approached yet another oppidum, Ragenos could sense an activity he hadn't seen until now. 'These people are preparing for war,' he thought. From his viewpoint on the narrow ridge overlooking the hillfort, Ragenos observed squads of horsemen

being put through their paces. Hundreds of foot soldiers, with their armor flashing in the sun, marched in formation. Ragenos admired the scene unveiling before him. His heart beat faster as he wished to join in the whirling commotion. While they sat on their mounts admiring the fervor, a patrol of mounted men approached.

"Have you come to enlist?" the leader asked as he drew up alongside.

Ragenos answered for the pair, embellishing his reply. "I am Ragenos, son of Ragelnos, of the Mayri clan of the Helvetii tribe, and this is my young friend, Danous, a bard from the Parisii tribe. We stopped merely to ask for information about the Belgae."

"We, the Nervii, are affiliated with the Belgae confederation. What do you wish to know?" the leader asked suspiciously. His query was not unwarranted, since the German tribes, particularly the Suebi, were known to hire Celtic spies.

Seeing the doubt in the inquisitor's eyes, Ragenos prayed that the Goddess Sulis would keep Danous silent. The youth, in his enthusiasm to locate his brother, could get them into trouble. Ragenos turned quickly to his companion and said, "Perhaps they can help us in our plight." Danous, never comfortable around armed men, kept his silence.

Ragenos, thinking quickly, asked to be presented to the leader of the tribe, so he might enlist in his service.

"You are fortunate. The King of the Belgae is here recruiting warriors. Because of your size and weapons, you appear to fit his needs," the Nervii leader replied to Ragenos as he turned toward the fort.

With the other Nervii forming an escort, Ragenos and Danous made their way into the oppidum. The line of applicants, lusting for warfare against the Suebi, greatly exceeded the space available, and many waited impatiently well beyond spear range of the walls. The Nervii patrol leader ignored those waiting and led the twosome to the vicinity of the King. The Nerviian caught the eye of one in authority and ushered the warrior and the bard forward. "These are representatives of the group that is camped ten kilometers to the southwest," he announced for all to hear.

"Welcome to the home of the Nervii and service of the King of the Belgae. Word of your approach reached us days ago. I am Autonix, leader of the Nervii. King Katrunix awaits your company."

Ragenos and Danous were led to the largest building in the compound. As they entered, messengers wearing the colors of many different clans were coming and going. While they waited for an audience with the King, Ragenos asked his escort, "What is the cause of all the activity?"

The Nevii looked puzzled. "Did not you bring a small force of warriors to help defend the land of the Belgae?" he asked.

Suddenly, Ragenos understood! Their questions about the Belgae did not go unnoticed. Each oppidum, and probably every farmer, reported their interest to the northern Celtic confederation. He quickly comprehended that they could best help Danous' brother Tomas by allying themselves rather than fighting the Belgae. As he looked at the great mass of warriors surrounding them, he realized they had little choice. Motioning Danous to maintain his silence, Ragenos vowed his support as well as that of the Helvetii camped some distance from the oppidum. "We did not wish to appear belligerent by approaching with an armed force, so the young bard and I came on ahead to pledge our allegiance," said Ragenos to Autonix in the presence of a very confused Danous.

Then they were ushered into the presence of Katrunix. Again they were welcomed with grace. "Word of your deeds, preceded your arrival," Katrunix said. "New songs overtake my swiftest messengers," the king added, laughing at his own joke.

After this pronouncement, Ragenos stole a glance at the young bard. 'I will get you for this humiliation,' he vowed. "I only wish I had accomplished the feats my young companion has attributed to me," he replied to Katrunix.

The King puzzled by Ragenos' frown continued, "Are you not the son of Ragelnos who defeated the Etruscans with a mere handful of troops?"

"I am he," confessed Ragenos. "I have yet to earn the right to call myself a son of Ragelnos, however, since I have yet to bloody my weapon against an enemy of substance."

"We will give you that opportunity," promised the Belgae king.

At the evening feast, Katrunix surprised the gathering of nobles by announcing that he selected Ragenos to answer the summons that their Druids arranged with the religious leaders of the Germans. "Though we would all dearly love to ride into battle against so worthy a foe, the Druids decreed otherwise. They commanded that we find one fit to face the enemy's most dauntless warrior in single combat. The gods have answered our prayers because today a swordsman from the south has joined our cause. He is Ragenos, the son of Ragelnos of the mighty Mayri Clan of the

Helvetii Tribe. Let us welcome him with honor." Every person at the feast rose and lifted their cups of ale in the direction of the man from the Mayri.

Ragenos felt trapped. Refusal would be taken as a sign of weakness and would more than likely cost him his life. On the other hand, he was ill prepared to engage a legitimate champion—a folly which would also cost his life. With his choice limited, he prayed to Sulis that he would die bravely.

As they traveled to the field of honor, Ragenos avoided ale for two days and nights preceding the battle, though many urged him to drink and fortify his body for the fight. Ragenos, however, followed the long-remembered advice of his father. "The person who survives a one-on-one challenge is the one with the clearer head. One does not win a single challenge between two champions. One survives it." He thought that a small measure of ale might chase away the demons that plagued his dreams and robbed him of sleep, but he reflected often on the advice of his famous father. "To win, one must survive," meant he had to fight a defensive battle.

By the morning of the combat, the rains of the past several days had rendered the ground slippery and muddy. Ragenos, knowing that it would be difficult to control a horse running full out under such conditions, decided to be extremely cautious. He chose a difficult strategy under these conditions. Well aware that his allies would demand a show of valor, Ragenos hoped that his opponent obtained courage from consuming brew in the days preceding the challenge. Taking another cue from his father, Ragenos knew that the one who makes the initial impression often wins the fight. Thus he took care to dress in his most fearsome armor. To hide the tremor of his hands, he allowed Danous to help him into his chain mail and mount the helmet with his totem, a soaring eagle with two-foot-wings extended. When viewed from a distance, the helmet added to his height and made him a formidable looking opponent. Furthermore, the wings flapped when Ragenos galloped, making it seem that both a rider and a bird of prey were attacking. Ragenos knew that he would need all the aid his dramatic costuming could provide as he displayed the vibrant green and white plaid colors that distinguished a Mayri warrior.

When the King of the Belgae presented his own spear to carry into battle, Ragenos realized the enormity of the situation. If the

German won the combat, then his people would become dominant in the area, perhaps even costing Katrunix the kingship.

Thousands of armed warriors surrounded the oval bowl that served as the field of honor. Each side beat leather drums and blew enormous war horns to announce the arrival of their champion. Single horsemen rode across the field and screamed at the enemy. Though Ragenos was too distant to hear the taunts, he almost felt certain that his clan name, Mayri, was repeated over and over. He knew the screaming was intended to intimidate the enemy and make him fear your champion.

'With the amount of ale consumed during the past several days, I doubt that mere words would intimidate anyone,' he thought, as he cantered down the long, narrow aisle of parted Celts. Looking across the field, he saw his opponent ride through the avenue of parted Germans. The solid German champion weighted over fifteen stone and looked like a giant sitting astride his massive horse. The Suebi had easily defeated every opponent that he had faced thus far. The sight of the German champion confirmed Ragenos' worse fears. Then a strange transformation occurred. With death as a certainty, Ragenos' fear faded away and calm returned.

He purposely shut out the crowd noise, a trick taught by Conel's brother, Rochlos. He remembered the lesson well. "The crowd can only distract you. Learn to ignore them and concentrate on your opponent. Look for weaknesses. Find out where he is most vulnerable. Then strike for that spot."

The two combatants walked their mounts to the center of the field where the cloaked religious authorities assembled. After a contemptuous glance at Ragenos, the German turned his attention to the authorities while Ragenos ignored them and studied his challenger. Once he saw his opponent up close, Ragenos found no obvious weakness. 'The Suebi is huge, but his horse will be the problem. The mount is a full head higher and broader than my own. He has the weight advantage, so I will have to rely on speed. Perhaps, his cockiness will work against him. Sulis knows that I need all the help that I can get. I must survive the horse charges and try to get this giant into hand-to-hand combat.'

When the Druids and their German counterparts completed the ceremony, the two warriors moved to opposite ends of the field. 'Goddess Sulis, I know that I have wronged you by killing in your sacred grove. Help me in this battle, and I will honor you for the remainder of my life. Please do not let my head adorn a German shaft tonight.' With that short prayer, Ragenos kicked his horse in the ribs, and charged at the oncoming Suebi. Chunks of dirt flew in the air as the horses drove their hooves into the wet turf. Both warriors held their spears above their heads in a throwing position. Ragenos faked a strike at the spear arm of the Suebi then drove his spear into his enemy's shield while he used his own shield to deflect the Suebi's thrown javelin. 'If I can get another spear stuck in his leather shield, I can make it awkward to carry.' Both horses pulled up, turned and charged again. Ragenos tried the same tactic, only to be met by a slashing motion against his spear arm. As his opponent sped past, Ragenos smashed him with his shield knocking him off balance and bloodying his face. 'Perhaps, his broken nose will interfere with his vision.' On the third charge, both riders splintered their spears against the other's shield. Ragenos sighed in relief as he drew his sword. 'It is only a matter of time until I wear him and his horse down,' he thought. Heedless of his own bleeding arm, he tried to slash any unprotected area as the German galloped past. He observed the speed of the other's charge and deliberately slowed his mount. He began to take shorter turns to save the horse's energy. Taking the sword impact with his shield, the force of which almost broke his arm, Ragenos saved his sword strokes for the German's horse. When first cut, the animal reared in pain but did not spill its rider. Ragenos required three more charges before the noble beast succumbed to the slashing attack of the Mayri. Both the German's horse and his own mount were tiring. The difference in the speed of the horses became more pronounced as the smaller Celtic pony dipped in and out, frustrating the wounded German champion. Finally, the enemy's horse collapsed.

Ragenos jumped to the ground, just as the German freed himself from his prone horse. Both men began to swing wildly, each trying to finish his opponent with one blow. From the direction of the stroke, Ragenos could tell the German was arm-weary. An overhead stroke struck early in the match now came from the side. With this knowledge, Ragenos sidestepped a wild swing and managed a thrust that critically wounded his opponent. The German fell to his knees, dropped his sword and removed his helmet. Only after the King demanded it, did Ragenos decapitate his fallen foe.

Danous immediately began to compose a tribute to the Mayri warrior, one that grew with each retelling.

Chapter 4
The Bonding of the Trio

Belgae Oppidum circa 408 BC
Following his heroic feat, Ragenos requested the release of Tomas, the brother of the bard. Katrunix, king of the Belgae, laughed along with Ragenos after he learned of the young poet's plans. "He has the will to be a great troubadour. Whether he has the talent to bring a mighty tribe to its knees by satire or even with a hunger strike has yet to be tested. I have no doubt, however, that the lad will try." In his good humor and as a favor to Ragenos, Katrunix granted pardon to Tomas.

Unknown to Ragenos and Danous, Tomas was no longer a prisoner. Because of the valor shown when his cattle stealing companions deserted him, the Parisian youth was pressed in service by the Atrebates, a minor tribe of the Belgae. Tomas ultimately showed enough skill to earn the rank of warrior. His good looks and warrior reputation made him popular with the females of the Atrebates. Unfortunately, two became pregnant and each of the girls' fathers expected Tomas to marry his daughter. When he was summoned to the king, he realized that his indiscretions were more serious than he initially believed. He speculated about the nature of his crime and quietly made peace with the gods. As he lay prostrate in homage, he wondered about the man, dressed in green and white plaid, seated at the king's right. Ragenos, upon hearing the name of the submissive Celt, descended from his position and took Tomas into his arms. "Your brother and I have looked long and hard for you," he said to the astonished warrior.

"My brother?" Tomas mumbled, "My brother, Danous?" Relief that he was not to be condemned and joy at the possibility of seeing his brother overwhelmed him.

Ragenos, who had been expecting that he would take on another ward, was pleasantly surprised to see a strong, mature warrior. "You'll make a fine addition to my squad."

"I'd be honored to ride with you," Tomas replied, and thought to himself as he smiled inwardly, 'And to escape my Atrebates predicament.' At that instant a cry rose from among the parting crowd, and young Danous charged to his astonished sibling.

Weeks went by when one day, Ragenos glanced across the low table at Tomas and thought, 'How did the Goddess Sulis ever match two more dissimilar brothers? Tomas is as tough a warrior as one could ever meet, while Danous, being a typical troubadour, can hardly lift a weapon. Yet they seem as content a pair as any that I have ever seen.' As Ragenos studied the two, he felt the same love for Danous as he would have for a younger brother or a nephew. For Tomas he felt kinship with a comrade-in-arms. He would protect the one and partner with the other.

Danous' natural shyness was vanishing quickly as the women of the Belgae tribes openly coveted the good-looking young troubadour. He knew that much of the attention showered on him was due to his close association with Ragenos. Nevertheless, he was determined to enjoy the adoration as long as it lasted. Though the women sought his attention, the men ignored him. As he wandered the campsite, he became aware that some were not pleased with the young knight of the Mayri. Groups of warriors would huddle in the shadows and question Ragenos' ability. "Our own champion could have done just as well or even better," some complained.

In other circles, courage became the issue. Cowardly supporters encouraged renowned warriors to challenge the new champion. "How tough can he be? He did not accept a direct charge. He ran until the great champion of the Suebi tired of chasing him. What kind of champion acts like that?"

Danous ignored the grumbling of the jealous Celts. Because of his inexperience, he deemed the griping unimportant, attributing it to the fact that Ragenos came from another tribe. As time went on, the comments became even more bitter and finally changed to outright threats. After he heard some drunken soldiers brag about what they would do to Ragenos, he became frightened at the menacing tone. He told his brother that he feared for Ragenos' life. Then he described the insulting remarks repeated around the campfires.

Tomas displayed a rare attribute for a Celt, one he inherited from his mother. He thought first then acted. Furthermore, he reviewed potential consequences before embarking on a plan. Calming down his young brother, he replied, "Let me think about your words and decide what actions we should take. In the meantime let's keep this between ourselves."

Unlike Ragenos, Tomas was rarely noticed, although he was always present. While Danous spent his time studying Ragenos, Tomas stayed in the background and studied the soldiers.

At the same time he was worrying about Ragenos, a change was taking place in Danous' outlook. The desire to become a full-fledged bard had reasserted itself, but he couldn't bear the thought of leaving Ragenos. Danous determined that he could only earn the distinctive blue cloak of the accomplished bard through self-study. To achieve his goal, he decided to remember all he could about the events surrounding his hero. 'I will compose great ballads to honor my friend,' he dreamed. 'So great will be my songs that my talent will win praise even from those who appoint bards.' To achieve this end, he avoided alcoholic beverages to keep his mind sharp and retain everything that occurred. Danous followed his hero everywhere to the extent that he appeared to be Ragenos' shadow. To earn the adored blue garment, he remained obscure and preferred to observe rather than participate in the camp festivities. From his lowly position near the wall, he took in all that he beheld.

Gigantic fires roared at the opposite ends of the two storied, great-hall of the Belgae. Smoke curled when it encountered the sod ceiling and drifted downward to find another escape. The banquet room reeked of the stale odor. Furry skins of immense brown bears lay scattered around the long low tables so the honored warriors might lounge in comfort while Danous had to be satisfied with dried grass mats to protect him from the damp dirt floor. Enormous shields and swords, adorned the walls. When the king imbibed, which was often, he would offer a detailed history behind each of the sets of shields and swords. These instruments of warfare were located just below the mummified heads of their former owners. Like all Celtic leaders, the king honored the enemies killed in battle, by displaying their shrunken heads as trophies. At the far end of the great hall, above a roaring fireplace, the head of the recently defeated champion of the Suebi hung in the place of honor.

Skewered hogs and sheep continually rotated as they roasted over the ash-covered coals. Cooks stirred the great caldrons hanging over the blazing embers emitting delicious smells which enhanced the aroma of roasting meats. Slaves continuously replenished platters of fruits and breads to satisfy the appetites of those lounging about. Amphorae of wine and jars of mead were emptied trying to quench the endless thirst of the guests. The consumption of vast quantities of beer and ale added to the volatility.

Bards from all corners of the Celtic world entertained those present with stories of past grandeur. The often-repeated saga of Ragenos' father caused many in the great halls to grow envious. The armed gladiators elevated bragging to the level of high art. Rarely did a guest get to finish a story without being interrupted. The high pitch of braggadocio steadily increased in volume. Long into the night, one warrior or another spent hours boasting of his deeds and those of his ancestors.

Turning to Tomas who served as his personal attendant, Ragenos said, during one of the banquets, "If one were to believe all one hears, there could not be any Germans left to fight." Tomas, like his brother, had sworn off alcoholic drinks to better watch his friend's back, erupted into a fit of laughter at the remark.

Rejoicing filled the air along with shouts from one cluster to another. Warriors wearing clothes of bright colors stepped on and over reclining diners, as they clumsily moved about to tell their tales in one group or another. Small scuffles were all the rage, as the individuals elbowed each other for additional room and attention.

Unaccustomed to Celtic partying, Danous sat silently, partially in fear and partially in wonderment, contemplating the sea of color and activity. On one such night, excitement rose to a higher pitch as those seated back from the tables stood to see more clearly. Rising with the others, Danous tried to peer over the great throng to comprehend what caused such a stir. "What is it? What's going on?" he demanded to know from those around him.

"'It's a challenge for the high end of the hog by the champion of the Atrebate tribe," came the curt reply.

Ragenos, as Belgae champion, had the first choice of meat. He chose the hero's portion, the finest cut of meat from high on the boar. He could not choose a lesser piece without losing his status. On this occasion, however, his status was not automatically confirmed because the Atrebate thought he was the better man.

Danous stood astonished when the actual challenge took place. He watched in disbelief as a huge Celt with sword drawn leapt over a table. He could not believe that a man was going to kill another over a piece of meat. 'Why didn't I warn him about the jealous knights?' Danous berated himself as he watched horrified, crushed against the wall by the massed humanity. Even the naive Danous knew a fight to the death usually settled such a challenge. Dismayed, he looked around for his brother as an unarmed Ragenos slowly turned to face his approaching challenger.

Danous' hasty prayers to the gods were answered. Looking over the shoulders of those in front, he saw the ever-alert Tomas appear at Ragenos' side with his sword and shield. Unable to gain complete surprise because of the quick acting Tomas, the Atrebate champion nonetheless showed his agility by leaping over the table and continued to press the attack. Those in the way scattered and tumbled into others seated around them. Confusion gave way to chaos. Fortunately for Ragenos, the Atrebate's normally swift reflexes were slowed by imbibing enormous quantities of alcohol to boost his courage. The Atrebate champion used his long sword to clear a path toward his still reclining target. Two of the diners who did not clear a path quickly enough to suit the armed Celt paid with their lives.

While Danous stared in horror, the partially inebriated Ragenos was at first perplexed when Tomas appeared at his side armed for battle. With uncanny speed, Tomas pressed his sword into his friend's hand. Then grasping the situation, Ragenos let his natural ability take over while the towering Atrebate continued to vault across the prone revelers with murder in his eyes. Gripping the handle of the sword, Ragenos scrambled to his feet and was in position before the other cleared the obstacles. Metal clanged against metal as the two champions fought for position.

Danous, contained by the crowd, was numbed by his inability to intervene even though an unarmed bard could do little. As an attendant to Ragenos, custom prevented the battle-hardened Tomas from directly interfering, but he made himself useful in other ways. With Ragenos' iron weighted shield, Tomas shoved friend and foe alike from the fighting area as he made pass after pass bashing into the surrounding crowd. The muscular Parisii warrior caused great pain and anguish among the spectators, who scurried for safety from the battering meant to insure that Ragenos had sufficient space to defend himself.

Many crawled on their hands and knees to flee the great hall while others, crushed against the stone wall, fell only when space became available. Bones, grizzle and fat from animal joints, tossed by thoughtless diners were spewed across the entire floor. More than once, Ragenos slipped on garbage, and only the automatic reflex, learned in childhood, of rolling from a foe spared his life.

In his alcohol-supported rage, the Atrebate hacked away as he steadily carried the duel to his opponent. The Mayri, on the defensive, expended enormous amounts of energy fending off ferocious charge after ferocious charge. Many of the onlookers were seriously injured by the swipes of the combatants' swords. Blood from the wounded in the crowd mixed with blood spilled by the participants and added to the precarious footing. Fortitude and luck replaced skill as the gladiators used their brute strength in a fight to the death. Breathing heavily with his energy about to expire, Ragenos resorted to a trick he learned as a boy. He drew back his right foot and kicked forward shattering the locked knee of his opponent, forcing him to crumble across an overturned table. Using his good leg, the Atrebate twisted as he tried to maneuver out of Ragenos' way. Despite his loss of mobility, the Atrebate still struggled to take the battle to the Mayri. Chasing the turning and tumbling Atrebate, Ragenos delivered the killing blow.

For the first time in his life Danous witnessed violence up close. He trembled then vomited over those around him. Finally, he forced his body to act and made his way to his wounded, but still standing, hero. Afterward, he wondered, 'How will I ever convey the noise and the smell of blood in my retelling of this saga?'

Those remaining in the hall stood and cheered the shaken Ragenos. Many, including members of the Atrebate tribe, lifted their glasses in a loud toast to the winner. Seeing others consuming bitter ale, after watching two soldiers try to kill each other, caused the young troubadour to lose whatever remained in his stomach. 'How can they drink when I cannot even hold what I had already ingested?' he wondered as the taste of bile burnt his throat. That night the young bard experienced the first of many strange activities associated with the warrior class. To his horror, the crowd began chanting, "Behead him!" Unfamiliar with the local custom, Ragenos at first refused to decapitate the dead warrior. "He is not my enemy, and I gained no honor from killing him," Ragenos declared.

He reluctantly agreed to commit the disgusting act, only after Tomas convinced him to follow the provincial practice. Without being beheaded, the Belgae believed the spirit of the dead would wander aimlessly and never make the journey to the otherworld. Ragenos' severed the head with a single stroke of his steel blade. Then holding the still dripping skullcap in both hands, he knelt before the king and presented his sovereign with the trophy. Trembling from the experience, Ragenos rose to his feet and left with dignity intact.

Fighting the returning tide of the curious, Danous pushed his way out of the great hall. Unfortunately, he stayed to watch the bloody head, separated from its protective helmet, roll across the floor, and he needed the better part of the day to regain his composure before he could face his wounded companion. Only later, when alone with his brother, did he confess to the fear that ate at his loins that he almost caused the death of his benefactor.

"Danous ever since your warning I have been vigilant," said Tomas, comforting him. Then Tomas explained. "Celtic champions, similar to the great bucks of the forest, must live in expectation of challenges, the greater the hero, the more persistent the challenges. It's the way of things. Until now, Ragenos never looked upon himself as a hero and considered himself lucky," Tomas continued. "Now he must learn differently, and until he does, you and I will have to watch his back," Tomas said, putting his arm around his brother's shoulder. "Not to worry little brother," he concluded with a smile. "I will be forever indebted to Ragenos for saving your miserable hide, and I will protect him as long as I am able."

Following the original challenge, other challenges came at a furious pace. Within a fortnight, Ragenos slew no less than three warriors. He did not look forward to a lifetime of warding off challenges from drunken Celts, who were trying to become heroes if only for a moment. After the third challenge, Ragenos told the brothers that he intended to move on, knowing that challenges would follow him no matter where he went. "Is there no way to stop these suicidal duels with fighters who have to get intoxicated in order to fortify their courage?"

Danous was terrified when he considered the odds of one of these drunks killing his friend, particularly if Ragenos was drinking as well. During a period of thoughtful reflection, Danous came up with a solution. Later that evening he decided to be with Ragenos, rather than sit slouched against the wall. To his surprise, his presence at the table went unchallenged. After the festivities were well under way, Danous took out his lyre and began to tell a story. His youthful voice captivated the boisterous Celts. He told of a great and wise monarch who lost many brave warriors to drunken challenges. The king knew if this loss of soldiers continued, he could no longer hold off an invasion by even his weakest enemy. As he relayed his tale, Danous paused to look at the Belgae king. Satisfied that he had Katrunix's attention, Danous continued, "One night after watching his second son lose his life to the tribe's champion, the king decided on a strategy. The king proclaimed that he would stage the greatest of challenges. All the warriors in

Druids, Celts, and Romans

his army would compete, though only dulled swords and blunt spears would be allowed, or else the entire army would disintegrate. This contest took place on the great meadow alongside the king's oppidum and consisted of three events, illustrating lance, spear and sword skills," continued Danous.

Katrunix understood the benefits of the tale and immediately approved. "As King of the Belgae, I declare a contest to take place before the next new moon."

To Danous' amazement, the often-bloodthirsty Celtic knights looked forward with glee to the upcoming event. Since he had never participated in warfare training, Danous never realized he had suggested a child's game. All Celtic clans used this one-on-one challenge with blunt instruments to train children to be warriors. Smiling broadly, the gleeful warriors slapped each other on the back and wished each other well in the coming contest.

On the day of the great challenge, the oppidum took on a carnival-like atmosphere. Banners identifying the clans and the multi-colored dress of the various clans added to the festivity atmosphere. Women, who did not participate in the contest, wore small ribbons displaying the colors of their favorites. Ragenos was astonished that so many maidens wore the green and white plaid of the Helvetii while others went a step further and added the distinct red and yellow stripe of the Mayri. Most of the single females would gladly bed Ragenos, hoping for a husband.

Huge fires roasted wild game and fowl. Food stations, including vast quantities of wine and ale, ringed the oppidum. The nightly banquet, on-going since the victory over the Suebi champion, simply moved outdoors. Bards strolled through the area, playing their instruments and entertaining small clusters of admirers. Danous joined the other bards in adding to the excitement, but he never ventured out of sight of Ragenos.

With all the enthusiasm that a gathering of Celts could create, the contest was staged. Loud bragging and playful taunting took the place of the vicious envy and duels reminiscent of the previous weeks. The contestants and non-contestants alike bet heavily on the outcome of the events, and the alcohol consumed took its toll. Before the contest began, several drunken contestants broke bones from falls while charging around the field showing off. Others were too drunk to mount their horses.

Tomas, who deferred from entering to serve as Ragenos' second, remained constantly at his side. In addition, he refused to partake of the ale that flowed freely. Furthermore, he didn't permit his charge to imbibe. Thus Ragenos was the only contestant clear-headed enough to compete effectively. The agility of his horse secured his first victory. His opponent lowered his head and, without looking, attacked straight ahead. Ragenos easily sidestepped this futile attempt by pulling his mount up short and letting the rider pass. Recognizing this maneuver the crowd laughed and cheered heartily to encourage the opponent. "The bloke never learned a thing from the German, has he?" one delighted warrior asked another.

"Bet he charges again without looking," another said.

Skill at a spear toss and agility to dodge those tossed his way carried Ragenos into the third contest. At this venture, he effectively used his weight, as well as his iron-weighted shield, to win contest after contest. The vicious blow from the shield often knocked an opponent off his feet, leaving him open to the pseudo-kill.

Although he never mentioned it, Ragenos knew he was indebted to Danous for developing such an imaginative solution to his dilemma. Danous in turn was thrilled by the contest and mentally created heroic epics about Ragenos as though the killings were conducted in earnest.

In honor of his great feat, Ragenos was presented the mummified head of the German champion of the Suebi. He hung this trophy from the pommel of his saddle, and carried it throughout his wandering.

Chapter 5
The Druid School

Mayri Oppidum circa 401 BC
With tears in her eyes, Meva stood on the rampart and watched the departure of nine upper class children. Turning to Conel, she pointed to the struggle that Hugh experienced, as he tried to prove to his mount that he was in control. "That boy never did learn to ride," she said with a giggle.

Her husband agreed as he returned her grin, "Think of the trouble he is in for when the group crosses the river. I asked Mick to keep an eye on him and not to let him get humiliated for being clumsy."

When the children cleared the slight rise and disappeared into the dense forest, the parents reminisced. "It just seems like yesterday, that I cried when they departed with the local Druid for their primary lessons," Meva sighed as she realized her children are growing up.

"It seems to me that you are always crying about the kids getting older," Conel replied. "Perhaps, it is because we are growing old as well. I remember the look of defiance on Mick's face when the Druid offered him his hand. He reminds me so much of your brother, Ragenos. Una, on the other hand, batted her green eyes at the flustered priest the entire time. She is going to grow into a true Celtic beauty, just like her mother," Conel said to his blushing spouse.

"Hugh reminds me so much of Munli," replied Meva, trying to change the subject.

"He does have many of our friend's mannerisms," Conel agreed. "But there is a difference. Munli was chubby and always seemed vulnerable, while Hugh is anything but vulnerable; however, he has managed to attain Munli's girth." Both parents laughed, picturing as they did the portly Munli standing next to their robust son.

"There is one thing. I noticed something strange about Hugh's behavior. He senses. No, he knows, whenever either of the other two is hurt. Yesterday, he and I were alone in the hut when he remarked that Una would soon be coming in crying. My ears perked up, but I didn't hear a thing. Within a few minutes, she came crashing through the door holding her arm after falling from a horse. That was not the first time that I observed his insight. It must have something to do with being a triplet."

The parents, though astonished, accepted the multiple birth as an omen of good fortune. The triple birth, one of the rarest of events, raised the status of the Mayri even higher among their fellow Celts. Only after the birth, did Munli secretly tell Conel of his bargain with the gods. Displaying a typical Druid trait, he did not share that certain skills were preordained for each triplet.

The children of Conel and Meva were among the favored few to receive a higher education at the Druid school. In fact, they were among the few to receive any type of formal education. Each clan's priest taught the essentials of letters and words to the children of the chieftains, warriors, Druids and skilled artisans. On occasion, other free people with expertise essential for the good of the clan were admitted to the ruling hierarchy. But only the children of a clan chieftain, and a few others, were entitled to learn to read and write. Conel took particular pride in how well his young children could speak Greek; learning that language was essential for the Celts did not possess an alphabet of their own.

The Mayri chieftain let his thoughts drift to a conversation that he had years earlier with his Druid friend. "You would be surprised at the infighting that goes on within the priesthood," Munli stated as he began the discussion. "The order uses many subtleties to retain their power. Druids maintain that loss of memory is a direct result of depending on written documents. That's why they restrict the ability to read and write beyond an elementary level for themselves. In fact, the priesthood frowns on anyone outside the order learning to read. Even we Druids rely mostly on our memory, instead of written material. I think that in order to retain our power, we make it almost impossible for the general population to learn to read and write."

"How about Turk, the clan's trader? He can read and write!" Conel interrupted his friend to argue the point.

"In recent years, the priesthood relented from their stanch rules," Munli replied. "But, they only yielded because of the advent of commerce and the need of the Celtic traders to document transactions with foreigners."

Munli's final statement weighted heavily on Conel, "Make certain that the children are educated as soon as possible. We do not know when their talents will be needed."

The schooling of the triplets began when they passed their second birthday. By his sixth birth year, Hugh was bored by the old priest's lack of imagination. Advanced subjects, such as science, art, and religion were taught to children nine years old and older only at the Druid campus. Conel, driven by a concern that he could not share with Meva, insisted his children receive an early education in those essential subjects and used his considerable influence to achieve this. So off the triplets went at age seven, much to the delight of Hugh.

On the first day of the new school year, Mick, Una and Hugh joined the other six children from their oppidum for the fifty kilometer trek to the school. There they would mix with over two hundred children from all over Helvetia.

Druid School circa 399 BC
At age nine with two years schooling under their belt, the triplets were experienced riders. Hugh, however, still had trouble controlling his mount on the raft across the river Saône that flowed

north of the Mayri Oppidum. Despite his lack of horsemanship, the twice-monthly trip was usually uneventful.

During their stay, they lived in a small hut attached to the school. The meals were edible and nourishing, but compared to the cooking of their household slaves, the triplets found the food to be bland and unappetizing. Hugh, with his hearty appetite, was the only one who never complained.

Like his parents before him, Hugh would learn what the Druids taught and, more importantly for the future priest, he would learn about the Druid priesthood itself. He already knew that Celts feared their priests more than they feared their many deities. This unnatural apprehension was instilled during mandatory attendance at the many rituals. During a conversation with his siblings, Hugh emphasized the importance of the Druids and the strategic role the priesthood played in the fate of the nation. "They are the keepers of the Celtic law, and are great natural scientists, who have an extensive knowledge of astronomy and physics."

"Why is that so important?" Mick challenged.

"By using their calendars, the Druids tell the farmers when to plant in the spring and when to harvest in the fall. Furthermore, the priests preside over all religious ceremonies, supervise animal and human sacrifices, and have the power to excommunicate someone and prevent them from participating in worship on the four feast days: Samain, Imboloc, Beltain and Rivos. Surely, you know that excommunication is the severest of penalties because it severs ties to the tribe as well as to the gods. During life, those punished are outcasts, and at death, they receive no burial without which their souls can't enter the otherworld. Without reincarnation, the person is chained to the earth forever."

In school, the triplets learned by verbal instruction. The nights were given over to memorizing by repetition. Teachers tested each student before they departed from the two-weeklong classes. If a student failed to pass this examination, he or she remained for an extra day and night under the tutelage of a wrathful schoolmaster. This punishment resulted in a long, lonely trip home. Arriving at their oppidum, the errant student was subject to further punishment administered either by parents or by clan leaders, whoever felt the most offended.

In the case of the triplets, their record of punishment varied by child. Una relied on charm to avoid punishment. Born with an artistic sense, she captured the essence of the lessons. With an ear for music, she spoke flawless Greek because she mimicked the instructor's inflection. Both traits made her the teacher's pet. She greeted each day with an effervescent enthusiasm, and her bubbly nature caused others to be delighted with her company. At an early age, she learned to use her female guile along with her good humor, to easily dupe others into doing things her way.

Hugh, who was always prepared for his lessons, never got into trouble. Wise beyond his years, he proved to be an ardent observer of human peculiarities. He studied the weaknesses of others as well as their actions and reactions. This insight provided him with a potent weapon to use against the taunts of his peers. Since he was shorter and less athletic than children years younger, he became a natural target. By knowing the very deed that would most upset an adversary, Hugh easily foiled many a prank, often by turning the tables on his antagonist.

The miller's son felt the impact of this sharp humor. The big lad, more slow-witted than most of his mates, prevented their picking on him by picking on others first. Hugh, one of his more frequent targets, became annoyed with the special attention. He studied McMiller's habits, waiting for an opportunity. Finally, he came upon the lad bathing in a nearby stream. After deftly collecting the clothes strewn about, Hugh took off in the direction of the meadow with the naked youth in full pursuit. Entering the pasture, Hugh tossed a piece of clothing to anyone within reach, all the while pointing to his pursuer and yelling that they had better run. And run they did, all going in different directions. It took all afternoon for McMiller to gather his belongings. A rumor that Hugh planned to set his horse's tail on fire the next time that McMiller bothered him proved sufficiently motivating for the taunting to cease.

Mick chose what topics he considered worthwhile and ignored all the others. Generally, the favored subject had something to do with fighting or riding. Unfortunately, this attitude had spilled over into his schoolwork and resulted in many an extra stay-over. But because of his innate ability to master warrior skills, he usually escaped the wrath of his parents but not that of his uncle, Rochlos. The warrior chief reminded Conel of Ragenos' many punishments that helped shape him into a superior warrior. With that said, Rochlos would assign an appropriate punishment to Mick, who accepted all chastisement without complaint.

Druids, Celts, and Romans

Mayri Oppidum 399 BC

The quietness of their home, due to the weekly absence of the triplets, enabled Meva and Conel to have long discussions about their children. Though both loved the children equally, each had a favorite. Perhaps like all fathers, Conel doted on his daughter. Meva, who knew how to the use beauty and charm to get own her way, recognized these same qualities in Una. She berated her husband frequently on the subject. "Conel," she would say, "You just can't give that child everything she wants. You will spoil her. If nothing else, have pity on the man she will marry. She'll drive the poor soul insane by desiring everything the world has to offer."

Conel, caught in an argument not to his liking, simply held his tongue not daring to point out the similarities between mother and daughter. Neither parent seemed to be aware of Una's remarkable intellect buried beneath a flock of red hair.

From the first day she held him, Hugh was closest to his mother's heart. Having grown up in a warrior household, Meva enjoyed the tranquil time spent with her youngest. His inquisitive mind led him to ask questions about the people that populated the oppidum. Whenever a stranger came to visit, Hugh spent hours quizzing his mother about the person. On rare occasions, he would share some insights about the strangers' quirks or temperament that Meva failed to observe. Without realizing it, Meva began accepting Hugh's intuition when dealing with others. As the wife of a clan chieftain, at no time could she gossip with those below her station in life. Even at the youthful age of eight, Hugh conversed as an adult and filled a void in Meva's life. He would describe the activities of his day, and share knowledge of his two siblings. At times, he would ask his mother to sing and accompanied her on a lyre. His favorite lullaby came from an old traveling bard. Though his mother had a beautiful voice, Hugh sang off-key. But a mother's love being what it is, they harmonized despite the differences:

> My boy, you remind me of a friend from my youth, one that I cared for and loved.
> A friend who was handsome, but to tell you the truth, he would never possess his beloved.
> He was destined to travel, a path far from home, but lingered on for my sake.

Until his calling forced him once more to roam, alone, I pine in his wake.
He took a voyage to a land far away, a land that's very remote.
I hope he'll return home some day, as I wait longingly for his boat.

During a quiet time, while the children were away, a remark Meva made brought tears of laughter to her husband. "It's a good thing that Hugh has an opportunity to become a Druid because he would never make it as a bard."

When he was just a wee lad because his father liked to see the fat little legs churn, Conel would send Hugh scurrying across the open compound of the oppidum. Possibly to gain attention from his father, but more likely it was because he never learned the meaning of quit, Hugh would repeat the dash as often as a dog would chase a tossed bone. In later years, older opponents failed to recognize the hidden strength behind the fleshly tissue. Nor would they take into account his inner-resolve to never let anything defeat him.

Of the three, Meva and Conel discussed Mick most frequently. "He reminds me of Ragenos," Meva would comment. "So much so, that one would think he spent years learning to imitate him. It may be a blessing that Mick never got to meet his uncle."

Then she would become teary eyed as she pictured her headstrong brother and wondered about his whereabouts. At times, a traveler, passing through, had a bit of news that Meva cherished. Looking at Mick, she would think back on her own childhood, and begin to wonder if the gods gave her a second Ragenos. Recalling the arguments, her parents had about her brother's exploits softened Meva's attitude toward her oldest child. Where Una could beguile people and Hugh would outwit them, Mick would physically run them over. His approach was direct, blunt and truthful to a fault. If he didn't like what someone did, he pointed it out to the person without hesitation, regardless of age or size. Each day, Mick ended up in a fight, which resulted in his returning home with more bruises than the considerable number he left with that morning. Never once did he explain nor did he complain about what happened. Either Meva would worm the truth out of one of the other children, or some unhappy mother would let her know of Mick's misbehavior. Even as youngster, the oppidum children followed Mick's leadership, regardless of the consequences. He would use his intelligence to plan elaborate war games. Schemes which so intrigued his older cousins, Roanlos and Roaylos, they supported his lead.

Rome circa 401 BC

Her mother disowned Julia on the day her sickly daughter was born. At every opportunity, she left her rearing to the many household slaves. Engaging a wet nurse to breast-feed the infant eliminated any chance for bonding between mother and daughter, leaving only her doting grandfather to spoil her.

Furthermore like all Roman females, Julia never learned to read or write; but unlike others of her age and status, she never learned to set a proper table or to decide seating arrangements. Unskilled servants were given the duty to teach the now spoiled child to spin, weave and sew. Distancing herself from her daughter meant that the mother did not instruct Julia how to manage the household staff or the household economy.

Julia, never given the opportunity to enter the sheltered world of a noble Roman lady, carved out her own niche. Once she had progressed past the crawling stage, the frail little girl cozied up to her adoring grandfather. Because Lucius Julius was the paterfamilias, he retained absolute control over the family, including his married children. His authority gave him the power to make life and death decisions for family members, slaves and tenants. Being a part of the Julian family proved to be an uneasy life because of the nature of the paterfamilias. Lucius, a member of the Roman Senate, was a throwback to the early Latin farmer noted for his harsh and rigid outlook. Similar to many in his class, Lucius craved power, hated his enemies, feared sharing power with the lower classes and did all he could to enhance the furtherance of Roman domination. The only love expressed in his life was showered on a little girl—who came into the world endowed with the same traits as her grandfather.

Julia, because of her gender, was unable to attend a proper school. Instead, she held her grandfather's hand as she knelt by his side, listening to his passionate discussions about the problems of the republic. The atrium of the Julian household provided an informal meeting site for Lucius and his allies in the Roman Senate and a classroom for Julia, who grew up quickly in an adult world.

Even at this early age, she knew the hold that she had over the old senator. "Why can't I go to school like my little brothers? I'm smarter than either of them!"

"Child, you know that I love you and I would do anything to please you. The law, however, is the law. Haven't we discussed the Twelve Tables of Law? Besides, even if you were male, you are still too frail to endure the long days of reading, writing and arithmetic. Your voice is too shrill for you to ever become a good orator. No my dear, you are better off to remain home and learn from your grandfather."

Lucius, the only member of the household who showed her any compassion, became her idol. The young girl saw herself as an ally and partner of the paterfamilias. As she listened, she relished his victories and was saddened by his setbacks. As she learned, she developed a deep anger against all who opposed him. She learned how the lower class plebeians in the popular assembly often overstepped their bounds. She learned that Rome's many enemies would stamp out the republic and take over its trade routes if the upper class patricians, to which the Julian family belonged, let down their guard. "We must be strong and vigilant, for we have only the marshes to the south preventing the Greeks from overrunning our city," Lucius Julius would remark at each meeting of the informal curia.

At the knee of this great statesman, Julia learned that the Greeks, Etruscans and Carthaginians were never to be trusted. In addition, the neighboring Samnites were to be feared. "We must demand that the Latin League unite and wipe out this menace once and for all," he would thunder in his deliberations. Then Lucius would digress from his thoughts and praise an ancient hero. "We need more men like Cincinnatus. A mere farmer who laid down his plough, wiped the sweat off his brow and answered the call to duty. Without him, we might be under the influence of the barbarian Sabines. In only a little more than a fortnight, Cincinnatus took command of our army, defeated the Sabines, captured much booty and led a triumphal procession to the temple of Juniper. Rather than accept the honors which were his due, he returned to the plough. Our republic is one hundred years old, but we must remain steadfast if we are to see its next birthday," was the usual ending proclamation of the curia sessions. The members signified their assent by shouting, "Long may Rome rule!"

Watching the old senator dispense justice, Julia learned to strike out against those who opposed her will. As the youngster listened, bitterness began to grow inside her. Julia saw her mother and some of the servants as her enemies. On her mother's part, the hatred she harbored for her daughter concealed any recognition of Julia's keen mind and wicked disposition.

Political insight was not the only lesson that Julia absorbed in her youth. She learned how to cruelly manipulate others. Knowing that her grandfather had the power to discipline any in the household, she would stage small thefts and accuse the servants of committing the crime. Then she would watch, and on occasion participate in, the beating that followed. Normally the household manservant, a freed slave, would be responsible for punishing the offending party. Whenever she blamed a favorite of her mother; however, Julia would plead with Lucius until he relented and let her punish the offender. On those occasions, Julia degraded the slave by making the entire household watch. "It will serve as an example for the others," she would say to her agreeable grandfather. To make the punishment even more severe, she used the many-tailed whip of leather thongs with the bits of animal bones attached and made the slave undress completely before administering the punishment. One time she beat a poor unfortunate so badly that she crippled the young slave for life. After a few months of exhibiting the lame vassal to teach the others a lesson, Lucius sold her at the slave auction. His only regret was the meager compensation that he received.

Druid School
This year's teacher was full of fire and brimstone. A stout balding man always dressed in his gold neck torque and white tunic. At first his thundering voice terrified the students, even though Mick would never admit it bothered him. The teacher frequently used a wooden staff, made from the thick branch of a blackthorn tree, to get the attention of an errant student. Mick, who had felt the rod often during his two years, never showed that those beatings bothered him. Such contempt for punishment infuriated the instructor, who soon tired of breaking the spirited obstinate student. Mick suffered in silence, and only Hugh realized the depth of his brother's pain. Discipline at the school was kept in strict confidence by all the attendees because a Celt was expected to endure physical hardships. Secondly, the students knew their parents would increase the punishment should they ever become aware of an infraction. The fact that Hugh and Una made up for Mick's inattention saved their brother from more extreme punishment, such as banishment from the school.

Hugh, the prize student, was always being praised by the instructor. Initially, this praise led to difficulties particularly with older students who took their jealous anger out by using their fists. In time, their anger evolved into rage. Though Hugh frequently received support from the other children from the Mayri clan, the beatings were severe and ongoing. But the threat of violence never seemed to deter him. He continued to amaze even his siblings with his grasp of every subject offered.

Because of their kinship, Mick and Una were included in the punishment. Unable to criticize Hugh and unwilling to submit in face of the threats from the older children, the two had no choice but to accept the beatings. Blood for blood without repentance was bred into a Celt at a very early age. Mick's offered condolences, particularly to his sister, and promised he would retaliate someday. "I'll make them pay, just you wait," he would say as he bound his sibling's wounds.

During this time of harassment, Hugh came to recognize his bizarre ability to know when either of his siblings was in trouble. He sensed it strongly one night in their second year. Una left their simple abode after dark to meet with a friend when Hugh felt a strange chill creep up his body. "Una is in some kind of trouble I can feel it in my bones," he said to his brother as he grabbed his staff and headed out the door.

A half dressed, muttering Mick grabbed another wood stave and followed his stout brother. "If this is just some more of your imagination, I'm going to trounce you when we get back," he yelled at the departing broad back.

Upon arriving at the meadow behind the school building, the brothers were aghast at what they saw. Una was being dragged on her stomach through a gauntlet of students while they beat her. Mick, the swifter of the two, let out a terrible war cry, as he slammed into the nearest tormentor. Hugh soon joined his brother in the mayhem, using his staff and ham-like fists to smash and bloody any tormentor that stood in his way. The early advantage gained by the surprise arrival of the armed brothers soon faded, and the opponents, superior in numbers and strength, gained the upper hand. Within minutes, the brothers became additional victims of the jealous rage of their schoolmates. They were knocked to the ground and suffered blows from sticks, fists and feet. After the tormentors spent their rage, they left the threesome lying in a bloody pool near the center of the field.

The Druids aware of the frequent beatings did nothing to prevent them. Instead, they decided to let nature take its course. Time and again the scene was repeated. Each time the beatings occurred, the innate ability of Hugh to recognize danger increased in intensity. The beatings would have continued, except Mick devised a retaliatory strategy. The children of Meva and Conel selected an older antagonist for revenge. Una would attract his attention and lead him into a trap where he received a severe beating. Though the Mayri triplets often paid the price, they persisted in their stratagem. In time, the ongoing threat of being singled out by the enraged triplets wore down the resistance of the bullies, and the Mayri kin were left alone. This rite of passage brought the triplets even closer together than their multiple birth.

The resultant comradely spilled over into their studies. "Una, the only way you are going to pass this topic on beliefs is to memorize it first and comprehend it later," Hugh said, restating an ongoing argument.

"But it doesn't make any sense," Una retorted.

"Why are the Druids, who can pass over to the otherworld at will, concerned about being out on the eve of Samain?"

"Okay, I'll explain it one more time," Hugh said, glancing at Mick who sat with an amused smile on his face. "On Samain's eve, when the veil between the two worlds is very thin, the gods travel this world and play tricks on any living creature they find out of doors, even pigs and goats. This hazing includes priests although for some reason cattle, sheep, and horses are left alone."

"That is why humans and small animals must stay indoors until the threat is gone," Mick added.

Hugh continued, "Don't you remember Roanlos telling us about being lost on Samain eve and digging a hole to hide for fear the gods would find him?"

"But that's my point. Roanlos isn't a Druid," Una declared emphatically. "Druids talk with the gods. Roanlos can't!"

"Just take my word for it. The gods can invade the spirit of a Druid on Samain eve," Hugh said, angrily responding to Una's argumentative tone. "Now let's get on with the lesson. Repeat after me...." Then each in turn repeated that day's mnemonics until they mastered the verse:

On the eve of all hallow with the harvest moon in the sky,
The glistening Pleiades glow is seen by the naked eye.

Then the gods depart their home and wander through our domain.
There is reason why they roam. They search for a soul to claim.
Even the Druids bow to their will, silently hovering behind closed doors.
They sleep with dogs, geese and swill, leaving the forest alone to the boars.
Some that can't find a black hole, close enough to escape a god's need.
May in the end lose their human soul when gods finish their dastardly deed.
So all humans beware of a hole in the splinter and never venture forth at the start of winter.

The siblings memorized this verse, one of hundreds, to understand the movement of the sun, which dictates the time of year. Through this form of teaching, they learned the Celtic year starts and ends with the appearance and disappearance of the Pleiades, a cluster of stars, six of which are visible to the human eye. They learned that the sun when it turns around the earth splits the year into two periods, one cold and the other warm. Each period has a center point at the shortest and longest day of the sun's year. The youngsters learned that each month began with the same phase of the moon. Furthermore, the ancients had devised an innovative method to keep their twelve month long lunar-year synchronized with the phases of the moon. They added an extra month every two and a half years to their calendar. The children looked forward to the four annual festivals, which were held under a full moon and normally fell in the middle of the month.

"Now let's concentrate on the sun year," Hugh said, as he warmed to his subject and began the familiar chant:

Hostile beings remonstrate at their birth. Too much we take from poor Mother Earth. Cold, dark nights are a sign of protest. Samain is the time when all claim their rest.
As we eat last year's bounty, oh goddess of fertility, milk begins to secrete. Imbolc is the first sign of relief. Massive bonfires welcome Beltain to drive the evil from all we obtain.
Earth begins to waken its seed, refreshed to grant all that we need.

Fruit ripens upon the apple tree. Warm is the air that lets us run free.
All that is wrong is for once set right. At Rivos, we beseech the god of light.

"Tell us about Roanlos being caught out on Samain," Una asked Mick, although she was as well-versed in this clan legend as was her brother. The threesome sat quietly together as Mick began. "Samain came early that year," he said. "The tree leaves had long since changed, but the sheep were still in the upper meadow. If left there, they would become victims of the ferocious wolves that roam in the winter. It was the younger brother Roanlos' duty to herd the sheep and get them to safety before the first snowfall. Normally, he would have over a month. But this year, he had nothing but bad luck. Twice, during the year, he failed to qualify for the warrior class. His brother, Roaylos, believed that some of the warriors were jealous of Roanlos' horsemanship; therefore, they made it extra difficult for him.

"Even Uncle Rochlos could not interfere because as warrior chief he had to be impartial," Hugh added.

"In any event, Roanlos tried three times before he made the grade, delaying the drive to winter the sheep." Mick continued. "I offered to accompany him, but he declined. 'I'll make better time alone,' he told me. Then he took four of the best sheep dogs and started out for the upper meadow."

A look of concern crossed Mick's face as he continued his tale, "Later that week the weather took a turn for the worse, starting with a steady cold drizzle. The ground froze and a thin coat of ice covered the branches of the trees. The following day, snow began to fall, blanketing the layer of ice, and continued until his dogs plowed through chest high drifts. He was fortunate that he brought his woolen cloak and had woolen socks to protect his feet.

"As Roanlos exited the sheltering trees, clouds descended so low that he could not see his hand in front of him. He thought about turning back, but he knew that many of the sheep would die unless he brought them down the mountain. So, he continued on. Unknowingly, he lost the trail. Roanlos then remembered that Samain was approaching. He had planned to be safely home before that night came. As a protection, he decided to dig a cave in the snow every night he was away."

"Thank goodness he did." Una said.

Mick continued. "On the third night following the snow fall, Roanlos had gathered all the sheep he could find and started down the mountainside. He stopped just before dark to eat a cold supper, the last of his dried meat and soggy oat-bread. He then dug a cave for himself and the dogs. Although he would have preferred to leave the dogs outside to prevent any sheep from running away, he was afraid of what might happen to them if they were left out." Mick hesitated to draw out the suspense.

"The dogs began to grow restless as though a bear or some other animal was about. It wasn't a bear, or he would have smelled it. Worse yet, the bear would have smelled him. Before long, the dogs' barking diminished to a low growl, and they became silent. At that instant a horrible odor, more putrid than anything he had ever smelled, invaded his sanctuary. The dogs were silent, and out of fear, Roanlos covered the small hole in the snow wall with his hand. He could hear something or someone crunching through the permafrost just outside the snow cave. The creature walked slowly, as though it waited for someone to come out of the cave. For the entire night, Roanlos knelt on the frigid floor of the snow cave and covered the hole. To keep his fear under control, he began to hum a rhythm he had learned as a child:

Lady of the spring watch over me. Keep me safe from those who prey. Become my protection, help me live another day.

"Finally when his arms grew too heavy, he had to let them drop. To his amazement, light penetrated the dark hole. He had survived the night. Wishing to be free of that location, Roanlos retrieved his horse and, with all the courage he could muster, began to herd the flock down the mountain."

Mick continued his tale while the other two listened silently. "He took the same precautions on the following night. But since he was below the snow line, he and the dogs sought refuge in the hollow of a rotted tree trunk. Snow, unusual at this lower altitude this early in the year, began to fall so heavily that Roanlos could not see. He had to dismount and lead his horse through the narrow openings between the trees in the dense forest. The snow mounted and formed deep wells around each tree, reducing the width of the path, and Roanlos struggled to retain his balance as he and his mount zigzagged between the trees. About to collapse from weariness, Roanlos spied a small hut in a clearing. He had never seen it before, but such apparitions commonly occur when spirits were

Druids, Celts, and Romans

about, or so he had been told. Though he feared for his soul, he had no choice but to approach whatever danger lay inside. Tying his horse to a branch, Roanlos whistled for the dogs and forced open the door. The hut, which appeared to be less than thrice the length of a horse, grew immensely once he entered. The single room had a large fire and sheepskins covered the floor. As Roanlos began to warm himself before the fire, he smelled the aroma of a delicious repast coming from a doorway at the far end of the room, a doorway that appeared out of nowhere. Hunger won over cold, and he ventured into the next room where he found a banquet, which only a king could afford, spread before him. Greedily grabbing steaming meat and warm bread, and after throwing a generous helping to the dogs, he began to gorge himself. As he reached for a cup of ale, he realized that he was not alone.

"'Welcome to the otherworld young Roanlos,' said a creature resembling a three-headed sheep. One head, sporting the horns of a ram, was black as night while another, white as freshly fallen snow, was hornless. The middle head looking as gray as a rainy day had a single horn was centered on its forehead. The creature sat with its legs crossed and a bevy of animals in attendance around it. 'Do not be afraid, we will not harm you,' said the beast.

"Roanlos looked around in apprehension and saw an enormous stag carrying the fullest rack of antlers he had ever imagined. A large black bear lay not two meters from him, opening and closing its mouth as though perpetually yawning. Turning his attention from the other animals, Roanlos observed that the creature, a god he supposed, did not have cloven feet like an animal. Rather, his feet were completely covered with the wool of a sheep from top to bottom. Not knowing what to do, Roanlos waited upon the pleasure of the god-creature, wondering if he was in a deep dream."

"Please don't stop," Una pleaded, totally engrossed in the story.

Mick continued. "The god-like creature then spoke to Roanlos. 'Your dedication to the sheep that you herd is commendable. More than a few shepherds would have left them to their fate when weather conditions such as you encountered prevailed. You did not. Why?'

"'If I left the herd to die perhaps some of my own people would die as well. I tried to get the herd as close to home as I could before my death with the hope that some might wander to the oppidum. Besides, my father would never forgive me if I let harm befall the clan's sheep.'

"'If you so honor the lowly sheep, why then is the horse your totem?' asked the god.

"'I am acknowledged to be the finest horseman in the Mayri clan, perhaps the best in the Helvetii nation. So naturally I took the horse as my totem,' the perplexed Roanlos explained.

"'You seem like an honorable fellow,' the god replied. 'So I will return you to your world on one condition.'

"'Anything that you wish, I will obey,' the youth replied in fear.

"'I command you to change your totem to a sheep so that this insignificant beast can be recognized for all it contributes to your clan.'

"Roanlos instantly agreed to comply with the god's bidding. 'Before I take your leave, would you tell me your name?' Roanlos asked.

"'They call me, Cernunnos.'"

"Then what happened?" Una asked, although she already knew from hearing this tale many times before.

"The baying of distant hounds awoke Roanlos that morning as he and his dogs lay covered with snow," Mick answered. "The entire clan searched for the shepherd because the sheep returned from the winter pasture on their own. When his dogs shook off the snow and bayed back to their friends, Roanlos looked around and saw that he was within sight of the oppidum. Neither he nor anyone else knew how he got there."

Chapter 6
Community Life

Rome circa 398 BC
Lucius, elated over an honor bestowed upon him, almost forgot to acknowledge Janus, the spirit that guarded his door. Only when he bumped into the chained door-slave did he remember the door-spirit. His mood soured when he came upon Julia in the atrium, playing with marked sheep knucklebones. "Are there no playmates or slaves to entertain you?" he asked in a harsh tone.

The child withdrew into a corner for her poppa never spoke abruptly to her. "No, Poppa. Mother is too busy, and the servants don't pay any attention to me unless I scream at them." The frail youngster broke into a coughing fit as she finished the sentence.

Watching his delicate granddaughter's slim body shaking with the cough, Lucius made a rash decision. "It's getting toward that time of year that the air in the city is worse than normal. Suppose we send you off to the countryside for a few weeks?"

The startled and surprised youngster imagined her mother's influence was behind the suggestion. "No, Poppa, I don't want to leave you!" Julia screamed as she ran across the room and wrapped her thin arms around his legs. "Please let me stay, I won't be any bother." Seeing that her pleas were going unheeded, Julia changed her tactics. "I don't want to go. If I am out of your sight, my mother will try to kill me."

"Hear, hear, my little puella, I will never let anything happen to you. Since the founding of our city by Romulus, the killing of a first born, particularly a pretty girl like you, is forbidden. Your mother is my vassal. If anything happens to you, she has nowhere to go. She can't run and hide. Why is that?"

"Because she has learned our family's secrets, we can never let her return to her own people." Next Julia asked very cautiously, "Poppa, why was Daddy forced to marry someone so spiteful?"

"I won't hear you say anything about you father. He is of our blood," answered Lucius sternly.

Julia pretended to be remorseful and folded her thin arms across her chest as if to protect herself. Seeing how fragile the child was, Lucius continued in a gentler tone, "You must know by now, because I have often told you, that we Julians have to intermarry with other founding families to maintain the little control that we still possess. Without a strong and pure patrician stock the plebeians will gain the upper hand. Your mother was the only worthy maiden available when time came for your father to wed. She also owned very valuable farmland that is now ours because all her possessions belong to her husband. Your mother is like a child and must be protected. In fact, in some ways she is more a child than you. Now see if you can beat me in a game of knuckle-bones," Lucius laughed as he picked up the oblong dice.

As they played, the timid youngster thoughtfully asked her kinsman, "The other girls say that I am not pretty, and that I will never marry. Is that true Poppa?"

"They are just jealous because you are a Julian. You can trace your lineage back to the founding of Rome. Many of those silly girls can't even begin to match your bloodlines. We are descendents of gens Julia Aeneas, son of the goddess Venus. Who is Venus?"

"Venus is the goddess of bloom and beauty, flowers and fruit."

"And who was Aeneas' father?"

"He was fathered by Anchises, a great warrior who helped win the Trojan War," Julia answered immediately.

"What city did Anchises found?"

"He founded Alba Longa, which is now ruled by Rome," Julia answered without hesitation. "Rhea was a descendant of Aeneas, and she was the mother of Romulus and Remus, who founded Rome."

"Who fathered the twins?"

"They were fathered by the God Mars," a satisfied Julia replied.

"Now you see how we trace our lineage back to King Priam of Troy, who was Anchises' father. With bloodlines such as these, you will be the envy of every girl when you seek a mate. Worry not, my little puella."

"But Poppa, I still don't have any friends."

"Some of those friends you desire are beneath you. They are merely plebeians in disguise and a curse on the Senate, which decades ago allowed plebeians to marry patricians. That is one of the reasons why the codes state that only boys may be educated. Girls, like the ones you talk about, are too frivolous. They need guardians even when they grow old."

Later that evening, Lucius had a long conversation with Vopiscus. "As my oldest son, you are going to have to assume more of a share in running this household. In addition to being a senator, I have been appointed one of the pontifices and will begin my term after the festival of the Compitalia, which falls at the end of the agricultural year. I am now one of the three most powerful men in Rome because I will control the Roman religion."

Vopiscus, who saw his own star rising along with that of his father, warmly received the news and suggested they celebrate.

"I am too busy to party," said his austere father. "Even though I am not yet in office, I must participate in the duties as though I were. Setting the dates of next year's festivals will not wait until this year is finished." It was then that Lucius told Vopiscus of his decision to send Julia to the farm.

"Is that wise, Father? Why, just today I overheard a senator telling about Etruscan bandits raiding his farm." Fortunately for Vopiscus, his back was turned away from his wife, who was starring at him with venom.

"No one would dare attack a holding of mine," Lucius roared. "Besides, isn't it time to send extra help to gather in the harvest? She can accompany them."

When they were finally alone, Vopiscus' wife berated him for not immediately agreeing to send Julia to the farm. Then she told her husband of an idea that had just come to her. The angry spat that followed between Vopiscus and his wife kept most of the household awake. None could distinguish the words, so they passed it off as a quarrel over lovemaking.

"How could you even think to do such a thing, when, after all, she's a child of your flesh?" asked the weak and oftentimes henpecked husband.

"She's a spawn of something from the underworld. She is no child of mine! Didn't you witness how she beats my slaves? My slaves! And the evil old man, your father, encourages her. She must be stopped!"

"How? You know my father will kill both of us if he even suspects that we wish harm to Julia."

"Now is the perfect opportunity. He has decided that Julia should travel to the country. Even you warned him against such a foolhardy move. Therefore, he can't blame you should some harm befall her."

"How can we accomplish such a thing? I don't know of anyone who would kidnap a child of Lucius Julius."

"Well, I do! There are plenty of people who will do things for the right reward. I will arrange it, so the captain of our guard will either kill her outright or turn her over to someone who will."

"Suppose he talks. We will be in his debt forever."

"I have given this a lot of thought since your father decided to send her to the country. You will lead the party that goes to investigate the murder."

"Me?" asked a terrified Vopiscus.

"Who better? After all, she is your daughter, and you did advise against her going. When you arrive, execute the obliging captain as the traitor that he is. Nothing could be easier. Now go to sleep."

Mayri Oppidum circa 398 BC

Just as Hugh knew when a sibling is in danger, Meva had a knack for knowing the day's weather even before she put her head outside the door. This morning, as she was braiding her hair following her daily bath, she chastised Conel on his choice of clothes. "It seems that you always want to delay the coming of a season," she remarked as she put down her bronze mirror and bone comb with its metal strengthening strip. "Spring was half over before I could get you out of winter clothing. Now winter is almost upon us, and you still dress for fall. What is it with you? Today is not the day to select a light garment. I do not want a husband coming home chilled to the bone."

Conel, who had yet to shave that day, just grinned as he recalled the many times when as a small boy his mother said the very same thing to him. But how Meva could predict the day's weather had been a mystery to him since the day they wed. Following her suggestion, he had donned his winter trousers and wool stockings. His knee-high, leather boots rounded out his winter attire. Even being so bundled up, the first taste of winter brought shivers to his spine. He was a handsome man with his reddish-blonde hair and just a hint of gray flecks around the temple. The flowing mustache, worn by Celtic warriors for as long as any could remember, covered the space beneath his long nose and upper lip and hid any imperfections in his cheeks. Like others of the warrior class, he was clean-shaven below the mustache. His long, somewhat narrow face, looking as if like it was made for his large blue eyes, was beginning to be creased by laugh lines around his mouth and worry lines across his brow. His father had not bothered to tell him about all the concerns of a chieftain before he accepted the job.

Meva looked up at her husband as he stood on the rampart of their fort city. Though she still loved him dearly, she realized that Conel had changed. He had become more moody, more withdrawn than he was during the days of their courtship. 'Maybe the responsibility of being the chieftain has caused the change. 'No,' she thought, 'It happened long before Conel was elected, even before Munli died over a decade ago.' She sensed the change occurred around the time that Ragenos inexplicably left the clan to roam unknown territories. Conel, who once would tell her his innermost thoughts, now revealed little of what concerned him. Knowing she could do nothing but support him, she slipped into her cloak to ward off the wind and proceeded on her daily errands.

Today of all days, Conel was grateful that Meva had insisted he wear his heavy woolen tunic and his cloak as well. The weather had taken a turn for the worst and winter wasn't long off. Looking south toward the saw-toothed Alpine mountain range, he knew it would be snowing in the passes. 'I wonder how Turk is making out on his return trip,' he thought to himself, as he re-secured his cloak with a large brooch inscribed with an boar, the emblem of his office.

His wife had presented him the brooch on his first day as chief. Since then, he had been re-elected so often that the annual election was becoming routine. His father held the post before him, and Conel hoped to have Una follow him when he retired. Smiling to himself, he thought about the reaction his normally delightful daughter would have upon hearing of his selection. 'I doubt that she will express joy. I wonder if I can convince Meva to give her the tidings. Fat chance of that ever happening, she will sit still and smile at my dilemma.' He would rather face an armed opponent in single combat than enter into a confrontational conversation with either of the females in his family.

In many ways, Conel resembled his father, both in looks and in outlook. Both worked to improve the welfare of their people without trying to enhance their own status. The philosophy that guided them may be best expressed by an old Celtic proverb, "the dog with the most meat is always in danger." Conel spent endless council meetings trying to teach the meaning of this proverb to his fellow members. In his even-tempered approach, he would often end a discussion, "I know we can afford such an extravagance, but to do so would be flaunting our wealth. For the most part, the Helvetii elders leave us alone because they believe we are barely getting by. If they ever think otherwise, our taxes will rise and the living standard for every member of our clan will go down. Mark my words."

Conel began each day standing on the upper bulwark of the oppidum decked out in the checkered cloth of his clan. He loved wearing the distinctive plaid of the Mayri with its wide green and white stripes intersected by thin yellow and red thread. The vibrant multi-color clothing allowed his people to stand out in a crowd, making the Mayri a clan to be envied. Being a male, he was prevented from learning about the process the women of the clan used to fabricate the colors that changed the drab wool into a cloth of splendor. Nor was it likely he would ever find out.

As he made his rounds, he discovered the north wind had indeed kicked up and the darkening clouds indicated that rain was on the way. In the distance, Conel saw choppy whitecaps on Lake Lucerne's misty waters, gray and apprehensive as his mood. On cloudy days, the windy vantage point on the east wall overlooked the gentle green of the meadow that swept to the edge of the foreboding forest. Only the glacier-fed streams rushing toward the lake disturbed this tranquil landscape. The distant snow-capped Alps made this scene, in Conel's mind, the most beautiful sight on earth.

Conel could never view the mountain pass, partially visible in the distance, without remembering his deceased friend, Munli. He believed what Munli had revealed, and his recurring dream reinforced the truth of the tale that foretold death and destruction would someday pour through the southern mountain pass. Only he, of all his clan, was aware of the prophecy. Therefore, he alone had the obligation to prepare his people to meet that great threat. This was the legacy left him by the Druid.

His thoughts of Munli weren't always as somber. They had been the best of friends although Munli, chubby and shorter in stature, was more adventuresome than either Ragenos or Conel. Whenever the threesome encountered trouble, they could blame one of Munli's plots. He smiled as he recalled the time they ignored the warnings of their parents and entered the forest near the shrine of the Goddess Sulis, where the Druids caught them spying on a priestly ritual. The sight of a Druid wearing his full regalia, a white tunic with gold accessories and carrying his wooden staff, could throw the fear of the gods into any child and most adults. Just as the lads prepared to make their getaway, a hand collared each by the scruff of the neck, and halted them in their tracks, a fright never to be forgotten. The three youths, upon being dragged before the chief priest, believed it would be their last day on earth. White with fear, Conel and Ragenos left the talking up to their more eloquent friend. He could smile now, some twenty years later, at the memory of watching Munli lie with a straight face. "We only came into the nemeton because we are interested in becoming Druids," proclaimed young Munli as he pleaded their case. The Master Druid gave them swift kicks to their rears and thumps on their heads with his staff before quickly and roughly ushering them from the vicinity of the shrine. Conel imagined he saw a smile cross the Master Druid's face as though the great one was recalling an episode from his own youth. Conel wasn't sure if he had a greater fear of the vengeance from the gods for his misbehavior or his father's anger should he hear of the youths spying on the priests. In time, the fear dissipated, and the trio went off on some other mischievous deed.

Despite the obligation Munli forced upon him and his family, Conel could only think fondly of his boyhood friend. Never one to be morbid long, today he was content to enjoy what he and his clan possessed. He looked toward the widespread forest, which protected his clan's holdings from those of the neighboring clans. Indeed, the Mayri clan was abundantly blessed beyond most others. They enjoyed cultivated land in both the high and low meadows. Their oppidum was located in a broad valley, astride a lake teaming with fish and other fruits of the sea. The neighboring hills provided iron ore and salt, which the men mined by tunneling into the earth. They collected small amounts of gold from the streams that flowed from the glacier above. The forest, in addition to providing protection, provided ample wild game and fowl that the clan hunted.

He thought of the days when his older brother, Rochlos, taught him to hunt boar, deer and other animals. Often when they were supposed to be tending the clan's domesticated cattle and sheep, the two siblings would sneak off into the adjacent woods and try to trap some game. Once when their spears brought down a young deer, they argued over what to do with the carcass. At first, they intended to leave it and return to herding the sheep. Further discussion on the matter made the two brothers fear to leave it to rot, lest they distress the gods. They finally decided to bring it home and face the wrath of their father. Praying they were not too late, the brothers slashed the throat of the animal and allowed its blood to spill onto Mother Earth. As they performed the ritual which allows the spirit to separate and depart from the remains, the young brothers chanted:

Oh worthy four-footed creature, accept our gratitude for your substance. Thy meat will feed the people of the Mayri and thy skin will clothe us. Gods of the earth accept as our offering this blood. Let it flow back into your bosoms. Cernunnos, swiftly transport the spirit of this noble beast into your realm.

On arriving home with their kill, the boys found their father upset with their shirking of their duty and furious that they had killed a doe. "Female animals replenish the earth," he roared. "From now on, look before you aim and then only kill the male of the species. Did you perform the blood ritual releasing the spirit of the creature to the Otherworld or did you forget to do that as well?" their angry father asked, only to settle down when the brothers swore they had done their duty. As furious as their father was over the slaughter of the female deer, the family enjoyed the fresh meat for many meals. "Not eating what you kill is a sin against the gods," his father said, rationalizing his behavior to the household.

Conel shook off the pleasure of reminiscing of days gone by and returned to the present. When he looked toward the west, he took in the varied colors of the cultivated plain, the breadbasket of the clan. He loved the flowering of the fruit trees in early spring. These woods, grains and fruits, plus the plentiful seafood of the lake, provided ample sustenance. 'Thank the gods there are those among us who take pleasure from this labor,' he thought aloud, following a short prayer he said for the workers.

Conel's real contentment came from looking within his clan's hill-fort. He took pleasure in the commotion and bustle, as dozens of people made their way to and from the open-air market. As was his habit, he took time to supervise the work of the artisans who were finishing the additions that would make the Mayri's hill-fort the strongest oppidum in the entire Helvetii nation. Strengthening the fort was not just a vain gesture and not one that Conel took lightly. Their fort, situated near one of the Alpine passes, must be made as strong as possible. He alone knew the reason. Time had not yet come to share the secret that burdened his heart. He insisted that the walled settlement include the bubbling underground spring that fed the clan's well. He further required that it be covered with a steel grate. Without disclosing his purpose, Conel secured precious water for his clan in the event of a long siege.

Conel was delighted that his brother, Rochlos, supported his plan to strengthen the gates, the weakest part of any hill-fort. Forcing invaders to gain entry through not one, but two gates would provide ample time to react to a surprise attack. Any unwary intruders trapped in the narrow area between the outer and inner gate would be vulnerable to the defenders stationed overhead. To his credit, Rochlos never wavered in his support, nor did he question the need for the additional barricades, two timber walls, seven-meters high sandwiching sun-dried mud bricks five-meters high. The upper structure rested on a stone and timber foundation three spear lengths thick. The combination of timber-lined walls and the brick medium provided a protected walkway for the defenders. Timbers nailed together and interlaced horizontally through the lower stone foundation provided additional support to the tall structure. The stone foundation protected against fire, and the timber supports made breaching by a battering ram impractical.

With the added space, a protected water supply and a six month food-reserve, Conel felt that his clan could withstand a siege by any of the rival clans or by any invading tribe. Smiling to himself, he doubted that any over-exuberant, attacker would have the patience to outwait the Mayri for a month, let alone six months.

The settlement of the Mayri clan, resting on the shores of Lake Lucerne, resembled a hamlet more than a fort. The merchants, metalsmiths, weavers, carpenters and artisans had already assembled their various venues within the stronghold. Only hunters, herders, fishermen and farmers remained on the land outside the walls. Conel could sense the energy of the townspeople as they performed their daily routines.

As the family of the clan chief, Meva and Conel ate from their own stores prepared by two slaves. Others in the upper class, Druids, warriors and master craftsmen also had slaves to prepare their meals. The families of less skilled craftsmen, freemen and slave laborers used common facilities and the clan's central stores. They carried the hot evening meal from the central fires to their living quarters. Even at this early hour with the sun beginning its path across the oppidum, cooks could be seen fishing animal joints out of the bronze caldrons with flesh hooks or pulling the large pots off the flames by the iron chains. The wind carried the smoke and fragrance of the cooking food across the entire town. Noise of children playing, or young herders chasing a runaway calf, rose to greet Conel's ears. He looked down on the path that led to the gate and watched the traders bringing their goods to town, the farmers carrying sacks of grain on their backs and the smiths hauling carts of the iron ore toward their fires. These were his people, and Conel felt proud.

As he walked the wall path, Conel could clearly see Meva, his spouse for over a dozen years, looking as beautiful as the day they declared their fidelity. Today, she wore her red hair in braids looking every bit a great lady of the tribe. Her hair was held in place by interlacing combs, made of animal bone strengthened by a thin strip of metal. As suited her station, the wife of the chieftain wore a large gold clasp, which gathered and held her cloak about her neck. Rarely did she make use of the hood of the cloak, despite inclement weather. Meva enjoyed showing off her natural elegance, and the hood would hide her beautiful waist length hair. Of all the upper class ladies in the clan, she was one of the fortunate few who did not need to color her cheeks or dye her hair with the berry juice. Despite the approach of middle age, not the slightest indication of gray could be found in the glorious crown of red. Though she would rarely admit it, Meva used enamel to paint her fingernails.

    Conel knew in his heart that his marriage to the daughter of the legendary warrior chief, together with the fame of his own chieftain father, got him elected the first time. Conel gave Meva her fair acknowledgement for his successes. It never hurt to have a beautiful woman escort him to the council meetings, but Ragelnos's daughter brought a lot more than a pretty face. She had been trained as a warrior and performed in that role up to the time the triplets were born. Therefore, at the council meetings she spoke with force that supported her wisdom. As he watched his wife, Conel pictured her twisting her necklace whenever she debated a point with the elders. This motion so distracted the opponent that he would lose both his train of thought and the argument. Meva was his counselor ever since they married. Someday, Una would fulfill that role. In the meantime, he had a most attractive advisor.

    At this time of day, Meva could be found bickering with the wine-merchant over the selection of the dinner vintage. The poor merchant would never win this debate, and well he knew it. Even from a distance, Conel could see that the merchant enjoyed the attention of such a gorgeous woman. Despite the cold, she allowed her cloak to part slightly, so the man could admire her full figure enhanced by a bronze linked girdle chain. Whenever, she wanted to make a point, she would pull up her sleeves and point to the other's face while clanking her gold bracelets. Conel believed that the merchant would give Meva the wine for nothing if only she would ask.

    Though he pretended he did not notice, Conel took pride in the looks the men and boys cast as they gazed at Meva in silent admiration. She was a true Celtic beauty, tall, some would say statuesque, with long tresses of dazzling red hair and emerald green eyes, complementing milky-white skin inherited from her mother. People of other nations would use these characteristics to describe a goddess. On this day, Meva displayed her finest golden neck torque along with the brooch of emerald clusters that matched the color of her eyes. Conel paid a handsome price for Turk-the-trader to acquire this treasure from the Greeks at Massilia.

    Concerned about showing off wealth, Conel wore his finest jewelry only when there were no visitors. He heeded well the words of his father, "The easiest way to turn a friend into an enemy is to outclass him and make him jealous." The riches of the Mayri remained a well-kept secret. To maintain this subterfuge, the clan traded their less worthy items with other clans of the Helvetii tribe and shipped their more precious trade goods south across the Alps to the land of the Boii and beyond.

Without needing to look up, Meva was well aware of Conel's attention. Whenever he looked her way, she automatically felt a warm thrill in her spine and a slight weakening of her knees. Little did Conel realize that Meva had set her cap for him when he was eight and she only six. He was the only man in her life then, and he was the only man in her life now. As the boy turned into a gangly youth, she remembered him loitering about.

Conel leaned his elbows on the outer timbers and studied his three children off in the training area of the meadow where they worked at acquiring the skills of horsemanship so vitally important to the Celts. 'They are making marvelous progress,' he thought. I will have to schedule more time with Roanlos if I intend to keep up with my children. Roanlos, Conel's nephew, was the finest horseman in all the Helvetii tribe. Getting Roanlos to teach such young children took all the influence he and Meva could muster.

Mick showed promise that he would surpass his father in height and bulk. Due to his aggressiveness, he was the natural leader of the adolescents, particularly those studying to be warriors. His inborn ability, at such an early age, with both horses and weapons astounded the most seasoned veteran. "He is the reincarnation of his Uncle Ragenos," was a comment often heard as he practiced his martial arts. Like his father, Mick was quick to anger, but just as quick to settle down.

Under their cousin's tutelage, Mick and Una were enjoying themselves as only youngsters can. Being thrown by a horse never seemed to hurt when the one who fell was showing off for friends. Mick simply laughed, brushed himself off and remounted. He was eagerly looking forward to the afternoon's weapons training conducted by his cousin, Roaylos, the younger brother of Roanlos.

Mick had the blacksmith fashion a mail shirt of interlocking rings that hung from two shoulder straps. His richly decorated bronze body shield, a present from his uncle, Rochlos, was wider than the traditionally narrow Celtic shield. "Although it's heavy and awkward, now is the time to get used to it. The extra width will spare you many a sword cut and maybe even save your life," the uncle advised. "A wise warrior learns to use his shield before he worries about using his sword. So practice well, my young man."

The craftsman combined a light, white-birch rib framed shield with oak inner-parts for added strength. Iron inserts at strategic points of the frame made the shield a formidable weapon when handled properly during a charge. Mick was taught to use his size and strength to rush with his shield, plough into and knock over an opponent. His sword, a present from his father, had a steel cutting edge welded to iron and hung on a bronze chain at his right flank. The metals combined strength and flexibility, making the sword an effective slashing weapon when wielded from horseback.

Until the day arrived that he was entitled to praise, he would have to settle for the round iron helmet for those slated to become charioteers. The others made do with padded leather helmets.

Una, the second born, combined her mother's beauty and stature combined with her father's captivating smile. The young men of the clan, and from other clans as well, had already made their intentions known. Only her cunning with both horse and sword prevented any from making a formal request for her hand. Few among the proud young males desired a bride who could outperform them. Though she has some of the warrior traits of her older brother, Una also possessed the calming influence so often demonstrated by her mother. This ability to get others to compromise made her a natural to replace her father as chief. But such an idea was far from Una's mind. In fact, she had never entertained such a thought. She loved being a warrior and envisioned herself as a mercenary following in the footsteps of her Uncle Ragenos. Una idolized Mick, and imagined she would forever be fighting by his side. Though she never clung to him, she was always in the vicinity admiring his every move. She mastered the warrior skills by imitating him, including the one-on-one challenges that were inevitable among the proud Celtic youth. A Celt's finest hour came when the enemy's champion challenged him to a deadly duel. Every youth yearned to be ready when the gods offered that opportunity. When her chance came, Una would not be found wanting.

The last born, Hugh was the runt of the litter. What Hugh lacked in height, he more than made up for in girth. Often visitors would mistake him for a blacksmith and ask him to shoe their horses. Hugh would only laugh at this insult and pointedly answer that he was only half the size of a Mayri blacksmith. With a sense of humor, an even temperament and a keen mind, Hugh provided the balance the over-achieving triplets needed.

As he thought about his family, Conel had reason to feel proud. However, on this day he was not stationed on the oppidum's wall merely to admire them. He was anxiously looking for a sign that Turk-the-trader's four wheeled wagons were approaching. 'If he doesn't get here within the month, winter will set in, and we wouldn't see him until the snow melts in the Alpine passes.' Turk had been instructed to go to the land of the Boii and buy an educated slave to train Una, who was destined to follow Conel as chieftain. Conel shuddered when he considered her reaction when she learned of his decision. Though not one quick to anger, she had the dogged determination of Hugh, once aroused, to hold her position no matter the cost. It will not be an easy time in the oppidum when that news breaks. "Her temper is like a roaring fire, and it well matches her hair color," he smiled to himself.

Nevertheless, that uproar would have to wait for another time because Conel was concerned over the delay of the merchant. 'Perhaps, Turk was having difficulty finding a candidate with the grace and manners of an educated Etruscan? Perhaps, the weather in the pass had turned stormy earlier than usual? Perhaps, there was a flare up in hostilities?'

These thoughts still disturbed Conel as he headed home for supper. Meals in the household of Conel and Meva were always a rollicking affair. Because of their station as the chief couple of the clan, they usually entertained guests. Tonight was a family-only event, but they still adhered to their tradition of dressing for dinner. Meva wore her cloak knitted from hare's wool and dyed to match the color of her eyes while the others dressed in comfortable wool trousers. The two slaves retained to handle the household chores relieved Meva from the duties of cooking and cleaning, allowing her more time to primp. Tonight's dinner consisted of roast pork accompanied by some grain and wheat cakes. The offering was flavored by a sauce from the land of the eastern slave and served on a terra-cotta platter obtained in a trade with the Etruscans. The wine, purchased earlier in the day by Meva, was poured from a silver jar and mixed with water. The silver jar, a prized possession, had been in Meva's family for generations. Her mother told her the famous silversmiths of Hallstatt had made it over three hundred years before. Because of its scarcity, silver was more precious than gold and to have a piece fashioned in Hallstatt was, indeed, a treasure. Hallstatt, a deserted hillfort near the great salt mines located miles to the northeast, was once the cultural center of the Celtic people.

Conel, sitting adjacent to the low table, did not like wine, and looked forward to washing away his thirst with a horn of ale. The family meal began with the children boasting of their day's accomplishments. Each tried to outdo the others, and all were duly praised by their parents. Mick and Una were by nature more vocal than Hugh, who often retreated into a quiet world of his own. They told and retold tales of the day's encounters as the family relaxed and enjoyed each other's company.

Chapter 7
Munli's Prophecy

Rome circa 398 BC
The Julius household bristled with activity as the caravan taking Julia to the country manor took form. The headstrong girl fought tooth and nail to avoid being sent off to the lonely life of a farm girl, and only her grandfather could calm her down. "Remember last week, when we spoke of how flighty girls were and why the laws were written to protect them?"

"Yes Poppa, I remember."

"Well, my puella, this is your opportunity to show your elders that you are more steadfast than your childish friends. Someone has to make certain that the proper homage is paid to the numina that protect the harvest. That someone is you. Now let me hear who they are and what they do."

The little girl recited the names and functions of the spirits in the rote-like manner that she had learned them, "When we arrive we walk the perimeter to pay homage to Terminus who secures the boundaries. Next we pay our respects to Janus, the door guardian, and upon entering the house ..." Her grandfather beamed when she finished the recital. "You did a wonderful job, far better than your father could do at your age."

"Remember, you promised that the next time I traveled, I would be carried in a litter. The ride in a wagon is very uncomfortable." The paterfamilias began to explain the complexities of being carried by slaves, but Julia pouted and stamped her foot. "You promised!" she whined. The exasperated grandfather made the arrangements, ignoring a sense of anxiety in the pit of his stomach.

Mayri Oppidum 398 BC

The triplets felt a tinge of pride, because they were being included in a family discussion. Normally their parents decided all the important matters. Pride turned quickly to anxiety as they began to wonder why they were included. "Is there a problem between Mother and Father?" Hugh quietly asked his siblings. "Otherwise, why was Father so agitated last night?" These and other considerations weighed heavily on the youngsters' minds, when they gathered around the low table reserved for meals. From the look of distress on their father's face, the children realized they were dealing with a crisis. Silence greeted Conel, as he gazed around. Each tensed, reacting in their individual styles. Hugh returned eye contact for eye contact eager to analyze every emotion. The overactive Mick fingered his belt knife in anticipation. Even the levelheaded Una sat on pins and needles.

After holding his counsel for the past five years after Munli informed him of their destiny, Conel agonized over how to explain that the fate of the Celtic race lay in their hands. He collected his thoughts before he broached the subject. "Munli was my boyhood friend," he said very peacefully. The family knew this and the anxious triplets met it with bewildered stares. "Munli loved this clan greatly and even sacrificed his life for our well-being," Conel continued.

"Sacrificed his life? When did he do that?" Hugh asked.

Without waiting for a verbal acknowledgement to the surprise announcement, Conel continued, "That is why he honored our family by selecting us and our descendants to carry the standard for the entire Celtic world." The children met this statement with puzzlement, their curiosity pushing toward concern. The longer Conel took to relate his story, the greater the dread grew. Even Meva felt uncomfortable at the telling of the tale.

Conel began by describing the secret meeting held by the Helvetia Druids before the triplets' birth. "Munli was chosen by the gods to carry a message to the priests of the Celts." The enormity of the situation began to settle on the ten-year-old minds. 'Munli, our Munli, was chosen by the gods?'

"He gathered the Druids at the shrine of Sulis, so that they might comprehend what he had been told about the Celtic fate. There were many unbelievers, but in the end Munli gained their assent." Conel did not go into the details of his and Ragenos' involvement for he did not want the story of Druid killing to be known. Instead he continued, "Munli had spent long years studying the temperament of the Celtic gods. One night, the gods summoned him, and he was shown the downfall of the Celtic race."

Sensitive to the dread on the faces of his listeners, he persisted for he had nothing to gain by delaying, "Munli requested that I accompany him to central Gaul for the annual meeting of the high priests. He swore me to secrecy. I was to tell no one what I had seen and heard until the appropriate time. Until tonight, I relayed this tale to no person, not even your mother; although, it lay heavy on my heart. I tell it to you now because I put in place the initial piece of my strategy. But first, I must describe the meeting.

"We arrived at the conference after traveling for many moons. I was amazed at the number of multi-colored tents that filled the valley. If it were not for the seriousness I read on my friend's face, I would have thought he brought me to a fair. The activity of attendants and the priests was beyond belief as they set up camp. The numbers of people present must have exceeded several thousand. There are many ranks from all the tribes, identified by their robes and insignia.

"I was not privy to most of the proceedings because Munli ordered me to wait in our tent. On the second day, an acolyte escorted me to a place of honor near a raised wooden platform. The young trainee whispered in my ear that Munli spoke next. I felt very proud and more than a little intimidated for I was the only lay person among so many clergy.

"When it came time for Munli to speak, strange apparitions in a multitude of different colors appeared in the heavens. Along with those present, I watched with apprehension while clouds in the shapes of humans and animals paraded across the face of the sun. Unknown to those present, Munli's acolytes added a dry weed to the fires around the campsite. This medicinal herb had a hallucinogenic effect on all those who breathed the fumes, myself included." Meva sighed and the children squirmed, as they imagined their father intoxicated.

"While the apparitions mesmerized the crowd, Munli stood motionless on the speaker's platform, situated in front of a semi-circular indentation in the hillside. From this position, his voice reached the vast multitude. I could see people nod in unison as his words rumbled through the valley. At first, I stared in wonderment as clouds moved in rapid succession to the cadence of Munli's voice. Then I found myself drawn to the words of my boyhood friend. The prophecy he related was frightening, and I could feel

Druids, Celts, and Romans

the dismay of the Druids as they listened to the damnation of the Celts."

"We're doomed?" Hugh asked aloud. The triplets groaned and Meva softly sobbed.

"Neither I nor the priests wanted to believe," Conel continued without responding to Hugh. "Then Munli, with a simple wave of his staff, caused the celestial bodies to return to their original positions. Silence fell over the multitude as though all stopped breathing. For the first time, I felt the icy hands of fear grip my heart. Never during my lifetime have I heard oratory such as Munli's discourse that night. When he finished, even the lord Druid, the highest priest of them all, maintained his silence and his distance. To my dying day, I will never forget Munli's last words."

Silence prevailed as if the entire family had stopped breathing. Conel continued, "'For the immediate future, the Celts will enjoy a period of ascendancy, during which all the rulers of the earth will quake before them like stalks of wheat bowing to the wind. For a long period, they will live in peace and contentment. Then their glory will fade. Their demise will be at the hands of people yet unknown. These people from the south will excel at warfare and master the entire world. The Celtic nation will be annihilated, and our history will be erased from the memories of the people who inhabit the earth.'"

No one stirred; although, Una took a coughing fit. "Dread like I have never felt gripped all in the audience," related Conel. Neither now nor at any other time did he tell about the vision he had of losing his hands to Julius Caesar. A vision that impacted him so emotionally, he preferred to take it with him to the grave.

Then he went on. "'What can we do to appease the gods?' the assembled Druids cried in unison. 'Help us Munli to save our people,' others shouted. The lord Druid absorbed this in silence. But from my position near the speaker's platform, I could see the hand gripping his staff was white with fear and perhaps fury.

"Munli waited with his head bowed until the immense throng stopped shouting and regained a semblance of composure. 'The gods offered one small glimmer of hope. They will bless a family among our people. Triplets will be born to this family, and triplets will be born to their descendants at each significant event in the future. If this family conducts itself with honor and valor, the gods may yet relent from their decision to destroy our race.' The Druids looked from one to the other as if to ask, 'Is it my family?'" A cold chill of recognition ran up the arms of the children and goose bumps rose on their skin.

"While each wondered, Munli turned his head in my direction. Then head after head across the length and width of the valley looked my way. Many noticed my presence for the first time. They realized that I, the only non-Druid present, must be the chosen one. I sensed jealousy mingled with dismay emanating from the distinguished priests," Conel said, as he continued, ignoring the anxiety on the faces of his family.

"Munli said nothing, nor did he look toward me again. I would have run, but my legs no longer had the strength to carry my weight. I had difficulty breathing, and tried to look as inconspicuous as possible. But none took their gaze from me. Finally after what seemed like an eternity, Munli spoke once again. 'To further appease the Gods, I, Munli, Master Druid of Helvetia, am compelled to offer myself as a sacred sacrifice.' I almost fainted when I heard this proclamation." The children listening to the gravity in their father's voice almost swooned as well.

"Munli's pronouncement brought a wail of protest that echoed and reechoed throughout the valley. Some, including the Lord Druid, believed themselves to be more important and offered to take Munli's place. But my friend would not be deterred. He concluded the service by saying in a low-pitched voice that carried across the floor of the valley and resounded up the hillside. 'The service must take place before the rise of the morning sun. Now I will retire with my friend, Conel, Chief of the Mayri Clan of the Helvetii Nation, to prepare myself.'

"I followed Munli when the assembly cleared a path for our departure. When he and I entered his shelter, he poured some dark ale from a container cooled with ice from the mountains. We spent the remainder of the night in earnest discussion and within earshot of the incantations while the assembly prayed to protect Munli's spirit."

When Conel stopped to draw breath, the triplets, captivated by the story, asked in unison, "What did he say? What did you and Munli talk about?"

Conel continued his account of the night he spent among the Druids. "Munli took my hands and held them to his face, and I felt hot tears moisten his beard. 'My friend,' he said, 'Although I bestow upon you a great honor, I place you and yours in grave danger. The future of the Celtic Race is in your hands and in the hands of your descendants. I have chosen you and Meva to birth the triplets and complete my pact with the deities.'"

Looking at each in turn, Conel thoughtfully announced, "You, my children, are those triplets." The siblings looked at each other in horror while Conel continued his tale.

"Munli told me that triplets would be born of my lineage prior to each important event impacting the future of the Celtic Nation. The female will serve as the vessel to pass on this sacred duty from one generation to the next until either the gods are appeased or the Celts no longer exist. Munli took me in his arms and looking squarely at me said, 'This, my friend, is a divine pledge that I must request from you and yours.'

"With tears streaming down my face, I hugged my old friend and accepted the obligation that he thrust upon us. Then, I fell to my knees and prayed that you, my family, would support me." Conel looked solemnly as these words registered on his loved ones.

Mick, with the entire fervor his ten year-old-heart could offer, placed a hand on his father's shoulder and pledged for all the children, "We love you, and we will always support you, no matter the reason."

Placing his hand on that of his first born, Conel continued with his narrative. "Then Munli confessed, 'Many struggles await you, but my heart is at peace knowing that a family of the Mayri will carry this burden, and that trust rests with the family of my friend, Conel.'

"This is a sacred trust, which must never be told to one who is not of our linage," Conel said with a solemn tone. He then turned to Una and addressed his daughter with a solemnity she had never heard. "Neither the father of your children nor the father of their children may ever be aware of the fate that awaits our people. Only the oldest female child can be informed of this family's burden until triplets are born. Then the triplets are to be made aware of their destiny and sworn to a solemn oath never to reveal their charge." Showing signs of exhaustion, Conel let the enormity of the events unfold and settle on his children. As often was their custom when they agreed on a decision of consequence, Meva provided a mixture of wine and water, even for the children.

"How can we carry out this burden if most of the gods are still angry with our people?" Hugh asked, after some moments of silent deliberation.

His father responded, "We will never be alone. Munli decreed that he had to be cremated, and in doing so, he willingly gave up his birthright to pass over to the otherworld."

The children nodded in awe because they knew that only the spirits of those who were buried crossed to the otherworld to await their turn to return to earth. "Munli will always be present to help us in our quest because he has never left our world," Conel said. Then, as though reciting a litany, he described the location of Munli's remains. I scattered his ashes:

> In the rivers and streams in order that our beloved Goddess Sulis may grant our people fertility and bounty.
> in the great forest in order that the horned one, Cernunnos, god of animals, will provide substance for Celts.
> in the great forge of our blacksmith, so the God Goibhniu might strengthen the Celtic weapons.
> in the meadow, so the Goddess Epona will make our horses plentiful.
> to the winds, so the divine god of the solar wheel will remain forever with the Celtic people.
> in the name of Euffigeneix, so the great boar god will help protect the Celts.
> within our oppidum, in honor of Nemetona to protect the Celts against ill health and barrenness.

After he completed this final stanza, an exhausted Conel paused to draw breath.

"How will we be able to save the Celtic race?" Una asked, pointing to her brothers. "We are but children."

"I've been told that each of you has been endowed with the strength, courage and talent to accomplish what is required. It will take, however, a joint effort on each of your parts to make this happen."

"What are these gifts that we are supposed to possess?" Hugh asked.

"I have never been told, but let me share with you what I have observed. All of you seem to have both the intelligence and the maturity of people much older. Mick has apparently been chosen to become a great warrior."

Una, after thumping her brother on the arm, said, "Even I can see that."

"To be faithful to his charge, Mick cannot only be a good warrior. He must strive to become a great leader. Only military dominance will help us prevail." Without waiting for the next question, Conel went on, "Una, you have been given a balanced personality. You have the ability to be skillful in warfare and knowledgeable in peacetime. Hugh, you have been given an inquisitive mind. I believe you will become a Druid. As my friend before you, you will rise to a prominent position in the brotherhood of priests. Those are some of the gifts given you by the gods. Learn to use them wisely," he concluded. Meva looked on with a smile of contentment.

"How did Munli die?" Una asked gravely.

With great reluctance, but never one to refuse a request from his beautiful daughter, Conel related the story of Munli's death. "Neither he nor I slept that night. When dawn came, he dressed in his finest robe, secured his gold torque about his neck and went out adorned in all his jewelry. I followed after him. As we left our sleeping quarters, torches illuminated the valley. As though to direct the eyes of the gods onto Munli, not one among the multitude wore anything but a drab gray, woolen cloak. I was witnessing a sacrificial offering, yet I did not know what to expect. I had only my traveling clothes to wear, but even these were more elegant than the dress of the assembled Druids. They cleared a path to allow us entry to the stage. Though I tried to linger behind, Munli beckoned me to remain at his side. Thus the two of us proceeded to the center of the valley where the assembled clergy continued their night long incantations. Rays of the morning appeared over the peaks of the mountains. The winds that normally blow through the valley kept their silence. Not a leaf on a tree stirred. Then Munli made his final request."

At this juncture of the tale, Conel broke down and wept openly. Each in turn tried to comfort him. Meva placed her arm around his shoulders. After a long interval, the chieftain of the Mayri clan finally gained control of his emotions and continued with the narrative. Then he said with all the sentiment that surrounds the death of a loved one, "My boyhood friend asked me to do him the great honor of performing the sacrificial ritual. Stunned, I tried to counsel and convince him that he had misread the intentions of the gods. I begged him to choose another, but he could not be dissuaded."

Again, Conel wept for an extended period and only after regaining his composure did he continue, "A young acolyte remained by my side and instructed me on how to proceed. To honor the gods a sacrifice consists of three deeds. I first took the garrote from an attending Druid. It may have been the lord Druid himself, but my eyes were too full of tears to recognize anyone. The chill I felt in my bones had nothing to do with the damp morning air, and the smell of death swirled around us. I flung the deadly instrument over the head of my friend and let it rest around his neck. I was then handed a thick branch from an oak tree, which I placed between the garrote and Munli's neck to increase my leverage. Finally I turned the shaft, twisting the garrote until my friend was strangled by my hands."

Upon this revelation, Conel broke down once again. Meva placed his head upon her lap. Mick took one hand and Hugh the other to help their father through this ordeal. All cried as he spoke about the terrible guilt, he carried in his heart. "Next I was instructed to withdraw my sword and send a crushing blow to the now deceased Munli's head to warn his spirit. The blow easily split his skull. Finally, I used my dagger to pierce his heart and enable his spirit to exit from his dead body. When these three deeds were done, I collapsed." Una, joining the family members in consoling her father; lay her head on his chest and cried along with him.

After what seemed to be forever, the family keened together. Then Conel continued, "A great pit was dug in the center of the valley for the cremation fire. The disfigured body of my friend was lying in state, and all those present paid homage. The bright rays of the noon sun blessed the corpse while each Druid said a prayer for the soul of their brother priest. The wind carried the ancient hymns to the far sides of the valley.

"Then I picked up the body and placed it on the fire logs. The young acolyte handed me a torch, which I touched it to the tar soaked kindling and dry mistletoe branches. We, the Druids and I, stood in silence as immense flames devoured the body of this holy man. When the fire grew cold, Munli's recovered ashes were entrusted to me for disposal." With these words, the tale of Munli ended. Because of the vow of secrecy, future bards would never retell the tale over festival fires. An emotionally exhausted Conel finally proved unable to continue. "We will resume our discussion at another time," he said.

Continuing to hold his hand, Meva looked proudly at her husband as the children silently departed. She then told the servants that the family wanted privacy for their meal that evening and sent them to eat from the common pot of the village.

Meva, along with her daughter, immediately took charge of the arrangements for the meal. Rather than allow the gloom of the revelation to linger, she announced that the family would celebrate the life and death of their good friend. Conel was sent off to rest while the boys butchered a small piglet. Una removed the inner organs and added them to the caldron along with the vegetables. The pig was placed on a spit and roasted over the wood fire. While the boys alternated turning the spit, they placed a rectangular pan under the pig to catch the drippings, which they then added to the vegetables. After kneading the bread dough, Una swept out the room. While the meal cooked, she spread new straw on the dirt floor, after which, she shook out the animal furs on which they would sit. Una and Meva hung elaborately decorated banners from the ceiling. From her private stock, Meva selected a special wine. The family took pains to dress formally. First they bathed with soap scented by flower petals, and then they lightened their hair with lime paste. Dressed in their finest, including the many arm bands, necklaces, brooches and rings they owned, they aroused their father.

In his youthful voice, Hugh welcomed the spirit of Munli to their humble abode with a prayer that his mother helped compose:

> Boyhood friend of my father, confidant of my mother, teacher of children, may your spirit join us in our meal. You have chosen a difficult path because you love your people. We honor your decision to remain among the living and to aid us in the difficult times that lie ahead. May we wisely use the wisdom, courage, strength, and other gifts with which we have been endowed. May we live up to your expectations.

The conversation became lively once the diners had devoured a few draughts of wine. His siblings laughed about the struggle Hugh had with the welcoming speech. "Thank the gods that mother helped him to compose it, or likely we would be listening all night."

The family used chunks of bread to soak up the saturated vegetables while ripping large amounts of meat from pig limbs. After satisfying their appetites, the children begged their father to tell them stories of the pranks he and Munli pulled when they were young. The family laughed long into the night as Conel recited one tale after another.

Chapter 8
The Priming of a Warrior

Julian Country Estate circa 398 BC
Two slaves died on the way to the family villa, one for stumbling while carrying the litter holding Lucius' pampered granddaughter. To quiet the squeals of the spoiled young lady, the captain of the guard reluctantly sliced off the unfortunate bearer's head and left the body lying along the roadside. In a fit of temper, Julia brutally whipped her former nurse and ordered her guards to enjoy the slave for the night. Before morning, the old woman committed suicide. Only the captain of the guard took any pleasure in the events by slowly nodding his head as if praying to a god.

The stay at the farm was short-lived. Nothing pleased Julia, and she demanded to be taken home. Only the diplomacy of the captain prevented her from using all the men for her escort. "Although the ride will be less comfortable than the litter, it will shorten the journey's time considerably. I will handpick the guard to insure your safety. The others, however, must remain for the harvest, or the wealth of your family will be severely diminished. If such were the case, even you might not avoid the wrath of Lucius Julius. Have no fear, you are in capable, Roman hands."

The captain selected four of the most experienced retainers and two newer ones, whom he formed into outriders. These, along with an armed driver, made up the guard for Julia's return to Rome. The leader veered off to the right at the first cross path instead of remaining on the main road. "I have chosen this route to avoid Etruscan raiding parties, who are known to frequent this particular road."

Julia bit her tongue, as she was about to complain that the path would be much rougher than the main road. She did not trust the captain because she felt he was too close to her mother. Therefore, she decided not to give the escort any unnecessary trouble. Darkness came early, so the party pulled off the trail to camp in a nearby grove of trees. Before dropping off to sleep, Julia thought of the pleasure the trip to the farm provided. 'I showed them who was boss. No one is stumbling now.' She reminisced about the killing of the slave, who almost dropped her when he fell over a rock and giggled over the fate of her nurse. 'I can't wait to see the fear in my mother's eyes when she finds out how her spy died. How dare that old cow remind me how she breast-fed me?' Still trembling with pleasure, Julia thought about how she whipped her old nurse. 'When my mother hears that her spy's body was left on the side of the road for the crows, she'll learn that I am no longer a little girl, but I am someone to fear.'

The young girl was barely asleep when rough hands bound, gagged and carried her struggling body out of the tent. Tossed over a horse, her feet dangled down one side and her head and shoulders dangled down the other. No one stirred in the camp, nor would they if they knew of her predicament.

The following morning, none of the escort seemed the least perturbed that their charge was not to be found, and only the two newcomers were concerned about the well-known temper of the patrician senator. "What will Lucius Julius say when we return without his granddaughter?" As they questioned each other, neither was aware of the captain's sword descending toward them.

"Slash them up even more, and cut each other," the captain commanded. "We will kill several of the horses as well. If this doesn't look like a fight, we are all done for." Returning to the villa with the dead bodies, the captain sent a single messenger to report to Rome that Etruscan bandits had captured Julia.

Rome

Vopiscus' wife had been waiting for the arrival of a messenger from the farm for the several weeks. Each day as she peered out the door, she became more and more agitated. 'What could have gone wrong? Did that conniving Julia find out about my plan? Did the captain take my money and flee with it? Why isn't word coming?'

Vopiscus, terrified of the plot they set in motion, tried to calm her. "The old man can smell a conspiracy. Stop looking out the door, or he will know you are up to something."

"If that captain failed in his duty, I want you to hunt him to earth if it takes the rest of your life. Are you listening to me?"

"Please keep your voice down. Lucius may have some of the slaves on his payroll as spies."

One morning while returning from the market, Vopiscus' wife noticed by happenstance a fatigued, bedraggled slave running up the hill toward the Julian household. Ordering her slave to carry the purchases directly to the eating area, she hurried ahead to warn her husband before his father called for him. "Vopiscus, come here," she ordered. "The messenger has arrived. Come here, I say!"

"What is it? I'm telling you if you keep being so secretive, you will get us killed."

"Act surprised when Lucius calls for you. Sound as agitated as you can with the incompetence of the guard. Let it slip that you warned the old man. Can you remember all that?"

"Yes, I can remember. You have been harping on me for weeks. How stupid do you think I am?"

Disregarding his last comment, his wife continued, "Remember, you want to lead the party to find out what happened. That is vital!"

"Yes, dear," Vopiscus said as his father's voice echoed through the house. "Vopiscus, come here immediately!"

"Coming Father, what is it?" the flustered son asked as he rushed to Lucius' side, while his wife whispered. "Don't forget, take the initiative. Demand to lead the questioning party."

"Julia has been kidnapped! Julia is gone!" cried the enraged senator as he moved toward his son as if to hit him.

"What do you mean, she has been kidnapped? Did someone attack the farm?"

"This feebleminded slave claims that Julia demanded to go home early and left with only a few of the guard."

"You there," Vopiscus yelled at the frightened messenger. "How many guards were with her?"

Counting on his fingers as he named the guards, the messenger said, "This many," while holding up seven fingers.

Ignoring his son's questioning, Lucius continued. "He says that the captain was wounded and two of the guards are dead."

"When did it happen?" Vopiscus asked.

"Three days ago," his father answered. "This idiot can't ride a horse, so he ran all the way. That is why it took so long for the word to reach us."

"Was it the Etruscans?" asked Vopiscus trying to sound natural. "Did the Etruscans who do this?" he asked again, more brazenly reminding his father of a prior warning.

"Who knows? Probably," answered the frustrated and angry senator.

Feigning rage, Vopiscus blurted out. "I'll take some real soldiers and find who did this!"

"Tell the consul that you want two cohorts of fighting men capable of tracking down treacherous dogs. I want all the surviving guards executed as well," Lucius screamed.

Mayri Oppidum 398 BC

Una looked around at the other youths, and felt her breast swell with pride as her heart fluttered. She was one of those selected to be tested for the warrior class. 'I'm no longer a child!' Only four youngsters were singled out, her brother Mick, which came as no surprise, his friend Brii, and an older youth, Malikii, who was trying for the third time. The triplets were just past their twelfth year, whereas Brii was a year older and Malikii was older still.

'My day has finally arrived,' thought Mick. He accepted his natural abilities in stride with never a thought of egotism. 'All four candidates should pass the trials easily,' he thought while he appraised the abilities of his classmates. 'Malikii will make the grade because of his perseverance. One could say he is similar to a plough ox that continues on a steady pace until the job is accomplished. Brii will be a warrior because he is solid in horsemanship and swordplay. Una will be successful because of her pride. She is not as skillful as even Brii, but like Malikii, she never quits.' Mick never doubted that he would pass. He based his potential not on arrogance but on a realistic appraisal of his abilities. During the past year he had competed on almost equal terms with his cousins, Roanlos and Roaylos, in horsemanship, spear throwing and swordplay. Both cousins were recognized as the best warriors among the entire clan. Seeing how Hugh was hugging Una to congratulate her on her wonderful accomplishment, he knew he had better do the same. 'Or else, she will never forgive me.'

In most clans the trial to become a warrior was less stringent than the one imposed by Rochlos. In addition to demonstrating master skill in riding a horse, each warrior had to excel as a charioteer. Rochlos would taunt, "What if your driver gets wounded? Will you beg the horses to take you home safely?"

Then turning to his brother, Mick asked, "Why do you think Uncle Rochlos makes it so strenuous for a Mayri to become a warrior? I'm told that in many tribes, it is a right of passage. We are not in any great danger unless father's fear of the Romans is warranted. The Germans haven't attacked the Helvetii for years, but I suppose that some day they will try to take some land from us. Other tribes are even further removed from fighting than we are. Uncle Rochlos calls them farmers with horses. We, on the other hand, are warriors who sometimes have to help with the farming."

On the day of the contest, the brother and sister sat quietly watching the entire clan gather. "Eat your rations during the first day. That way you won't feel the hunger for the remainder of the meditation test," Mick cautioned his sister.

"I know that. Don't you think I have wits about me?" she asked.

Though this test was not a contest against each other, each participant took it very personally. Their friends and supporters added to the pressure by betting on the outcome. Una was heartened, when her mother whispered the amount that she had wagered on her daughter. 'Please do not let her finish last!' Meva whispered to the clan's goddess as she watched with pride when her daughter was called to begin the first event.

Rochlos, who served as the event's over-all judge, called the contestants to order. Lots were drawn to determine the direction each person would take. The luck of the draw often determined the severity of the trial. Una faced south, which meant she would spend the next four days and nights in the difficult, damp confines of the tide-flats along the banks of the lake. Mick drew the easterly direction toward the high meadows leading into the mountains.

Each candidate had to travel on foot for a day in the direction given, and spotters made sure that they covered a sufficient distance. Their allotted rations consisted of less than one day's provisions and several pouches of water, but each had to obtain his or her own needs when the pouches were depleted. No flints were provided because lighting a fire for warmth was prohibited. To keep warm, each candidate dressed in a woolen undergarment covered with a woolen brat. The brat, an oversized cloak, served as a blanket as well as a tent. All four contestants carried a short dagger for protection. Following a blessing from the clan's Druid, each began the lonely trek.

Before Una had traveled a half day, her feet were thoroughly soaked. The trail continued down an embankment into the swampy ground that led onto the lake. She was grateful that the ever-vigilant Meva insisted she wear double thick woolen socks, which would help prevent blisters. 'Thank the gods for Mom,' she thought.

Traveling through the marshy soil was exhausting as every other footstep was sucked into the muck. Several times she stepped into knee-deep ponds obscured by the brambles and brush. Soon thousands of swarming insects made a bloody mess of her unprotected skin. Slapping them consumed more energy than Una wished to expend, so she coated her bare skin with foul smelling slime in an attempt to discourage the bugs. Sticky thorns protruding from bushes along the overgrown trail scratched her legs through the trousers as she walked by. Often the thorns penetrated so deeply that she had to remove them with her belt knife. She covered the small wounds with mud and hoped they would not fester.

Tall weed-like growths, which exceeded her height and obscured her vision, added to her feeling of isolation. The only signs of life were birds chirping and the occasional swamp rat scurrying across her path. Fortunately, her thrashing through the brush kept larger swamp animals at bay. To maintain her direction, she occasionally traced the route of the sun as it arced across the sky to her rear. To maintain her spirits, Una broke the lonely solitude by humming her favorite songs as she strode along.

Often she thought of her brother and wondered how he was doing on his ordeal. "His terrain may be more difficult and colder, but I would trade him instantly," she commented aloud. "He doesn't have to put up with all this mud and bugs." Surprisingly, she found comfort in hearing her own voice, so she spoke to herself often. Her long legs helped her make good time even walking through the slimy loam. "Thank the gods it isn't raining," she said aloud.

As the sun began to set and as darkness swept across the landscape, a cold chill crept in from the lake and the wind picked up. Una knew she better find some type of shelter and began to look for a dry location to make camp. She soon found that it was impossible in the marshes to find protection from the wind.

Without any high hills to use as a guide, she had to be very careful, or she could easily become lost, since all the animal trails looked the same. To ensure her whereabouts, she marked a path with her dagger. In addition, she placed three sticks on the ground, every hundred meters, to form an arrow facing the direction from whence she came. That mark would serve her well in finding her way back. Finally rather than continuing down the water logged trail, Una walked in ever widening circles, always arriving back at the marked starting point before starting again. Finally on her fifth circle, she spotted a cluster of downed, moss-covered saplings and chose that location for her lodging. Taking advantage of the remaining daylight, she arranged three of the water-soaked logs into a triangle, having to drag one of them a distance over ten-spear lengths. To complete her campsite, she gathered the driest moss she could find and stuffed it between the saplings.

After eating her remaining provisions, she crawled under her cloak to wait out the night. Never had she experienced such total blackness. The stars blinking through the dense growth offered little comfort. "If there is a moon tonight, it is avoiding me," she mumbled to herself. The noise of creatures slithering through the marsh, accompanied by the occasional splash of an amphibious reptile, robbed her of any sleep. Dawn came early and brought with it a covering of cold dew. Looking out from her woolen brat into the blanket of fog that obscured everything from her waist down, she envied her brother's high altitude.

To wile away the remaining time, she searched for fresh water, all the while bartering with the God Lugh. She thought about leaving the bartering until nightfall, but was afraid that the veil to the otherworld might be thin at such a time. No one wanted to meet the gods on their own territory. Late that afternoon, she discovered a thin stream of water trickling toward the lake. 'This looks drinkable. At least, it isn't all slimy and green.'

With a water supply secured, the second night proved easier as Una became accustomed to the bog's noise. Hunger pangs set in on day three, and feeling faint as a result, she almost gave up her quest. Only the confidence her mother showed by betting on her ability to survive enabled her to keep up her courage. She increased her singing to ward off loneliness. 'If anyone was about, they would take me for a crazed person,' she thought, but continued to sing nonetheless.

Finally, the day for departure arrived. She often wandered off the path because Una was afraid to hurry lest the judges question her lack of distance. The key to succeeding in this test is to return just as the sun began to sink on day four. Premature arrival proved to be an unfounded fear for Una because it was well into dark before familiar landmarks came into view. "Thank you, Lugh, for providing the light from your moon to aid me," she prayed, knowing that the safety of home was not far away.

The baying of their hounds alerted the worried Mick and Hugh. Racing in that direction, they reached their tired and forlorn sister—the last of the contestants to return. Hugh picked Una up and

Druids, Celts, and Romans 113

carried her to their parent's dwelling. For once, Una did not insist that she could get there on her own. The hot meal and a solid night's sleep revived her tired spirit. Before falling asleep, she found out that all four candidates survived the most frightening of the trial events. Upon awakening, she learned that Mick found an unoccupied cave below the snowfields, whereas the other two made their lodgings in hollow tree trunks.

Mick excelled in each of the upcoming events and anticipated being the winner each time. He hit the target on the first try, but the others were not so fortunate. Finally on the fifth and final try, an arm-weary Una bounced the shield into the circle. To her great relief, the judges counted her throw. The many hours of target practice paid off for all the contestants as they sailed through the remaining projectile events, almost without mishap. But even the skillful Mick got wet while attempting to vault across a broad stream using the shaft of his spear.

Both brother and sister enjoyed a decided advantage for the horse and chariot events. Being children of the clan chieftain, they had access to excellent training from the day they could walk. All the contestants who had a mount of their own could use that horse, which proved to be an added advantage for Una. She and Thatch, named for the tender growth in the meadow that the animal loved, easily cleared the six barriers and carried out the intricate maneuvers. She finished second only to Mick in this stage of the trial.

The chariots told a different tale, Una knew she lacked the strength and agility to control two racing horses while holding her balance on a bouncing vehicle. She needed and took the full three tries to accomplish the extremely difficult task of turning the team on the downward slope. When she mounted the chariot for the final try, tears of frustration streamed down her face. Only the look of confidence, accompanied by a wave from Mick improved her spirits and enabled her to take a deep breath and try again. As the vehicle bounced to a halt, a successful Una jumped off and draped her arms around her smiling brother. With tears of joy, she thanked him for his gesture and told him how much his support meant to her.

In the sword trial, the first opponent usually is the most experienced to face each contestant. Should they lose that match, they then faced a lesser opponent. Should they defeat their first opponent, or, in the judges' view, hold their own, they faced better foes in each succeeding event. If they failed to win once within five contests, they lost their opportunity to advance to the warrior class. The wood swords used for this event were often broken against the iron boss of the opponent's shield, leaving the unarmed contestant with only a shield for defense.

Instead of drawing an intermediate adversary, Mick was initially paired against his older cousin, Roaylos, a master at single combat. After bowing to his competitor, Mick raised his shield in his left hand and withdrew the wooden sword. The pair parried for position when suddenly Mick took advantage of an opening, and tried an overhand slash. Roaylos shifted his shield so that the iron edge took the brunt of the blow. This maneuver shattered Mick's wooden weapon. Rather than face the disgrace of yielding to his cousin, Mick pretended to retreat. Once his adversary responded and advanced, Mick shifted to his right. Then holding his shield as protection, he immediately charged, ploughed into his cousin and knocked him to the earth. A laughing Roaylos conceded the match. Una finished second in this event, although she faced her fourth opponent before she could declare a win.

On the first day of the hunting contest, the four carried a single spear, a sling with five shot and a short sword. The warrior candidates had three days to accomplish their kill. Each evening as darkness approached, the unsuccessful hunter returned to the oppidum to continue his pursuit the following day. A successful opponent gained bragging rights for the night, which often drove a competitor to try harder. The forest teemed with game, making for an easy kill. However, only the ferocity of the animal mattered. To earn a rabbit as one's totem, often limited the warrior's ability to acquire the spouse of choice.

The contestants spent the first day looking for tracks of savage animals such as the boar or bear. At times, they tossed stones into the branches of tall trees to see if they could stir an eagle. Mick, an experienced tracker, happened upon the spoor of a large boar. He had to wait, however, until day three to catch up with the animal. His natural hunting skill enabled him to spear the beast in the eye and penetrate its brain on the first throw. Afterward, he slit the throat of the animal to allow its blood to soak into mother earth. He then prayed to Euffigeniix, the great boar god:

Take the soul of this great creature to his rightful place in the otherworld. Release his replacement to enter our world and keep the great population of wild boars in balance. Bless the bounty for our use.

On the final day, Una brought down a young female deer. The teenage warriors offered gratitude to the gods for their good fate and boasted a little to each other.

Finally, the day each had trained for arrived. Lined up in a solemn procession, the warrior class of the Mayri clan followed the clan's Druid into the forest to the spring of the Goddess Sulis. Here each contestant swore a solemn oath to obey the code of the warrior:

I vow: to maintain my skills and physical ability,
I vow to perform the required service each year,
I vow to defend the Mayri clan and the Helvetii tribe.
I vow to earn the respect and honor of my totem.
I vow to never be cowardly or abandon my companion warriors.
I vow to keep the sacred laws of my people.
I vow to raise my offspring to attain the rank of warrior.
I vow to die the noble death of a warrior.

After reciting the solemn pledge, each was presented with the symbol of a warrior, a golden neck torque, which was elegant but also protected against slashing swords in battle.

The successful candidates took their neck torques to Leemn the blacksmith who heated the prize to make it pliable. Then, he placed a wet piece of leather on the inductees' skin. Next, he reheated the torque and wrapped it around the warriors' neck. This symbol of the warrior class was removed only upon death, and often not then. Once properly adorned, the proud competitors could attend the feast of the warriors. Mick's boar was roasted on a spit and fed all who participated in the celebration.

Meva, once again successful with a wager, added her winnings to the growing pile of coin she had acquired over the years. Conel was as proud as a father could possibly be, and he acted accordingly by bragging about his warrior children. Surprisingly, Hugh, the triplet who did not participate, seemed to be the most delighted of all.

"No time to dally, there's training to be done," Roanlos yelled as he entered their quarters early the following morning.

Una, whose mouth had never felt so dry, suffered her first hangover. "Don't we even get a day off?"

"No, because today we are going to select proper mounts," answered Roanlos. "You will need at least three horses, and now before the others recover from their feasting, is the best time to choose."

"Why? I like my horse and my horse likes me," Una responded angrily.

"Your mare was chosen for beauty, not for endurance. Warriors challenge their mounts to carry them over long distances and to do battle when they arrive. Do you really think your mare is capable of that type of rigorous campaign?" Roanlos asked. Then without waiting for an answer, he shouted, "Enough talk! Today you will get your first lesson in choosing a horse reared to carry a warrior." Then he escorted the siblings to the grassland where the clan kept the horses bred for warfare.

Over the next several hours, Roanlos assisted the brother and sister in choosing mounts. Using his own as an example, he pointed out the dapple of a healthy coat. Next, he made Mick and Una rub the coats of dozens of horses to learn the subtlety of a good warm coat. "You must avoid one that is too shaggy. Do you see how this one sweats? Its coat is damp after a short run. You do not have the luxury of carefully cooling down a horse in battle."

Next, they discussed the proper angle of a horse's foot and the density of its bone. They chose horses with well-set necks, strong backs and a proper bite. Initially, they separated about eighteen from the herd. Though each was partially broken, Una and Mick rode the selected mounts to determine the animal's temperament. Finally, each haltered the three they selected and led the animals to the training corral, an enclosure set aside for the final breaking of the warrior's mount. It consisted of two areas. One was large and allowed the horses to roam freely, but a deep ditch around the perimeter prevented them from wandering. The other was a smaller field surrounded by fallen tree trunks. Here the warriors were getting accustomed to their mounts, eager to start training despite the affects of the previous night's celebration.

Late in the season, Mick wondered why his uncle insisted that he withdraw from the afternoon's cavalry charge. When he finally caught up with and questioned the warrior chief, his uncle replied. "You have excelled in the training-in-arms since you were a child. Now you must learn the lessons for which you were born and bred."

"What lessons are they, Uncle?" Mick asked in a puzzled voice. "Aren't I to become a warrior like my Uncle Ragenos?"

"No, Ragenos is a mercenary. You were born for a loftier role. You are to become a warrior chieftain," Rochlos replied most emphatically. "As your training progresses, you will soon see the difference. Our clan needs someone who can replace me, and your father has chosen you."

"Why can't I be like Ragenos?" Mick persisted. "Let one of my cousins either Roaylos or Roanlos replace you. I am destined to become a hero, to have my deeds sung by the bards."

Rochlos answered with a smile, "That is a dream to which all warriors aspire. As capable as my sons are, they are not the leader you could be. Both your father and I see that ability in you. Roanlos is the finest horseman I have ever seen, and Roaylos may be the next champion of our clan. But a cavalryman or a champion need think only about himself. A warrior chief must think about everyone because the responsibility lies on his or her shoulders. Whether or not you admit it, all your compatriots followed you since you were a youth. They looked up to you to protect them. Even those who are many moons older followed your commands. That is the first mark of a true leader. In any case, the decision has been made and blessed by the clan council. You are the chosen one."

Of the triplets, Mick became the first whose wishes would be denied. Only Hugh, destined to become a Druid since birth, would be happy with his choice.

From that day forth, Mick followed in the shadow of his uncle. Everything that the Uncle saw, Mick saw as well. He learned the vast difference between an unorganized cavalry charge and the proper use of this offensive weapon. He was taught the importance of keeping a reserve to counter the enemy's unexpected move. "Your grandfather played this role in the rout of the Etruscans," Rochlos explained as he tried to make the young man realize that a hero sometimes has to wait for the proper moment.

Mick learned to use the armored knights to full advantage, before committing the leather clad foot solider to battle. He learned how to use stones to count the number of soldiers under his command. As each participant departed for an encounter, he or she would place a stone on a designated pile. Upon returning, each soldier retrieved a stone from the pile, enabling Mick to determine the number that did not come back.

He was challenged, on a daily basis, to develop better ways to defend the oppidum. Some of his ideas were implemented while some were not. He was most remembered for his suggestion to plant pointed stakes in the pit surrounding the fort and to cover the stakes with a moat. He also advocated training hounds to guard the forest trails. Their baying at the approach of strangers would warn the distant guards.

Julian Country Estate

Before Vopiscus entered his family's compound, he stationed two centuries of soldiers with their full complement of archers around the perimeter. "If you see anyone either galloping away, or trying to sneak off, shoot to kill." The following morning, he approached the farm and met immediately with the captain of the guard. "Tell me in detail, the success of your assignment."

If the captain was concerned with the cohort of soldiers that accompanied Vopiscus, he did not mention it. As if speaking to a fellow conspirator, the captain took Vopiscus aside and related his story. "I did as I was told and entered into a contract with some Etruscan mercenaries; ones who had done chores for the family in the past. We agreed on an appointed site where the terrain provided cover. I assigned my most trustworthy men for guard duty that night with orders to ignore any sound they might hear. The next morning, we found the girl missing. I executed the two younger members of the escort, just as I was ordered. Each of the remaining guards slashed themselves to make it look like we put up a struggle. We pretended to search for a period of time, and then returned here to await any further orders."

"Reward the members of your guard with this Etruscan coin. They had better lie low for the time being. Afterward, we will rehire them into our service. Have them depart one at a time each hour. Order some to sneak out, while others should boldly ride away from the compound. I will meet with you in the morning. You have done good work."

That night Vopiscus met with the commander of the cohort, after hearing that a number of guards tried to leave the premises. "Are you certain that none of these traitors escaped?"

"I'm certain! We counted the dead and added them to those who are still here. The tally matches those known to be present at the time of the kidnapping. I might mention that all killed had Etruscan money on their person." This last discovery confirmed in the commander's mind that the escapees were indeed traitors.

Vopiscus nodded as he understood the unspoken accusation. "Having such a large number of traitors means only one thing, the captain must be involved as well. How else can anyone explain a kidnapping taking place under his nose, and he being unaware?

Bring him to me and disarm him as soon as he comes into my company."

When the captain entered the room, he felt a slight shove, as he was pacified. Before he could complain about the commander removing his weapon, Vopiscus stabbed him through the heart with his sword. "Hang this turncoat from the gate to remind others that Romans do not tolerate traitors. Then assemble your men. We are going to seek revenge for the kidnapping of my daughter."

For the next month, over two hundred armed marauders roamed the countryside in search of Julia. They torched small Etruscan villages and burned their adjacent grain fields. Vopiscus' men poisoned wells and quickly stamped out any resistance. Innocent farmers and non-combatants including their women folk were hung. Children were left to starve.

Rome
When he committed sufficient mayhem to satisfy the bloodthirstiness of his father, Vopiscus returned to Rome and announced. "Let all that hear of the cruel deed done to my daughter remember the terrible price that was paid. No one shall ever again violate the rights of a Roman citizen."

As he mounted the speakers' platform, dressed in his finest toga, outlined in the royal purple extracted from a sea urchin, Lucius Julius wondered what kind of reception his speech would receive. 'I must speak to the patriotic heart that beats in all true Romans if I am to arouse my city before disaster descends upon us.' Lucius knew his visits to the Senate had decreased considerably since he became a pontifice. Therefore, he realized that he had to make each visit count. "Members of the Senate, news of the Etruscan retaliation for their punishment for kidnapping my granddaughter has reached my ears as they have reached yours. I can not tolerate Roman farms being burnt and slaves being freed, and neither can you!" A great roar of approval followed as he uttered this last remark.

"I come before you, not as a grandfather who sorely misses his first-born. If only that fact troubled me, I would stay away and deal with it in my own fashion. If your farm has been destroyed, I would allow you to extract your own justice and aid you if you should ask. I know that many of you have suffered grievous losses, for which the Etruscans must be held accountable. I come for none of those reasons. Although, the action I am seeking can atone for all of them. I am here because the Etruscan has taken a citizen of our city. Forget for the moment that she is my beloved granddaughter, instead, bear in mind that first and foremost she is Roman. As a citizen of Rome, she is entitled as we all are to the protection that the name Rome stands for." Cries for revenge rose from the crowd, as the listeners showed their support.

"If we fail to retaliate in a fashion that will deter future crimes against our citizens, we have failed to uphold our heritage. We have failed Lucius Quinctius Cincinnatus, who left his plow to save the republic. We have failed Horatius Cocles, who in his finest hour stood alone at the Bridge of Sublicius and defied the armies of Lars Porsenna of Clusium, an ancestor of the same Etruscans who now dog our very footsteps. Nay, we do much worse if we do not respond. We have failed Romulus, the founder of our city." The noise, and cries of, "Not I, not I," drowned out any following comment.

Lucius knew that he now controlled the hearts of the Senate, and after quiet returned to the assembly, he continued, "Tell me, my Roman citizens, which of you will go home tonight and offer sacrifice to his ancestors and not blush in shame? I, who can trace my lineage back to Troy, dare not until we make amends. Tell me, Romans; are any of you any less a man than I?" "No, no," the senators answered. "Tell us what you need, and we will comply."

"We must stop being the laughing stock of the world. For seven long years, we have set siege to the Etruscan City of Veii, and for seven long years, they have defied us. That city not only shelters the very men that attack our farms, it also blocks any expansion out of the Tiber valley to the north. That city must be destroyed." Lucius said, touching on the very sore subject of lost commerce. Pandemonium broke out among the now angry Senate. "Destroy Veii, destroy Veii," the senators cried.

"If you mean what you say," Lucius continued, "we must prepare an army that is up to the task. We must name a statesman to lead such an army. I recommend Marcus Furius Camillus. He is the only general who has the trust of the people." "Marcus, Marcus, Marcus," the Senate roared in cadence.

"We must provide Marcus with the finest soldiers. We must free his hands to campaign throughout the year. We must take the greatest weapon away from the Etruscan, the knowledge that our troops will leave in the summer to harvest the crop. That means we must capture, or purchase, a sufficient number of slaves to enable our citizens to leave their farms and participate in the military action." "Slaves, slaves, more slaves," became the battle cry.

"My fellow Senators, we must teach the world a lesson. Rome is not to be trifled with. We must illustrate our resolve with the citizens of Veii. To set an unforgettable example, we will enslave the entire Veii population, all fifty thousand people. The world must learn that a day of reckoning await all who defy Rome." In his desire to inflame the Senate, Lucius was well aware that he overlooked the ambitions of another powerful leader.

Marcus Fabius Ambustus, whose gens lost three hundred men to the Etruscans in a great disaster, prayed for the day he could get even. Turning to his son, Quintus, he said, "Look at how that old fool goaded the Senate into naming Marcus, when you, a Fabii, should be in charge. We must never let such an opportunity slip from our hands again!"

Chapter 9
The Arrival of Julia

Po Valley circa 398BC
Shivering with fear, Julia watched two Etruscans and four barbarians bargain over her body. Her terror was barely held in check by an unquenched anger because the newcomers ignored pleas to ask her grandfather for ransom. "Why should we take her off their hands?" Roith of the Boii asked his father. "She is nothing but skin and bones. I have seen pigeons with more meat."

The Etruscan captors countered by pointing out her qualities. "Chief Dhulack, we have traded with you honestly for many a decade. Would we lie to you now? This maid is the daughter of a great Roman noble family."

Julia, although, unable to understand the language, knew they were haggling over her as though she were some type of cow.

"Why do I care about this Rome? They are your enemy, not mine," Dhulack answered.

"Did you say Rome? Is this girl a Roman?" asked a voice from the darkness, as Turk of the Mayri joined those bickering.

"Yes, she is from Rome."

Pointing to the girl, Turk commanded her to speak, "Say something in Latin!"

Julia was surprised that the stranger who just joined the group could speak a civilized tongue. In keeping with her upbringing that a Roman citizen never pleads with a barbarian, she answered defiantly, "My poppa will reward you handsomely, if you return me safely. Furthermore, he will pay you a fortune if you turn over those who captured me. He will torture them until they tell the truth of my abduction."

The promise of a small fortune drew the attention of Dhulack, and the concern of the ones who abducted her. "Don't listen to her! Everyone knows that Romans kill females. Even if you take her back, who can say they won't capture you instead? You can't trust a Roman."

Roith convinced his father to forget about the prospect of immediate gain and give the girl to Turk. "He has been trustworthy for many generations as have these Etruscans. Why destroy these relationships just to get a few more goods? Besides, she may not even survive the trip back to Rome."

After listening to the logic of his second son, Dhulack turned Julia over to Turk who agreed to pay the Boii in trade goods. They debated the terms for some time, before they gagged Julia and tossed her into a nearby wagon.

'My mother must have paid them to kidnap me! It had to be her,' Julia thought. 'A bag of coin must have been given to the Etruscans to take me. By the gods, I will live to see the day she rots in prison.' Julia began to imagine the pain that she would cause her mother, before the old hag earned the cruel death she deserved.

Mayri Oppidum
One evening as Conel's family finished dinner, Una asked, "When is Turk returning, and is he bringing back any jewelry for me?"

Conel had been worried for the past month about the delay of his friend and could no longer contain himself. Without thinking, he blurted out, "Maybe it's taking longer than we anticipated obtaining the slave"

"Why do we need another slave?" Meva asked a bit vexed because she had not been involved in the decision.

"To instruct Una in the language and culture of the Etruscans," Conel stammered, suddenly realizing he had opened a subject best kept secret for now. Furthermore, he was very contrite for not discussing the matter with Meva beforehand.

At the mention of her name, Una reentered the conversation. "Why do I have to learn about the Etruscans?" she asked. "Let Hugh learn about them. He's the one who always wants to know everything." With this comment she made a face at her husky brother, a habit she developed when bantering with her siblings.

Conel usually enjoyed a rousing debate, but this one had him very badly on the defensive. He didn't wish to explain their need for a slave at this meal. Embarrassed because he had yet to confide in Meva, he took the only option he deemed open. Raising his voice and slamming his fist on the low table, he thundered, "We will cover the whys and wherefores in the morning. This discussion is over."

Because Conel rarely lost his temper during a family matter, even Meva thought it wise to let the matter drop for now. She would, however, have her say before they would sleep that night.

Later that evening, out of earshot of the children and slaves, Conel told of his dream-like encounter with Julius Caesar. "We have to learn more about these people called Romans. Since the Etruscans are their neighbors, I thought that an Etruscan slave would be a wise addition to the household."

When her husband had finished, Meva was of two minds. On one hand, she was upset that he did not tell her sooner, but on the other she was alarmed at what his vision revealed. For some time, Meva had been aware of Conel's dark mood. She was beginning to imagine that his love for her had diminished. Finally, her concern for Conel's welfare took precedence over her budding anger. Taking his hand, she led him to their sleeping space, and made love to let him know that he was still worthy of her affection.

The early morning arrival of Turk relieved Conel of his immediate family dilemma. Word spread quickly, and the entire clan gathered as the heavily loaded wagons pulled into the oppidum gates. The triplets, waiting since dawn, were most eager to see the new addition to their domestic staff. So was Meva whose lack of sleep drained her of her normally cheerful personality. Still, she kept her usual distance from the activity. Even when under a strain, Meva was too proud to reveal her curiosity.

As chieftain, Conel was the first to greet the trader. For a few minutes while the entire clan held its collective curiosity, the two old friends discussed Turk's adventure. Finally, the goods so carefully covered in the wagons began to be unloaded, including the human cargo. The six male slaves, destined to be traded to other clans, were the first to put in an appearance. Julia, the last to crawl from under the tarp, looked around at the gathering. 'They all have such white skin. Don't they ever see any sun? Look at that red haired female staring at me as if I were a strange animal. She's the one who's as bulky as a horse.'

The chieftain and the trader escorted the slaves to a holding area and continued their conversation. Una, who stationed herself as close to her father as she dared, was astonished to see how small and frail the female slave seemed. 'She looks like a sickly child. How is she going to survive the harsh winters? And what can such a scrawny person teach me?' During the remainder of the morning, Una quizzed her mother about the nature of the slave's duties. "Why did father say that I needed to know something about the ways of the Etruscans? What can that slave teach me? She's so delicate, she as skinny as a squirrel after a hard winter. How old is she?"

"I know as little about the slave as you do. When your father decides the time is right, he will tell us why he acquired her," Meva answered.

At times, instead of a question, Una would throw a dig at her mother in hopes of gaining additional information. "Does Father plan to marry me off to one of those Etruscans?" she asked, emphasizing the word father. "Or perhaps, he plans to trade me for some of their wine crocks," she spoke loudly, just to annoy her mother.

Finally, an irate Meva ordered her daughter outside. Una spent the remainder of the day wandering the oppidum waiting for her father to bring the slave to their living quarters. Hours passed before Conel finished his work and entered the family quarters with Julia. As the family and two current slaves gathered, he introduced the new slave and explained that she was from a place called Rome.

"Where and what is Rome?" asked Mick.

"Rome," his brother Hugh patiently explained, "is a city-state once governed by the Etruscans, now ruled by people called Latins."

Julia, quiet and small of stature when compared to these huge and boisterous people, stared at them with fear and trepidation. She was surprised to find that she could understand many of the words they spoke. 'It's as if they speak Latin with a strange accent. They must be barbarians,' she concluded for only uncivilized people would speak Latin so poorly. From their expressions and movements, Julia determined that several of these giants were unhappy with her presence. The younger of the two women, with hair the color of blazing fire, seemed particularly distressed. The scene frightened and confused the young slave. They all talked at once, and the man that she assumed to be the head of this family did nothing to prevent it. Julia knew such behavior would never be tolerated in a Roman household where the paterfamilias word was law. Silently, she prayed to her Roman gods for deliverance from these savages.

After the introductions were concluded, the household slaves were ordered to bathe Julia and find some decent clothes for her to wear. Conel gathered his family around the low table for a very serious discussion. Looking directly at Una, he said, "Yesterday you asked why you had to learn about Etruscans. Now I am ready to explain why I added this additional slave to our household. She is more valuable than the Etruscan slave that I initially sought because she is Roman."

With his next words, he shocked his listeners to the core of their being. "A while back, I told you about the Munli's dream. Well, I, too, had a dream. Whether it was a revelation of the gods or a forewarning, I do not know. In my dream, I saw Celtic armies go down in defeat at the hands of a people they called Romans."

Impetuously Mick spoke abruptly, "We should kill the slave and slaughter all other Romans."

Smiling sadly and looking at the boy who had just become a warrior, Conel quietly admonished his son. "Mick, how many times have we been through this? Indiscriminate killing is not the way of our people. It would anger the gods and make what I am about to relate a difficult task to achieve. No, we must never lose our Celtic traditions. Should we digress from these time-honored practices, we would not be Celts. We would have lost our identity as a people. Do you understand what I am saying?" Conel asked as he looked at each member of his family.

When he had restored order to the conversation, Conel continued, "I bought a slave from the south because I want to learn as much as I can about these Romans. The slave that Turk fetched is young, but she is the only source of knowledge we possess. Therefore, we must indulge her differences so we can obtain information about her society."

Then he began to assign tasks to each child, "Hugh, I want you to find out all about their religion. Do they honor the same gods as we? What are their Druids like? Mick, I want you to learn about their military might. Find out the size of their army. Find out how they train their warriors. Find out how well they're armed. Una, you must learn all about their government and commerce. How do they administer their city?"

At that part of the conversation, Meva added, "Now don't gang up on her. You will scare her to death and we will learn nothing. I will feel her out by asking about her family. Then Una can take the next step. Being a female, she may be better able to get the slave to talk. Do I make myself clear?"

"Yes, Mother," each answered

The next day while learning from the other slaves how to serve the family meal, Julia sensed a different mood pervading the household. Yesterday's loud behavior seemed to be replaced by curiosity. Julia suspected that she was the reason for the change. On the hopeful side, she noted the lack of animosity on the part of the young redheaded female. Furthermore, she sensed a new respect on the part of the two younger males. 'I must have something they want,' she thought. Though the realization that she was needed did not weaken her resolve to escape, it did reduce her immediate apprehension.

After giving her several days to settle into the household routine, Meva sat down with Julia to have a serious discussion. Given their language similarities, and assisted by the use of hand signs, they communicated reasonably well. "If you will teach our family all about Rome and Roman customs, I will have you returned to your people unharmed," Meva said. "This is my promise."

At first, the young slave was overjoyed with the prospect of eventually getting back to her grandfather, but the naturally suspicious girl wondered about the offer. 'I better be on my guard, for I doubt they will ever let me go.' In the most solemn voice she could muster, Julia promised to teach them all she could. In the coming days, Julia performed the duties for which she had been procured. Although she agreed to give lessons, she vowed to learn everything she could about these barbarians. She knew her family would extract a great price for their taking her captive and making her a slave. 'I need something to trade or my mother will convince my poppa that I am worthless.'

Meva made it a point to spend some time each day quizzing the slave about her family. "You say you come from the Julian family, but your name is Julia? I don't understand. Is Julian a clan belonging to the Roman Tribe?"

Julia didn't reveal contempt for this ignorant foreigner as she described the family structure. "The Julian family lives in a great city with over a hundred thousand other citizens. Therefore, we devised a method to identify which citizen belongs with which family," she said as the twelve-year-old decided to impress Meva with the knowledge she learned at her poppa's knee. "Every man has two names, and every woman has only one. Sometimes if a person is famous for some deed or has a prominent feature, he is given a third name. The praenomen is the personal name that is used at home. For example, my parents call my poppa Lucius at home.

"If your poppa isn't one of your parents, then who is he?" Meva interrupted, thinking to herself that the slave was either repeating something that she heard or trying to deliberately confuse her.

"He is my father's father. He is the paterfamilias of our family," the young girl said with a hint of disdain. Meva recognized the irreverent tone but dismissed it for the moment.

"As I said, Lucius is his praenomen, while Julius is his nomen." Knowing that the barbarian didn't understand, she added. "A nomen indicates the family or gen. Non-family members and people who are not personal friends use the nomen, not the praenomen. We are the Julius gen, and we are one of the founding families of Rome," Julian said proudly. Then she concluded with her explanation of the third name. "My poppa calls our neighbor Gaius Vibius Brutus. Brutus means idiot. He added the third name as an insult. Poppa only uses Brutus when Vibius is not around, although one day I called him that to his face after he displeased me."

For the first time, Meva became aware that the slave might be a valuable possession in spite of being mean-spirited. "You mentioned a term with which I am unfamiliar, paterfamilias. What does that mean?"

"The paterfamilias is the oldest male and the head of the family. My poppa can do anything he wishes with the family. He can order my father and his family to leave the house. Of course, he won't do that because he loves me. When a man marries, he owns all the possessions his wife brings with her. Poppa can't actually sell my father into slavery because my father was the firstborn and has to consent. I don't think that is too likely, though, I wish he would sell my mother into slavery. Isn't that funny? My poppa can sell my mother as a slave, but he can't sell me because I am a firstborn. Also, my poppa can have a slave or a child killed if he wishes. That's how powerful he is. Sometimes he lets me whip the slaves who do not do what I want." Julia was breathless when she finished because she remembered the pleasure she derived from beating her mother's personal slave.

Meva ended the conversation after Julia's last remark to have a chance to reflect on the young girl's revelations about Roman society. The sadistic attitude of the youth toward slaves bothered the matronly Celt.

Later in a conversation with Conel, Meva called Julia a brat. "She is the spoiled child of some noble family. I think we should ransom her back to those awful people."

"Perhaps we will when we have learned all that we can from her," Conel replied.

Julia spent her spare time studying her captors, so she could impress her poppa with all that she learned. The size and stature of these Celts scared her. 'They are all so big and gawky!' The fact that Una aspired to warrior status sent shivers up the spine of the young Roman. No female in Rome would even think about being anything other than a wife and mother. She avoided Una whenever she could. The males won't hurt me, but I don't trust the girl. I think she is jealous of me because I am civilized.' Though the jewelry and colorful woven capes impressed Julia, she thought little of the culture. 'Who would be content to live in a wooden house with only one room?' Furthermore, she was unimpressed with the small size of the oppidum with its dirt paths, a poor contrast to the paved streets of Rome. Their dining habits, sitting on the floor instead of lying on a couch and eating greasy meat instead of bread, figs and fruit, appalled her. 'Though they are clean, they don't have a single bathhouse. How can anyone live without those? Where do the women socialize?' However, Julia adapted to some of the habits of the Mayri household without a thought. Each day she washed with soap, brushed her hair, and admired herself in a hand held bronze mirror. 'I must remember to tell poppa about soap. It is much gentler on my skin than sand.'

Julia wondered about Celtic laws that permitted females to own property and have some say in government. It dumbfounded her that Meva had as much status as Conel. 'I doubt that my poppa would put up with that.' In addition, she was jealous of Una and other females who received a formal education. She found it difficult to believe that no individual family owned land, nor could she fathom why anyone would work hard if everyone shared in the bounty. Most of all, Julia was astounded that she was allowed to keep her golden bulla.

Druids, Celts, and Romans

The young slave accepted her job of sharing her people's culture. "Our city is very ancient, and the laws set up by Brutus the liberator, the founder of the republic, are the most just in the entire world," Julia emphasized for the benefit of her students, who now included not only Meva but the triplets as well.

"I thought you said that Brutus meant idiot," Hugh said in a sarcastic voice.

"It does now, but it didn't during the time of Brutus the liberator. However, my poppa believed that Brutus the liberator was an idiot because when the city became a republic the plebeians got some rights."

"Who are the plebeians?" Hugh asked.

"There are two types of citizens in Rome, the patricians and the plebeians. The patricians are wealthy landowners, and only they can become senators. The patricians also control the state religion. My poppa, for example, is both a senator and a pontifice. That means he controls the law and dictates when we celebrate religious holidays. Also, the patricians run the government and control the army."

This latest remark got Mick's attention, but before he could ask a question, Hugh asked once again. "Who are the plebeians?"

Julia looked at her inquisitor as though he were a simpleton. "The plebeians are the common people, of course. They can't hold public office, but they now can marry into a patrician family. They were given this right about fifty years ago, though only the lower class patricians would think of marrying a plebeian." Because Julia never paid heed to slaves, she failed to mention that one-third of Rome's population live in bondage.

"Isn't that nice of them?" Una remarked sarcastically, as she listened to Julia's description of Roman class distinctions.

"How old is Rome?" asked Hugh.

"Rome was founded over three hundred and fifty years ago on the twenty-first day of the fourth month of the year. On that day, a bull and a cow pulled a bronze plough to form a furrow which marked the city limits. Following the marking of the ground, dwellings on the highest of the seven hills were assigned to the gods. These gods protect our city."

"Who founded your city?" Una asked.

"The city was founded by the twins, Remus and Romulus, children of the gods who were suckled by a she-wolf and fed by a woodpecker until humans found them in a wicker basket floating on the Tiber River," Julia answered.

The Celtic family held their silence, and listened in disbelief. The triplets passed knowing looks, because they would discuss this further among themselves. Una then asked about the laws of Rome and Julia replied. "There are twelve tables which cover trials, debt, acquisitions of property, rights concerning land, torts and public law," Julia said, using the same manner and tone as her grandfather. During the succeeding months, she explained how the Romans administered each table of the code of law.

When the triplets were alone, they showed their dislike of Julia by making fun of her stories and beliefs. "Did you hear her tell about the founders of Rome being children of a god and nursed by a she-wolf? What nonsense!" said an amused Una.

"I was intrigued by the part of the story where Remus jumped over his brother's wall in jest, and the brother killed him," said Mick.

"Here is what I believe happened," Hugh, wise beyond his years, added to the conversation. "Julia said that the mother of Romulus and Remus was a vestal virgin. Later she admitted that a vestal virgin was supposed to remain chaste and took a vow of chastity. Now the woman becomes pregnant, so what does she do? She claims their god, Mars, raped her, and everybody believes her."

'I liked her tale of Tarpeia, who wanted the gold bracelets that the enemy soldiers wore," Mick said. "After she betrayed her own people, the Sabines gave her everything that she desired. Their captain took off his gold bracelet and his buckler and he threw them at her. All the other soldiers did the same. They buried her under a mountain of gold. That is what should happen to all traitors."

"The Romans could tell such a tale for another purpose," interjected Hugh. "They could be warning traitors of their fate. Didn't they name the rock after her, and don't they throw all dissenters off Tarpeian Rock? Doesn't that remind everyone never to be a traitor to the city?"

"Whatever we do, let us not divulge anything about Celtic life to Julia that will be useful to the Romans when she returns," Una said. "I don't trust her."

"We must destroy Rome before it destroys us. I think it's a mistake to return Julia," Mick added. "When I invade Rome, I intend to close the doors of the Temple of Janus."

Druids, Celts, and Romans

"You mean the temple whose doors never shut while Rome is at war?" Hugh asked. "Do you plan to start and end the war all by yourself?"

"I think you want to invade Rome because you have those vestal virgins on your mind," Una said with a snicker as the other two siblings joined in with a hearty laugh.

While their children discussed Julia's tales, so did their parents. Rather than deriding the young Roman's stories, the parents grew deeply concerned with what they had learned.

"These people seem to be despicable, maybe even evil," Meva declared. "What kind of father would order the execution of his own son? And worse yet, what kind of people would let a child whip a slave?"

"I don't like what I hear either, but we must be patient. We are learning a great deal about these people, how they live and how they think. Besides, I believe it is important that Julia teach us Latin."

Now Meva was beginning to get nervous. 'Is Conel thinking about going to Rome?' she wondered. "Why do you need to learn how they speak?"

"If we ever deal with these people, we need to talk with them. You heard Julia when she scorned people who did not speak Latin properly. If we are ever going to trade with the Romans, we can't be objects of scorn. There are a lot of things I don't like about them."

"I wouldn't appreciate the way a woman has to turn over her entire fortune to her husband," Meva remarked angrily. "That makes the woman a slave to his wishes. Speaking of slaves, whoever heard of having the slaves fight each other just to entertain their owners? According to Julia, these fights continue to the death. I don't understand why the gods sit by and let that happen."

"She didn't say the Romans enjoyed the sport of seeing their slaves fighting," Conel rebutted. "She was talking about the Etruscans. Don't you remember how she held the Etruscan women in such disdain because of their sexual freedom? I wonder what she thinks about us?"

Meva got up and poured a glass of wine for herself and her husband just to have something do. She was growing irate as she thought about the unfairness of Roman law.

"Their city has survived for hundreds of years, and it isn't going to destroy itself because a woman can't marry the man of her choice," Conel replied, smiling to himself at what he considered his wife's illogical position. "I am more concerned with how they share authority. It makes little sense to me to have one group in charge of declaring war, another in charge of funding it and a third group in charge of conducting it. Our system of having the council of elders select a chieftain of the tribe, who appoints a brennos as the overall general to conduct the war, is a lot easier to administer."

"From the description of the triumphal parades that Julia mentioned, it seems that they go to war for glory rather than for need. In addition, rather than have everyone involved, the original families retain most of the power. They control the army."

"But they are just one city. How can they be a threat to us? Besides, they are far away," Meva said, trying to dissuade Conel from entertaining any thoughts of traveling to Rome.

"From the point of view of a warrior, Rome can be a very formidable enemy," Conel replied. "According to Julia, twenty thousand occupy the city proper. Their numbers grow to two hundred and fifty thousand when you include her allies. That's as big as the entire Helvetii nation!" he said as he sipped some more wine. "I would be wary of treachery in negotiations if I understand what Julia's telling us. Remember her tale of how Romulus captured the wives of a friendly neighboring tribe? He invited them over on the pretense of seeing the altar of some god. Thinking they were going in peace, the men came unarmed. Romulus quickly killed them and captured their womenfolk. He defied the gods and broke a sacred pledge!"

"That is just what I am talking about," Meva countered. "Suppose we offer to return Julia for ransom and they accept. What if the acceptance is false? What if they intend to capture the people who brought her back? Wouldn't they want to punish those who enslaved one of their citizens? Doesn't Julia tell us about how secure a Roman citizen feels, and how the city would go to war if even one of their citizens is harmed? 'Rome will do anything to get even.' Those were her exact words."

"Just because we can't trust someone is no reason not to trade with them. To really learn how well they are prepared for war, we have to look."

Meva, who by this time had developed a bad feeling about returning Julia, once again tried to persuade Conel to forget about seeing Rome for himself. 'I know in my heart that he wants to go there,' she thought. "These people sell their own children into slavery. They are not to be trusted. Even if we return Julia, how do we know they won't sell her as a slave anyhow?"

Conel replied, "For the time being, let's learn all we can. Later, we can decide what to do about returning her."

Each member of the family learned to read and write Latin to supplement the Greek they already understood.

Chapter 10
Beltain Feast

Mayri Oppidum circa 394 BC
The triplets were getting ready for the annual feast of Beltain, which occurs midway through the sixth month of the Celtic year. While his two siblings relaxed nearby, Hugh spent most of the morning trying to describe the significance of the event to Julia, "Of the four main feast days, Beltain is the most sacred and the most important. On this day, the Druids lead the people in rituals to protect the crops from drought and blight. Livestock must be protected from evil forces in order to foal," he explained to the uninterested slave.

"Why don't you pray or make a vow to the lares. The munina that I told you about, Seia, Segetia...?" Julia asked, as she recited the names of the Roman spirits.

"Because the Celts don't believe in these spirits, or if we do, we call them by different names," an exasperated Hugh replied. "The Celts believe that the earth is indestructible, and either fire or water will take a turn at being the dominant force. Therefore at different times, we must honor either the fire or the water gods. At the beginning of summer solstice, fire dominates. That means at Beltain, the Druids use fire in honor of the God Belenos to purify the herd." There is a special significance to this year's feast because Hugh, for the first time, would participate as an apprentice Druid. As members of the warrior class, the fourteen-year olds, Mick and Una, will join in the adult contests.

"Hugh, forget about trying to explain our religion to her. Look out for yourself." Una advised as if Julia wasn't present. "You don't seem to be excited, but you should be. This is the first time that you will wear the robe of a Druid. Aren't you the least bit nervous?"

"I have been prepared for this since I was ten years old. Even if I do poorly, which is unlikely, no one will notice."

Suddenly changing the subject, Una asked "What do the Druids do at the oak sanctuary during solstice time that we don't do at our local festival?"

"The rituals are the same," Hugh answered. "We don't, however, convict any violent criminals here, nor do we establish any new laws. We recite the old laws, so that they will stay fresh in our minds and in the minds of the people. If any of our clan has a major complaint, they have to go to the oak sanctuary to have it addressed since our local Druids only deal with minor concerns."

"Maybe we should send Malikii to the big summer solstice at the oak sanctuary since he is always complaining about something," Una said with a laugh.

"Well, let's get started. We have work to do!" Hugh then picked up the end of a large rolled cloth to cover one of the carnival games in case of rain, a likely occurrence at this time of year.

Una answered with good humor and a little sarcasm as she picked up the other end, "We have work to do? Now that one of us is an apprentice Druid, he gets to boss everyone around." Hugh ignored the retort.

Una smiled when she listened to the excited youngsters talk about the festival. "Last year Roanlos played the part of Lug, the God of Light," said one adolescent, making faces as she described how ferocious he looked. "A mask covered his head, but we knew who it was because he wore the same shoes that were torn during the horse race. He didn't fool us a bit."

"I like watching the jugglers," said another, "particularly the ones who perform after dark and set the ends of their staffs on fire. That is really spectacular."

Meanwhile, Mick helped his cousin, Roanlos, measure the track for the horse racing, even though the distance hadn't changed from the previous year. Roanlos, a perfectionist, insisted they check anyway.

Each year before the start of the festival, the last of the winter grain, stored in the four-posted wattle and daub granaries, is disbursed to all the families. People use this cereal to make honey cakes to be shared by all at the banquet. Meva and Conel had final say over the non-religious programs whereas the Druids decided on the rituals and law-related ceremonies.

Fortunately the rain held off, although, a cool spring wind kicked up just as the sun was setting in the west. The clan gathered in the field in front of the oppidum with a good view of the hills and the shallow valley. From the edge of the great forest, the people could see the flickering light from the Druids' torches while they walked in solemn procession. Two by two, the line of white robed priests emerged into the clearing, chanting as they headed toward the small oak grove.

From conversations with Munli, Conel knew they were looking for the most abundant source of mistletoe, a parasitic plant nourished by the mighty oak. Some of the mistletoe would be used in the ceremony, while the remainder would be reserved for medicinal purposes. The gods would be offended if any were to fall onto the ground, and any offense to the gods would mean hardship for the following year's crop. The head Druid used a golden scythe to harvest the sacred plant. While he performed his holy duty, the priesthood ceased chanting and only the sound of the wind could be heard. Even Conel held his breath as the priest made a careful cut. The clippings were caught in a large piece of white cloth spread underneath the selected tree. In relief, the clan released its collective breath.

When the cutting ceremony was concluded, four priests wrapped up the mistletoe and returned to the forest. Then a Druid lit a small fire in a shallow vessel into which he sprinkled mistletoe. Torches lit from this blaze sparked the sacred fires that would continually burn during the ensuing week. Each Druid placed his or her hand into the hot container and made a mark on their forehead with the blackened ashes. Then they formed two lines and climbed adjacent hills, chanting as they processed. The eyes of the congregation focused on the sacred torches for the anger of the gods would be felt if even one were to flicker out. After the white robed priests assembled on the hills, the leader on the north hill chanted an invocation that was answered by his fellow priests on the opposite elevation. This recitation continued until two Druids lit the fires simultaneously.

Following a silent meditation, two white bulls were driven toward the entrance to the valley. Everyone knew that the bulls were culled from the herd at an early age and raised in pens attached to the Druids' compound. Each day, young acolytes would massage the selected beasts with special malt made from a closely guarded recipe to tenderize their flesh. Tonight, the horns of the bulls were bound in leather to protect the handlers while Hugh and an associate chased the bulls through the opening between the two fires. If either bull faltered, the gods would be displeased. Unknown to Conel and his family, Hugh and his associates had spent hours practicing how to control the movement of the bulls to prevent any possibility of their balking as they proceeded on their ritual journey.

When the animals successfully completed the purification passage, two Druids descended from the hilltops, and with golden knives pierced the artery in the bulls' necks, insuring a rapid death. Control over the animal was crucial at this juncture lest they bolt. To prevent just such an occurrence, Hugh injected a substance before the ritual piercing. The medicine quieted the animals and reduced the possibility of a major catastrophe. Those who watched believed the power of the Druids calmed the stricken animal. Following the demise of the bulls, Hugh and his associates butchered the carcasses of the sacrificed beasts and boiled the bones to make a broth, which will be consumed by the gathering at the closing ceremony.

The next event blessed the livestock. To ward off all pestilence and disease, the clan herded its cattle through the low flat valley that lay between the fires. Since the animals belonged to the entire clan, everyone was involved. Those on horseback drove the herd from the lower pasture. As they entered the low flat valley, others on foot joined them to drive the cattle between the sacred fires to purify them.

In the games that followed, Hugh showed off his superior strength and almost bested the son of the blacksmith in tossing the iron ingot. In addition, he also took the lead role in several humorous plays depicting the wrath of the gods descending on unsuspecting buffoons. His size and training aided his performance. The children in the audience rolled in laughter and shivered in fright, all to the delight of their parents.

Later that week, the triplets discussed their activities. "Why are you looking so smug? You didn't win even a single event," Una and Hugh both said sharply to Mick who ignored their jest.

The fun and games ended when the Druids brought the proceedings to completion on the seventh day. After drinking the broth from the sacrificed bulls, the lead priest proclaimed the sacrifice concluded and stated that the gods were pleased. Knowing that the Druids could interact directly with the deities, the clan was content, and looked forward to a fruitful harvest.

During the summer after the planting was finished, the triplets would sit under an apple tree in the nearby orchard and talk about their progress in learning from Julia. "The Romans are a strange people," Hugh said. "They are afraid to let their hearth-fire go out.

Druids, Celts, and Romans

Each tribe has a public fire that the Vestal Virgins keep lit constantly. According to Julia, the virgins live in a small temple shaped like one of the Roman old-fashion huts."

"Didn't Julia claim that she's descended from a Vestal Virgin?" Mick asked before Hugh finished. "I understood that Vestal Virgins were buried alive if they weren't true virgins."

"How come you're an expert on virgins?" Una asked, and then continued without waiting for an answer. "Now that I think of it, she would make a perfect virgin. Who would want to marry the skinny witch anyhow?"

"Ignoring the interruption, Hugh continued with his description of Roman beliefs, "I was taught that the gods Julia described as Jupiter, Juno and Minerva were originally Etruscan gods. Janus was the original Roman sun god, but Jupiter replaced him."

"How can you replace a god?" Una asked of no one in particular.

"Gods aren't replaced. They are just renamed," Hugh said.

"They seem to have dozens of different gods. Don't any of them watch over living things, such as trees and animals?" Mick asked.

"Diana is a wood spirit who also is the goddess of fertility, the cycles of the moon. Sort of like our Goddess Sulis," Hugh replied. Then weary of explaining, he announced, "It's all very confusing and I am getting tired. Let's call it a night."

The next day Una wanted to continue the prior discussion; therefore, she put Hugh in a position where he could hardly refuse. "Why don't you ask Hugh what he has learned about the Romans and their beliefs?" Una said to her father while she made a face at her aggravated brother.

"That is a good idea. Why don't you tell us?" Conel asked as the family sat around after finishing their meal.

"The biggest difference is their calendar," Hugh announced. "Each day is separated into twelve parts. They divide their year into months of which they have ten. For some reason they ignore the two winter months when they don't farm."

"Doesn't this confuse those using the calendar?" Meva asked.

"Of course it does. Julia says that at times their first month of the year, that should mark the start of winter, eventually ends up in summer. I think this makes the whole calendar useless. I wonder why they even bother using one."

"What has this to do with religion?" Conel asked.

"The calendar determines how they set their religious festivals." Hugh replied.

"I think that will be enough for now. Thank you, Hugh," Conel said, smiling at his son, who in turn made a face at his sister, the instigator of the discussion.

"Were you listening as Hugh explained the differences between the Roman and Greek gods?" Meva asked Conel as they retired.

"Not really, I have enough trouble remembering all the gods that we worship. Right now, I am only concerned with my sleep," Conel said. "I have a busy day tomorrow, goodnight, dear."

A less than satisfied Meva mulled over, what her husband wasn't telling her.

Chapter 11
Intrusion by the Germans

Mayri Oppidum circa 393 BC
\When the word came down for the Mayri warriors to prepare for war, the seventeen year old Mick immediately stopped helping to plant the spring crop. No one in the entire clan welcomed the invasion with more enthusiasm than the oldest triplet. Rochlos had promised him that he would accompany the warriors the next time they were called. As a further sign of Mick's maturity, the warrior chief assigned him to be his adjutant and arrange for the materials, weapons and food needed for an extended combat.

For the first time in over a decade, the Suebi, a warlike German tribe from beyond the northern border, had demanded permission to settle in part of Helvetia. Because the nomadic Suebi hunt until the wild game is depleted then move on, they periodically probe the Helvetii strength. This time the threat was so great that the nation called up every warrior, even the young and the old. The clans were ordered to have their troops converge on the southern plain of Manching by the beginning of the new moon.

Never had the Mayri engaged in such frenzied activity. Rochlos and Mick seemed to be everywhere, directing the massive production of the craftsmen. Every tradesman operated on a war footing. Ironsmiths produced neck torques and arm bracelets, as well as the harness for the horses. White smoke covered the landscape as the muscular smiths kept their forges burning day and night to produce chain mail, body armor and helmets. The sound of hammers clanging against the red-hot metal to make spears and arrows echoed throughout the compound. In all this mayhem, Mick saw to it that the heads of the spears were notched to tear the enemy's flesh.

Wheelwrights used an abundance of nails to secure the iron tires onto spoke wheels for wagons and chariots. Outside the hillfort's gates, carpenters repaired and constructed chariots and wagons. The younger children gathered osier willows and twigs for the wicker sides of the great chariots, shields for the infantry and baskets to carry supplies. Older children combed the forest for straight ash and willow saplings for javelin and arrow shafts. Women cut strips of leather for infantry shoes, shields and helmets

The bronzesmiths had their hands full forming the wings, horns and animal images that would adorn the helmets. Warriors waited in line to order their totem decorations for their armor. These they believed would protect them from harm and terrify the enemy. Most of the bronze helmets of the warrior class had only a guard in the rear to protect the wearer's neck, although some were outfitted with hinged ear protection. As if the noise of creating and assembling weapons was not deafening enough, testing gigantic battle horns added to the clamor resounding throughout the oppidum.

Roanlos saw to it that additional horses were selected and broken-in to provide extra mobility and each cavalry soldier received two mounts. Furthermore, he put the cavalry through their paces until the unit performed their maneuvers precisely. Then he taught javelin tossing from both horse and chariot. Javelins, with their lighter heads and shorter shafts in contrast to the longer and more awkward spears, were the preferred missiles of the Celt.

Roaylos directed the infantry squadrons in their daily sprints up and down the surrounding hillside. Even the farmers and herders were recalled from their chores, armed with long shafted spears and taught how to thrust this vicious instrument of death.

Mick had charge of the adolescents who would serve as archers. Normally, children of this age were left behind, but the enormity of the enemy's challenge demanded that all able-bodied clan members participate. "Take the wind into account. You don't want your shots to fall short and land on our troops," he constantly reminded them.

Surrounded by this din, the women of the clan maintained the public caldrons to feed the village. People took their rest whenever and wherever they could. Bodies of exhausted craftsmen were sprawled across open areas, to awaken soaking wet from the morning dew. Meva enforced a routine for eating meals at established times. After the first cold rain of the fall season, she had the youths of the clan construct a huge pavilion, covered with thatch to serve as a general sleeping quarters, and she assigned a portion of the pavilion to serve as a hospital for work injuries. To keep production moving, Meva rounded up the bards to provide music and song to bolster the spirits of the workers.

Una inventoried the food stocks, cooking implements, water containers and other non-military supplies that an army traveling a great distance would require. One day while looking at the pile of weapons, she noticed that one sword was shorter than the others. "Why is one of the solid steel swords shorter?" she asked Mick.

"That is for you. I want you to have one of the best swords, and I thought a slightly shorter one would be easier to handle," he answered with a smile. "Besides, Father would have my head if something happened to you."

In his own mind, Mick thought himself invincible. He dreamed of attacking the enemy completely naked as a Gaesatae, wearing nothing but a gold torque and armlets. These mercenaries became famous because they ignored caution and charged the enemy with reckless abandon. His mother, on the other hand, knew that such pride could be a weakness. She insisted that Una be always in position to support Mick's back, assuming the position that she had taken beside her brother, Ragenos, since childhood.

"Are some of us going to have to carry an extra sword and spear?" Una asked, noting the many extra weapons that were being bundled.

"No, we'll store these behind the lines," her brother answered, "to keep our troops armed in case they lose their weapons."

After a night of little sleep, the day of their departure dawned. Conel, Rochlos and Mick stayed up late pouring over the plans they had devised. More than two thousand combatants and support personnel formed a great line, as wagon after wagon followed the troops. The noise of the horses and wagons often obscured the parting cries by the warriors, which in turn were drowned out by the bellicose sound of the battle horns. The warrior class, astride their horses and chariots, led the parade followed by the supply wagons. Columns of foot soldiers, moving through clouds of dust, trotted closely behind. Druids, dressed in the various colors distinguishing their rank, rode in front of the rearguard. A small number of infirm and older warriors were left to provide security.

Of the immediate family, only Meva remained behind. In the absence of Conel, she governed the oppidum. Surrounded by other wives and non-combatant family members, she stood on the upper rampart adjacent to the main gate. Filled with pride, she waved until Hugh in his white cloak trimmed in green, looked up to receive her parting blessing

The Plains of Maching
Upon arrival at the war camp, the Mayri clan was assigned its location in the battle line. Rochlos was proud beyond belief when they were given the honor of supporting the personal guard of the Helvetii chieftain. They would backup the middle of the Celtic strength. The Germans refused the Druids' offer to engage in a single warrior challenge, opting instead for full scale fighting. It was agreed that the battle would take place in three days, which provided the leaders of the Mayri contingent additional time to survey the battleground. After studying the terrain, Rochlos, Conel and Mick met, time and again, to refine their battle plan. On the night prior to the fight, Rochlos made certain that the combatants consumed an ample supply of ale to provide additional vigor.

Their commanders woke the Mayri before dawn on the day of the battle. After eating a heavy breakfast of meat and bread, they assembled to hear their leader. "Warriors of Mayri, I speak to you as our ancestors did before me," roared Rochlos. Then he recited the customary challenge to inspire the Celtic warriors. "You are the best armed and best trained force that will enter the battle today. Your leaders have inspected the battlefield and will place you where you will be most effective. The green and white of the Mayri will make a spectacular sight, and the foe will flee from your onslaught." Shouts of approval arose to greet this last remark. "I will not have even one of you disgrace the name of the clan that fathered the great Ragelnos." A mighty roar went up at the mention of the name of the renowned warrior hero.

"I expect that before you rest at the end of this day, every mounted trooper whether in chariot or on horseback, will penetrate the battle line of the Suebi at least twice."

This order encouraged the bragging rights of the Celt to take center stage. "I will penetrate five times," said one. "I will penetrate eight times," said another. Mick brought laughter to the assembly when he announced. "I will be in their lines so often, they will think I am bringing them reinforcements."

For a time, Rochlos encouraged his army to boast about the feats they would accomplish, and to belittle those they would be battling. Then he raised his sword to command silence, so that all might hear his words. Those warriors standing by their war chief repeated what they heard to those behind until the full contingent had been told what to expect. "We will line up directly behind the personal guard of the Helvetii leader. Our horns, shouts and resulting din will encourage them to withstand any German charge for they will not want the warriors of Mayri to take their place."

A howl of anguish followed, as many in the audience realized they would serve as a reserve unit. Mick looked at Una. "This means that we will have to wait on the sidelines and watch others fight."

"Don't worry. We will be given an opportunity. I can feel it in my bones," his sister responded to her visibly upset brother.

Again Rochlos called for silence. "When the word is given, we will proceed through the lines of the Helvetii guard and with our great power and strength smash the middle of the Suebi line." The roar was deafening, Rochlos again called for silence.

"Await my signal before you advance. The infantry will meet the enemy head on, and they will take the blunt of the first charge. While our foot soldiers occupy the enemy, then, and only then, will I engage the cavalry. Chariots will attack first, and then Roanlos will lead the mounted troops." With their blood hot for want of battle, the Mayri Celts roared their approval.

"No one, and I mean no one, will attack without my orders. Is that clear?" When he asked this, Rochlos looked directly at his nephew and waited for his nod of agreement before continuing, "As I said in the beginning, no one will disgrace us. I will personally execute anyone who runs from battle. No matter what the other clans do, the Mayri will stand strong. May the totem of the Mayri, the great Boar God Euffigeneix, stand with us as we destroy the invaders of our land." With that final declaration, the clan's Druids passed among the warriors, and bestowed their blessings on each participant.

When they arrived at the assigned battle station, Rochlos ordered his troops to stand fast. He placed the infantry in a slight decline between two hills, which shielded them from the enemy's sight. Stationed directly behind the infantry, the archers had orders not to shoot until their own men reached the middle of the field. Hidden by a small rise were the chariots, the cavalry and the extra mounts and supplies. The Druids arrayed themselves near the

Druids, Celts, and Romans

reserve horses, standing on a small hill between the supplies and the troops. His position with the assembly of priests provided Hugh a view of the entire battlefield.

The Mayri could hear but not see the action. As each combatant heard the noise, they imagined what was occurring. Only the fear of disobeying Rochlos prevented Mick from partaking in the taunting ritual that occurs before a battle. The Mayri warriors stood in envy of their fellow Celts when a lone individual charged the German line and bragged of his ancestors, while belittling the mighty host of invaders. The moans, coming from the Celts on the right and left flanks, spoke of the death of each brave warrior with such sounds breaking the hearts of the Mayri. At other times, the Celtic lines were goaded to fury by the insults of a single German warrior, who stormed their position. The Mayri cheered, along with their fellow Celts because they pictured the solitary Suebi being cut to ribbons.

After the individual bragging ran its course, the leaders decided their troops were sufficiently excited and ready to fight. The next encounter involved the charioteers who raced across the field and tossed their javelins into the front lines of the foe. Some drivers stood on the yoke separating the two horses to put themselves in a better position to launch their spears. These charioteers flaunted their skill in an effort to disrupt and dishearten their enemy. As was the case with the individual braggarts, the wheeled vehicles, wildly dashing back and forth, did little damage to the soldiers of either side. The shields of the rank and file successfully deflected the tossed spears.

As though in lock step, the great battle horns from both contestants sounded simultaneously, creating an enormous din. The actual battle now began. The cavalry from the ranks of both sides, except for that of the Mayri, charged into the lines of the opposition's infantry. The Germans' horses were a head higher, broader across the chest and far more powerful than those of their adversaries. However, the agility of the smaller Celtic mounts evened the score. The screams of the wounded steeds ripped the souls out of the horse loving Mayri.

Not until the German cavalry unit crashed into the ranks of the Helvetii guard did their leaders realize that the invader was winning and called for reinforcements. Sitting astride his horse on the hill overlooking the mayhem, Hugh could sense the distress of the Celtic infantry. He quickly rode to his brother's nearby location and told him of the circumstances. "Mick, Mick," he shouted. "The Suebi are breaking through the Helvetii guard. You have to do something quickly or the center of the line will collapse."

Mick made a snap decision. He called for the archers and directed them to take up a position just in front of the Druids. "If you see a large horse shoot it," Mick shouted. "Remember, the horse is the enemy, not the rider. Shoot the horses." Turning away from the young archers, Mick said a silent prayer for the spirits of the magnificent animals that were soon to be butchered. From their vantage point, the Mayri archers picked their targets with impunity. The space between the two opposing armies was soon covered with the bodies of the fallen. The response by the youthful archers to their young leader took the spirit out of the Germans and their attack slowed. The stallions' agonized screaming would remain with Mick for the remainder of his life.

With the charge of the German cavalry blunted, the battle entered another phase. Answering the appropriate call from the trumpets, the foot soldiers lifted their shields and spears to run recklessly at the opposing side. Mick knew that a flying arrow could not distinguish between friend or foe. Turning to the archers, he ordered them to cease firing although most had already launched all the arrows they possessed. Carefully selecting a score of fleet-footed youngsters to accompany him down to the battlefield, Mick and his supporters collected as many spent arrows as they could carry. Many of these young archers broke down and cried as they got a close-up look at the bedlam they had caused. Only the presence of Mick kept them from running away in despair.

The Mayri could only vent their anger by sounding the terrible war horns. Cries of vengeance mixed with dying screams as thousands lay wounded and slain. Neither side gained control of the struggle. Only the Druids situated above the fray, watched the ebb and flow of the armed combatants. While the Celts maintained their long lines, the Germans concentrated their forces in the center and once again overwhelmed the Helvetii guard. With shouts and waves, Rochlos and his lieutenants instructed the Mayri to open their lines, and let the exhausted Celts through. The Mayri battle horns were silenced as their holders dropped them to take part in the fight. Their lines consolidated to meet the astonished foe charging over the top of the rise. The Suebi had expected to chase retreating soldiers, not face a solid wall of spears. The Mayri ran to meet and blunt the German thrust. As the front line was forced to halt, those following ploughed into their comrades and drove them into the pikes of the waiting Celts. Warriors on both sides, with their sword arms extended, reached over their slain comrades to strike their opposition, but still the Germans came. The small squad of Mayri fighters broke under the onslaught of their determined foe, and the soldiers ran in terror. Roaylos, who abandoned his wounded horse, was among the many Mayri who gave their lives. While his own comrades fled, he died fighting alongside a small force of infantry who tried to stem the tide of the oncoming Germans.

When he saw the line rupture, Roanlos, unaware of his brother's death, drove forward on his charger, followed by the Mayri chariots and cavalry. This sheer mass of horses and riders broke the front of the German assault as the cavalry sliced through. Mick took to horse, and joined his fellow cavalrymen. In spite of his youth, his leadership further energized the outnumbered Celts. Using his shield, sword and horse, he slew all who stood in his way. Una knew she could not let Mick be surrounded when he charged into the horde of invaders; therefore, she rode at her brother's left side. Using her horse to trample, and her sword to strike, she cut her way through. Other Celtic warriors followed in the wake of this fearless twosome, and the German line bulged.

Mick rode with vengeance, trampling any enemy who impeded his path. He failed, however, to see the German foot soldier lower his shield and charge from the right. Fortunately, Una swerved into the space between the foot soldier and her brother. As the Suebi looked up in surprise, he vainly raised his shield to protect himself. This failure cost him his life, when Una slashed her curved-steel sword into the exposed neck and silenced him forever.

From his vantage point on the low hill, Hugh saw that the relatively few mounted warriors couldn't turn back the mass of enemy that had penetrated the Celtic lines. He yelled for his fellow Druids to light their torches and stampede the extra horses into the oncoming Germans. The hoofs of the panicked horses kicked both friend and foe as they galloped into the horde of men struggling for survival. The momentum and sheer weight of the animals cut a path through the on coming Germans and turned aside their attack. After creating this distraction, Hugh picked up a second torch and held his arms preventing any retreating Celt from getting past. Soon other priests followed suit. The fear of penetrating the line of Druids proved to be more than the battered Celts could handle. Those who were retreating turned once again to face their attackers. When the Germans crested the rise and saw the line of white-cloaked clergy with flames shooting from their outstretched arms, they turned and ran. Those Germans fleeing the Druid-inspired warriors rammed into their comrades who were still attacking.

Having cut his way to the rear of the enemy line, Mick, halting momentarily for his sister to join him, turned his mount and began to fight his way back. Those enemies facing the Celtic line were easily decapitated by the returning Celts.

The Celtic flanks, which held under the central charge of the German, folded inward, surrounding the main body of the enemy and slaughtered all in their path. The Suebi army was annihilated, ending the threat to Helvetia for generations to come.

Following the battle, immense bonfires consumed the slain foot soldiers from both sides. Only the bodies of the renowned warriors or chieftains were recovered for burial. Bloodied during their fierce encounter, Una and Mick were thrilled and humbled by their contribution to the successful charge. They felt in their hearts that Hugh kept them in his prayers. After checking on the condition of their father, their relatives and their friends, they gathered around the campfire, trading tales of glory with anyone who would listen. The two knew that Hugh would not join them because he and the other Druids attended the wounded and carried the corpses to the great bonfires for cremation. His absence did not prevent them from including his name among those who deserved to be recognized for glory. Bards listened to the heroic conversation and would carry the tales of this battle far and wide.

The following day the Helvetii chieftain honored the Mayri for their decisive role in the fray by ordering the poets to record the feats of this honored clan. The triplets were prominent in the songs and stories that would be sung for generations. A young bard, who watched the battle from the rise occupied by the Druids, composed the most popular version, which made every subsequent singer seem as though he or she personally witnessed the triplets' heroics:

> I stood near the crest of a hill, on the eve on that fateful day,
> looking at the confusing battle scene that seemed so far away.
> Suddenly, our lines broke under the crush of horse and men,
> The brave soldiers of the Helvetii guard were routed from the glen.

Druids, Celts, and Romans

I gathered up my faithful lyre and made ready to take flight,
when a savage cry went up from the Druid, standing on my right.
He rushed across to his brother near and made a holy sign,
'Arouse your archers while the Helvetii are still able to hold the line.'

The young archers attacked until all their arrows were spent.
I delayed my departure to observe what followed this event.
When reserves of the Mayri cavalry charged to turn the German tide,
giving their all to slow the advance although many a hero died.

Then two of the Mayri triplets filled my heart with pride.
The brother led the charge and his brave sister rode at his side.
The Suebi ranks parted for the Celts to complete the attack.
With no foe to face, the triplets turned to fight their way back.

I stood frozen with amazement when the Druid on my right
picked up a torch and a flint in order to make a light.
He tossed the torch at horses, standing tethered in the glen,
sending the crazed animals dashing into the melee of men.

Then as I watched from my perch, the battle's tide began to clear.
The Druid's mighty arms stopped any from running to the rear.
More fearful of the priest than they were of the enemy that day,
the timid reversed their flight and bravely reentered the fray.

As night fell, I watched the stubborn enemy finally yield.
Next, I saw the multitude of corpses that lined the battlefield.
The chieftains and warriors, heroes all, were lying head to head.
Under a moonlit sky, I watched the living and prayed for the dead.

I tell you this tale, not to make you sad, nor to make you mourn,
but to describe the triplets serving the purpose for which they were born.
This day they were needed, and we are grateful they were on hand.

May we bless the gods that sent them to defend our native land.

Mayri Oppidum
Meva, who spent most of her time on the upper rampart, was among the first to see them come home. She easily recognized the distinct and triumphant battle horns. Then with a mounting dread, she looked through mist-filled eyes for her family. Only after she recognized Conel surrounded by the triplets did she relax.

Mick, chosen to become a member of the Helvetii Guard, was given several weeks leave to recuperate from the battle. As her children sat talking earnestly with each other, Meva looked on from across the room. She marveled at the maturity of both Mick and Una ever since they returned from their first battle. 'I guess I have to face the fact that my children are growing up.'

Chapter 12
The Return of the Mercenary

Mayri Oppidum circa 390 BC
The same dream reoccurred, only this time it was so strong that Meva decided to tell her husband. Over breakfast she spoke up before she lost her nerve. "Conel, I think Ragenos is coming home."

He shook his head in disbelief. "Whatever brought that up?"

"I have been dreaming about him, and the dreams are coming more frequently, I'm certain it is a sign that he will return soon."

"Put it out of your mind. I don't believe that we will ever see your brother again."

"Why do you say that? Is there something you are not telling me?"

Not certain how he should answer her query, Conel decided to change the subject, but he did not want to discuss the only topic that could possibly take Meva's mind off her brother. They had to have the discussion at sometime, however, and now seemed as good a time as any. "We need to talk about something else."

Conel's tone of voice made Meva wary of what was to come. "What do we need to discuss?"

"I have decided to accompany the slave when Turk returns her to Rome," Conel said, almost sighing with relief now that he had introduced the subject matter.

A chill overcame Meva when she heard the words she had been dreading. "Why in the world would you go to Rome?"

"Ever since Munli told me about the Romans, I knew that I would have to see them for myself. I still carry a vision of torment in my heart. I have to go."

The finality in Conel's voice let Meva know that she could not change his mind. Almost immediately, her protective instincts took over, and she began to scheme about how she could minimize any harm that could come to him. Even as they finished their meal, she thought about who could accompany him and watch his back. She knew that it was almost impossible to get the Druids to allow Hugh time off. Based on her maternal instincts, he would be her first choice. Mick, with his temper, might cause more harm than good. That left only Una who, her mother thought, was unprepared for such a responsibility despite her success in battle. "If you insist on going, then I will support your decision. I would, however, like you to consider taking Una with you."

Conel, who loved his daughter more than life itself, shuddered at the thought of putting her in harm's way. "Don't you think such a journey will be a little dangerous for a young girl?" Looking around, he was grateful that Una wasn't in sight. She would vehemently protest, but to her father she would always be a young girl.

Meva continued, ignoring her spouse's reference to the danger he would face. She understood why he still thought of Una as a young girl because her own father had the same fault. "You want her to replace you as the clan chieftain. What better experience can she get than to see the strange customs of other people? Besides, didn't she perform admirably in the battle against the Germans?"

After long years of marriage and knowing when to end a discussion with Meva, Conel said meekly, "I'll think about it."

Mayri Oppidum (several weeks later)

The journey across the continent from Alba went swiftly, after Ragenos wished Danous and Tomas farewell. The brothers promised to rejoin him, after Danous succeeded in obtaining his bard's blue cloak. Ragenos wished him well, then turned his thoughts to his return home. He wondered what kind of reception he would receive. After all, it had been decades since he departed without explanation. 'Would Munli welcome him?' Ragenos hesitated under cover of the tree line at the edge of the immense forest. Looking ahead, he could make out the immense hill-fort that he once called home. Aware that he had been under observation ever since he crossed into the land of the Mayri, he knew that word of his arrival had likely been sent ahead. As he halted his mount, the gates of the oppidum opened and five riders left the hillfort to make their way across the vast meadow. Three of the riders were moving at such a swift pace that they appeared to be racing.

These, thought Ragenos, had to be the triplets. 'How old were they now?' Counting on his fingers, he guessed about eighteen. "Has it been almost nineteen years since I left home?" he wondered aloud.

While waiting for his nephews and niece to reach him, Ragenos looked at his childhood home that began to take shape in the rain and mist. "It's bigger, a lot bigger. Conel has made an oppidum that even the King of the Belgae would brag about," he said to himself as he urged his horse forward.

Mick greeted his uncle first, followed swiftly by Una. Hugh, as usual, came in a distant third. The first youth dismounted without slowing the horse, and ran beside the running animal under his uncle's admiring gaze. Una while riding at full speed stopped her horse abruptly then leaped off to run beside her uncle. 'So these are the triplets, whose deeds bards are praising throughout the land. Already, I am being shown their skill at horsemanship,' Ragenos thought. Hugh ignored the desire to impress his uncle and sauntered to a stop. "Welcome home, Uncle," he said, trying to be heard over the voices of the other two. "We had received word over a week ago that you entered the forest and were headed in this direction. Father had his spies out scouting ever since."

Smiling as he pictured silent Celts following his every move, Ragenos motioned his mount toward Hugh, all the while dragging the two of the welcoming party still attached to his arms and legs. Leaning forward, Ragenos enabled the still mounted Hugh to embrace him.

"You must be Hugh? How is my favorite Druid doing?" he asked his obviously pleased nephew.

"I'm doing all I can to keep these two in line, but as you can see I am a failure."

Ragenos dismounted and affectionately embraced his sister's children in a huge bear hug. Meva and Conel rode up while Ragenos was still trying to disentangle himself from the youths. With tears in her eyes, Meva jumped from her horse and dashed toward her brother. The two embraced for what seemed to the triplets to be an eternity. Finally, Ragenos turned to the chieftain of the Mayri and hugged his brother-in-law. Conel ordered his children to take it easy with their travel weary uncle then said in greeting, "It has been too long. Welcome to your home, my brother. May the Goddess Sulis insist that it be a long stay."

"Are you all alone?" Una asked looking at her uncle who had only his horse, armor and the clothes on his back.

"My retainers are bringing the chariots and supplies along. I rode ahead," Ragenos replied.

"Your retainers?" an astonished Meva asked.

"Yes. I have acquired my own mercenaries, and then some." Ragenos then turned to Conel and gave him the sad news that the three Mayri mercenaries who accompanied him at the start of his journey had joined those in the otherworld.

"May the God Euffigeneix return them as newborns to our clan when they have completed their term in the otherworld," Conel said solemnly as he made plans to visit the families. "They were good men, one and all."

"They were very good warriors," replied Ragenos. As though he could read Conel's mind, he added. "I would prefer to break the news myself. Besides, I have several skulls, mementos of their valiant deeds, which I need to deliver."

Conel looked skeptically at his brother-in-law and asked, "Each of them earned the right to possess an enemy's skull?"

"In two decades of warfare, a man can earn a great number of skulls. He needs only a few as memorials."

"Have you skulls of your enemies?" Mick asked in awe when he overheard the conversation.

"When my supplies get here, I will show you many strange and wonderful souvenirs," Ragenos said to the triplets. "Now let's go home. I am tired of the cold and the wet. I look forward to having a roof over my head when I sleep."

"And some good Mayri ale," his sister said as she recalled her brother's preference for the alcoholic drink. With that said, the family group set off for the oppidum.

Many clan members, even at this early hour, were standing in the fields observing the riders as they approached the hillfort. Rumors of Ragenos' coming were widespread since the first scout's report, and his friends were licking their lips in anticipation of the feast that was certain to be held within the week. The triplets, realizing they would be the envy of their friends, proudly accompanied their uncle through the gates. Neither Meva's insistence nor Conel's authority could convince the triplets, and their envious friends, to allow Ragenos some well-earned rest. Ragenos' promise to tell the tales of his adventures finally did the trick. After a hot meal washed down by strong ale, Ragenos was ready for sleep. As he drifted off, he wondered about the significance of the small slave with the bronze colored skin who hid in the background when he entered.

'Thank the gods it is not harvest time,' Conel thought as scores left the fields, laid down their tools and gathered in a gigantic circle around their prodigal son. Barrels of ale were opened, and the slaves served wheat cakes to the gathering. Conel made it a point to mention that this was not the banquet a returning warrior hero should expect. "The banquet is yet to come," he announced happily.

Ragenos found little time to himself. Sitting in the middle of a crowd, he began to tell about his adventures. "We were first engaged by Druids to guard wagons of gold that was mined on an island west of Gaul. Then we journeyed to the land of the Belgae who were warring with a bloodthirsty people from the northeast." Ragenos embellished the reputation of the Germans, knowing it would make his tale more interesting. He then paused a few moments to collect his thoughts and quench his thirst. "The Belgae welcomed the men of the Mayri and all those who accompanied them for even the Celts in that distant land had heard of the brave deeds of Ragelnos." He paused again before continuing. "When they were told that I was the son of this great warrior, their King received me with great honor. The Belgae are the bravest and fiercest fighters I have ever encountered," Ragenos emphasized, then he paused to sip some ale.

The vast audience sat in wonderment as he described his first sight of the stupendous warriors who invaded the land of the Belgae from across the Rhine River. "These Germans seemed to be larger than those of the same race residing north of our border. Their leader sat on a horse half again the size of mine, and even then his legs almost touched the ground."

"Was he bigger than my father?" Mick asked, interrupting his uncle.

"He was the biggest person I have ever seen," Ragenos answered. "His hair was almost white, a natural blonde and not lightened with lime. He was naked to his waist, carried a full body shield, his bronze helmet embellished with horns extended over

Druids, Celts, and Romans

half a spear length. He rode alone into the meadow. A magnificent specimen, his voice bellowed as he shouted his challenge to the champion of the Belgae, belittling their ancestors and questioning their courage." Again he paused while his cup was refreshed.

"Tell us more," his many admirers called.

"Let me tell you why I was selected," and again there was silence. This time, it seemed that no listeners even breathed.

"The night before the battle the Belgae King confided to me the problem of picking a champion from among his worthy warriors. Unlike our small clan, the Belgae are composed of many tribes, each with a man who could be champion. Because of his quandary, I suspected the King might choose an outsider to accept the challenge. I was dumbfounded when he chose me.

With this pronouncement, the hushed crowd leaned forward to hear every word of this heroic tale. They quickly realized that the speaker had become a legend in his own right.

"The Druids surrounded me, as I silently prepared myself to do honor to the gods. Their incantations filled me with pride and made me feel as grand as my opponent. Not a man of the Belgae would shy away from an honor so great. As an outsider I was doubly honored. I sensed their envy, as the Belgae wished me well." Pausing to catch his breath, Ragenos considered what he would say next.

"Please continue, Uncle," a hero worshiping Una begged.

"Facing so formidable a foe was not a welcome task, but as I gazed across at my opponent, I realized that so large a man would tire more easily than would a smaller man like myself," Ragenos said. Some of the crowd smiled at this last remark as they looked upon a man who easily was the biggest man in the compound. Then they fearfully pictured the size of his opponent.

"Furthermore, if the German had eaten his full and drank heavily to quench his great thirst, he would tire more quickly still. So, I settled on my battle strategy while the Druids stood in position between the two armies. Looking across the terrain at my giant challenger, I mentally reviewed all that my father had taught me about single-handed combat. I knew that my strength lay in my speed of arms and the rapid response of my horse. I decided not to attack, but to evade, until he committed himself, and only then would I respond. I was aware of the discipline such a strategy demanded, and I prayed to Euffigeneix to give me the will to execute my plan." Everyone listening to the tale nodded his head in agreement with this well conceived scheme. Each could envision Ragenos contemplating the matter before taking on the giant.

"The German and I entered from different ends of the field so that my supporters formed on my right. As the Suebi and I sat mounted, the taunts from the spectators vibrated and echoed across the hills surrounding the valley. Each side blew large trumpets and cursed their opponents. I could see the small assembly of Helvetii waving white and green banners, and my pride overwhelmed me. I prayed continuously to Euffigeneix to assist me in making my plan work. I also prayed that I had the courage to die like a man." Silence greeted this last remark as those listening realized that their champion could have died.

"As the giant and I faced each other, a Druid dressed in a white cloak, held sway in the middle of the arena. At his signal, the great giant swiftly charged, closing the distance separating us, as if to dispose of me in with one great sweep of his sword. His horse rushing toward us made my mount tremble in fear, as it strove mightily to escape this beast bearing down on us. While my opponent's mount chewed up huge amounts of turf as it attacked, I held hard onto the reins and whispered into my horse's ear to steady him." Again Ragenos hesitated to collect his thoughts.

"Rather than meet the giant head on, I feinted a charge at his sword side, which he turned to meet. My horse's training then overcame its fear. With my mount performing admirably, I swiftly changed direction and took a swipe at my opponents' unprotected arm, as I raced past him, bloodying the limb that held his shield. From that short encounter, I knew I had the best of him. His monstrous mount could not turn swiftly enough to counter the agility of my smaller steed." A sigh of relief went up from the listeners.

"The assembly, both German and Belgae, was outraged that I did not meet him head-on as was their custom. The giant took a long sweeping turn to prepare for his next assault, a motion that further drained the energy of his monstrous warhorse. Resting as I awaited his approach, I saw that I had wounded him severely. The sight of blood running down his side more than made up for the Belgaes' dismay and the loud booing of the enemy. Even in the din of that field, I could hear the foes' taunting, 'Is this boy the best that you have to offer?' 'Send a man to face us,' screamed others. Finally they began to shriek. 'You insult our honor. We hold you in contempt.' These and other insults were hurled at me, at my ancestry, at my tribe and at my supporters. I could feel the scorn of my allies, who were shamed into silence by my tactics. Only the men of the Helvetii continued to cheer me on.

"My opponent sallied, and I parried his move. Each time he passed, I would swipe at an unprotected part of his body. For a time, he had yet to taste my blood." A sense of relief spread over the crowd engaged in the tale and in their anxiety for the hero, forgetting for the moment the speaker's involvement in the challenge.

"It seemed the German rested more frequently between sorties, indicating that he was beginning to tire. My arms grew weary, and I could feel the sweat of my mount run down my legs. I took advantage of every opportunity to rest between clashes because I knew the encounter would not be brief. My horse began to gasp for air.

"As the uneven match continued, I could feel the spectators' mood shift. My opponent's mob grew less boisterous while the Belgae grew bolder for the crowd sensed that my giant opponent was beginning to tire. His horse took wider and wider turns as it struggled to catch its breath. The time between each charge grew measurably longer. By comparison, my mount remained well rested because I did not waste its energy by madly charging my rival. I merely sidestepped my opponent's rush and continued to maneuver within a small area." Admiration for the hero's scheme swept through the crowd.

"For the first time, I began to see doubt in the giant's eyes. He feared losing to a seemingly inferior opponent in front of his countrymen. I knew his thoughts, and I evaded the recklessness he exhibited when he tried to kill me with one fatal blow. I had to be careful for by this time I too was both bloody and exhausted. My horse, a noble beast, was beginning to tire as well." Heads of the listeners nodded in agreement.

"The end came when I sliced his sword arm, cutting off his hand and forcing him to drop his weapon. He will be long remembered because he fought hard and died a champion. After dismounting and dropping to his knees, he offered his neck that I might take a clean stroke. I approached my opponent with all the admiration that I have ever held for another person. Before I raised my sword, I prayed that this worthy adversary would die cleanly. With one stroke, I cut off his head." The sound of released air from dozens of lungs resounded through the crowded space.

"The followers of the loser left the field with their heads hung low and quietly returned to their homeland. The Belgae, on the other hand, celebrated their great victory for days, during which the King awarded me the title 'Champion of the Belgae.'"

Following that comment, Ragenos shook his head to the chant, "More! more!" Finally Conel ordered the audience to return to their duties. As the crowd began to disperse, Conel motioned to Ragenos that he wanted to have a private chat. "I'm dumbfounded that you returned. Not that I'm not delighted to see you, but I thought when you had left that you left for good."

"I thought the same on that fateful day when I rode through the gates. I was partway through the forest when Munli met me and bade me stop. He told me that the day would come when my services would be needed. He said, 'I would feel it in my bones.' Actually, I saw it in my dreams. The thought of returning began to nag at me night after night while I tried to sleep. One night, my longing for Meva was so great that I packed the following morning and began my trek home. Well, it really didn't happen that quickly. I had to wait for Danous to return from Ierne, the sacred island."

"Who is Danous and where is Ierne?" asked Conel.

"Tales of my travels would consume the better part of the next several months. I will share a little bit over a horn of ale if we can get away by ourselves. I have not seen nor heard about Munli. How is the Druid doing?"

Conel looked surprised, and then realized that Ragenos did not hear about Munli's death. "The spirit of Munli wanders in the earth world. He chose to be cremated rather than buried in order that he may remain in our presence and assist the Celtic people."

Ragenos did not know how to reply and decided that silence on his part was the best answer. So he just nodded.

A few stragglers from the assembled members of the clan sat in silent admiration of their famous mercenary as he and Conel spoke privately. Ragenos picked up a cloth sack that he had in his possession and withdrew an article. Almost reverently, he approached his sister and her husband. Kneeling before them, he presented the mummified head of his valiant enemy. The interior of the skull was lined in precious silver. Astounded by her brother parting with his most treasured trophy, Meva broke down and cried. Conel, on the other hand, vowed to give a feast that only a warrior of renown deserved.

Druids, Celts, and Romans

Each night as the family ate dinner, Ragenos told story after story about his exploits. "You must be the best storyteller in the world," his niece exclaimed with wide-eyed admiration.

"Wait until you meet my friend, Danous, the bard of Parisii. He can embellish a tale to such a degree that I, the main character of the story, wait with bated breath to find out how it ends," Ragenos laughed as he fully enjoyed bantering with his kin.

"You have your own bard?" Meva asked as she stared incredulously at her brother, "Your very own bard?" In her enthusiasm, she failed to notice Conel shudder at the mention of the bard's name. Nor could she know that it brought back memories of a vision that he strived to keep buried.

"Well he's not really a full-fledged bard, at least not yet," Ragenos answered. He then told how he found the starving boy unconscious in the forest and waiting to die. "As sorry as the lad looked, his mount was in worse shape. I never knew that a horse could live to such an old age and still be useful transportation. When we found a better mount, I had to put the poor animal out of its misery because Danous did not have the heart. He could not harm a barnyard mouse."

For long periods, Ragenos would not speak because he insisted on hearing each of his kin tell of their experiences while he was gone. The triplets gladly obliged and happily relived their childhood for their uncle's entertainment. Meva and Conel used Ragenos' first weeks at home to prepare for a lavish feast. They divided the task according to the talents that each of them possessed.

Conel tended to the liquid to be served. His brew master was instructed to pick only the best ale available. Conel often invited Rochlos and Ragenos to join him as they tested the brew. "We wouldn't want our guests to be disappointed, now would we?" was the excuse for the private party. After much practice, they had this down to a science. First they opened a barrel of mead, a fermented beverage concocted of water, honey, malt and yeast. Consuming too much of this sweet liquor often left a person with a headache beyond belief. Therefore, the mead needed to be washed from one's system with ale. The males of the clan favored this rapidly fermenting liquid, made from a blend of malt and hops, over the sweeter mead. The three, enjoying each other's company, left most of the preparation to Conel's wife.

Because the feast was clan business, Meva did not need to haggle with the wine master over the selection. Still she haggled because she knew the great pleasure he gained from such an encounter. The wine master in turn delayed presenting his more exquisite wines because he was well aware of the pleasure Meva experienced whenever she uncovered a vintage of unique taste. The two chose several gross of amphorae and put them aside for the great feast. Under the supervision of their cousin, Roanlos, the triplets traveled to the upper meadows and choose for slaughter the finest of the sheep and cattle. Small bands of mounted hunters entered the forest to track down the wild boar, so loved by the Celts, and to kill the plentiful deer that inhabited the lower mountain meadows. They rode horses especially trained to avoid the charge of a cornered boar and to run the deers to earth. Trained dogs pursued the numerous hares and broke their necks. To satisfy the hunger of the lower classes, domestic pigs were slaughtered in vast quantities and fowl of all types were hunted to accompany the other dishes. The fishermen readied their nets and traps, but they delayed the harvest of the lakes' bounty until the feast drew near to insure absolute freshness. The early spring crops, emmer wheat, fat hen and tic bean, were flayed to remove the beards from the grain before it was ground. Farmers obtained additional grain by cracking open the clay tops of the granaries. Beekeepers washed honey from the honeycombs, which their wives combined with the flour to make sweetened wheat cakes, a special treat. Families polished silver jars with spouted tops, especially crafted to serve wine, while children cleaned bronze platters that would hold the entrees. Families wove wicker baskets for the bread and fruit while hollowing out soft stone bowls and wooden saucers for the cooked vegetables. Children gathered eggs and milked the lowland cows. Tripods for holding large cauldrons covered the large fire pits dug in the meadows surrounding the oppidum. The smell of the soups and stews drifted over the area reaching the edge of the forest. Carpenters worked around the clock, manufacturing low tables. Brightly colored tents erected in the lower meadow of the oppidum served as coverings to protect against the sun and the rain.

Nervous energy permeated the clan, as other Helvetii clan chiefs, minstrels, bards and entertainers of various types arrived. Each honored guest received his or her just due at small feasts, but the main festivities had to await the appearance of Ragenos' entourage in accordance with his wishes.

Chapter 13
Arrival of the Bard

Parisii Oppidum circa 390 BC
Although the muddy road to the Parisii oppidum seemed as bleak as ever, the company of his brother cheered Danous. "After enduring the rigors of my adventures with Ragenos, any attempt to attain full stature as a bard should be an easy affair," Danous said as they rode toward their childhood home.

"Don't worry. You are the equal of any bard that I have ever heard," Tomas said, agreeing that Danous' plan seemed reasonable though he knew little of the ways of troubadour.

Urging his horse along, Danous relived his long-held anger at his dismissal and replacement in the bard college. In the next moment, fear along with a bit of common sense replaced anger. 'How could I have been so naive as to write such a silly satire of the process of judging bards?'

> Three old men sat on a bench, pondering the evidence before them. The one with talent was brushed aside, The one with none was chosen.

'It's not likely, even after two decades, that they have forgotten, and it's doubtful that they are forgiving.' Danous smiled to himself as he thought of his replacement from the lesser clan trying to memorize all the songs and legends. 'He was tone deaf! A fine bard he would make.' During his travels, Danous drove himself to memorize a multitude of legends, songs and stories to perform for the required year and a day without a repetition. Although, he knew that no one was tested for more than a few hours.

At night, the two brothers plotted about how to make the most of their opportunity. While Danous challenged the chief bard to a hunger-strike, Tomas would engage the Parisii warriors and try to get them to support Danous' effort. Only farmers and herdsmen took note of their approach when the fighter and the apprentice bard rode through their homeland. Evening was quickly falling, and several parties passed them in their hurry to get through the oppidum gates before dark. Danous and Tomas barely made it before the single set of wooden gates were closed. "The leaders must be expecting some type of trouble," Tomas remarked. "If not why would they even bother to close the gates?"

The brothers stabled their horses near the smith's forge before making their way to the gathering hall. The meal laid out for visitors was plain and unappetizing when compared to the feasts to which the brothers had grown accustomed. The brothers didn't recognize anyone at the hall and few recognized them. As was the way with Celts, no one asked them their names or business until after they had eaten. Murmurs of astonishment were apparent as the identity of the two was whispered from diner to diner until it made its way around the room.

Few realized that Tomas had survived the cattle raid, but all remembered the younger brother's satire. Because of his behavior toward the chief bard, Danous was shunned. Instead, the diners questioned Tomas about his adventures. Some, who had accompanied him on the ill-fated raid, tried to make their own part seem more important. "We went back and looked for you," said one who had been on the cattle raid. "We waited for you," another said. They could not look Tomas in the eye, however for in truth, all fled as quickly as they could.

Tomas appeared to be unconcerned about their childhood cowardice and told of his adventures. The quiet crowd listened attentively as the tales from the past decades unfolded. Many knew of the beheading of the dauntless Suebi champion, but few were willing to believe that one of their own witnessed it. None challenged the muscular warrior, but they doubted all that they heard. Bedding arrangements sufficient for two were prepared for Tomas. No one in the assembly dared to talk to Danous.

Before the early morning mist cleared, Danous made his way to the door of the bards' college. He wanted the benefit of surprise. Since his adversary would not know the precise time that Danous took up his position, he would be at a disadvantage in not knowing how long he had to respond. According to custom, if a person offered a hunger strike challenge, the one challenged had to respond within two days. When the bard teachers and students arrived, they were dumbfounded to find Danous seated outside the structure. Clothed in the green and white cloak of the Mayri, he sat, leaned against the wall and rested his lyre on his lap. Sitting on the right side of the door, he neither looked nor spoke as those entering passed him by.

"Who is he? "What does he want?" the younger pupils asked, although, his intent was immediately obvious to the older students.

Those who heard of the brothers' arrival were well aware of the contention and quickly informed the others. "That's Danous the lampooner, and he appears to be on a hunger strike."

Danous sat for the better part of the day before the elderly chief bard took a position across from him. 'He probably spent the time eating,' Danous surmised. 'Little does he know he will suffer hunger pangs sooner because of a large meal.' Danous smiled as he recalled often being famished during his vast travels.

Although they sneaked furtive glances at the pair as they passed, none of the townspeople dared get involved. They were well-versed in the seriousness of the tradition. The participant who lasted the longest without breaking his fast was deemed by the gods to be the victor. This event was the most exciting thing to happen to the small oppidum, and word of it spread quickly. Finally, the schoolmaster nodded at his opponent and Danous spoke for the first time. "Do you know why we are seated opposite each other?"

"I was on the panel that refused your credentials. My joining this farce will confirm our decision to be the correct one."

"That may well prove to be the case, but it's not very likely. Surely you have heard about the time that my brother and I, along with Ragenos the Belgae champion, lived on water for the better part of a month?" The chief bard refused to acknowledge whether or not he had heard the tale, knowing his young opponent would relate it in any case.

Danous ignored his opponent's silence and continued with his story. "We found ourselves trapped in a siege by the Iberians at a hill-fort on the opposite side of the Pyrenees." As Danous began to speak about his travels, a large number of the curious sat down to listen. Most had never witnessed a hunger strike. "After the third week passed, the only nourishment we received came from chewing on the soles of our boots," Danous exaggerated the tale for the benefit of his audience.

"The Iberians, as fierce as the Belgae, outnumbered the small clan that defended the fort at the head of a large bay. Fortunately, there was a fresh water stream nearby, so we could add liquid to our meager diet. During the first few days my brother, Tomas and Ragenos would sneak out at night and snare small game. The last time they tried this feat, an Iberian guard noticed the hidden entrance to the oppidum and warned his fellow fighters. For the next several weeks the enemy attacked without letup, but the brave defenders threw back every advance." Danous, who by this time was an experienced storyteller, procrastinated for a moment to build the suspense. While he delayed, he noticed that the chief bard was paying close attention.

"Just before our food ran out, Ragenos advised us to eat it all immediately rather than try to stretch it out. There were those that did not listen. In a short period of time, this group went mad with hunger and leapt form the walls to engage the enemy, hoping to die swiftly." Danous looked around to make certain that he still held his audience's attention.

"Ragenos, a member of the Mayri clan of the mighty Helvetii tribe, understood all aspects of warfare. He knew that if we held out for just another week, the enemy would lose patience and return to their homes. In this instance, Ragenos was correct."

While the antagonists faced each other, Tomas followed through with his part of the plan. While Danous was getting settled for his long ordeal, his brother joined other soldiers at warrior practice. Tomas quickly proved himself to be a seasoned veteran, proficient in all of the martial arts. Furthermore, he let it be known that he would not take kindly to any one interfering in the contest of wills taking place in front of the bards' school. The young males and many of the older ones openly admired the skulls he had attached to his horse's reins. After exhibiting his skills against all who accepted his challenge, Tomas described the bravery shown by each former owner of the now shrunken heads. Soon thereafter, a group of younger warriors imitated the mercenary's stride, and they began to wear the colors of the Mayri, instead of the traditional plaid of the Parisii. Even as his brother was collecting an audience, Tomas acquired his own group of hero worshipers. During a practice session, while he talked with one of his young admirers, Tomas learned why the gates were closed nightly. "It happened shortly after the ill-fated cattle raid on the Belgae. One of their confederate tribes, the Atrebates, began to collect a yearly tribute. If we fail to pay, which we did one year, they steal our cattle and rape our women."

"Why don't you fight them?" a shocked Tomas asked

"They are much stronger than we are. We don't even have a champion, let alone a decent fighting force."

This last statement left Tomas with a great deal to consider. Finally, he proposed a course of action. "If I were to help you prepare to fight such an enemy, would the Parisii people support my brother's selection to become a bard?"

"We are already behind him. He is the only person to ever stand up to the college for the bards. He is a local hero, but everyone is afraid to support him openly. If you help us, no one would dare deny him his due." The next day, Tomas began to train the warriors of the Parisii in earnest, and each day their numbers increased.

As dawn of the seventh day approached, the old bard weakened and collapsed. Danous was vindicated. The review board had no alternative but to hear his request. He began his defense with his brother and his followers, all fully armed, in attendance. "I, Danous, son of Annous of the tribe of the Parisii, petition this board to test my skills as a bard. I have seven years of formal training. Furthermore, I have an additional ten years of practical experience, during which I competed against the most notable bards in the world. Epics that I composed are being sung around the campfires," he boasted. "I stand before you in my hunger-weakened state prepared to demonstrate my ability."

The board did not miss the implications of the armed warriors in the audience, nor could they disregard the fact that the hunger strike gave Danous the right to perform. After a whispered consultation, they agreed to hear his presentation.

The following day, the entire population turned out to witness the testing of the rebellious bard. Wagers were offered on whether or not he would win the coveted blue tunic, but there were few takers.

The board of bards faced a dilemma. They wanted Danous to be disgraced because of the satire he composed decades ago, and because he prevailed in the hunger-strike. If Danous were not treated fairly, however, they faced the wrath of the armed warriors. After much discussion between the board members, they decided to give him a most difficult epic. Not knowing the extent of Danous' travels, the board asked him to recite, in full, the "Cattle Raid of Cooley." Although, they referred to this epic of ancient Ierne, none had sufficient knowledge to recite it in its entirety.

Danous, on the other hand was pleased at the selection. "Before I begin, I would like to take a moment to describe the sacred isle where the mighty Cuchulainn lived" When Danous spoke these words, the board knew they had been outsmarted. For the next hour, the young apprentice portrayed a land where the fog rolled in off the mighty Atlantic Ocean and kept everything green. He described the landing of the fairy people, the Túatha Dé

Danann, as told to him by the blind poet Kelii. After totally mesmerizing his audience, he took up his lyre and began his recitation. In keeping with the spirit of his story, Danous spoke in the quiet, sing-song lilt of the inhabitants of Ierne Island. As he spoke, he strummed softly, increasing the tempo to emphasize specific points. He sang to the audience rather than the board of bards. This action brought disdain from the bards, but the townspeople listened attentively:

> Long ago in a far off land, there lived a youth; the son of Lugh Long Hand, the god of light and grandson of Daghdha, the 'good god.'
> At her wedding feast, the youth's mother swallowed a mayfly who was, in reality, Lugh himself. The god transformed the mother, Dechtire, into a beautiful swan along with her fifty attendants. The swans were whisked to safety to await the birth of the child.
> Great heroes, Master Druids, talented poets and most worthy law givers assembled to instruct him. The boy excelled in all he did.
> One day while he was engaging an entire hurling team, the king summoned the youth, who was called Setanta. Upon entering the hall, the vicious watchhound of Culann attacked him. Setanta defended himself with his hurling stick. Then he grabbed the beast by its legs and bashed its head upon a rock.
> Through no fault of his own, the dog's owner, Culann, found himself without a watch hound. In his wisdom, the king ordered Setanta to take the place of the dog and guard the champion's quarters. In the process, the youth obtained the name Cuchulainn, which in old Celtic means the hound of Culann.

Danous kept his audience's attention when he described the lad's training under the magic warrior woman on the isle of shadows. As he plucked on the strings of his lyre, Danous proceeded to narrate the famous "Cattle Raid of Cooley."

> At this time, there was a king and queen of balanced ability. Each had equal wealth and equal beauty—except for one item. The king possessed a great white bull, the envy of the land.

Druids, Celts, and Romans

To even the score, the queen sent envoys to Ulster to procure the services of the great brown bull. If not given freely, the envoys were to take the bull by force. Upon hearing their intention, Daire, the owner, would not part with the animal.

The scorned queen traveled throughout the land to acquire a great army. She expected little competition from the warriors of Ulster. Because at this time of the year, they were under a spell of sleeping sickness, Cast by a goddess that Ulster King Conchobar's ancestor had once insulted. Only the youth, Cuchulainn, was available to defend the honor of Ulster.

In single combat, Cuchulainn, only seventeen at the time, slew all his opponents. So great were his accomplishments that the Goddess Morrigan sought his love. Upon being turned down, the goddess threatened Cuchulainn. When he drew his sword to retaliate, she turned herself into a crow, her totem, and flew from the scene.

Years passed and Cuchulainn reigned supreme. He killed many of the queen's champions, including unknowingly, his only son Conlaoch. The son would have dearly loved to reveal his lineage to his father, but could not because he was under Morrigan's spell.

Morrigan next sent for the three daughters of a great magician to extract her revenge on Cuchulainn. Time and again, the three tried their magic on the youth only to be denied.

Then they connived to turn his totem against him. The three daughters, disguised as old hags, invited Cuchulainn to dine. When he accepted, they fed him a portion of a roasted hound, the totem of Cuchulainn. Immediately, half his body was rendered useless because he feasted on his own totem.

In the final battle, Cuchulainn carried three spears, each created to kill a king. The three magic sisters had Druids, each, ask for a spear. A true Celtic warrior would never deny the request of a Druid.

In each instance, Cuchulainn gave the spear to a Druid by throwing it at him and killing him. Cuchulainn used one spear to kill the first Druid, but an opponent retrieved the spear and used it to kill Cuchulainn's charioteer. He was known as the king of charioteers.

A second Druid, who requested a spear, was also killed. But, an opponent retrieved the spear and used it to kill Cuchulainn's horse. It was known as the king of horses.

The final spear killed a third Druid, but once again, an opponent retrieved the spear and used it to kill Cuchulainn. He was known as the king of champions.

For the first time, many among the heralded bards of Parisii heard the full tale of Cuchulainn. Even after hearing the tale, the board of bards hesitated in granting Danous the title of a bard, but the clamor of praise from those assembled rose to such a pitch that he could no longer be denied. In a great ceremony, he received the cherished blue tunic denoting a bard.

The brothers had decided to move on; however, before the sun rose, Atrebates assembled near the gate of the oppidum to demand their annual tribute. They displayed their disdain for the Parisii by appearing with few warriors. The Parisii trainees approached Tomas and pleaded with him to intervene on their behalf. Despite their appeal, Tomas had intended to stay out of the local quarrel until Danous interceded. "Since we have been home for a time, I have begun to reconsider my contempt for our people," Danous said. Then he added, "What would our father say if he were alive today?"

Shaking his head at his softhearted brother, Tomas dressed in his full complement of armor and picked up his trophy bag. Then, he went forth alone to meet the enemy who were astonished to see that one of the spineless Parisii would dare challenge them.

"Have you a champion among you, or has your tribe sent children to collect the tribute?" Tomas shouted as soon as his horse cleared the gate.

"Have the cowardly ones hiding behind the wall hired a mercenary to do their bidding?" asked one of the Atrebates in an insulting tone.

"I was born a member of this tribe," Tomas answered while looking around to seek out the one who spoke. Finding him, he directed his next remark to the youth. "And you are correct. I have spent time as a mercenary in the company of Ragenos, the champion of the Belgae."

Many in the raiding party knew the name of the Mayri warrior, though the spokesman for the group questioned the truth of Tomas' statement. "Even if you are who you claim, why should we believe that you are a warrior of renown in your own right?"

"Perhaps when I add your head to my collection, you might become a believer." Reaching into the sack he carried with him, Tomas pulled out a shrunken head. "This is the head of a German, who tried to take the gold we guarded for the Druids. As I recall, he fought bravely when the rest of his party fled. Because of his bravery, I possess his spirit." Tomas tossed the head in the space between his mount and those of his adversaries.

As he reached for the second head, the gate of the oppidum opened and his trainees rode through. They assembled in a parallel line behind the brother of the bard. Tomas heard their approach but did not acknowledge their presence. "This one carried the spirit of a ferocious Iberian. I relieved him of his fierce pride." He tossed this head near the first.

As the assembled war party looked at the two heads on the ground, several hundred foot soldiers made their way through the gate and lined up behind the cavalry. Tomas ignored these as well and put his hand into the bag once more. "This one tried to sneak up on our leader, the great Ragenos of the Mayri clan of the Helvetii tribe. I acquired his spirit to remind myself to always protect the back of my leader." He tossed this skull in the vicinity of the other two.

The next skull had to be held by the cavity opening since it retained little of its hair. "This is the head of a fighter from Massilia, the Greek colony lying alongside a large body of water to the south. The Greeks are knowledgeable people, so I captured his spirit in order to retain that knowledge for myself." Again he threw the skull to the ground, and again Tomas reached into the bag. He added six more shrunken heads to the pile before he stopped. "Does that answer your question regarding my credentials as a warrior of renown in my own right?"

The number of skulls lying on the ground shook the confidence of the Atrebate spokesman. Still, he did not want the Parisii mercenary to win the debate, nor did he want to lose his head. Thinking swiftly, he announced loudly for all to hear. "If my brother, Gordos, were here he would spit on your paltry number of kills."

"Ah, but your brother Gordos is here!" exclaimed Tomas as he reached into the sack once more. He then pulled out the biggest head any in the crowd had seen and threw it toward the insolent Atrebate. "Perhaps you would like to take him home with you?"

The visibly shaken opponent turned white. Then he pulled on the reins of his horse and retreated from the field of conflict, followed by all his men. A loud cheer rose from the ranks of the Parisii who had emerged from their fort to support their leader. That night, the finest celebration in the history of the oppidum was held in honor of the new hero. The newly appointed bard was called upon time and again to sing of the travels of the trio.

Once they recovered from very bad hangovers, Danous and Tomas left the company of the Parisii, and began their journey to linkup with Ragenos. Just beyond the shadow of the Parisii oppidum walls, Danous sought the information that he had been burning to hear. "Did that head really didn't belong to Gordos?"

Tomas laughed and laughed. "It may have. After all, how does one know the names of those he has killed?" Mayri Territory

As they neared the land of the Mayri, Danous could sense Tomas' anxiety. "What is the matter?" he asked.

"This forest has an atmosphere of foreboding, a feeling like I've never had before. For the past several hours we have been followed, but the parties are keeping well back. Every time I slow up, they slow as well. I fear we are riding into some kind of trap," Tomas said with concern showing in his voice.

"How can we be riding into a trap? We are in the land of the Helvetii, Ragenos' people," Danous answered thoughtfully, trying to calm his brother. "In any case, we are veteran enough to take on any bandits." This statement came from a person who had never raised a weapon in anger, except for his lyre.

"Now there appear to be runners tracking us on each side," Tomas replied, as he backed his horse toward a rise in the ground. Tomas positioned Danous at his back to complete the defensive stance and waited for a response from the trackers. They didn't have long to wait as the thunder of hooves announced the arrival of a war party from the direction in which Tomas was headed. Relief and sheepishness instantly marked the face of the Parisii warrior when the white and green plaid of the Mayri confronted him.

"I, Rochlos, brother of the chieftain Conel and friend of Ragenos, came to guide you to our oppidum. You were taking so long in coming, I was afraid we might witness a riot by those waiting for the feast to start." He then laughed at his own humor, a sound similar to the familiar laugh of Ragenos.

After listening to the familiar accent, Danous knew they arrived at their destination and burst from the encirclement to greet the clan brother of his great friend. "I, Danous, a humble and recently commissioned bard, and my overly-concerned brother Tomas, accept your gracious welcome."

"Ragenos said you would try to be humble, but humility doesn't suit you," laughed Rochlos.

"Why did you have us tracked?" Tomas asked as he tried to recover from his fear.

"We track everyone who enters the forest of the Goddess Sulis," Rochlos answered. "Only friends, however, are allowed to realize they are being watched," he said with a smile.

When the riders broke through the shelter of the great trees, throngs of people greeted them, some mounted, many on foot. The moment that Danous and Tomas spotted Una, they both fell instantaneously and hopelessly in love. Danous felt his heart stop and his breath shorten as he gazed on Meva's beautiful daughter. Tomas in his quiet manner looked on with awe. Una rode up to Danous, leaned over her horse and kissed him on the cheek. The youthful bard blushed when he received the kindest welcome in all his life. In a voice as sweet as the song of a bird, she said, "You must be the wonderful bard that sings praises of my uncle." Una gave a similar greeting to Tomas once the stammering Danous pointed him out. She said affectionately, "And you, sir, have saved my uncle's life on many an occasion, for which I will be eternally grateful." Unlike his glib, but for the moment tongue-tied brother, Tomas was a person of few words, none of which he could recall. For the second time in less than an hour, he felt like a fool.

Una, who was accustomed to having young men fall in love with her, shrugged off the brothers' awkwardness. Aware that her uncle, Ragenos, was waiting impatiently to welcome his friends, Una encouraged them to hurry. Neither brother could retain his composure as Conel's impetuous daughter challenged them to a race. Then, without waiting for a response, she immediately set off in full gallop for the oppidum, with the brothers quickly taking up the chase. People scurried aside as the riders raced through the entryway between the two gates.

"Uncle Ragenos, look who I brought," Una shouted as she jumped from her horse before it came to a complete stop. Ragenos rushed out to greet his friends. Within an hour of their arrival, the long awaited feast for the Mayri hero began. Tomas completely relaxed for the first time in decades, his brother and his friend were in good hands. Tomas noticed that about one-third of the warriors, at any given time, did not join in the revelry. Rather, they guarded the walls, went out on patrol or simply kept order. His final observation explained the friendly, outgoing nature of Ragenos. 'These people really like each other,' Tomas realized.

Conel, Meva and their children made it their business to make each and every guest comfortable.

Both brothers stayed close to their newfound love. Though delighted with their attention, she made it her business to embarrass them at every opportunity. When a noted bard of the Helvetii finished his recital, Una put Danous on the spot to match the performance. She thought that the lovesick bard would be ill-prepared to equal the performance of more a experienced troubadour. An embarrassed Danous responded to the crowd's shouts of encouragement and began to strum on his lyre. He then composed the following verse as he showed off for his true love.

> Etruscans invaded, arrayed in splendor, and covered the valley for all its fill. But this was only one-half of their number. Others hid behind a tree-covered hill.
> 'Wait in yonder glen' ordered the chieftain, 'and see for yourself how warriors must fight. We defend our valley, homes and our honor. These before you speak of the Boii might.'
> They took the field, amid noise and bluster, and challenged the Etruscan to send forth his best or die from the shame of failing to answer the might of the Celts. The gods sent on this quest.
> Ragelnos and his handful of Mayri took shelter. Well-hidden, they overlooked the mayhem below. Disappointed they had come so far to battle, only to let the glories of warfare elude them so.
> The chariots of the Boii struck for first blood and sent the Etruscan retreating in terror. The Celts then committed their force as a whole, sealing their fate with this terrible error.
> With their blood running hot to finish the task, the Boii charged forward to partake of the slaughter. With the bright sun blinding the eyes of the Celts, the hidden Etruscans descended in order. Suddenly, cries of the dying revealed their sad plight. For the Etruscans surrounded and hacked from on high. All turning as men knowing the foes at their back, Boii warriors stood their ground and waited to die.
> From his concealed spot, Ragelnos saw danger below, and called for warriors to follow his cue. The trumpets of the Mayri resounded through the valley. Etruscans never realized the attackers were few.
> The charge of the Mayri raised the hope of the Boii, Who stood with honor and died like men. But the ferocity of the Mayri carried the day, the valley never saw the Etruscan again.

Druids, Celts, and Romans

Let's drink to the glory of the mighty Mayri. Ragelnos, their leader, showed us the way. The men of Mayri are never found wanting. Their valor is honored, long live that day.

A roar of delight saluted the talent of the Bard of Parisii. Toast after toast followed in his honor. Danous returned to his seat at the low table, trying not to stare at Una. Though he had experienced many women during his travels, Danous had not met the match of the beautiful Mayri. Una, a little surprised at Danous' ability to respond to her attempts to embarrass him, immediately challenged him to do similar justice to her uncle's exploits. The audience grew silent as they awaited the performance of the bard. Plucking the strings of his lyre, Danous' beautiful voice stirred all present.

The King of the Belgae, his face ever grave for the Suebi champion challenged his brave. No man among many, his kingdom could save when entered Ragenos of the Mayri.
Pressure of the Suebi on his kingdom ever tightened, for the loss of honor, left all his warriors frightened. At the son of a legend, the Belgae King brightened when entered Ragenos of the Mayri.
Have I the field to myself?' bellowed the Suebi. He pranced on his great horse, his sword held steady. His followers shouted, 'our champion is ready.' When entered Ragenos of the Mayri.
The German sneered then followed with this comment, 'I'll crush him in an instant.' He delayed just a moment. This was no ordinary foe that feared his opponent, thus waited Ragenos of the Mayri,
On the far side, the enemy shouted in glee, expecting any moment for his rival to flee, but the Mayri held his ground as all could see, patiently waited Ragenos of the Mayri.
Shifting his mount to avoid the great spear, the Suebi champion pulled his reins to steer. Ragenos slashed at the horse with naught to fear, so fought Ragenos of the Mayri.
Again and again, he used the same ploy. His strategy was first to annoy, worked so well, he had to destroy, and thus he won, Ragenos of the Mayri.
A single stroke decapitated the Suebi. He held the head aloft for all the world to see. A valiant enemy had no choice but to flee the champion, Ragenos of the Mayri.

Una gloried in Danous' attention and quick response. At the same time, she knew a bard's attention to a pretty lady was fleeting. Her sense of duty to her people warned her that she must choose a warrior for her mate, even if her heart lay elsewhere. Until such a warrior turned up, however, she would entertain herself with Danous' affection.

Sitting quietly in the background, Tomas looked on with love and a bit of jealously. The woman's beauty captured his heart. As forceful as Tomas could be in battle, he acted the opposite in the company of beautiful, confident women like Una. He had all the more reason for him to feel uncomfortable in her presence because Una's presence sent shivers down his spine. "She is beautiful, isn't she?" Hugh commented as he took a seat beside Tomas.

"Is it that obvious?" Tomas answered as his face turned a bright crimson.

"Not to most people, but I make a habit of studying others," Hugh answered. "I have spent my life hearing bards exalt, and I don't believe a word of they say. Please tell me in your own words about the adventures of which your brother sings."

The two met daily for over a month, during which time Tomas and Hugh became close friends. As time went on, Tomas, who also studied people, began to question Hugh about Julia the Roman slave. "I feel uneasy when she is around," Tomas observed as the young slave passed them on her way to perform an errand.

"And I as well," Hugh answered. "Even though she does everything expected of her, I sense a foreboding, almost as though she is the source of some great evil."

Ignoring Una's cavorting, Ragenos sat beside Meva and her husband and talked of the days when they were young. "Are you happy?" he asked his sister.

"As happy as a person can be on this earth," she answered forgetting for the moment that Conel would soon depart for Rome.

"Perhaps, this will make you even happier," Ragenos said as he took the covering off an item he had been carrying all evening. When Meva looked at the beautiful white gold urn, she broke down in tears.

"It is the most exquisite art work that I have ever seen, even more delicate than my mother's silver vessel," she said as her hands gently traced the surface of the urn, stopping and fondling each piece of inlaid glass. The she held it up to the fire to admire the craftsmanship and let the light flicker off the resplendent etchings.

"The person who sold it to me said it was hand crafted on Insula Sacra, the island we call Ierne. When I saw it, I knew that only one person deserved such a present." With tears running down their faces, the brother and sister hugged.

Chapter 14
Crossing the Alps

Mayri Oppidum circa 388 BC
Una reflected on yesterday's tedious task of overseeing the manufacturing while she and her mother lunched on a grassy knoll outside the oppidum gates. The early thaw allowed a whirl of activity in preparation for the journey. "This might be our last opportunity for quite a spell to have a conversation together," Meva said. "Sit and enjoy yourself."

For the first time, Meva shared stories of her own life as a warrior chieftain's daughter. "Your father and I were far less strict with you children than my parents were with me. I know that must be difficult for you to believe!" Meva said, smiling slightly. "Though they respected Conel, my parents thought little of him as a prospective husband," a revelation that came as a complete shock to Una.

Nodding her head, Meva continued. "In my teen years, Ragelnos wanted to marry me off to Finel, the Allobroges' chief. At the same time, my mother had young Kilti of the Vindelici clan in mind. Imagine those choices, a toothless old man far past his prime or a boy too young to grow a beard. I was stubborn. I would have none of their matchmaking," Meva continued. "Once, I even went on a hunger strike, but my dad held my arms while my mom force-fed me. I loved Conel, and I was determined to marry him ever since I first saw him. I was probably only six or seven, but I had a will of my own. No one, not even my own parents, could ever change that! Thank the Goddess Sulis that I had Munli to confide in." Meva smiled as she pictured the short, rotund Druid.

"In his quiet way, Munli compared the other candidates to Conel and pointed out their many deficiencies. 'Because we possess wealth beyond our needs, the Mayri has no need for alliances with other clans,' Munli explained. 'I agree that Finel is a fierce warrior,'

Munli would say. 'But consider that he has two wives already and children by both. Meva would not be an honored first wife, and he may not be able to bless you with grandchildren. Would you want Finel's other sons vying to rule the Mayri clan?'"

As she spoke, Meva lovingly ran her hand through Una's wavy red hair. "I remember the time he said, 'If Meva marries into either the Allobroges or the Vindelici clans, they will learn about our silver and gold. The Mayri would never know a moment's peace. It's better that they think we can just barely scratch out a living on the shores of this desolate lake. The Druids have a saying, 'A dog with a bone can never feel safe from hungry rivals.' So with my parents' approval, I connived a proposal out of Conel."

"Father wasn't reluctant was he?" Una asked in amazement. "I thought he loved you?"

"In some things men have to be led, and marriage is one of those things. They're more than happy to bed you rather than commit to a life of living together," Meva answered, giving her daughter a bit of her wisdom.

"Have you got your cap set for anyone?" Meva asked her daughter in all seriousness.

"No Mom. I haven't met anyone who can compare with my father or my brothers."

"When that changes, we will need to talk! There are more than our clan's needs at stake." For the next several hours, Meva carefully explained a spouse's role to a Celtic chieftain. "At times, the chieftain could be female, which may be true in your case. You were trained both as a chieftain and a warrior because the spouse needs to guard her husband whether in battle or in politics. In my own way, I convinced the elders of the tribe to see the wisdom of making Conel the chief. He turned out to be a better chief than even I would have guessed." Una smiled as she saw the love in her mom's eyes.

Her mom continued. "I must remain here and continue the vital work that your father has started," Meva explained, "You must become the guardian to look out for his welfare while he observes the Romans. There will be many enemies on this journey, all of whom must be feared." Meva continued, "First, you will encounter maverick tribes with their own agendas. They pose a serious threat to all wagon trains that cross the mountain passes. Next, you will meet the Po Valley Celts. The land south of the mountain pass is rarely peaceful. Even now, I hear of fighting between the Celts and the Etruscans.

"You may be able to avoid the Etruscans, but you will inevitably encounter the Romans. You must return the slave to the safety of her family, ensuring that she cannot be recaptured and enslaved by another. We promised her a safe return. Our pride allows no other recourse." Una pledged to respect the agreement.

Meva continued, "I picture Julia's people as being without honor. Never doubt that they might strike out in vengeance because of the enslavement of their kin. Your duty is to see your father safely home." Una consented with a nod.

As the mother and daughter talked privately, Danous, took up a position not far from the two women. For all intents and purposes, he entertained the young children that gathered at his feet.

While she listened to Meva, Una wondered, 'If Danous is so interested in the children, why do his eyes never leave us? For that matter, why does his brother Tomas always carry the heavy loads past this spot, when there are shorter distances between the storage sheds and the wagons?'

Meva noticed her daughter's eyes wandering even as she listened. "I see the two Parisii brothers make a habit of being seen by you as often as possible," Meva spoke with a mischievous smile. This comment made Una's blush, turning her face as red as the color of her hair. "I think any serious romance should be delayed until your safe return. Then you and I shall talk in earnest," Meva said with emphasis, persuading Una to quickly agree with the order.

The urgent need to hear news from beyond the mountains drove Conel to join the first, and therefore, the most dangerous trading caravan scheduled to head south. Turk took the lead, while Una sat at her father's side in one of the trailing wagons, their horses hitched to the rear. Before attempting to cross the mountain pass, the Mayri group will join a larger caravan. With Mick and Hugh away, Danous and Tomas escorted the wagons until they turned into the great forest. After a quick hug and a silent wave, they returned to their duties at the oppidum. Conel noticed the tenderness the two Parisii' brothers showed toward his daughter and remarked on it to Una. "I like both those young men; however, neither is suited to become your spouse!"

Una, a little irritated at her father for trying to determine whom she should marry, decided not to have an argument. So, she diplomatically replied, "I understand! Mom and I discussed this yesterday."

A satisfied Conel nodded his head, and smiled at the maturity shown by his oftentimes headstrong daughter and contently urged the team to stay close to Turk's wagon. He knew the party would not encounter danger until after they left the territory of the Mayri because Mayri' guards observed the main road from lookout positions along the less traveled, parallel trails in the deep forest.

Julia, wrapped in a blanket, sullenly tried to escape the bitter chill of the early spring morning. Embittered by her captivity, she plotted terrible retaliation. Her upbringing would not allow her to appreciate the Celts' honor, and her heart cried for revenge against their imagined atrocities.

On the first day, the wagon train halted early in the afternoon and camped at the edge of the tree line where the trail rose from the forest floor to ascend into the surrounding foothills. Turk assembled the drivers and handlers of the eight Mayri wagons and outlined what they should expect. "Once, my father and I traveled with the trails still covered by snow and ice, and I have carried that frightful journey in my heart ever since. We lost over half of our wagons and their drivers. My father swore, and I after him, never to attempt such a journey again. I am only doing this at the bequest of my chief." Turk paused and nodded toward Conel.

Una began a spirited defense of her father, but Conel placed a hand on her knee, and bid her hold her tongue. "I have appointed Turk to be the wagon master. From this point on, he's in charge," Conel whispered very sternly in her ear.

After waiting a brief moment for silence, Turk continued. "This will be the last rest stop without the need for night guard duty. Henceforth, I will assign rotating watches, which will be continued until our safe return. Even when we join the caravan, we will maintain our own watch. We carry goods of great value, and there are those who would prefer to steal even at the risk of their lives. So stay alert! If any among you have issue with my leadership, return to the oppidum in the morning," the wagon master declared. "Once we break camp, my word becomes law. Any who disobey will be abandoned on the trail without any supplies or shelter and will surely die. Have I made myself clear?"

"You have made yourself very clear wagon master, and I for one will submit to your authority," Conel answered. None of the others dared make a sound.

With his authority firmly established, Turk began to explain what the travelers might expect. "The trail through the mountain passes will be hard-packed icy-snow during the early morning hours.

When the sun breaks out, the trail will quickly turn to a gooey muck. Those at the end of the wagon train will have the most difficult time. I will attempt to get our wagons near the front to minimize the ruts that we will encounter."

Turk continued. "Whenever the trail narrows and becomes treacherous, I want you to hug the inside, nearest the cliff, away from the steep slope of the mountainside. This vital position helps to avoid the onrush of melting snow from higher levels. This condition occurs when fresh snow accumulates but doesn't adhere to older hardened snow. Snow gathers force and moves down the mountain as though it were a wave crashing on the shore. Should it hit either you or your wagon, it likely will sweep you over the side to your death. If I foresee such danger, I will have you bind the horses' mouths because even a small noise can bring a mountain of snow down upon us."

"Will there be there any warning?" Conel asked.

"Should you hear a great noise that sounds like a gigantic rock breaking in two, immediately leap from the wagon and drag the horses as close to the inside cliff as you can," Turk continued in his description. "If you become buried in snow dig your way out as quickly as possible, or you will suffocate and freeze to death," Turk emphasized.

"Listen carefully. First clear a passage around your eyes, nose and mouth. Then spit to determine which way is up. When hit by an avalanche, often times a person ends up buried face down. When this occurs, the spittle goes straight down. If you dig in that direction, you will only dig yourself deeper into the snow. Shovel away from the fall of the spittle. Do I make myself clear? As we venture through the mountain passes, you may find your shovels are more valuable than your swords," Turk said. "Follow my lead, and I will get you safely across."

Alpine Camp

Upon arriving at the point of convergence with the other traders, Turk led his group through the other wagons to the far edge of the camp. He ordered his followers to level the ice and snow before setting up sleep coverings, or else the entire camp could slide down the mountainside into the campsites of those below them.

During the night while sleeping on the frozen tundra, twice Una found herself rolling downhill into her father who slept at her side. When she groaned about the rough conditions, he admonished her,

"You had better get used to sleeping on cold snow, or it's going to be a long journey." Because of her fragility, Julia was allowed to remain in the wagon with the supplies.

Just as the scouts, sent to determine the conditions of the trail returned, and reported that it was passable, the last of the merchants reported to camp. Turk came back from a meeting with the other wagon masters and informed the Mayri traders, "Kneal of the Insubres has been chosen grand master. He's a good wagon master, maybe even the best. He has traveled this pass many times to and from his home in Milano on the far side of the mountains. The caravan has chosen wisely," Turk contended.

"Despite my confidence in Kneal, I wouldn't trust too many of the other Insubres," Turk whispered to Conel, receiving a knowing nod in return.

Then he spoke aloud for all to hear. "Kneal's wagons are directly below ours. We will move aside to let his group pass, then position ourselves immediately behind. Pack the wagons tonight and prepare to move quickly, lest another party sneak in before us."

At daybreak, Turk ordered the trailing wagon of the Mayri to station itself as though it were the last wagon in the Insubres' train. When the Kneals' wagons passed, the Mayri driver blocked the trail, and allowed the seven wagons of his train to proceed ahead of him, much to the chagrin of the wagon masters behind him.

The succeeding days consisted of hard, brutal work. Icy wind constantly blew directly toward them, making the travelers cover their faces with woolen scarves and try to breathe through their mouths. As the train proceeded upward, the lighter air made breathing harder and reduced their endurance, which made each task increasingly more difficult. At the time when their cold ears and hands became numb, many travelers stuffed straw, hauled along for animal feed, into their footwear for added relief. "Should we be doing that?" Una asked Turk.

"There's no need. Stuffing straw, a tradition of the southerners, comes from the days when they first crossed the passes. We now know wool stockings will keep our feet warm. If your feet don't get too cramped, it may be useful to put on two pair of stockings."

Just as Turk had predicted, the trail bed turned from permafrost to gooey muck as the day progressed. When the temperature dropped at night it would refreeze. Yesterday's hoof prints and wheel ruts become icy ridges, jolting both wagon and rider. The drivers shoveled the upper layers over the side to keep the wagons moving as the snow melted. The iron shovel raised raw blisters on the hands of the Celts unused to this type of work. After several days, the brute work of trying to push or pull a wagon through the gooey mud so thoroughly exhausted the horses, drivers and handlers that the entire procession had to be halted. "Unless we begin to make better time, we will perish on the trail," a frigid driver said while he blew on his hands in the vain hope of warming them up.

"Father, would it make any sense to strip some of the wood from the wagons and cover the path?" an exhausted Una asked. "That's what we do at home when the muddy road becomes impassable."

Hitting himself on the side of his head for not having the thought himself, a delighted Conel answered. "Of course, we should plank the road." Then pushing his weary body up from the semi-frozen ground, Conel went off to find Turk.

The wagoners spent the next day stripping all unnecessary weight from the wagons. They laid the wood planks across the trail until the wagons passed over them. Then they gathered the used roadway and hauled it to the front for reuse. In this manner the wagon train slowly made its way toward the higher elevations.

In the process of crossing an ice field, Turk pointed out to Una that they were passing over a river of ice. "When this slides down the mountainside, it will melt and form the Rhine River that runs through Helvetia."

Before long, the sky clouded over, and the rain turned to snow. Almost two feet of new snow covered the ground when the campers awoke. To make matters worse, a gale force wind roared through the mountain pass directly toward them, forming massive snow drifts. The blizzard-like conditions reduced the visibility, blinding people and animals. Even in these dismal circumstances, the wagons continued their trudge forward. "If we don't keep moving we will be buried in the snow," Turk yelled.

"What about the boulders that are bouncing down the hillside. Aren't they dangerous?" Una asked.

"They are," Turk answered. "Rolling rocks pose the great danger of starting an avalanche. So be alert." When Kneal, the wagon master, ordered a break, Turk gathered his party and passed out mufflers to be placed around the horses' mouths. He again cautioned the Mayri that vibrations from loud noises cause snow and ice to slide.

Several days later, the long feared calamity struck. As the wagoners rested during the mid-day break, a fierce cracking sound, like a clap of thunder, roared through the pass. Resembling salt pouring out of a barrel, tons of snow mixed with ice and rocks tumbled down the slope and covered the trail. Without hesitation, Conel jumped from the wagon seat and tightly held the reins of the horses, meanwhile Una grabbed their overcoats and shoved Julia into the space between the wagon and the cliff. The trio sat with their backs against the hillside while a massive wall of snow rumbled down the hillside and across the top of those huddled on the ground, crashing down onto the path. Holding her breath as long as she could, Una lay stunned in the dark, bitter-cold until she felt her father stir beside her and begin to push upward. Conel used both his shovel and sword to create an air hole in the ceiling of snow. Snapping out of her stupor, Una aided in widening the opening, allowing light and air to penetrate their snow-bound cocoon. Looking at her dad, she nodded as she noticed the frozen saliva across his mouth.

The horses shook with fright and began to pull away from their holders. In their efforts to get free, the animals caused the bulk of the snow covering the threesome to break loose and tumble down the mountainside. Conel grabbed both females, and hauled them into the space created by the agitated livestock. Una used her superior weight to keep the terrified Julia from bolting. Only the quick effort on the part of father and daughter saved the nearly frozen slave's life. As an added precaution, Conel tied Julia across the back of a horse to reduce her life threatening shivers.

"Why did you do that?" his inquisitive daughter asked.

"It's an old mountain trick that Turk taught me. If someone is shivering, the only way for them to survive is by returning heat to their body. What gives off more heat than a horse? Besides, it will keep her out of our way, and out of harm's way."

Before the danger passed, most of the horses and oxen were put to use in a similar manner to prevent other deaths from hypothermia. Unbeknown to the Celts, the terrified Julia did not understand that being restrained on the horse could save her life, and besides, she was terrified of horses. A deep hatred of her captors, bred during her captivity, exploded into white anger during this short period of confinement. Julia vowed she would survive this journey to wreak havoc on those who imprisoned and humiliated her. "I will obtain vengeance for this outrage!" screamed

Julia in her native tongue while plans for revenge spawned in her mind.

Looking once to assure himself that the females were well, Conel worked his way toward Turk's wagon. For the next several hours, those who were free struggled to save those who were trapped beneath tons of snow. Fortunately, their location on the side of the mountain enabled them to easily shove the snow over the side. Without this site advantage, even more people and animals would have died from the shivering cold. A full quarter of the wagon train lost their lives, most suffocating as the snow first clogged their breathing passages, then froze solid.

Fortune shone upon the Mayri party for the avalanche's bulk hit before and aft of their position. Kneal of the Insubres failed to survive. So Turk, due in part to his position at the now head of the train, assumed the role of wagon master. He ordered the dead livestock butchered, the meat preserved and the bones tossed over the side. Next he ordered the bodies of the dead stripped of their clothing and other valuables. After a short prayer to assist the spirits of the dead on their journey to the otherworld, their corpses joined the animal carcasses.

A low hanging cloud forced the party to rest at the disaster site for two full days, helping them to recover both their strength and their spirit. "This cloud, called white death, prevents us from seeing farther than our hands in front of our faces. If you have a need to leave your wagons, always keep a hand on the wheel or sides or you may wander off and tumble over the edge. Pass this on," the wagon master commanded.

During the delay, Turk ordered the damaged wagons repaired. Stripped wheels, harnesses and other utility items served as spare parts. The scavenged trade goods were distributed among the remaining wagons.

The few surviving Insubres from the front of the train found themselves scattered among the remaining wagons. "Why didn't the wagon master provide us with our own vehicles?" one questioned. "I'll wager that we will be gypped out of our share of the trade goods as well," another complained. Turk, aware of the disgruntled Insubres, chose to remedy the situation at a later time.

As the party moved forward, the trail turned downward, and the weather improved considerably. "Are we getting close to the Po Valley?" Una asked Turk as they walked alongside each other.

"We are closer but not exactly close. Look ahead and you will see how the trail is no longer straight but begins to zigzag indicating that we are heading upward again. We have several high elevations to pass over, though none as high as the one we just encountered," Turk replied.

Following a few moments of silence, he continued, "We may expect trouble as we make the next climb. So be wary. The spring snowstorm kept the wild mountain Celts close to home. They wait until a wagon train is most vulnerable before they strike. I'm going to have the party rest for a day just up ahead before we attempt the next climb. Join Conel and the other leaders as we discuss our strategy for clearing the next mountain ridge."

Within hours of the continuance of the expedition, the avalanche disaster became a distant memory. Every step was torture as the bitter cold, oxygen-depleted atmosphere sapped everyone's strength. They could only put one foot ahead of the other and pull the terrified horses.

Just as Una began to feel composed once again, loud trumpets sounded just as the traders began to break their humble camp. Then large rocks fell near those huddled next to the hillside. "It's the mountain Celts," Turk yelled. "Take cover under the wagons. Block the wheels to prevent the animals from stampeding."

Hiding under their wagon, Una looked to her father for direction. Conel seemed calm considering the seriousness of the situation. "Stay relaxed," he counseled. "They are unconventional, mavericks. They do not intend to harm us. As you heard from Turk, this is how they begin bargaining."

"They have a strange way of negotiating," Julia said during one of her few remarks, causing father and daughter to burst into laughter.

"What can we do?" Una asked.

"We must hold our position until dark and confer among ourselves," Turk replied as he crawled from his wagon to theirs. "I will scramble back and tell the others."

"Do you think we will be safe until dark?" Conel asked.

"As long as we don't try to move, we are safe for the time being," Turk answered. "Look at where the rocks land. They intend to keep us here, not to harm us. Those above us have been at this game a long time, and they want to avoid fighting their way down the mountainside to claim any valuables."

Under cover of darkness, the drivers met beneath one of the center wagons. Turk invited Conel and Una to attend because of

Druids, Celts, and Romans

their warrior status. Of the lot, Turk was the most despondent for failing to place scouts out in front of the train. "I knew we would be hit, but I thought we had another day before they would attack. Perhaps the winter was cruel and the mountain Celts are starving," Turk suggested. His chance ascendancy to the role weakened his status as the wagon master, and arguments, even from the least knowledgeable, consumed most of the night.

The next day proved to be no different than the previous, except the train was in greater danger. The attackers' anger increased as the day lengthened and the negotiations lingered. Rocks accompanied by spears came ever closer to the huddled defenders. The wind chill factor increased as an intense southerly breeze blew through the pass directly at those huddled under the wagons.

Turk ordered each small party to bundle together to conserve their body heat. This enabled the group to make it through another day, and the weary leaders met again as evening fell. If anything, the arguments became more heated and less useful. Finally, after biting her tongue for hours, Una spoke up. "I considered what my brother, Mick, would do in this situation. When the mountain Celts take up their positions tomorrow morning, Mick would be above them," Una announced.

Silence greeted these words from one whom many considered inexperienced. Then they all agreed, when they realized the strategy made sense. Conel assumed command of a party of five armed with swords, spears and arrows. Carlos, a slight lad in his mid-teens, climbed up a small gully formed by the large rocks that blocked the front of the caravan. Armed with a short dagger, he had instructions to cut the throats of any guards on the upper bluff. Despite the fact he had played at stealth with his younger kinfolk, Carlos had never killed anyone. His heart pounded more from fear than exertion as he scrambled from one foothold to another. When he neared the top, he expected to be stabbed, or at least shoved back down the hillside. To his astonishment, no one guarded the gully. The guardians of the pass went home to their dwellings when night descended. Carlos secured a rope around a rock outcropping and dangled it toward his waiting companions. Next to climb up the cliff face, Una added her weight to the youngster's, which enabled the heavier males to easily ascend. After they recovered from the exertion, Conel commanded them to climb even higher. Then turning to Una, he ordered her to take the lead.

"Why doesn't Carlos go first?" she asked. "He's the lightest."

"Have you looked at his hands?" Conel asked as he pointed to Carlos' blood stained and frostbitten fingers.

Una easily began the climb up the less severe second slope. She jammed her woolen wrapped fingers into cracks on the rock face. Then she used her arm strength to pull herself up. Suddenly, her foothold gave way, and she dangled from the precipice by the hand she had jammed into a small crack in the ice. Her arm felt like it was being pulled from the socket as her fall halted abruptly. "Drive some nails into the ice and secure the rope," someone yelled up from below.

'How am I going to do that when I can't get to the bag holding the nails?' She wondered. Perspiration ran freely down her back, even in the sub-zero temperature. The fingers supporting her weight began to cramp, and her breath came in gasps as she tried to get either a hand or foothold on the slippery surface. Ignoring her pounding heart and after taking several deep breaths to get sufficient oxygen from the thin air, she finally wedged her free hand into a hole and steadied her position. After waiting a few moments to gather her wits, the gallant warrior located a foothold by stretching her leg to the left and continued her climb. Una pulled herself over the lip of the cliff by plunging her dagger into the ice to secure a handhold. She then crawled on her belly away from the edge.

Only her exhaustion prevented her from falling into a crevasse, just a few feet from where she collapsed on a relatively flat surface. Una had plunged her spear point into the snow where it penetrated the soft covering of the fission's opening. The snow gave way, but her agility saved her life. Missing falling into a deep glacier fissure proved to be more luck than skill. The near catastrophe shook her composure, and she lay on her back for a few minutes until she regained her confidence.

Carefully searching for solid ground by stabbing through the snow with her spear, she took off her outer garments and placed them on the ground along the edge of the breach. The slippery ground sloped upward, forcing her to use both her dagger and her spear to stop from sliding backward. Using her weapons as ice picks, she gradually made her way forward to provide sufficient space to secure a belay line. Next, she reached into her pack and retrieved some iron nails. Using her sword pommel as a hammer, she drove the nails in a diamond shape pattern through the frozen earth, and secured a rope around the implanted pegs. After tying the rope around her waist, she sat, and while using her feet and spear to prevent further sliding, she tossed one end of the rope to the climbers below. As she pulled the others over the edge, she warned them of the opening only a spears length from her position. Conel, the last to make the climb, ordered all to tie themselves together with the rope used to climb the cliff face.

"Where is Carlos?" she asked.

"We had to leave him behind. His hands were too badly damaged to climb any further."

Conel immediately took charge of the group. "Should anyone fall into the crevice, the others must immediately fall down and stab their spears into the ice to prevent themselves from sliding in as well. We will hold that position until the one who fell in can climb out again. Do I make myself clear?" he whispered hoarsely. "You must act quickly because you will last only a few minutes in the hole if we don't get you out."

While Conel and his armed squad attempted to get the upper hand on the mountain Celts, the Insubres who survived the avalanche began speaking among themselves. "Have you noticed how the wagon master relies on his own people and ignores us?" one of the Insubres asked. "They deprive us of the glory, even though we know more about this crossing than they. I have no doubt the wagon master will cheat us of our just share of the trade goods!"

By first light, Conel's patrol had secured the site above the position the mountain Celts used for their daytime sorties. When the maverick Celts arrived, they looked in amazement at the wounded Carlos lying on their ice shelf, wondering how he got there. Conel had one of the patrol sound a large Celtic horn. The noise ricocheted down the mountainside and carried across the valley below. Fear struck the mountain Celts who looked up and saw the war party above them. Upon a signal from Conel, Una loosed an arrow at the feet of the enemy. "Put down your weapons and parley with us or your widows and children will starve this spring," Conel shouted so his voice could be heard by all.

As Conel's patrol watched, one of the wild mountain Celts pulled his sword and charged toward the prone Carlos. Una's second arrow pierced the neck of the young Celt, the tribal chief's son, who had chosen to go for his weapon. The speed of this death shook the lethargy from those looking up, and they quickly agreed to a truce. Using the rope, Conel pulled up Turk while his small band above the mountain Celts maintained the upper hand. "I'm sorry I had to kill him," Una said aloud.

The mountain Celts asked the gods to accept the spirit of the young warrior before they agreed to parley. Amid threats and promises both sides hammered out an agreement. The goods of two wagons would be left, along with the meat of four slain horses, to reward the mountain Celts for allowing the party to use their pass. As the parties rose to bow in agreement, an arrow struck between the maverick chieftain's feet.

Standing with his sword held above his head, Conel yelled to the group. "I look with anger upon any who attack my people and dare to place the life of my daughter in harm's way. Look at my marker!" Conel then held up the colors of the Mayri clan. "My traders will pay a token price for your permission to use these paths. However, should any wagon flying these colors be attacked in the future, I will return with my entire army and wipe your people from the face of the earth. Now be gone from my sight before I have a change of heart."

The next morning, the train moved toward the last elevation in the pass before entering the magnificent valley of the Po. The trail narrowed as it approached the last elevation. Turk halted the train and took one of his young attendants along the route until it widened on the other side of the sloping hillside. There Turk stationed himself to prevent a train heading north across the pass from entering this dangerous precipice at the same time his train moved south. The young assistant returned to the train to inform Conel that the way across was clear. For added safety on the narrow path, Conel had the participants fasten themselves by a rope to the wagon in front. He reasoned that if a mule or oxen reared and pulled a wagon over the edge at least the driver would be saved by the preceding wagon. Each driver kept a knife handy to sever the lifeline in case the wagon in front experienced disaster. As Conel started up his wagon, he experienced a sense of relief. "Thank the gods, we made it through safely," he mumbled to himself, or perhaps to Julia who huddled in back of the lead wagon. Just past the halfway point, he noticed some movement on the steep leeward slope in front of him. Several hundred meters above the moving wagon train, the grieving mother of the slain youth used her foot to push on a layer of hard pack. Within moments, she started a slab of ice cascading toward the departing wagon train. It was of little consolation to those below that her act of revenge cost her life as well. Conel shouted as he watched the wall of snow picking up speed and rushing toward them.

In the following wagon, Una heard the thunderous crash of ice chunks mixed with snow that broke loose on the mountainside. Before she could scream, she flew airborne, along with her wagon while her father, holding onto the Roman slave, looked back in horror. The Mayri chieftain whipped his team in an effort to outrun the steadily expanding snow-slide. At the same time, he dragged the dangling Una along in his wake. After clearing the end of the slide, Conel's brute strength brought his oxen to a swift halt. The momentum of the wagon continued before the animals stopped precariously perched over the edge of the cliff. Conel quickly realized the danger and screamed at Julia not to move. Any shift on the part of either one would send the wagon and its passengers over the edge to certain death. As the Mayri chief waited for help to arrive, he had to endure the screams of terror of his daughter dangling from the safety rope. So tenuous was his position that a slight movement to see what was taking place around him could send them over. Fortunately, the traumatic experience was too much for Julia, and the Roman slave fainted in her terror.

As the wall of ice and snow hit her wagon, Una was dragged off the seat by the improvised safety halter her father rigged up. Then she bounced off the icy cliff as her father's mule team raced to safety. She used her right arm to protect her head as blocks of jagged of ice glanced off her body. Her crushed left hand, pinched in a coil of the safety rope, had lost all feeling. The avalanche lasted only a few minutes, leaving Una hanging by a thread.

"Father, save me," she screamed.

"Hold on, and be as still as you can until some assistance arrives. You don't want to pull this wagon down on top of you. Only the body of a dead mule prevents us from tumbling over. I am keeping Julia with me to balance the wagon to prevent it from tipping over. We are that close to the edge."

Time passed slowly as the midday sun melted the snow, sending a stream of ice cold water pouring over the dangling maiden. As he leaned forward to prevent the wagon from shifting, Conel continued shouting encouragement to keep her spirits up. While waiting, he prayed devoutly, perhaps for the first time in a great while, to the Goddess Sulis to protect his beloved daughter. Turk, the first to reach the wagon, arrived after Una, overcome by hypothermia, dropped off into unconsciousness.

Chapter 15
The Druid Priesthood

Helvetia Druid Seminary circa 390 BC
Although he dearly missed the companionship of his sister, Hugh soon found himself far too occupied with studies to dwell upon it. Each night for the past year, he thought of her as he tried to sleep on the padded pallet provided for a bed. For if truth were told, Una adored Mick but loved Hugh, and he loved her.

The old Druid droned on and on about the origin of the Celtic peoples, a lengthy subject that Hugh and the fifteen other apprentices were expected to memorize. But lacking a written language, the Druids conducted all the lessons in accordance with an oral tradition. Furthermore, they combined the more practical lessons on law, astronomy, genealogy, medicine and history with studies dedicated to their religion.

Hugh's classmates made up an unusual mix for the priesthood since half were female. Rarely did females make up so large a percentage of trainees. One of the few female teachers presented this day's history lesson. Hugh and the others listened intently to the lesson before reciting what had been taught. The instructor emphasized her fervent belief that the Celts were the most favored of the universe. Most of the students sat on the dirt floor and listened with rapture while she captured their imagination. Hugh, however, heard the tale at the feet of his idol Munli, and hearing it rehashed by a less talented instructor failed to awaken his enthusiasm. "The gods created our forefathers by merging three unique traits they deemed essential. First of all, their people must be attractive. Secondly, they must be fearless warriors and finally, they must be authoritative leaders of the world," she continued.

"In the northern regions lived an island-people who ruled the far seas, and provided the leadership trait the gods sought. These long-faced islanders, large of frame and attractive beyond description, were driven from their homeland by the will of the gods. They moved south, conquered and intermarried with the native round-heads. By which time, the round-heads, noted for their ability to govern fairly, had developed from migrating hunters into settled farmers and miners."

Silently Hugh said to himself. "I wonder if she classifies me as one of the round heads."

"The final piece of the triad emigrated from the vast grassland far to the east. These were horse people, feared across the known world for their prowess in warfare, drawn westward to mix with those already chosen. But the gods still were not satisfied." Again she paused before continuing.

"The people lacked attributes that only the gods themselves possessed. After centuries of debate, the deities finally shared these essential ingredients. The gods gave intelligence and creativity to a magical people who inhabited Irene Isle. The gods wished their people to possess boundless perception and fantastic artistic skills. These island-bound fairies sent some of their members east across the sea to intermarry with the creatures of the gods. Only with the talents of intelligence and creativity could the people pay the expected homage. The gods studied their creation and were satisfied. Our people, known to the world as Celts, were created to bring order and reason to the universe!"

To his joy, Hugh discovered that all learning did not center on classroom instruction. The students were paired off and cut adrift to fend for themselves on the vast territory allotted to the seminary. Hugh was paired with the fair Katlyn. Unlike many of his classmates, Hugh had been trained as a warrior and not likely to fail. Katlyn of noble birth never ventured beyond her town until she answered her summons to the Druid school. This third daughter of the family had little choice but to study to be a priestess since the family holdings would go to the oldest son, and both sisters were married off to further the family's position. The extent of their dowries left little to provide for the youngest.

Forest area within the Druid compound

At first intimidated by her companion, Katlyn soon found herself grateful when she watched as Hugh demonstrated his keen insight and skill in outdoor crafts. In the first hours of their pairing, Hugh took Katlyn to a distant corner of the Druid forest far from other students, and constructed a crude shelter next to a bubbling brook. Then he designed and built weapons for hunting. "Come with me," he said. As he tramped through the nearby woods, he pointed out various animal tracks and explained how to recognize the best locations to set the traps. While waiting for a small animal to be snared, the two spent their time collecting kindling. Hugh didn't indicate his surprise, though he felt it when he had to teach Katlyn how to use flint to start a fire.

Hours later, the comely noblewoman watched in amazement as Hugh skinned and cleaned the two rabbits that fell prey to his simple snare. He then indicated that Katlyn should cook the meal. "No one ever taught me to cook," she said.

"If we are to survive, you must learn!" Hugh said as he demonstrated how to skew the plump carcass with a tree branch, and place the rod on the Y shaped branches he stationed at each end of the fire. The delicious aroma arising from the cooking rabbits reminded Katlyn of her growing hunger. While the meat roasted, Hugh placed ground up grain, mixed with water, in a metal container to bake. After a time, he made several knife slits in the rabbits to be certain the juices ran clear. "Now we can eat without getting the stomach sickness," he announced.

Pulling handfuls of meat off the bones, the shelter-mates enjoyed the meat and bread, washing them down with pristine water. Following the simple meal, Hugh collected the stripped bones and tossed them in a trench that he had dug far from the shelter. "Leaving food or bones lying around will only attract wild animals, and we have neither bow nor sword to drive them off.

Turning in with a full stomach, a hesitant Katlyn joined her associate in the small lean-to for their first evening together. Because she was destined for the priesthood, her mother neglected her education on dealing with men. Despite having two brothers, Katlyn's knowledge of males came from local gossip. Her fear of forcible rape dissipated as Hugh rolled over on his side and fell asleep instantly. The young Katlyn lay awake for most of the night puzzling over the sad turn of events. There were others more attractive and of higher birth than this Celt from a small provincial clan. After praying to her gods for a fortuitous outcome, she finally fell into an uneasy sleep.

For his part, Hugh was dazzled by the prospects of spending twelve months with such an exquisite creature. From the day Katlyn came into his life, Hugh felt attracted to a female for the first time. During class, he often gazed longingly at her oval face with its generous mouth, dimples and cleft chin. She came from a tribe that favored black hair, snowy-white skin, a sprinkling of freckles and deep blue eyes, a stark difference to the red hair, green-eyed maidens of his own clan. Her friendly smile, however, captivated him the most. He knew it took a full year to trace the movement of stars in the heavens and just as long to follow the growth of plants

Druids, Celts, and Romans
191

from seed to maturity. He thanked the gods for designing such a lengthy time period and for allowing him the opportunity to spend it alone with Katlyn. The great distance Hugh placed between them and their other classmates was not an accident.

Because Druids were expected to fend for themselves, the teachers designed this period to make the apprentices self-reliant. With winter quickly approaching, the couple spent their time dealing with survival concerns. They replaced the small lean-to with a larger structure composed of mud-covered wattle walls and a timber roof. Katlyn designated a site, downstream from the dwelling, for their natural functions. She gathered nuts and dried berries while Hugh salted the carcasses of small animals to preserve them. He also dried animal skins and stored them for later use as clothing. Katlyn aptly applied the sewing skills she learned as a third daughter.

Once during the first month, the couple ventured to the community to pickup the allotted supplies. The survival skills and knowledge to coexist with nature exhibited by the male and his reluctance to mingle with the other apprentices made a second trip unnecessary. Swift in spite of his size and with the surprising stealth gained in the childhood pursuit of his siblings, Hugh proved more than a match for most game. Once, he attracted a small black bear to a waddle-covered hole by placing pieces of rotting meat around its perimeter. The slick sides of its prison prevented the bear from escaping after it crashed through the thin covering. Following a laborious struggle, the bear finally died of exhaustion. Because the bear's deadweight made retrieving it more trouble than trapping it. To hoist the carcass out of the trap, Hugh designed an elaborate pulley, which he attached to nearby trees. He preserved the meat in dandelion wine, providing nourishment for months. Katlyn, who learned quickly, dried the fur and skin to provide additional clothing and covering for the dwelling.

Despite her inexperience, Katlyn proved to be proficient in finding, and gathering, the various herb and plants needed for medicinal purposes. To heal eye injuries, she collected moss from evergreen leaves, which she burnt in a small fire pot for the ash. Hugh told her how mistletoe, a parasite of the mighty oak, served as an antidote to many poisons and a cure for minor wounds. He also knew the verbena plant extraction cured snake and insect bites and proved useful in preventing fevers. Katlyn stored the herbs in wooden bowls that she gouged-out and marked with the name of the contents. Both she and Hugh could decipher the Greek lettering she used to identify the medicines.

Whenever the weather permitted, the pair studied the position of the celestial bodies and repeated, in unison, the location of the constellations. Using a section of ground they scraped clear for the purpose, Hugh inscribed the movement of the heavenly bodies in the dirt. He included the number of nights between each movement, the position and size of the moon, as well as the corresponding position of the sun. Dried skins of small animals covered the drawings to protect them from inclement weather. Together the two studied the passage of time reflected by the dirt sculpture. On the wall of their simple abode using stains from different berries, the couple recorded the number of nights in each lunar interval.

As their trust of each other grew, their nightly conversations flourished. Katlyn replaced Una in Hugh's life. Katlyn gained a companion who listened to her needs and whims, something that was foreign to the youngest daughter from a family of four. As often happens in a continuous relationship, one's beauty becomes less important as does the unattractiveness of the other. Such was the way of things with Katlyn and Hugh. He became less inhibited by her stunning good looks, and she less intimidated by his sheer size. Their personalities and sensibilities rose to the forefront. Over time, simple acts of kindness, as well as the close proximity, led the twosome to mate as lovers. The budding Druid found himself supported by a devoted and skillful partner. Two young people went forth on the rustic adventure. By the end of the term, two mature adults returned.

Helvetia Druid Seminary circa 389 BC
Upon their arrival back at the college after completing the twelve month-sojourn, the two apprentices were joined into a triad with the oldest looking Druid Hugh had ever seen. He was small of frame and timid looking as though the years had robbed his body of both height and vitality. The man's sun-spotted hands and leathered skin added to his frail appearance. Hugh looked on with apprehension, afraid that the old man might stumble and die on the spot. "My name is Seamus, and I have traveled a far distance to become your teacher. I am delighted that you have survived your nature internship. Now, I plan to expand on your learning. You may call me master."

"Master, you have a strange accent. Where did you come from?" the dubious Hugh asked as he silently wondered why they got someone so old.

"I come from Ierne Island, the Insula Sacra because of a promise I made to the Druid Munli long ago. He sent a message telling me that one day a triplet would become a Druid, and I was to teach him all that I knew. I believe you are the third of a single birth, are you not?"

"I have a brother and sister who were born on the day that I entered the world. That is true. But I wonder, when did Munli ask you to become my tutor?"

"He came to me in visions, dreams if you will. Perhaps he had already passed on to the otherworld. That I do not know. During the third dream, despite my advanced age, I agreed to travel to Helvetia and become your teacher. Several moons ago, Munli appeared again and told me it was time to pass on all that I know."

"How old are you?" asked a bewildered Katlyn.

"I have lived through one thousand lunar periods. Though I look like I should have gone to the otherworld ages ago, I can assure you that I am in excellent health and will survive your tutorship. You will soon wear the special tonsure of the Druid for your knowledge will come swiftly." Seamus then had his charges sit beside him as he began their formal education.

"You must let go of your ego and all that other Druids have taught if you are to absorb that which I will pass on. This is knowledge that must descend to the next generation, to your children, nephews and nieces if our Celtic world is to survive. Bear in mind that a tradition endures only as long as its memory survives." The two students looked intently at the piercing eyes of their master as he emphasized the role they would play.

"My age benefits me as I speak to you because I have knowledge of a chain of memory to life forms other than man. The life forms that retain the oldest memories are those that live the longest. Man, though he lives long, is but an infant compared to life forms around him. The Druid priesthood has long known that knowledge can only be retained by honoring our ancestors. From them, we inherit all our wisdom. Are there any who choose to strip us of our wisdom?"

"Master, there are the spirits who invade our realm during Samain," Katlyn answered as Hugh pondered for a more obscure reason.

"That is so. Now what do people do to prevent the spirits from the otherworld from stealing their spirit and with it their knowledge?"

"They stay indoors," Katlyn answered.

"They don disguises to confuse the wandering dead and make them think the human behind the mask is one of them," Hugh added.

"This is so," answered Seamus. Then the old man arose and hobbled toward the corner of the room where he picked up two huge boulders and handed one to each student. Hugh easily hefted the weight but had to help Katlyn secure hers. Both students were dumbfounded by the ancient Druid's strength. "For the remainder of the day and the night, you will each go to a separate memory hut that I will assign. Once you close the door no light will enter. You will lie on the bed with this rock resting on your stomach and recite all that I have told you. Perhaps you will sleep, perhaps not. It matters little. The stone, which will become your constant companion whenever you retire to the hut of memory, will prevent hunger pangs. Now follow me, and I will direct you to your quarters. When I appear sometime during the night, I want you to recite everything that we discussed today."

"Can I help you carry your stone?" Hugh asked Katlyn, as he watched her struggle with the heavy boulder, half-afraid that she might drop it on her foot.

"No, I am capable. But I expected it to be much lighter since the master picked both up so easily."

"I, too, was astonished at the strength of such an ancient person. I believe we are blessed in being chosen to be his subjects. We have much to learn, and I for one intend to be a most attentive student."

Over the following weeks, Seamus gifted them with herbs and plants which assist healing. He provided nuts for knowledge, apples to discover eternal life, and sticks and stones for divination. After each gift they retired to the hut of memory to reflect on what they had learned. When he sufficiently stimulated their memory, Seamus changed to a topic more spiritual in nature. "Have you ever wondered why the moon doesn't fall down upon the earth? Or considered that blood continually runs within your veins to nourish your body? All of this is proof that we are part of a grander scheme, a scheme that gains its structure and harmony from the unknowable god." The two young apprentices sat in awe as they listened to the ancient Druid's wisdom.

Druids, Celts, and Romans

But Seamus wasn't finished. Later that month he inquired. "Have you ever wondered why you, and not another, have been selected to study for the priesthood?"

"Because, I am the third female of a noble family," a flippant and self-confident Katlyn answered.

"If every third female of a noble family is destined to become a Druidess, then these halls would be overrun by females," a smiling Seamus said. The two stared in shock. It was the first time they had ever seen him smile.

"I'm here because it is my destiny," a very serious Hugh responded, not wishing to fall victim to Seamus' humor.

"Have either of you determined why you differ from your siblings?"

"No, not really," Katlyn answered.

"Thank you. That is an honest answer. Now let me explain one of life's greatest mysteries. Every infant is born with three cauldrons, which, depending on the cauldron's position at birth, determines the knowledge, creativity and physical health of a person." Using his fingers Seamus drew the form of a human figure in the soft soil of the floor. Then he placed three small, shallow vessels upside down, one in the head of the drawing, one on the chest, and the final one on the stomach. Taking a water pitcher he attempted to pour the liquid into the three vessels. Each time it spilled on the ground. Seamus turned the shallow dish, resting on the head area, upright and filled it with water. "This cauldron is the most vital if one is to be a leader, a Druid, a warrior chief or a king. This receptacle contains knowledge and wisdom, the residence of the soul and the link to our ancestors. Warriors cut off the head of a revered enemy and drink the blood from the skull to gain the wisdom their enemy possessed."

As the year and their training progressed, the students learned about the interrelationship of life and death. "Explain why a warrior does not fear death?" Seamus casually asked one spring morning following his usual light breakfast.

"Because death is a continuation of life in a different form," Katlyn answered. "The soul of a worthy Celt enters the otherworld for a period determined by the gods. After which, the soul returns to this world."

"What is the greatest death a warrior can seek?" Seamus asked.

"That he or she die bravely in battle," Katlyn answered.

"After slaying many of his enemies and in the presence of a bard who can tell of his glory for generations to come," Hugh added.

"Quite so," Seamus said, smiling at his students' acquired knowledge. "Death is merely a continuation of the wheel of life. Where do we acquire such knowledge?"

"The trees are repositories of knowledge. The oak gathers knowledge through its roots and from the heavens by attracting lightning. Also we find knowledge in the hazel, the yew and the mountain ash," Katlyn said in response to his prompting.

"Well done. Today I want you to wander through the forest and using your senses try to communicate with the gods residing in the trees. Learn how nature makes our very egos gain a sense of serenity." With that command, Seamus finished the lesson for the day.

The following day when the threesome met again, Seamus changed the discussion from nature gods to spiritual gods. "We have dwelled on nature, the world of living things around us, and we have discussed the otherworld. Where else do the gods reside?"

"The residence of the Supreme Creator is unknown and unknowable," Hugh answered.

"That is the correct answer, but why is that so?"

"Because none of the known gods rank above any of the others; therefore, there must be more than we know," he answered with assurance.

During the next several weeks, the triad covered a myriad of subjects, including the use of an incantation which allows a Druid to foretell future events. This verse enables the user to view the circumstances surrounding anything hidden, even a future occurrence, and it serves as a practical tool when used to plan a campaign or choose a war chief. In addition, Seamus taught his students how to interpret visions and dreams, then surprised them by acclaiming, "In all my years of teaching, you two are the quickest learners I have ever encountered. You complement each other with one being knowledgeable about healing and the other being equally knowledgeable about the spiritual world!"

For the next several months, the old master concentrated on the laws of the Celts, which the Druids administered. This stage of his training proved to be a refresher course for Hugh who had been admonished by his father to memorize these laws since youth.

Druids, Celts, and Romans

"No matter how distasteful these laws such as the incineration of criminals may seem, they exist for the benefit of the clan as a whole. The Druids hold the Celts together as one people. The preservation of our race must be our foremost objective."

On that same gloomy rainy day, Seamus announced his guidance was nearing an end. "Our next topic will be the final one for this level of your training. Come prepared to learn,"

"Yes master," both replied.

At the end of the following week, they could see the seriousness of the subject reflected on the master's leathered facial expression. "We will now study the Druids' calendar so that you may instruct your fellow countrymen on the order of events." Seamus then unrolled two long, treated calfskins with strange columnar markings burnt into the material by the use of a hot spike.

"For thousands of years the Druids and their predecessors, the ancient wise ones, studied the celestial universe. After years of documenting the wheel of the sun, moon and stars that revolve around us, they determined a pattern existed. The ancients discovered an orderly process governs the celestial universe. I am about to share that knowledge with you. This is one more proof that there exists some unknown god who governs all things." Even though they felt like their cauldron of knowledge was overflowing, the two sat patiently and listened to their master.

"The new moon marks the beginning of each lunar period that lasts twenty-nine or thirty nights. When the wheel of the moon completes a cycle and becomes a new moon again, a lunar period is complete. The sun takes longer to complete its cycle. To detect the movement of either the sun or moon, we start at a fixed position and measure how long the heavenly body takes to return to that same spot in the sky. Do you understand me so far?" Both students nodded in agreement.

"The length of night, as does the length of day, changes as the wheel of the moon moves around the earth. Therefore, we have to study the rotations of the moon and sun for an extended duration if our efforts are to be of value. This knowledge ranks among the most important information that you will ever learn."

"Why is that, master? You have taught us how to govern, how to heal and how to enter a trance in order to cast a spell," an inquisitive Hugh asked. "What can you say that is more important than all those things?"

"In my homeland at a site known as Knowth, an ancient person carved the phases of the moon on a boulder. It shows using circles and other markings sixty-two lunar periods. I have interpreted these marks and copied the findings on leather skins. The universe determines a favorable time to conduct a certain act. For example, the universe's movement determines when corn should be planted. Planting too early would mean the seeds would never sprout, whereas planting too late would mean the stalks would never bear fruit. Imagine the effort it would take during every lunar phrase for Druids, all over the world, to make a prediction on when to plant, when to herd cattle and sheep, or when to start a military campaign."

"Yes master," each answered.

"Now I am about to reveal a method to make the determination of a favorable time much easier." Seamus then unrolled the two scrolls of leather and gave one to each.

The two students looked at long columns of figures and letters before glancing at the scroll held by the other. Different words were written next to some of the figures and letters in the columns. The students studied the documents, remarking on occasion when they understood the meaning of a word. Seamus interrupted and explained what they held in their hands. "You are looking at a map of time, a calendar that merges the revolutions of the moon and the sun. Each lunar period is broken into two, the light side and the dark side. The months of thirty days are described as matu meaning fortunate. Those of twenty-nine days are marked as anm which means unfortunate or unlucky."

"Most events, therefore, should start in the first fortnight of a lunar period," Katlyn said gleefully.

"That is correct. The first half of lunar periods with thirty days, such as the month of Samain are the luckiest portions. If you look closely, you will see special days that are noted as well. The fourteenth day of a lunar period is the best to hold festivals."

After counting the number of months, Hugh asked, "What is the meaning of thirty-one months?"

"You are looking at one-half of the total period," Seamus answered. "Katlyn has the other half. There are sixty-two periods in total because the map covers a period of five years. What else do you see that is remarkable?"

"One of the months on my scroll is not named," Katlyn answered.

"Nor is one named on the scroll that Hugh holds," Seamus pointed out. "These months were inserted to bring the revolutions of the moon into agreement with the revolutions of the sun. Remember that I told you the two celestial bodies move at different speeds. If the calendar weren't brought into agreement with the movement of these two bodies, snow would fall during the summer months after decades of using the calendar."

"How did the ancients know that adding a month every two and a half years would bring them into agreement?" Katlyn asked.

"On Ierne isle and adjoining Alba isle the ancients built enormous structures where they could measure when the sun and the moon pass time-lines carved in the rock. After centuries of study, these stone circles assisted them in bringing the workings of the moon and the sun into agreement." Hugh nodded his head as he remembered learning of these great stone circles when he listened to Munli describe them.

"Retire to your huts of memory and learn what is written on the skin that you have been assigned. We will meet in three days, and I will have you recite them from memory."

After three days, they recited their assigned halves and they traded skins. Then they began memorizing the other half of the calendar. The final recital covered its entire sixty-two month scope.

After he was satisfied, Seamus gave each of the students two leather calfskins. They departed again to draw from memory time maps on their own. Each used caution to inscribe correctly, or else they might error and ruin the skin. Though they did yet not realize it, Hugh and Katlyn would treasure the knowledge given by this precious gift for the remainder of their lives. After presenting the finished product to Seamus for his inspection, the students sat and awaited his appraisal.

He gave them the finest acknowledgement he could provide. "You have acquired all the knowledge that I can impart. Now you must practice what you have learned to become proficient at your profession. I shall report to the chief Druid that you have excelled far beyond my expectations and can take the next step on the path to full priesthood. My time with you is now finished."

Helvetia Druid College circa 388 BC

Months after Seamus' departure, the two were deeply engrossed in studying religious rituals when a strange apprehension overtook

Hugh. "I don't know why, but I believe the gods are calling me to return to my family," he announced one day to Katlyn.

"How can you be certain?" Katlyn asked.

"Perhaps, I can use the foretelling trance we learned from Seamus to gain knowledge of hidden things," he replied. Katlyn knew Hugh used this trance at every opportunity.

That night, Hugh chewed on the raw flesh of a freshly killed pig and went to bed early. He slept soundly but did not dream. "I have failed!" he announced upon awakening.

"Perhaps you did not focus properly. Thus the gods did not know where to direct your dream. Remember that Seamus told us the spirit must be allowed to freely flow from the body. Maybe you have been holding back. I will prepare a medicinal drink to help you relax."

That morning, he chanted mystical incantations while taking certain gifts, treasured from childhood, to bed with him. He held the gifts in each hand against his face, and with the help of Katlyn's concoction he immediately fell into a deep slumber.

"What did you see in your dream?" a worried Katlyn asked as he arose.

"Una is in mortal danger. She is swinging from a rope over a vast ice chasm. A frigid waterfall is pouring over her body. She is dying. I called out to her spirit and vowed that I would hurry to her rescue. She pledged to hold on to life until I arrive."

Without a word, Katlyn packed their sparse belongings. After they asked for the blessings of the priests, they began the long trek to the oppidum of the Mayri.

Chapter 16
The Po Valley

Po Valley circa 388 BC
Midday arrived before a warming sun burned off the morning fog. The grandeur of the vale of the Po River spread before the welcoming eyes of the weary and wounded trading party. Julia in particular perked up as she gazed over the side of the wagon toward the familiar fruit trees, the broad leaves of the grape vineyards and the groves of olive trees planted on cleared forestland. 'I have lived through my torment. I soon will be in Rome, and then I will have my revenge,' she silently swore when the last of the snowfields receded behind her.

Druids, Celts, and Romans

As the wagons rambled down the mountainside, the small tributaries feeding the river roared past, and white water torrents carved deep channels into the slopes of the Alps. Conel stopped his wagon, stepped down, stretched his legs and walked over to the edge of a steep bluff. He gazed toward two large lakes, one on each side, where the turbulent rivers seemed to both terminate and originate. 'Lake Lucern could easily fit in either of these lakes,' he thought. With his homeland never far from his mind, he stood daydreaming and enjoying the warmth of the sun upon his face. "I should be feeling comforted after surviving the perilous crossing, but I only feel cold fear wrapping around my bowels," he murmured aloud, not realizing that the nearby Julia listened to every word. He returned to the wagon and removed the tarp covering the still unconscious Una, hoping the warmth of the sun would penetrate her haze. As Conel looked on his beloved daughter, tears of sadness ran down his cheeks.

Turk halted his wagon and joined Conel. To distract his friend from dwelling on his daughter's fate, the trader pointed toward a fair-sized herd of cattle pastured in a nearby narrow green alpine valley. "You will be amazed at the size of these animals. The cheese is as rich as any you tasted. The large lake on our left is called Como. I don't know the name of the one on the right."

"After seeing nothing except white and gray for the past weeks, I could sit and look at this green for all eternity," the large chieftain said pleasantly to his traveling guide. In an effort to shake off his lethargy, Conel asked about the land they were entering.

"It's similar to our side of the Alps," Turk explained. "The river Parus, which most people shorten to Po, resembles the Rhine flowing through our own country. Except the Po flows west to east on its journey to the sea, whereas the Rhine flows east to west then turns north. This river, the Celt's southern border, runs alongside the Apennines Mountains. I have not seen the river's mouth, but I am told that it splits into five channels as it crosses its delta and enters the Adriatic. The Po Celts have settled on a plain between two rivers originating in the Alps, one empties into the Po, the other enters the Adriatic to the northeast of the Po's delta. At times the ground is as swampy as the land alongside the Lake Lucern. We will pass ancient people's homes built on stilts where the marsh is soft. Though still in use, the homes are decaying, but you can appreciate the skill required to build them."

Then looking south, Turk changed the subject. "I can see from the dust rising below us that our arrival has not gone unnoticed," he said, pointing to several miniature figures moving in the distance. "These people, the Insubres, are the most populous of the many Celtic tribes living on this side of the Alps," Turk warned Conel. "They claim to be the first Celtic settlers south of the mountains. In fact, they claim to have settled here over six hundred winters ago. Because of their denser population, they consider themselves rulers of all the land. They have no love for our allies, the Boii. So, we must be wary of what we say and do. We will trade with them, but we want to save our most precious items until we reach the Boii. Therefore, it behooves us to keep the more valuable goods under cover, away from the prying eyes of the Insubres who have traveled with us."

Concerned about Una, a distracted Conel nodded to indicate his understanding.

"Gather the leaders for a parley," Turk said to his young assistant. "The last I heard, the Insubres and other Celtic tribes are on friendly terms. Still we must be vigilant and maintain our guard until we reach our Boii allies."

Standing on the backboard of the lead wagon, Turko spoke to the wagon masters. Pointing toward the south, he told them that the natives of the valley were already making their way toward the first trading party of the season. Turk explained the Mayri clan's wagons would spend several weeks with the Insubres before proceeding on to the land of the Boii. "We hope to have profitable trades with both tribes," he continued. "Many will complete their transactions with the Insubres while others who need to trade further are welcome to accompany us. The choice is yours," he emphasized. "Once we come within sight of the first oppidum, the Insubres are responsible for our safety. Until then, we provide our own protection. Therefore, the guard rotations are as follows..." Turk continued until he posted the guard detail.

"How are the traded goods going to be divided?" Lavos one of the disgruntled Insubres traders asked. Although, he had often complained behind Kneal's back, Lavos now traded on his rival's name to gain an advantage. "Most of our valuables went over the cliff when the first avalanche crashed into Kneal and the lead wagons."

Turk replied, as the wagon masters from the surviving parties nodded their heads in agreement. "The law of the trail provides that each surviving wagon will share one-tenth of its goods with any party that lost goods either through an attack by an enemy or because of a natural disaster. Since an avalanche is a natural disaster, we will settle up when we arrive at the Insubres' oppidum," he concluded, expecting nothing more to be said on the matter.

"That is not just," the offended Insubres replied. "Kneal had traded well and was returning to his land with goods worth as much as all your wagons contain. We should be entitled to half the remainder!"

"As wagon master, I have spoken," Turk said. "If you insist on being paid now, then take the last wagon of the Mayri for your share. This is my offer. Take it or lose everything."

Realizing that they would gain nothing further, the Insubres turned to the other traders and asked for an immediate distribution of their shares. The goods were stacked onto the single wagon offered by Turk, and the Insubres left the train in anger. No one noted that Julia was most interested in the dissention among the Celts.

Turk did not have to remind the Mayri party that the valuable cargo was purposely stored at the bottom of the first two wagons. "We have not heard the last from that bunch," he said for the benefit of those who remained. "Bear in mind that we have made enemies during this journey, and they will not soon forget. We're in their territory. So until we are well clear of the Insubres' land, we should be on our guard."

Rather than push on to the Insubres' oppidum, Turk ordered the trading party to prepare camp on a level spot near the rushing river to await the arrival of the herders who were seen approaching.

"Conel, we have to rest the men and teams before we can continue. It would be wiser to send Una on ahead to the nearest oppidum to be treated by the Druid healers," Turk said. "I need you, however, to remain here to guard the Mayri's wagons. As a clan chieftain and warrior, you have the respect that no one else can command. I recommend that we send young Carlos along as her guard. He has shown his worth on the mountain." A disappointed and worried father agreed with the wisdom of the clan's trader.

The meat preserved from the animals lost in the avalanche had long since lost its appeal, so the party was grateful for the opportunity to eat fresh game. The first trade of the year consisted of providing weapons to the herders in exchange for cattle and lambs.

For their part, living in a land with few mineral resources, the Insubres' herders yearned for the few iron weapons offered in return for their sheep and cattle. After they shared some food and drink with the herders, the wagon train was circled to keep the newly acquired livestock from rejoining their herd.

Carlos and three of the herders were assigned to escort Una to the nearest healers. Conel took Carlos aside and gave him private instructions. "This is my only daughter whom I love dearly. I entrust her life to your hands. Can you pledge that you will keep her safe?"

"I pledge my life that I will keep her safe," Carlos answered.

The small party took off before the improvised banquet began. Though he participated in the activities, Conel's thoughts went with his beautiful daughter.

In route to the Mayri Oppidum
"Don't you think you should warn someone that we are coming?" Katlyn asked her companion.

"You know that I have been spending all my energy, using the incantations taught by Seamus, trying to communicate with Una. Why don't you try to get in touch with my brother, Mick?"

"I don't know Mick. How am I to get a message to him? I can't picture him, let alone know where he might be."

"Give me time to rest. Then I will try to send a vision to him to meet us at the oppidum."

Insubres' Druid Temple
Carlos took his duties so seriously that he wouldn't allow the party carrying the unconscious Una any rest until they arrived at the first oppidum. As well as he could, he explained Una's comatose condition to the imposing Insubres' Druid. Una and her guardian were instantly dispatched to a temple, a half-day's travel on the far side of the Po, situated in a narrow valley in the foothills of the Apennines. There the young Celtic maiden was immersed in the healing waters of a sulfur spring that bubbled upward from a smoking hole. For two days, Una was fed a combination of goats' milk and herbs mixed by the healers and alternatively immersed and then laid unclothed under the warmth of the suns' rays. On the third day after her arrival at the healer's compound, she awoke to a painful blistering burn from the hot sun. The healers immediately moved her within the temple walls and began to treat her sunburn with a mixture of olive oil and lamb grease. Within a day's time,

Una had regained a partial memory, but the sunburn took longer to heal. She questioned Carlos who remained constantly at her side. "Where am I, and how did I get here?"

He described the vengeance wrought by the woman for the death of her son. "You got harmed, because you saved my life. I owe you everything that I am," the young love-struck Celt declared.

The Druids treated her as royalty and protected her privacy, allowing only her traveling companion to view her. Upon hearing of her rare beauty, a number of young Insubres' nobles had come to admire the maid but were sorely disappointed to find her off limits to visitors.

Carlos filled her in on the aftermath of the avalanche and assisted her in any way that he could. Even though she listened with interest, she could not recall anything about the incident. "I can remember everything up to and including the treaty we signed with those wild people but little more."

The few times she dropped into a deep sleep, her moaning pervaded the small temple. She told Carlos of seeing Hugh in her dreams telling her to hold on, that he was on his way. "He had a female companion traveling with him. It must be a vision, or at least something more than a recurring dream because I see the same person every time that I fall into a deep sleep."

Carlos did not understand the significance of Una's vision. Being a simple lad, he knew little of a Druid's ability to disturb dreams. So, he positioned himself outside her door each night, fearing that even the local Druids could not provide the protection his lovely companion deserved.

After the sunburn's pain subsided, Una had to learn to be reconciled to her useless left hand. Two fingers tangled during her fall on the mountain suffered severely damaged nerves, making the hand useless with chronic pain almost beyond enduring. Every movement involved bumping into something.

Helvetia's Northern Border
For the third time in Mick's captaincy of the frontier guard, the Germans tried to penetrate beyond the forest that separated the two peoples. The patrol that he had posted reported that a large party of mounted warriors was moving swiftly south along the main trail toward their camp. "Assemble the leaders. We must go over our plan once more. Hurry, we don't have much time."

When the squad leaders arrived, Mick described, for the final time, the trap he wanted set. "We will conceal the main trail and open up the secondary one. Once the enemy has taken the wrong path, place the spiked wooden posts in the holes dug to prevent their horses from retreating. I want two squads of archers, one stationed where the false trail ends, and the other posted behind the spiked wood. Do not allow those at the end of the false trail to start shooting until the enemy is almost upon them. If the arrows come too soon, they may retreat before the trap is sprung. When the enemy is sufficiently confused, I will sound the horn for the mounted troops to enter the battle. Now listen to me carefully. I will kill any man who charges into battle before the sound of the horn. Pass this on to your warriors." The Celtic warriors quickly assembled in the assigned areas and waited for the German raiders.

The first barrage of arrows hit the leading raider squarely in the face as he tried to halt his horse. Blood splattered on those charging behind him before they realized their leader was mortally wounded. As he fell from his horse, his followers began to screech, "Turn back, turn back. It's a trap." Their unheard shouts mingled with the triumphal clamor of the archers as they zeroed in on their prey.

Mick led the charge before the bunched up cavalry could reform and react to the danger. Unimaginable screams came from their flanks as angry Celts, guarding their homeland, crashed into them from both sides. Swinging his massive steel blade Mick killed with impunity. Those in the rear of the raiding party turned their horses around and rode to escape the slaughter, only to encounter the murderous wooden stakes. As horses and riders impaled themselves, the archers safely hidden behind the barricade, cut down the survivors. The battle was swift and the result as certain as the young captain expected.

Around the campfire that night, he explained why the horses had to be sent back with headless riders. "If we just leave them to rot, their tribe may think that they succeeded and send more invaders. This way they will know that they not only failed, but their spirits did not return with them. We can delay future invasions until the German works up his courage again." In celebration Mick and his squad got very drunk that night.

Rolling over, with a head that pounded with pain, Mick screamed at his brother to remain quiet. "Why are you making so much noise?" Then he woke, and realized he was still in the border patrol's camp. 'Could I have been dreaming about Hugh or was it something more? He seemed so real, so concerned. What did he say? It had something to do with Una. Is she in some type of danger?' Mick could not keep his mind on his duties as the likeness of his brother returned time and again. Finally, he decided to pay heed to the images appearing in his head. 'I must go home to the oppidum and find out if it is more than a dream.' Without further delay, he packed up his belongings, assigned the patrol to his second in command, and explained that he had been summoned. With that short comment, he mounted his horse, and taking the reins of a spare mount, he rode off.

Insubres' Oppidum

While his daughter was recovering from her near disaster, Conel neared the first densely populated holding of the Insubres. Not wanting to appear empty handed when he entered the established settlement, he engaged a small hunting party to scour the hillsides and small valleys in search of game. With the assistance of native guides, the hunters killed two wild boar and several mountain goats. The goats were left with the herders, but the carcasses of the boars were tied to poles and carried on the shoulders of four Celts. Conel had Turk re-assemble his two-wheel chariot that somehow survived the trek across the mountains. He wanted to enter the settlement as a warrior instead of as wagon tender.

Conel took the opportunity to wash his clothes in the chilly mountain water as well as shave the beard below his flowing mustache. After dressing, he strapped on the great sword and positioned his shield at the front of the chariot.

Although he maintained a calm demeanor, the clan chief secretly feared for the health of his only daughter. 'Meva will surely kill me if anything happed to Una', he thought to himself.

Despite the valley being lush, it was also swampy because of overflow from the many streams coming down from the Apennines to enter the Po. The muddy roads hindered the traders' train almost as much as the mountain snow had earlier. Though they could see the oppidum in the offing, they took more time to cover the distance than Conel would have imagined. As the party neared the hill-fort, he took note of the orderly canals that crossed the landscape. The nearer their destination the drier the route because the water ran off into the canals, leaving rich soil to grow grapes and olives.

At long last, Turk had an assistant blow the great Celtic horn to announce the arrival of the first trading party from the north. The wagon train, led by a warrior's chariot, turned down the hard-packed road toward the distant oppidum. The northerners were amazed by the grandeur of the settlement. The walls were made of solid stone surrounding a hillfort far larger than the capital of Helvetia. Conel noted that the interior structures were made of stones laid on top of each other and held together with a type of mortar. "They use this hard material because trees do not grow as plentifully on this side of the mountains. Their predecessors destroyed the forest in order to plant grapevines," Turk stated as he noticed the amazement reflected in the eyes of his traveling companion.

While Turk completed the trade transactions and set up the wagon camp in the space provided outside the walls, some of the traders continued on to other nearby Celtic tribes. Lavos lead the surviving members of the original Insubres trading party in accusing the Mayri of being unfaithful to their bargain and cheating them out of their fair share of the trade goods. He made sure that these false rumors were passed from tribal member to tribal member, contributing to the animosity the southerners held for the Celts from the other side of the Alps.

Druid Temple
After they got settled, Conel left the wagon train in Turk's charge and set off for the temple site to find his daughter. His first sighting of Una terrified him. She appeared quite thin, and her skin seemed to be peeling off her body. Furthermore, she concealed her left hand when she entered her father's presence. Conel could tell that she was embarrassed by the injury and did not inquire about it. The love of the father and daughter was evident in the embrace they shared. Since her father rarely showed the affection that was now evident on his face, Una began to appreciate the peril she had experienced. Settling down on the chairs provided by the Druids, each described their encounters since the avalanche. Conel wept as he told of his frustration at having to remain absolutely still to balance the teetering wagon while his only daughter dangled on a thin rope, bobbing like a spider on a web, suspended over nothing but open space.

"I threatened Julia with great atrocities if she dared move the length of an arrow point. She was so frightened that she swooned in terror," Conel said, emphasizing his fear that the wagon would roll down the slope and crush his daughter.

"Would you really have punished her if she did upset the cart?" an amused Una asked, knowing that her father never laid a hand on any of his offspring or his slaves.

"You will never know the dread that pulled at my heart when you where in danger. She would surely have lost her life if she endangered yours. More than likely, she would have followed you over the cliff." As the two parted, Conel told Una that she would have to remain and that Carlos would stay with her. Because of their treatment of Una, Conel decided to be most generous when he bestowed gifts upon the Druids.

Insubres Oppidum
During the following weeks, sitting around the campfires at night, Conel spoke with the leaders about the political situation. "Because their oppidum at Veii has been captured by a city-state called Rome, we are presently at peace with the Etruscans," the Chief of the Insubres told Conel.

"Their other oppida don't appear to lend support. Like Celtic tribes, each Etruscan city-state is on its own," the man said with a shrug.

As he listened, Conel learned that the Etruscans established a highly-advanced culture at a dozen city-states, along the western side of a mountain range which divides the peninsula into eastern and western regions.

On the last evening of their stay, the Mayri trading party was entertained lavishly in Etruscan style. The Insubres copied the habits of the Etruscans and reclined when they ate and served an abundant supply of fresh fruits and wine. The northern Celts were amazed at the few torches needed to light the vast banquet room. Looking around at the small lamps, Conel could not help but ask what provided the light. "We burn the oil from the olive, a most useful product," his host replied.

Conel spent the remainder of the banquet quietly contemplating all that he learned.

Within the week, Turk finalized the trading. At Conel's urging, he included some of the finer items, originally reserved for the Boii. In return, the party received escorts, along with the promise of one hundred amphorae of wine and numerous barrels of olive oil for their return trip. Along the route, groves of olive trees covered the hillsides, and Conel learned the southerners used the oil to flavor their bread and to aid in cooking. He soon discovered that olive oil tasted more delicate than animal lard used by the Mayri women in their cooking.

Although the Etruscans lived at peace with the Celts, they were not above raiding a lightly armed trading party so all were cautioned to remain vigilant. For the first time since her capture, Julia ate with relish. As she approached her home, she purposely remained in the background to avoid drawing attention to herself. Moreover, her association with Conel's household prevented her from enduring the sexual advances of the wagon train drivers. The slave did not understand the protection that Conel's proximity offered, nor would she appreciate it if she did. Outwardly she seemed submissive, but her internal thoughts told a different story. Her hatred directed toward Conel would have warned the Celtic chief had he been observant, but his thoughts were busy elsewhere. Julia listened in on every conversation to gather information on the Celts. 'My knowledge of these barbarians will be the only coin I possess to buy myself back into my poppa's good graces,' she thought.

"Because the country is relatively flat and the path is broad, we should shorten the length of the train by riding three abreast to better protect ourselves" Conel ordered.

A guard rode ahead to alert the Boii, who sent an armed party. Roith, son of Dhulack the Boii chief, led the escort with horses thundering over the terrain, and horns announcing their coming. The Insubres guard left when the attendants arrived. After paying to homage to Conel, Roith led the party to his home.

Boii Oppidum

Dhulack received the Mayri trading party with open arms. The feasting was every bit as elaborate as that which the Insubres offered. For over seven decades, the Boii remembered the heroic attack by Conel's father-in-law. These deeds were sung nightly around the campfires, making Conel uncomfortable. He confided to his friend, Turk, "One would almost believe that it was I, and not Ragelnos, who saved the warriors of this tribe in their battle against the Etruscans."

Turk just smiled and told his friend to enjoy himself, "The Boii became the main southern trading partners of the Mayri. Both our peoples have benefited from the arrangement, one that has made other Celtic tribes jealous, particularly the Insubres. They would

Druids, Celts, and Romans 211

like to dominate this part of the world." Conel grunted his understanding.

Roith was most enthralled by the giant from the north. He followed Conel wherever he went and engaged him in the daily combat exercises of the warriors. Though he did not yet carry the weight and strength of manhood, Roith conducted himself with valor. One day he expressed his gratitude. "I feel honored that a great chieftain would even consider me a worthy opponent."

Conel immediately liked the young chief's son, and promised to take him north to the Mayri oppidum to receive additional training under his brother, Rochlos. "On my return trip perhaps, our clan can take you in fosterage to help improve your skill as a warrior and bind the ties of our two tribes even tighter."

"Thank you for your kindness. I am certain that my father will agree to such an arrangement."

After discussions with Dhulack, Conel and Turk left the majority of the trading wagons in the care of the Boii. On their way to Rome, they would use one wagon to carry the slave, supplies and the disassembled chariot. Roith was selected to lead a group of warriors who would accompany the Mayri Chief to the Boii's southern boundary in the foothills of the Apennines. There they would wait until the two Mayri tribesmen returned from delivering the slave girl. With his parting words the chief of the Boii told Conel that he hoped to see his son's swordsmanship upgraded to the level of a Mayri champion. "The days ahead will call for trained warriors, and unfortunately, our skills have eroded. We haven't had the need for extensive combat, and the warriors grow weary of fighting each other."

"I will do the best that I can for your son," a grateful Conel replied.

"I want you to keep your eyes open and observe all that you can about these lands, about any Etruscans we meet, and about the Romans," Conel instructed Turk before they set off.

Insubres Oppidum
Within a week of her father's departure, Una was moved from the protection of the Druids to a small hillfort. She began to regain her strength, exercised daily, and participated in the normal activities of the clan. After returning from a small-game hunt, she looked at herself in a mirror and wasn't pleased with the image she saw. 'I look depressing,' she thought. Then she bathed and dressed.

Carlos entered as she was combing her flowing red hair before she tied it with a green ribbon and let it dangle over her shoulder. "After all, I am the granddaughter of Ragelnos, and I have my own image to project," she explained to her companion who broke into a joyous laugh. Because her left hand was useless and she was in his care, Carlos always carried a sword and shield for their protection.

Una became a symbol of curiosity and envy for the females of the Insubres. Female warriors were rare in the Po valley, particularly ones as attractive as Una. "They retain the farming and livestock raising methods of our clan, but they lack artistic inspiration. Is it because they can easily trade for scarce items?" she asked Carlos one day as they were preparing for a picnic.

A few hours after she had gone to bed, Una awoke drenched in sweat, despite the fact that the night was cool. She dreamt that Hugh was calling to her to beware of those coming for her. The small cottage the Insubres assigned her lay outside the wall away from the main gates. The young woman had rolled over on her back, making certain that her sword was within easy reach, when she heard the sound of a struggle outside. Her aching left hand slowed her attempt to rise and toss off the night covering, which allowed the assailants easy access. One stomped on the hand holding the sword while a second threw a sack over her head. Hindered though she was, the two intruders needed all their strength to subdue her. They succeeded only when one intruder struck her on the head. "You better not have killed her, you fool!"

"I didn't hit her that hard. Besides, what does it matter whether we kill her now or later? We are supposed to kill her. Aren't we?"
"Lavos wants her dead, but I know some Etruscans who will pay dearly for a female slave of this caliber. Besides, our kidnapping her will teach the Mayri not to cheat honest traders."

The unconscious Una was spared the sight of the decapitated Carlos as she was roughly dragged from her sleeping quarters.

Chapter 17
All Roads lead to Rome

Eturia circa 388 BC

After leaving the Boii oppidum, the first days on the trail to the south were uneventful, except that Roith emulated Conel's every movement. "That lad, Roith, certainly has taken a fancy to you," Turk said in jest, during one of the few moments when he and Conel were alone. "Why don't you begin his training while you have the opportunity? Who knows what troubles await us down the path."

"Thank you old friend, I can always count on your counsel. Roith acquires knowledge quickly, but he still has much to learn. I've been thinking, we need alliances on this side of the Alps, and if Roith were my son-in-law, it gives us an easy way to secure that alliance," Conel said to his sometime teacher as he began to grasp the possibilities.

"He could well be the father of your grandchildren. But keep in mind, you have to contend with a headstrong daughter. Those that make grave decisions hurriedly usually live to regret their rashness."

"I won't forget your caution. Besides, Meva will have the final say, regardless of my feelings." The two old friends laughed as each pictured Meva's wrath should her desires not be considered. "All that in good time," Conel concluded.

"Roith, come here, if you please," Conel requested in the form of a soft command. "I want us to ride together so that I may learn more of your countryside. The two rode a short distance ahead of the small party. "Tell me all that you know of the terrain that we cross and the dangers that may face us."

"Our land is cold in the winter because of the northerly winds from the Alps," Roith began his commentary. "In summer, the southerly winds blow from a hot barren land hundreds of leagues away. My father has visited this vast desert where even the lakes and rivers dry up. It lies over two hundred leagues to the south on the far side of a large sea that the Greeks named the Ho Pontos."

Conel displayed his impatience. "I care not for the weather or for a land far to the south. I want to know what we will face between here and the end of the Boii territory."

"Travelers face danger from brigands who rob the weak and unwary. Because we are mounted and armed, none will bother us," Roith answered, puzzled by the Mayri's chief's temper.

"In my homeland, we are constantly on guard for an invasion by the Germans who live in the great forest north of us," Conel related. "At times, clans raid each other to capture women for wives. There is nothing more shameful than others capturing women of a Celtic tribe. To prevent such a disaster, the Mayri constantly patrol our territory." Conel quickly changed the emphasis of his lesson. "Pretend for a moment that our small traveling party is facing danger. Where would you place your lookouts? A wise chief knows those who ride on the other side of his border. It is not prudent to just protect up to an imaginary line." Then turning toward the blushing youngster, Conel suggested that he station guards sixty-spear-lengths in front of the wagon, the same distance on each side, and a similar distance from the rear.

"Each hour, you as their leader should ride the perimeter and check on what they have observed. Often it is useful to point out something to keep them alert, lest they daydream and overlook a danger. For example, have you noticed that churned up grass over to our left? That indicates to me that a large wagon, accompanied by mounted people, had passed through here recently. A herd of animals wouldn't follow each other in such an orderly fashion," Conel said as he pointed to the tracks leaving the area.

Roith saw the tracks for the first time. "I will post the guards as you suggested," he replied to his mentor. "But what are we to do about the ones with the wagon?" he asked. "They may still be in the vicinity." He was determined not to be made a fool of again.

"Send some scouts ahead. Warn them to be on the lookout for strangers or anything that may look out of the ordinary. Tell them to examine any warm campfires to determine how long since a party departed the campsite. Often a thoughtless war party leaves clues of their presence. They may have forgotten to bury their waste, or they may have left spoors when they departed the trail. If the party splits up, they may intend to attack from more than one side. We should know of their presence before they know of ours."

The normally lax Boii guards were dumbfounded when their young leader ordered one third of the troop to mount. Roith put these warriors on full alert while the others rested, waiting their turn to guard the perimeter of the moving party. He directed those at rest to look after their weapons and make certain they were ready for use. He told his men about the habits of the Mayri and warned his warriors to be vigilant and not dishonor the name of the Boii while the Mayri were in their charge. Finally, he selected two companions, adept in following a trail, to accompany him on the spying mission.

As Roith rode off on his sortie, Conel shortened the length of the train and widened the positions of the surrounding guards. He further instructed the men to return immediately to the wagons in case of an attack. Conel did not want these inexperienced soldiers to go off fighting on their own.

He rode around the perimeter and said to each sentinel while looking him straight in the eye, "Since Roith is scouting the trail ahead, I will take command. Anyone who disobeys me will have to deal with my wrath. If you have any thoughts of showing off your fighting skills without my permission, I wish you would inform me who will inherit your possessions because if the enemy does not kill you, then I surely will. Anyone who disobeys will find that their head is not fit to even grace the saddle horn of an enemy. Do I make myself clear? Return immediately to form a circle around the wagons should you detect an enemy presence. Our concern is to protect the slave Julia until I can deliver her safely. I am honor bound to do so."

Conel heard the horse returning long after the night camp had been set up. "The party consisted of a wagon and three riders," Roith said. Then he explained how he had calculated the size of the party based on the number of different hoof prints he found and by the spoor of the horses. "There were only four of them, and by their pace they seem to be in a hurry to clear this territory," the lad said to reassure Conel.

"More importantly, we encountered a small Greek trading party on the path. I have left several guards with them. We should easily overtake them in the morning," Roith reported as he became more comfortable in his leadership role.

The next morning as he crossed a ridge, Conel saw ten wagons tethered together. Sitting placidly at the wooden wheel of the lead wagon was the oldest man that Conel had ever encountered. He neither looked up nor did he quiver in fear as the rest of the party joined those guarding the Greeks. The leader, a weather-lined Greek answering to the name of Maharis, had wandered these byways since he was young, and there was little that he did not know. The Celts were flabbergasted to find a Greek traveling overland, and the old man was equally astounded to find Celts fluent in his language. When Turk asked why he traveled on land, and not by merchant ship as did most of his Greek compatriots, Maharis replied, "My father was the captain of Athens' finest vessel until he allowed the Carthaginians to defeat him in a sea battle. My people are not kind to those who do not succeed. From that day forward, he and I became outcasts and have made our living as land traders. My father is now dead. For decades, I have traveled the inner route from Syracuse on the southern tip of Sicily to as far north as the land of your people."

"What and where is Sicily?" asked Conel.

"It is a large island situated at the end of this peninsula," he replied. "It is a land of fertile soil and plentiful rainfall with forests of timber, orchards of grapes and olives, along with pastures for sheep and cattle. It is as fair as the Po Valley."

"How long have the Greeks been living on this Sicily?"

"The early traders arrived there about the same time Rome was founded. These events occurred three hundred years after your people began to filter through the mountain passes. Toda, you can find a hundred Greek settlements scattered across the southern part of this peninsula and Sicily."

Then the startled Maharis pointed to Julia as she emerged from Conel's wagon. "She is Roman. By the looks of that young girl, you are in the slave business. What are you doing so far south?"

"That is not so. We rarely engage in slaving for trade," Conel replied in anger at the accusation. "I am Conel of the Mayri clan, and I come from across the Alps. This young slave has been in my charge, and I am on an errand to return her to her family. Tell me. What do you know about Rome?"

"I know little of Rome. Although, I have often traveled through the city," the old trader answered. "Except for salt, the Romans have insignificant items to offer in trade. However, I know Etruria well. You have to survive the Etruscans before you engage the Romans," Maharis advised the Celt.

"Then tell me about the Etruscans," Conel said, disappointed with Maharis' knowledge of the Romans.

"Only outsiders refer to them as Etruscans, they call themselves Resanna. Since my greatest danger is an ambush by highway robbers, I offer you a trade. If you provide me the protection of your mounted men, I will impart all my knowledge of the Etruscans."

Conel quickly agreed to the bargain. "You can travel with us as far as Rome. Then we will drop off the slave and return to our own lands. I wish, however, to learn all you know of Rome, as well as Etruria, and a fair bit about your own people as well."

"Rome is farther than my travels will take me this time. I need to depart this trail when we cross the road to Clevsin, which is about halfway to Rome from where we sit. When I leave, you need just remain on this path which runs parallel to the Tiber River to find Rome."

Satisfied with the arrangements, Conel asked, "Why do you trade among these people? Why don't you return to your own fabled land to enjoy your old age?"

Maharis answered, "Greece is no longer my home. I am content with the life of a nomadic trader. Greece has been trading with the Etruscans for hundreds of years, ever since we established a colony in Campani, several days travel south of Rome. In recent years, Rome cut off the sea routes to the south. Because I was already situated here, I became the main trader between the twelve Etruscan cities and my own people. I travel east of the Apennines Mountains in order to pass safely through Roman territory. It is dangerous to move goods across the mountains, but I am accustomed to danger," Maharis replied.

That night as they sat around the campfire, the Greek broke out amphorae of wine, and began to tell about the Greeks living south of Rome, "In Greece, we live in city-states, which are similar to the territories of your tribes. Each city-state is independent. They have different forms of government and make war upon the other city-states. Most of the wars are fought over trade. We live on poor soil, and therefore, we must earn our wealth by trading across the vast waterways. You asked about the southern part of this peninsula and Sicily. As I said earlier, we first settled this land at the time of the birth of Rome. There is an old fable, which I will tell if you are interested in such stories."

"Very much so," Conel answered. "We Celts depend upon bards to remember our history and genealogy. Many consider their stories to be fables. However, I find much truth in them."

Maharis began his tale. "Ages ago, there lived in Greece a most famous sculptor, named Daedalus. He was such an artist that his sculptures looked life-like. Some claimed that they had to be chained to their pedestals or else they might walk away. Now Daedalus had a temper that got him into trouble. Following a night of heavy drinking, he slew his nephew. The people were so outraged that they banished him. Daedalus and his son took refuge in the island kingdom of Crete.

"His love of the ladies got Daedalus in trouble at the court of the Cretan King Minos when the queen showed an interest in him. The king put Daedalus and his son, Icarus, into a man-made puzzle known as a labyrinth. It is said that a person can wander around this maze for his entire life and never find his way out. Daedalus, more intelligent than the ordinary prisoner, fashioned wings from bird feathers held together with the beeswax. Both he and his son escaped by flying away. But Icarus began to think he was a bird, and flew too close to the sun which melted the beeswax, sending the youth falling to his death. A broken-hearted Daedalus flew until he reached the island of Sicily. He became the first Greek to settle there, or so they say."

"You have a wonderful way of storytelling. Why don't you become a bard?" a pleased Conel asked while he and Turk listened with pleasure to Maharis.

"Does Greece occupy the entire land south of Rome?" Conel asked, steering the conversation back to the peninsula's settlements.

"The Carthaginians from across the Ho Pontos, a sea that we treat as a road, also have colonies on the isle of Sicily. About eighty-five years ago, Gelon from Syracuse defeated the great Carthaginian General Hamilcar at Himera. Hamilcar arrived with over three hundred thousand men. Gelon easily won the battle although he had a mere fifty-five thousand troops."

After puzzling over the massive figures in his head for a time, Conel finally asked. "How is it possible that so large a force could be defeated by a much smaller army?"

"It is said that Hamilcar did not observe the battle. He spent his time praying to his gods while his army fought. When defeat was obvious, he leaped into the flames of his offering and was consumed by the fire. I don't know the whole truth of it, but there are many such tales. Let me tell you a tale of a battle between two Greek settlements that perhaps will help you understand how a small force can defeat a much superior opponent.

"Sybaris, a city-state almost as far south as Sicily, went to war with the neighboring city of Crotona. Sybaris was a rich society and professional in everything they did. Its army of three hundred thousand soldiers taught their horses how to dance to a certain tune, so they would look splendid in a parade. When the Sybaris army arrived at the gates of Crotona, they heard music and their

Druids, Celts, and Romans

horses began to dance, causing great confusion among the invaders. They were slaughtered to a man, their city sacked and the remaining inhabitants taken as slaves by the victorious Crotonians."

As the Greek finished his tale, Conel and Turk were holding their sides from laughter as they pictured the horses dancing as their riders were killed. Julia sat in ignorance of the tale, and wondered if the two Celts had gone mad, for laughter did not come easily to the stoic Romans.

"You are a lively storyteller my friend, but these countrymen of yours, especially the Crotonians, seem to be a bloodthirsty lot," Conel replied when he recovered his composure.

A displeased Maharis misunderstood the remark and defended Greece's contributions. "Crotona is known throughout the Greek world for its excellent school of medicine. It is so famous, in fact, that the great Pythagoras decided to make it his home," the affronted Greek continued.

"Who may this Pythagoras be?" Conel asked.

"He is one of the greatest philosophers who ever lived, and he lived over one hundred years ago."

"What made him so great a philosopher?" Conel inquired.

"Pythagoras believed that the soul doesn't die. Instead, it is cleansed and returns to another body. Isn't that a strange concept?"

"Why would you say it's strange? We Celts believe the same," Conel replied, a bit agitated that Maharis would think it strange.

"We teach that the soul is taken to Hades when the body dies. Perhaps your people learned your belief from Pythagoras. He was supposed to have visited many foreign places, including the land north of the Alps," Maharis answered.

"Because our beliefs existed hundreds of years before your Pythagoras was born, it is more than likely that he learned his philosophy from our Druids," Conel countered as he thought about his good friend, Munli.

"Enough about beliefs, and who learned from whom, is there peace in your lands or are your city-states still fighting?" Turk asked interrupting the conversation.

"Peace will never come to Sicily because it lies at the crossroads of many great powers," Maharis answered.

During the next hour, the tone of the conversation changed from a discussion about war to topics covering the weather and the terrain. The Greek and two Celts finished the wine they had opened and retired for the night, each with his own thoughts and each well on the way to inebriation.

The following day, while they rode along the trail, Conel inquired about Maharis' dealings with the Etruscans after deciding he shouldn't ask any more questions about the ill-fated Greeks of Sicily. "Why do you trade with the Etruscans? I would think that trading among your own people would be sufficient." Conel asked because he suspected that Maharis was spying for the Greeks.

"Why do I trade with the Etruscans? I trade with them because they are so numerous, and their cities are lined up all along the western part of this peninsula. Tarquinia is their cultural capital. So I make certain I visit that city of twenty thousand inhabitants."

"I also trade for paintings in Vulci, as well as for pottery and bronze figurines. These are among the finest art in the world. I take these goods to the Etruscans at Populonia, where I arrange for iron ingots to be shipped to Syracuse."

"Why don't the Etruscans trade between themselves?" a perplexed Conel asked.

"Maybe they prefer to play at their political games and bury their dead. I don't know! At one time they were among the greatest traders in the world, but today they party, drink wine and wait for their civilization to die."

Based on advice from Maharis, the party remained on the more forested path east of the Tiber. "The path on the other side is wider and more firmly packed down, but this side is safer since the Romans and Etruscans are in conflict. And the Romans fear the forest."

The old man explained that in the beginning the Etruscans were farmers and lived in hovels, until the day the sea-people came among them. "These sea-people were not plentiful. Therefore rather than overrun them, they ruled the natives and in time intermarried with them. With their skills in producing iron weapons and their love of the horse, they easily became the dominant people from the Po valley to far south of Rome. In fact, the Etruscans ruled Rome for over a century." At the mention of her city, Julia perked up and listened intently.

"Please go on with you story, as I have a lot to learn before you depart our company," Conel said.

"I do not know the full truth of Etruscan history for the natives do not discuss the arrival of the strangers. Instead, they tell of a young lad, Tages, who sprang from the earth and outlined their

Druids, Celts, and Romans 221

ritual and religious scriptures. These scriptures were written down, and Etruscan diviners, the priests of their people, use these criteria to foresee the future. They believe the heavens are divided between sixteen gods. Hence they divide the entrails of the sheep into sixteen sections. Each section is used to predict a particular need."

"The diviners foretell the future by reading the livers of sheep? This is amazing because the vates, a segment of our Druid priesthood, read the entrails of sheep as well!" an astonished Conel expressed, remembering the long discussions he had on the subject with Munli.

As they continued south on the trail bordering the Tiber River, Maharis continued his tale, "Their buildings are made from stone and unburned bricks. The walls of these structures are coated with radiant white marble stucco. Terracotta decorations representing gods, attached to walls of the buildings, are whimsical in style, as though, the artist poked fun at his gods. Decorations are not their only accomplishments. Their largest city, Populonia, has been producing iron for several hundred years. The furnaces are constructed along the waterfront, and the iron ore is transported by boat. The fires are fed by wagon trains carrying wood from the nearby forest over paved trails, built purposely to carry the heavy loads." He ceased with his description when Turk signaled that they would stop to camp alongside the river.

Later, after camp was set up, Maharis continued the conversation at Conel's insistence. "The Etruscans build conduits to channel water from the mountain streams directly to their cities, which are built on plateaus surrounded by walls of stone. Their roads continue uninterrupted across rivers using arched bridges, which can handle great stress. I implore you to come with me to see these marvelous structures."

"I would if I were not obligated to bring the slave to her family. I have never been this long away from my family, and I am beginning to sorely miss them. What is family life like among the Etruscans?" a homesick Conel asked. He longed for his beloved Meva more and more as the distance separated them.

"The sooth-sayers teach the people that their culture will last a total of eight hundred years and then it will disappear. 'Seize the day' is a greeting between natives as they pass each other. They are far too pleasure-minded to fit the morality of a normal Greek citizen. They feast often and eat the finest of foods. Their womenfolk dine with the men and copulate with their husbands or any male that is available. Musicians play lutes, a stringed instrument, and blow on a double pipe to make the feasts merry."

"What's a double pipe?" a curious Conel asked.

"The Etruscan double pipe consists of two hollowed wooden branches attached to the musician's mouth by a strip of leather tied at the back of his head. The player blows into one end and changes the tune by covering or uncovering the holes."

Maharis continued discussing the Etruscans' frivolous behavior. "Their women are free to own property in their own right, and they even arm wrestle and gamble with their men folk. The men shave daily and the women use polished brass mirrors to adorn themselves with brooches, necklaces and earrings.

"They are a merry people but cruel as well. They beat slaves to the tempo of musicians playing on double pipes. Furthermore, they force the slaves to participate in wild, extravagant contests against each other and at times against savage beasts. The Etruscans make wagers on which of the slaves is likely to survive the contest."

"Tell me about their warfare skills," an obviously upset Conel asked in order to change a subject that he found distasteful.

"The Etruscan is a fine warrior. However, their naval trade is all but eliminated, and they have not developed an extensive overland trade in iron, wine and olive oil to take care of any excess. As I related, the cities act as independent entities, which means they can easily be picked off one by one as the Romans are inclined to do. The Romans besieged the Etruscan city of Veii for over ten years and only recently overwhelmed the inhabitants, destroyed the city and enslaved all that resided within."

A sick feeling from a flashback of his vision of the defeat by Caesar came over Conel when he listened while Maharis related this portion of the story. "You said the Etruscans once ruled Rome. Did they do anything practical? Did they build a strong gate for their hillfort?" The ever attendant Julia crept closer to listen in on the discussion whenever the name Rome came up.

Maharis' answer indicated he had more interest in history than construction, "The wall surrounding the original city is in dire need of repair. During Servius Tullis' reign, Rome signed a treaty with the Latins, a people that may be related to the Celts."

"Why do you say they may be related to the Celts?" Conel asked.

Druids, Celts, and Romans

"There are many similarities in the languages of the Celts and the Latins. That is just my own thoughts on the matter," Maharis answered.

"Tell us more about this treaty," Conel said.

"My thirst has addled my brain," a rather inebriated Maharis said. "My head will never forgive me in the morning," an unsteady Maharis said, as he held out his wine cup for the Roman slave to fill.

The following morning the rain clouds, which dogged the path of the travelers, finally let loose. Sitting under dense tree branches to avoid being soaked Conel, Turk and Julia gathered around the old Greek to hear him complete the tale.

"I believe that I was talking of Superbus' evil reign when my head and tongue no longer could communicate." The Celts laughed as Maharis joked about the amount of wine he had consumed the previous night. "This last, and most brutal, King of Rome ruled for thirty-five years before his own family actions did him in. His son raped a noble woman by the name of Lucretia."

As Maharis revealed the tale of sexual exploitation, a naive Julia gasped in horror.

"After Lucretia had her family swear an oath to revenge her dishonor, the young lady grabbed a knife from her father's belt and committed suicide.

"Her cousin, Lucius Junius Brutus, was so incensed by the senseless death that he aroused the anger of the populace, who then rebelled against Superbus and overthrew this evil king. The Etruscan King of Clusium, the city to which I am bound, raised an army to put down the rebellion, but he was repulsed at the bridge of Sublicius that crosses the Tiber. A larger than life Roman, named Horatius Cocles, led two companies of soldiers to protect the city and prevented the Etruscan Army, led by the King of Clusium, Lars Porsena, from crossing the bridge. According to legend, all the Romans from the first company, with the single exception of Horatius, were killed, but he stood his ground until the second company could destroy the wooden bridge. One tale has him surviving by jumping into the river and swimming across while another has him giving up his life for the love of his city."

"Which do you believe happened?" a smiling Conel asked as he watched the look of awe on the face of his slave.

"If the story happened as it has been told, it is not likely even a Roman hero could swim while fully clothed in armor. But I can only share one more tale of this time period. I must be gone if I expect to be safely inside the gate of Clusium before it is shut for the night.

"The Etruscans are no longer as carefree as they were when I first started trading with them over a half-century ago. They now realize that their days as a power are drawing to a close. I fear that the Romans will be the next great threat on this peninsula, a great threat to the Greek colonies in the south and on the Isle of Sicily. If I were a Celt, I would not sleep too easily in the Po Valley either."

"You would not say that if you were aware of the vast numbers of Celtic people living on the far side of the Alps," Conel stated defiantly.

"I have traveled this peninsula for over five decades, and I have studied its inhabitants with great care," Maharis answered, taking no notice of Conel's outburst. "Every time Rome defeats an enemy, it accepts most of the people as citizens and incorporates their territory into the city of Rome. This increases their numbers, as well as that of the pool from which to draw. People who aren't taken in as citizens are put to work as slaves on farms to feed the ever increasing multitude. Furthermore, such a practice allows more citizens to go to battle and fight for longer periods of time because slaves are at home tending to the planting and harvest. Rome is a power to be reckoned with. Mark my words."

None around the campfire noticed Conel shiver when Maharis completed his remarks.

The next morning Maharis took his leave where the road to Clusium crossed their path. Conel last saw his Greek acquaintance when he and his party turned onto a road through a small volcanic canyon. This amazed the Celt, whose people never considered leveling the land to make traveling easier.

Several days further down the trail to Rome, Conel came across structures that truly amazed him. The Etruscans built a road across the Tiber. The road stretched between two hillsides and spanned the river with a stone bridge. The bridge, built on pillars, used a stone arch for support.

Roith's campsite in the foothills of the Apennines
By the time he and Turk began their trek on the level, hard-packed roads of the south, Conel learned many things about the Etruscans and some history of the Romans. Before they departed, Conel insured that Roith's camp was well situated for the terrain and defensible against an attack by a small raiding party. His last words to the youthful commander were. "Keep alert. We are

nearing Rome but have not yet left Etruria. If you cannot easily overcome an attacking party, return to your father's oppidum and bring help."

Roith solemnly agreed to follow his orders to the letter. With that commitment the mentor and student bid their farewell. Turk painstakingly reassembled the chariot and decorated it as stylishly as he could. "Because our numbers are so few, we're better to bluff our way rather than fight our way through."

Conel eagerly accepted this recommendation. Julia was stationed in the front of Conel pinned in by his body. Conel's horse was tied to Turk's mount. This arrangement provided the most flexibility and gave them an escape on horseback should the chariot become disabled. Despite the need for a contingency plan, Turk never doubted that the fearsome look of an armed and helmeted Celt, driving a two-horse chariot at full speed, would deter any bandits. Besides, the Celts were presently at peace with the Etruscans who had their hands full with the Roman army. Julia served as their token of passage should they meet any Roman soldiers. The small party purposely avoided the Etruscan settlements at times delaying their journey considerably to avoid a potential conflict. Their patience was rewarded, and they swiftly journeyed through the remainder of the Etruria.

Chapter 18
The Betrayal

Etruria circa 388 BC
The days following her capture were a blur as the blindfolded Una, tied to her horse, rode bareback. She was allowed no privacy even when she had to relieve herself. The party moved swiftly and rarely rested while driving the tiring horses almost to the point of exhaustion. In addition, the pain pulsating from her left arm robbed Una of what little rest she could achieve.

Despite her captors' attempts to remain anonymous, even a fool could tell they were Celtic, and Una was no fool. She listened carefully to detect differences in their speech patterns as each whispered their aspirations and their fears. She easily recognized the voice of the leader as belonging to one of the disgruntled Insubres from the wagon train. He had a slight lisp when he said certain words that he used frequently. The trek across the Alps preyed on his mind because he believed he had been cheated of his just compensation. He complained without letup, "The new wagon master ignored us. He provided a broken down wagon and goods of little value."

The other two voices were unfamiliar, but she made an oath never to forget them. A day of reckoning would come, and Una fantasized on the pain she would extract from these traitors. 'The one who always complains will scream like a wounded crow when I begin to slice the flesh from his bones.' Her fantasies became the fabric that kept her from falling into acute depression.

As each day passed, she entered further into a world of hatred, which provided her with the energy to endure. Whenever one of her captors would whisper, lest Una would hear and recognize him, she would form an image the person's appearance. Furthermore, she assigned names to each of the voices. The leader treated her more harshly than did his companions, reminding Una of a young Helvetii schoolmate. So she silently named the leader, Complainer. A second captor spoke in a high pitched voice, which reminded her of a pigeon and was so named. The third member sounded young so she called him, Sparrow. When the motion of the horse enabled her to daydream, she fantasized that she turned the tables on her captors and subject them to the most excruciating pain she could conceive.

Today, Sparrow tied her hands tightly, after allowing her freedom to urinate. 'For this cruel act he'll lose his fingers. I'll force the others to watch as his bodily parts are being fought over by hunger crazed canines. As for Complainer, I'll stake him out in the swamps along Lake Lucerne with his manhood smeared with honey to attract the beavers and other swamp animals.'

While the other two did not sexually fondle her, Pigeon rubbed his genitals against her whenever the opportunity arose. Her experience crossing the Alps left Una with a fear of heights, so she prayed that Pigeon would be dangled by his manhood from a rope strung across two cliffs over a raging river. 'Pigeon would die wondering if his body or his manhood would drop into the current first.'

"I'm going mad," Una cried out one night as she lay on a rocky outcrop above a river. "I must get control of my emotions or I will become a bumbling simpleton good neither to myself nor to anyone else. I must learn to calm myself in the manner taught by the Druids. Although, I swear on the love of my mother that I will see these dogs suffer for their betrayal."

Following this decision, Una focused her vivid imagination on her situation, sometimes speaking aloud in her frustration. "Who among those that I love and trust can I count on to rescue me? I have been the cause of Carlos' death, of that I am certain. My father had already left the oppidum of the Insubres; therefore, he's ignorant of my predicament. Someday he will be informed, and on that day these kidnappers will pay. That means, I can rely only on Hugh and his gift of knowing when either Mick or I am in pain."

Then she became aware of a horseman near her and grew silent. With the cold, calculating mind of an administrator she began to plan her strategy. She decided to delay as much as she could. Doing everything at a deliberate pace, whether eating or walking, she would pretend to be grievously injured and require help even to mount a horse.

This purposeful slowdown frayed the tempers of her captors, who began arguing among themselves. Pigeon threatened violence, but was restrained by Complainer who commanded, "Ignore her, you fool. Even a bruise lowers her value."

This comment raised her hopes, as Una learned that she was being held for ransom.

Insubres Oppidum

Even as Una dreamed of rescue, the Insubres tribe discovered that she was no longer in the hut they provided. The body of Carlos was transported away and given a swift burial.

Etruscan raiders were the first targets of their suspicions, and search parties covered the area looking for clues. A party of Insubres confirmed the suspicion by tracking four horsemen and a wagon as far as the Boii tribe's border. In reporting back, the trackers concluded, "They avoided any settlements of either our people or the Boii. They were moving fast in the direction of Etruria. Because you ordered us not to be seen, we did not track the kidnappers any further."

The concerned elders were puzzled. "How could a random band of raiders pick the one hut where the daughter of a revered clan was recuperating?" they asked each other.

"What are we going to tell her father?" Some felt this would lead to war between the Insubres and the Boii, allies of the Mayri.

Finally one elder sent the trackers back for a second look. "We know the tracks leave the hut and are bound for Etruria. Find out where the tracks came from!"

The council was deeply disturbed when they learned that the only tracks leading toward the hut came from their own oppidum. "If we are found to be in collusion with the Etruscans, we might not only face the Boii but the other Po tribes as well."

An order was immediately given to interrogate every family living in the oppidum. It took time before the elders discovered that three Insubres, one of whom was associated with the wagon train, were missing. Lavos's screams carried across the oppidum before he finally confessed to his part in planning the kidnapping. After extracting all he knew, the elders of the Insubres turned him over to the Druids for their judgment.

The Insubres council assembled an amply supplied war party of several hundred and ordered them to venture deep into the territory of the Etruscan and retrieve Conel's daughter. At the same time, members of the upper echelon traveled to the Boii's main oppidum to inform Dhulack of the sorry event. They brought sacrificial gifts for the gods in an effort to pacify her distraught father, and were thankful to the gods when they found out he had already departed. The last command they were given before they departed came from the tribe's Druid. "Do not tell them that Insubres were involved in the kidnapping. Blame it on Etruscan raiders. We will punish our own when we have them in our custody."

Boii Oppidum
The leaders of both tribes agreed, for the sake of preserving peace in the valley, to keep the kidnapping a secret until they could free Una. They also agreed that if they failed to free the girl they would jointly go to war against the Etruscans. Many among the Celts viewed combat as an opportunity to gain additional territory. Others, particularly the restless, younger members, felt it had been too long delayed.

Etruria
Una could feel the pace slowing and the journey becoming less strenuous. The horse cantered over a smooth surface, rather than along the rough winding trail they first encountered. She learned to detect the approach of other travelers, some mounted, some on foot. But, she could no longer listen in on conversations because Complainer posted Pigeon several dozen spear-lengths in front and Sparrow the same distance in the to the rear to serve as lookouts. Whenever a mounted party approached from either direction, the

lookout would signal, and the party would ride off the smooth trail to pause until the danger passed before continuing on their journey.

'We must be nearing an oppidum,' Una realized as the number of pauses increased. Finally, Complainer called a halt to their progress. After the party made camp, Una was tied with her arms touching the bark of a tree, but not so tight that the ropes bruised or ripped the skin. Other than not permitting her to see, she was treated gently as though her captors did not want to damage the merchandise. Her weariness robbed her of her instincts, and she did not comprehend that Complainer had left her alone for a time with the other two. The voice of a newcomer, with a strange dialect, brought her out of her stupor. "Take off the hood and allow me to see her face," demanded the stranger in Greek. To the keen ear of Una, the language was not his native tongue.

At that moment, while tied to a tree, she realized she was going to be sold into slavery. For the first time since the early days of her captivity, Una became despaired, despondent and stricken to her very soul. 'Me a slave!' resounded in her mind time and again whenever she allowed herself to think.

After enduring weeks of darkness, the bright light drove sharp pains directly into her brain when the light penetrated her still closed eyelids. "Have her stand and strip off those repulsive clothes, so I can see what you brought me."

Rough hands pulled her to her feet and ripped her clothes off her body. The day was warm, and standing in her undergarments was embarrassing but not unpleasant. Being judged as though she were a piece of meat, however, was degrading for the proud daughter of a Celtic chieftain. "She'll do. Bring her along!" the newcomer ordered. This command was followed by a discussion between Complainer and the stranger. As the weary and sore maiden picked up bits of the argument, she became aware that her captors wanted to be paid and be off immediately. But she soon learned that was not to be.

"My master makes the decisions as to the worth of a slave. If you wish payment, then accompany me to him." Only the promise of payment provided the incentive for the captors to follow the slave purchaser.

Clusium

After hours of travel during the heat of the day, the party arrived at their destination. The slave master, burned black by the sun, was the cruelest person that Una had ever seen. His long nose was pushed against his face, apparently from numerous beatings. His evil looking eyes, instead of being blue or green, had the darkest color brown that she could imagine. The slaver asked questions in a number of different languages, and she responded in Celtic, Greek and Latin. "Ah! We have an educated noble on our hands. Let her keep that gold neck torque. It will highlight her status and bring more than it is worth. Strip her of the rest of her rings."

After being touched, poked and prodded by the slave master's meaty hands, Una was taken to a filthy shed and shoved into a narrow space already overcrowded with sweaty, foul smelling male and female captives. Her last wish to the Goddess Sulis was that her captors would receive the same fate as she. "Please let them end their lives as slaves," Una pleaded to the benefactress of her clan.

Through the iron bars on the door, Una overhead a heated discussion between the Celts and the slavers. The discussion turned into yelling followed by the noise of fighting. Within moments, three unconscious Celts were crammed into the shed. Una gained some satisfaction as she used her feet to crack the ribs of the nearest. The other prisoners, taking their cue from that action, beat the unconscious men unmercifully. This was not done out of cruelty but for self-preservation. Time spent attacking someone else allowed less time for someone to attack them. Her savagery toward the helpless men earned Una fearful respect from the other captives who left her alone. All hope of rescue evaporated as she leaned up against the iron door for safety and tried to get some rest. The moans and cries from her former captors did little to improve her morale.

Few of the captives got any sleep during the night. The guards would enter the prison and kick or prod everyone to make certain that they still lived. Bodies of the fortunate who committed suicide by hanging themselves with pieces of leather were dragged away. Before the sun had cleared the horizon, the slaves were pulled from the shed, chained to each other, and forced to march across a dusty field just below a path leading up a cliff to a walled city.

The location of the city on top of a well-protected plateau reminded Una of the strategic location of the Mayri oppidum in her far off homeland. Her one ray of satisfaction came when she witnessed her motionless captors being dragged along the ground and dumped onto a tangled pile of inert bodies.

"Thank the Goddess Diana that we are not with that bunch," said a prisoner in a Roman dialect while others muttered similar sentiments.

"What is going to happen to them?" Una asked in her schoolgirl Latin.

At first the woman was not going to reply because of Una's poor use of the Latin language, but finally she said. "They are going to become fodder for the gladiator games, stupid." With that rebuke, Una decided to keep her questions to herself and wait to see what developed.

The survivors were stripped naked, inspected by the slavers and segregated into groups. Una had a garland wreath placed on her head, and a scroll tied around her neck to warrant that she was healthy and disease free. The slaver would be held responsible if his guarantee proved false. Her feet were coated with a white chalk to indicate that the slave tax had been paid. Then she was fed. Breakfast consisted of sour wine and stale bread, which Una, who had not eaten for several days, gratefully consumed. Eating helped pass the time until the buyers arrived.

Una, along with a dozen handsome young boys and girls, was taken to a tent away from most of the common slaves. Only privileged buyers were invited to bid on those within the tent. Una did as she was ordered when the slavers and the buyers eyed the human merchandise, who one by one were forced to stand, turn, squat and jump. More than one buyer forced her mouth open to look at her teeth as though he was purchasing a horse. Fondling private parts of her body became standard practice, and Una learned not to pull away after the first several touches. Each time she tried to protect herself, a nearby slaver would hit her across her buttocks with a wooden rod. "If you don't stop moving, I will beat you to death," he warned.

Finally, Una abandoned her dignity and pride, and allowed the buyers and sellers to do as they wished. Never in her life did she feel more helpless, and the helplessness led to a deep despair. Even then, her warrior upbringing would not let her sink to the level of hopelessness seen in the young women, and in some of the boys, many of whom swooned from fright, despair or hunger. Una did not know which nor did she care. Like all the others in bondage, she thought only of herself and her plight. Even the anger that sustained her to this point abated when her former captors, the focus of her anger, were dragged off for the gladiator games.

The moment the master sculptor Vulcan saw the tall, slim Celt with the flaming red hair, he knew he was destined to buy her. At first, his desire was artistic. He wanted to obtain a model for a frieze that he was commissioned to create. But a second glance at the gold neck torque convinced him that this one could become a replacement for a slave, an inadequate teacher of his children, now destined to be put to death.

The more he looked at the beautiful Celt, the more he desired her. Vulcan pictured the image of the slave adorning the temple at Volaterrae. He would dress her in a toga and allow her hair to frame her face. Turning to the physician who accompanied him, Vulcan ordered a physical examination of the Celt. When the doctor returned with an overall favorable report, Vulcan decided to buy her.

"I must advise you, Citizen Vulcan that her left hand has been injured and is almost useless. She will not make a good servant," counseled the physician in an effort to soften his advice in case anything went wrong.

"I don't plan to use her as a common household slave. Her looks captivate me," the sculptor replied.

Enraptured by the slave's regal neck and exquisite profile, he almost missed the opportunity to bid. However, a soothsayer foretold good omens for this day when he read the entrails of a sheep an omen Vulcan had purchased that morning at the temple. Perhaps, it was the good omen. Or perhaps, it was the eager waving of the highest bidder that brought Vulcan out of his absent-mindedness. Waving his gold-headed staff, Vulcan raised the stakes, to the dismay of the other bidder. The other, not wanting his prize to slip through his fingers, continued bidding until financial circumstances, brought on by current indebtedness, forced him to bow out. The outrageous prize paid for the Celtic slave was the talk of the slave market for weeks.

Vulcan beckoned, and the newly acquired slaved followed in silence. The sculptor approached a litter, marked with the same insignia that graced his toga, and climbed in. Four bearers lifted the litter and moved off toward the plateau above the slave pits without a backward glance at the human purchase. Una could do nothing but follow her new master's conveyance.

As they entered the master's oppidum through a massive arched gate, Una turned and looked in astonishment at the size of the city and the mass of humanity that pushed and shoved its way across a mammoth courtyard lined with booths of merchants. In her amazement at all the activity, she almost lost sight of her litter-borne owner as his bearers cried out for the populace to scatter and make way for their master. She hurriedly moved to catch up, lest she be swallowed up by the crowd. Whatever her fate with the new master, she realized she would endure far worse if she appeared to be trying to escape, even unintentionally.

The litter stopped in front of a single rectangular building consisting of several stories and covered by a gabled tile roof, a far cry from the thatch roofs of her homeland. Even this unworldly maid recognized the engineering skill needed to construct such a residence. Upon entering the abode, Una beheld an interior of three rooms looking out onto an atrium courtyard containing a statue of a nude woman holding a vase from which water flowed. She was unaware that the fountain was, in reality, a pan to collect rainwater, recycled during the wet months to create a vision of cascading water. Looking upward, Una observed several stories of roofed galleries overlooking the courtyard. Arching trees and shrubs bearing clusters of an unfamiliar yellow flower circled the perimeter of the courtyard. The instantaneous transformation, from the depravity of the slave pits to the grandeur of a noble Etruscan home, was more than the young Celt could absorb.

As Una stared at the residence, she became aware that she was the center of attention of three adolescents, one male, two female, and an attractive noble lady reclining on a sofa. No one spoke. The children gaped while the matron wore a judgmental frown as she viewed the tall, red-haired Celt. Finally, after a delay of some time, the young male queried his father in almost understandable Greek, "Where did you get her?"

A young female asked, "What is her name?"

Vulcan replied in Greek in a vain attempt to help his children become bilingual. "She is a Celt from the Po Valley," he explained. "She does not understand us; therefore, I have not decided what to name her."

To the amazement of all, Una spoke in near perfect Greek, "My name is Una. I am the daughter of Meva and Conel, chieftains of the Mayri Clan of the mighty Helvetii nation. Our people are not from the Po Valley but rule the land across the Alps." Then she retreated into silence.

At that instant Vulcan knew he had a find worth all the gold he laid out to purchase her. "What other languages do you speak?" he asked.

"I speak Celtic, read and write Greek, and I know a little Latin, both reading and writing."

Knowing that the world of commerce required knowledge of Greek, he was not surprised that a barbarian of noble blood could converse in that tongue. However, he was dumfounded that a Celtic slave could speak Latin. "How did you ever learn Latin?"

"Our slave, Julia, came from that city," she answered promptly.

Vulcan decided on the spot that Una could serve both as his model, and as a language teacher for his children. He was delighted with his find, and speaking in his native tongue said to Ramtha, his wife. "Now we can get rid of that useless servant that we retain to teach Greek to the children. I stand corrected she does not teach Greek, she babbles Greek. Or perhaps, we should wait and have her cremated at your mother's funeral, which should be coming up soon," he added, not letting an opportunity to criticize her overbearing mother or her female lover pass by. During this banter he achieved both his objectives at the same time.

"Since you did not know that she spoke Greek when you bought her, did you intend her for your model or your concubine?" Ramtha asked, in response to his mocking as she poured another draught of wine into a translucent, alabaster cup.

"Why, both of course," a laughing Vulcan replied, aware that he got the better of the repartee.

Learning to read and write in Etruscan came easier to Una than did Greek to her youthful charges. After mastering three languages, a fourth comes naturally, particularly when the alphabetic characters with minor changes, were copied from the Greeks. It took some time, however, for her to comprehend that the writing was done from right to left on one line, then left to right on the succeeding line. Later, Una learned from the children's former teacher that the alphabet originally came from a sea faring people called the Phoenicians.

After she settled into her new life, escape was the first thought that entered the mind of the proud chief's daughter, 'I will not live in bondage nor will I be subservient like Julia and await my deliverance.' Using her quick mind, Una decided to grasp everything that she could master to be prepared when her opportunity to escape arrived. With the liberties the teaching assignment offered, she had no doubt an opportunity would present itself. Applying the training method she acquired at the Druid school, Una repeated over and over everything she learned. Each night while she lay in her corner of the slave's quarters, she would mentally reconsider everything that happened during that day.

In the beginning, the changes occurred rapidly. Una had to shed the cloak and trousers of a Celt and don the toga of the Etruscan. This loose oval-shaped material with its many folds was inconvenient to wear, but the young Celt had little choice in the matter. So day after day she fumbled into her toga, while Vulcan's family retained a slave to help them dress.

Because she was the prime teacher of the children, Una did not have to participate in the preparations of the family meals, nor did she serve them naked as the other slaves were forced to do. Una was assigned the duties of governess to the three children. At times, she cut their meat with a small axe, dipped their bread in olive oil and hand fed them the legume soups. Her duties allowed her to dine with the family, where she freely partook of roasted pig. Nor did she refuse any of the strange fresh fruits which did not grow north of the Alps. Her favorites were grapes, cherries and wild plums. She dined in luxury while the common household slaves survived on roasted cereal and beans and their weekly ration of meat, usually a poor cut boiled in a cauldron.

Una took her duties as the children's language teacher very seriously, employing the techniques the Mayri Druid had used to teach languages to her and her brothers. The children eagerly responded to her ability to coax people to do things for her, amid a fear that she had a harsh temperament and would display it if not obeyed. The desperate Una used the teaching of Greek as a subterfuge to gain information about Clusium's state of affairs. In addition, she learned to write on scrolls, although most of the lessons were done on boards covered with wax. The children easily adapted to the practice of using pebbles to count and to do math problems, which surprised and elated Una. Along with her teaching duties, she was expected to serve guests at banquets, model for Vulcan and, when requested, satisfy his sexual urges. When called upon, Una did not shy away from the sculptor who was a kind and skillful lover. As part of her role as a slave, she often had sex with other Etruscan males as well.

Ramtha did not appreciate the attention her husband gave to the beautiful Celtic slave, perhaps because Una did not return the loving glances that the wife sent her way. One evening after their lovemaking, her master began to unburden his fears to the lovely slave. "Your free spirit belongs to an age older than the present," he announced in Greek

"What do you mean?" Una asked.

"When our ancestors first came to this land they were fun loving and free, now we lie about and await our doom."

"I do not understand what you are saying. Aren't they still? They seem that way to me," Una said. "Everyone seems to enjoy themselves at your parties and banquets."

"Perhaps it is that I have become melancholy in my old age as have my people," Vulcan continued. "Now our priests, repeating the Greek philosophers, tell us there is an underworld where demons await to capture our souls. Once our gravesites were painted with fun loving dragons, now blue demons prowl with snakes in their hands and winged black demons wait on the other side of the River Styx to claim their prey. The priests even have names for these demons, though none will tell how they learned the names. Charun is the demon of death. This winged creature, with his vulture beak, finishes off his victims with a hammer. Vanth, his female companion, has eyes on her wings so she can see all. They say she is everywhere. Some claim she is the herald of death, and the sight of a snake near a deathbed is a sure sign of her presence. I must confess that I have been praying for such a snake to visit my mother-in-law for quite some time," he concluded, laughing.

Una modeled daily for Vulcan. Her image, when completed, would become a massive display of winged horses being given a drink by a beautiful goddess-like creature. She held an alabaster jar at an angle to spill its contents in front of the horses' mouths. Once he completed the scale model, Vulcan would chisel the final life-size statue out of limestone. The final image would adorn the exterior of a temple being constructed in the capital city of Tarquinii, the headquarters of the Etruscan league, a judicial body for settling disputes between city-states.

By taking them for daily walks, Una used the children as her excuse to wander and learn more about the city. Her straightforward logic easily convinced Vulcan of the need for such errands. "How else are they to learn practical uses of a language if they cannot see it demonstrated to buy items at the market?" After receiving permission, Una and her three charges roamed the city with impunity. It was a fair exchange. The children learned both

Druids, Celts, and Romans

Greek and Latin while Una acquired knowledge about the layout of the town.

In route to the Mayri oppidum

The old mule supplied to Hugh was less than responsive to the tugs and oaths of the bulky Celt. Fortunately for Hugh, Katlyn was more familiar with pack animals than he, and she swatted the animal on its haunches whenever it declined to move. "There is no reason it should refuse to move forward," she proclaimed. "I believe that stable boy was jealous that we were leaving, and gave us the worst pack animal he could find."

The good natured Hugh was quick to agree there was little either could do to hurry the beast, so the two slowly rambled along at the speed set by the animal. Neither he nor Katlyn were aware of the increased danger that Una and Conel faced in the south.

Clusium

The most exciting event in Una's slavery came when Vulcan's mother-in-law died. Una was assigned to bring the midday meal to the workers employed to ready the family tomb. Laden down with pails of wine and trenchers of food, she made the long walk from the city gates across the valley floor. Then she trudged up the hill on the far side to the house-like necropolis cut into the soft rock cliff beneath the arena. This daily ritual enabled the impressionable maiden to watch in fascination as the artists, employed by Vulcan, captured the life story of the deceased on the crypt's walls. Using white chalk, black charcoal, red iron oxide, and a blue compound made from a mixture of silica, calcium and copper, the artisans painted on the moist lime plaster.

A full sized rendition of the woman's life covered the four walls of her tomb. The first illustrations began with adoring parents ogling their newborn while holding a large egg, the symbol of life. The second scene showed a young girl reading from a scroll followed this view. A panorama of life-size scenes of courting, marriage, child birthing and feasting told the story in the order of their occurrence. The final scene, the one being painted for the funerary services, conveyed a battle between good, represented by an angelic creature with wings, and evil. Snakes, crawling up the arms of a winged demon, made Una shiver every time she observed it. Possibly, the red-haired and bearded creature of evil, dressed in plaid trousers much resembling those of a Celt, annoyed the young woman the most. 'They picture my people as evil,' she supposed. 'No wonder the children look at me with dread.'

Before the tomb could receive the remains of Vulcan's mother-in-law, workers moved in replicas of furniture. Doors, windows and columns were carved out of the soft, porous, volcanic rock. A table, carved from rock, was covered with platters of food, amphorae of wine and golden mugs. Luxurious cushions lined the replicas of the bed and chairs. The various countertops contained personal items, including a bolla of perfume, a bronze mirror, necklaces, brooches, bracelets, earrings, rings and the clothing of the deceased. Only when the fixtures of the tomb captured the warmth of a normal Etruscan home was Ramtha, the lady of the house, satisfied.

The bereaved daughter kept herself occupied by selecting the musicians, ordering the food and wine, overseeing the weaving of dark mourning togas for the family and slaves; and most importantly, staging the gladiator games. Additional attention was paid to her personal effects. Jewelers by the score attended the noble lady as she studied their offerings in the reflecting side of an exquisite bronze mirror. The opposite side of which was etched with sensual figures of Etruscan mythology. She finally settled on an impressive matching pair of granulated gold pins highlighted with a fine wire of silver. The daughter was determined to make her mother's funeral one that others would try to emulate for eons to come. Multi-color tents were set up surrounding the racetrack with each containing an array of food and beverages befitting the station of the citizens invited to enjoy the festivities. The slaves of the guests would make use of the plain tents on the outside of the perimeter. Those of the highest rank could enjoy the festivities without having to leave the comfort of their tents to watch the amusements.

While his wife worked to increase her social status, Vulcan used the opportunity to improve business relationships. He established a separate tent to host all his current business associates and potential clients. Vulcan enjoyed a bit of irony when he invited Lucomo, an aristocrat, and Arruns, a businessman. These nobles quarreled constantly over which had constructed the most elegant temple. Vulcan knew having the two in such close quarters might lead to trouble. He could not invite one; however, and ignore the other, nor could he afford to ignore both. Besides, he wanted to see what would happen.

When Lucomo was invited, he questioned Vulcan's intent. "How can I be assured that you wouldn't use this as an opportunity to spy on my business dealings with the others present?"

The quick-witted Vulcan replied, "I will assign a Celt, who has no knowledge of Etruscan to be the only servant in the tent."

"How do we obtain service from a dim-witted Celt?" asked the noble.

"She understands a little Greek. Speak to her in that language."

"Where did you obtain a barbarian capable of speaking a civilized tongue?"

"I purchased her at the slave market to serve as a model," Vulcan answered. This answer satisfied the suspicions of Lucomo and the many others who would attend.

When Vulcan explained the assignment to Una, he warned her with a threat to her life not to reveal that she understood Etruscan. He then told her to report back to him everything that went on and everything that was said within the tent. After he was satisfied that Una perceived the gravity of the situation, he attended to other concerns regarding the funeral arrangements.

Una, astonished and a bit unnerved, discovered the lover of Vulcan's wife was to be cremated while still alive for the entertainment of those assembled. The slave's ashes were destined to occupy a beautiful funerary urn depicting two miniature female lovers drinking wine while lying naked on a couch. Vulcan made the urn to taunt his spouse upon the loss of her lover.

Una was rewarded with her prodding for details when she realized the opportunity the gladiator games presented. The vilest of the contests consisted of blindfolded slaves being pitted against wild animals. Vulcan's excited children described this particular contest in the grimmest detail. The children assured her that the limbs of the slaves would be ripped from their trunk as the beasts challenged each other for the largest portions. Seizing a splendid opportunity for revenge, she begged Vulcan to make sure that her betrayers took part in that portion of the games. Ever willing to please his favorite concubine, her lover readily agreed to purchase the Celts for the games.

Una was deprived of sleep on the night before the funeral festivities because the children interrupted her to prepare them for their big day. Being the grandchildren of the deceased, they had the privilege of walking at the front of the parade. The marchers lined up in front of Vulcan's house before the sun had cleared the distant fog enshrouded hills. Lute players and pipers, a dozen strong, arrived first on the scene. Several positioned themselves at the house before the sun had gone down the previous day in order to be first in line. As the dawn broke over the hills, they began to warm up their instruments. This music brought the neighbors streaming from their nearby houses to participate in the events.

Silence prevailed when the priests arrived and entered the house of the deceased to pray for an uneventful voyage to the other side. Waving chain mounted vessels of burning incense, the priests led the slaves carrying the elaborately dressed corpse toward the necropolis. Family members followed next, then musicians, dancers, invited guests and finally the household slaves. In excess of four hundred people filled the procession train that wound through the narrow streets of the living toward the hillside homes of the dead.

Only the slave who was to be cremated showed any signs of anguish. The female strode sluggishly along as though she has been drugged, which the priest had arranged to avoid a scene at the burial site. Upon arrival at the appointed place, the unwilling victim was tied to a wooden pole around which was piled dry brush. As one priest tossed a blazing torch into the brambles, others emptied their vessels of smoldering charcoal. The smoke helped to conceal the smell of burning flesh when the slave screamed in pain as the flames consumed her. The slave's ashes were carefully scooped from the earth and placed into the urn.

Only members of the family and priests were allowed to enter the catacomb on the day of the burial. Una and the others waited outside as the ceremony continued beyond their sight. Finally, she could tell by the heightened noise of the crowd waiting with her that the rite was nearing a close. A cry of delight went up from the mourners as the door opened, and the family rejoined them.

Following the burial, horse racing around an oval track provided the first event of the day. Each rider wore the colors' of a noble house and carried a small fortune in wagers. The losers after each race paid off handsomely, drank to the fullest and bet on the next race.

The remainder of the day brought a confusion of images, which danced in and out of the memory of the Celtic maiden. The only mental picture, which remained crystal clear, was the slaughter of her captors. The three Celts were dragged out onto the sandy area in front of Vulcan's family tent. Una was allowed to stand outside the open flap as the slaves were presented to plead their case. This formality provided the cruel Etruscans a cover of respectability for the slaughter.

The Celts, standing naked with their hands tied, stared in disbelief at the beautiful red-haired woman who denounced them to their fate. Then they turned and looked in horror with their bowels losing control when the chained wolves were dragged into the ring. Una arranged that Complainer be the last to face his doom, giving her a greater sense of vengeance. Vulcan allowed Una the honor of placing the hood over the head of each Celt to blindfold them as their hands were untied.

Each flailed at the growling wolf pack, which charged whenever the slave turned to ward off an attack from the rear. The crowed booed lustfully when Sparrow tried to run away instead of standing to face his attackers. The second victim, Pigeon, was every bit a coward when he ran in circles screaming until the wolves finally disemboweled him. Only Complainer, made an attempt to fight the wolves. By waving his arms in a whirlwind fashion, he kept the brutes at bay for a time. Ramtha had set a high standard for her party by declaring, "None should survive the games." Dissatisfied with the lack of ferocity shown by the animals and afraid the crowd would pardon the gladiator for his bravery, Vulcan's wife ordered a servant to splash the juice from a meat dish over the man's exposed groin. Following the servant's action, Complainer's combat was short and futile. While Una looked on without pity, the wolves charged across the small ring drawn by the smell of the meat-laden gravy and ripped away the Celt's manhood.

Only when the man lay writhing in agony on the blood soaked sand did Una return to her duties. Blood for blood without contrition is considered a sign of strength among the Celts, and Una displayed this strength for all Etruria to admire. This trait did not go unnoticed by Arruns of Clusium.

Wrestling matches provided the next performance on the agenda. First men fought with men and women with women. Later women wrestled with men, and dozens of wagers were placed in the tent in which Una was stationed. Some among the clients wanted Una to wrestle because of her size, but the host wouldn't allow it. "Her left arm is useless," he announced.

"That would only make the bout an even bet," one of the inebriated clients answered.

Numerous priests and acolytes, announced by a blast of triumphant horns, descended upon the arena, each holding a writhing snake. The procession of snakes began to move in a winding fashion around and through the tents. After drinking wine and other alcoholic spirits, the vicious bloodletting of the performers aroused the passions of the on-lookers. Women ran from the tents to form a human chain, which paraded around the grounds of the arena following the priests. Slaves, as well as free born, were encouraged to enter the dervish maneuvers unfolding before those being entertained. Winding in snakelike fashion through and around the tents, the women began to disrobe and toss their clothing to the cheering males who lounged on the sofas and taunted the dancers. Often the dancers allowed themselves to be grabbed and dragged onto the couches by the aroused males, who lusted for their pleasure. This activity consumed the remainder of the events, which lasted throughout the night.

In the commercial tent where Vulcan's business associates were entertained, trouble erupted. Lucomo seized his rival Arruns' wife as she passed and pulled her down onto his couch. The intoxicated noble lady went willingly into his arms, much to the anger of her ever-watchful husband. The action of his rival destroyed Arruns' ego and left his manhood open to ridicule by his business associates. Arruns secretly swore revenge. Even in his drunken state, he was afraid to challenge Lucomo directly because the aristocrat was known to have dealings with the Romans. Whenever one involved the Romans, murder and armed intervention was well within the realm of probabilities. Arruns was aware that his city, Clusium, did not have the armed strength to enter into such a struggle. At that moment, Una stooped over to refill his wine cup, exposing her voluptuous breasts. Arruns, jealous over his wife's betrayal, immediately pulled the slave down onto the couch and quickly entered her. The deed was consummated without satisfying either party. The Etruscan, however, recaptured his lost ego by having control over such a bloodthirsty savage. Then an idea formed in his wine-sotted brain. Hauling Una out of his rival's sight, he queried her in Greek about her tribal status, "You wear a gold neck torque. Does that mean you are an important person among the Celts?"

While pretending to stumble over the use of a foreign language, Una replied, "I am the daughter the chief of the Mayri Clan of the mighty Helvetii Nation."

"If your people know where you are being held captive will they pay to retrieve you?"

"Celts rarely pay to retrieve hostages. More likely they will seek retribution and exterminate the offenders," the defiant slave replied.

"If I assist them in finding you, would they place an armed force at my disposal?" Arruns asked, seeing an opportunity to get even with his rival Lucomo.

"My father will be most grateful to any who assist his daughter and most ferocious with any who have enslaved her," she replied.

"I will be in contact," Arruns replied. Then he returned to his drinking while planning revenge on his blood enemy, Lucomo.

Una, along with the other slaves, was pressed to cleanup the area while their masters crawled home to their beds. When finally arriving at her sleeping chamber, she dared not get her hopes up, nor did she mention the conversation to Vulcan.

Chapter 19
Retribution

Mayri Oppidum circa 388 BC
An exhausted Hugh and his companion, Katlyn, arrived at the Mayri compound with the balky mule in tow. Mick, coming in answer to the extrasensory message sent in a dream by Hugh, greeted them warmly. "Welcome brother," the warrior shouted as he ran toward the couple emerging through the gate of the oppidum. In his exuberance at seeing Hugh, Mick ploughed into and over the more rotund of the siblings to the astonishment of both himself and the female traveler.

"I didn't think a horse could knock over Hugh," the fatigued Katlyn laughed as Mick included her in the embrace meant for his brother.

"Who have we here?" Mick asked as he introduced himself. "I am the warrior brother of this disheveled cleric, and who might you be?"

"This is my friend, Katlyn, and keep your groveling hands off her," a prone Hugh laughed, too tired to attempt to regain his balance.

The overwhelming enthusiasm of other tribal members welcoming the two in typical Celtic ebullience ended further attempts at conversation. Meva observed the scene from the door of her home and wondered what brought her son home from his studies. Just yesterday, she had asked the same question of Mick, who was most evasive in his reply. Praying silently that the visit was a cordial one and not a prelude to his discharge from the priesthood, she hurried across the open space to greet her still sprawled son. But most importantly, she wanted to have a closer look at the female who accompanied him.

While Mick stood chatting with Katlyn, his mother offered Hugh a hand to get up. Then she ushered the three toward her home. As much as other clan members wanted to use the visit as an excuse for a celebration, Meva wouldn't hear of it. "Hugh hasn't the energy to stand on his two feet, and this poor woman looks like the last petal to fall before winter." She quickly hurried the both of them home, fed them and ordered them to bed. "The morning will be sufficient time to discuss matters," Meva admonished the protesting Hugh, who quickly went to sleep, only too happy to let someone else attend to the pack mule.

In the morning before Hugh could state his concern, Meva grilled him about leaving the priesthood. "Have you done anything to disgrace yourself? You know I have much on my mind with your father gone on that trading venture and with Una accompanying him. Now, tell me what brings you here?"

"Ma, I received permission from the head Druid before I withdrew. He also gave Katlyn permission to accompany me," Hugh said, defending himself against his mother's critical stare and onslaught of questions. When Meva finally calmed down, he related his concern over Una.

"What do you mean you can tell when either of your siblings is in danger?" his suspicious mother asked, not wanting to hear any bad news. "Whatever put that nonsense into your head?" Although like all mothers, she had known since Hugh's childhood that he had possessed such a gift, she did not want to let on all that she knew about the lives of her children.

"Honest Ma, it is a talent that I have. Even when we attended the Druid school, I could tell whenever Mick or Una got into trouble."

"Tell me what you see in this vision of yours!" Meva demanded.

"It's not a vision, well not really. It is more like a feeling that something dreadful has happened, or is about to happen. When I get this feeling, I sense it concerns either Una or Mick. This time it turned out to be Una. Occasionally, I get flashes of images of what may be taking place."

"What do you see regarding Una, and where is your father?"

"I know nothing about him. I can only perceive happenings to Una and Mick. First, I sensed a place that was very frigid. Then Una appeared holding onto a rope with her right hand, and for some reason she is not using her left hand. Perhaps, it is injured."

"Can you feel things as well?" Meva asked, interrupting.

"Sometimes, Ma please let me continue. It's important. I could feel her getting so cold that her spirit was leaving her body. I screamed for her to hold on because I was coming and would warm her."

"What else can you tell me!" the distraught Meva demanded.

"In later dreams, I saw a time of darkness. Una was struggling with someone. Her arms were bound behind her back and her shin was rubbed raw as though she had been dragged across rough ground. After that scene, I saw a very hungry and scared Una crowded in a wooden shelter with a group of other people. I could smell their sweat and sense their fear." Hugh continued, "I know something has happened, and I must go to her. Mick, Katlyn and I just stopped to obtain some supplies."

"Young man, if you think I am about to let you trek off alone to a land where your sister and your father are in danger, you are sadly mistaken! I am going with you," a determined Meva announced.

Only the counsel of her brother-in-law, Rochlos, and the clan elders prevented her from packing and leaving immediately. "Mick is a proven warrior, who has earned the right to venture after his sister. You are needed by your clan," the elders concluded.

Meva's intervention concerned Hugh. In her effort to get the rescue party to the setting as quickly as possible, she suggested that Hugh be left behind. "He is not as qualified on a mount as you," she said one morning to Mick. "There are others we could send, like my brother."

"Mom, we can't wait until Ragenos returns," he said in exasperation. "Hugh can detect Una's location when he gets anywhere near her proximity. We need him! Now sit down and take a deep breath. I know that Father is also on your mind. We will find him and bring him back safely. I promise on my word as a warrior." Mick wasn't certain whether Hugh could, in fact, determine the whereabouts of Una, but he felt it was vital that his Druid brother accompany them.

Her warrior son's confidence calmed Meva, but it did not prevent her from getting involved in choosing the rescue party. In the end and after much discussion, the rescuers consisted of Mick,

Hugh, Katlyn and four warriors, two females and two males. One female and male warrior pair where chosen because they were small of stature and did not resemble typical Celts, which gave the party both diversity and the opportunity to gather information that they may not be able to obtain otherwise.

Danous insisted that he accompanies the rescue party as well, "I have vast experience from my travels with Ragenos. Also, I bring the added advantage of being a bard, one who can obtain information when even a Druid is suspect." He did not offer to explain that his reasons included his infatuation with the beautiful Una, nor did he need to for even Meva was aware.

Rochlos saw to the arming of the party, and Meva attended to their supplies. Following a short blessing from the Mayri Druid, the eight rescuers set off just as the sun broke across the horizon.

Rome
Several days later when they neared the city, Julia began to give helpful directions. She pointed out the lowest point for crossing the Tiber. "It is best if we cross at Tiber Island and enter the city from the west. Only commoners would use any other bridge."

The bridge, named after Sublicius, led onto an open area between two of Rome's seven hills, the Aventine and the Palatine. Jostled by dozens of people entering and leaving, their entry into Rome proper brought no more than a glance from the guards at the gate. The legionaries presumed that the young Roman girl was returning from a country outing with her barbarian slaves. A change took place in Julia's demeanor as her confidence grew upon being in the safety of her city. Julia began sensing that she, instead of the Celts, controlled the situation. The trio passed through a cattle market near a wide and lengthy oval path, which Julia described as the location for the city's horse racing. "My papa owns a stable of horses and has servants who race chariots under his colors. Most often our team wins."

Conel's first impression of the city was not pleasant. It was noisy, busy, smoky and dusty. Soldiers in shining armor stood out among the workmen dressed in their dark belted tunics. Litters, borne by slaves and carrying the rich, fought for passage through the wagons laden with goods. Even though the marshes were adequately drained by the Cloaca Maxima, the stench of rotting sewerage still prevailed. "No wonder the citizens reside on those high slopes," Conel said to Turk. While gazing across the flat field at the rising hills, he observed that most of the citizens lived in small hovels, whereas the Palatine Hill consisted of more stately stone buildings.

Ignoring Conel's reference to the odor, Julia pointed to an open area and remarked. "That's the forum where they hold the free festivals to keep the poor content." Both Conel and Turk looked at each other, but neither commented on Julia's remark.

Looking off to his right, Conel observed what must be the docks where the maritime trade took place. The maritime area held Turk's interest, and they agreed to meet there after Conel dropped off Julia. "I'm going to get in touch with some Celts from the Aedui Tribe, who have been trading with the Romans for years." With that short statement Turk left, and Conel turned to Julia for further directions.

"Our family, being one of the original families of Rome, naturally lives near the crest of the Palatine Hill, which is directly in front of us," the bold Julia stated as though she were the noble and Conel the servant. "Carry on, and I shall correct you when you make a wrong turn." Confused by the size of the city, Conel did not take offense at the cocky mannerisms Julia displayed.

The chariot negotiated the narrow lanes, finally arriving at rectangular sets of attached buildings on both sides of the street. With a motion of her hand, Julia pointed to her residence, down the street and the third door on the left. As they approached the entry, Conel was disturbed to see a chained slave, who rose to open the door for them. Another servant promptly came out, but he was afraid of the horses that pulled Conel's chariot and called for someone to assist him with the strange beasts.

"Mater will be infuriated when I tell her the door slave was resting. One would think that a returning daughter deserves a more cordial greeting," Julia stated as she completed her role reversal from slave to master.

As they stood before the entryway, the door slave at a signal from Julia blew a long note on a small horn. "Give the slave boys a hand with the animals, and you had better disarm," she ordered, while pointing to the squads of armed men running onto the street from both directions. "They belong to the city watch, and they will kill you if you do not do as I tell you."

Assuming all would be straightened out when he clarified his mission, Conel unbuckled his sword belt and listened to the clash as the weapon hit the stone street. Raising his hands in a sign of friendship, he began to explain, "I am Conel, my reason for being here is to ...,"

But he was rudely cuffed across the head by a wooden club swung by the first of the arriving guards. The unexpected blow staggered him, causing him to lose his balance. "Secure him. Then drag him in my house for the paterfamilias to do with him as he sees fit," ordered a joyful Julia.

Even in his semi-conscious condition, a half-dozen of the short stocky guards had to work together to shackle the large Celt. Without ceremony the Celtic chief, chained with arm and leg irons, was handed over to the Roman male-dominated society.

Julia's reception, instead of being the triumph she anticipated, bordered on the cruel. Her mother refused to see her and retreated to her bedroom in tears of shock. Her father sternly ordered her to leave his sight. Only her papa showed any sign of compassion. The paterfamilias had his granddaughter whipped with a single rod because of her stupidity for being captured. Turning to Julia's father, Lucius said, "You will find a suitable match that will benefit the Julian house and name. Do I make myself clear?"

In his naivety regarding Roman customs, Conel stood in shock and amazement while Julia was whipped. 'What kind of people are these Romans who beat a female instead of welcoming her. I hope that Turk hears of my predicament and quickly comes to my rescue.'

After learning there was a second Celt who accompanied Julia, he ordered his son to find and enslave him. Then Lucius commanded that Conel be brought to him, so he might determine the punishment.

"There has been a terrible injustice done," an agitated Conel declared as servants pulled his chains. "I brought your child back, because I was honor bound to do so."

For speaking in the presence of Lucius, Conel was whipped with a flagellum consisting of leather cords to which bits of bone were attached. "I believe that a newly acquired slave needs to be taught his place," reprimanded the paterfamilias. "I will have no slave speak in my presence without being requested to do so!"

"In my culture, we feed a person before we ask their purpose for entering our oppidum. Is it your custom to beat a person before asking their purpose for entering your city?" Conel asked while purposely ignoring Lucius' last comment.

Turning to the bloody and bruised Conel, Lucius sneered. "You speak a poor imitation of our tongue, even for a barbarian. But

Druids, Celts, and Romans

because you can speak our tongue, I will forgive you this one time. If you speak again without permission, I will cut out your tongue." Realizing that Lucius would make good on his threat, Conel remained silent.

Then speaking to those who held the prisoner, he said. "Know this. Savages have no rights! Take this man to the shed behind the atrium and feed him half a slave's rations until he is housebroken."

Before Conel was dragged off, his gold neck torque was cut off and replaced with the leather collar of a slave. The gold was added to the family's money chest. Because the Julian family had the maximum number of slaves regulated by the State, another slave was chosen by lot to be killed to make room for Conel.

Turk was easily found, but his enslavement was another matter. The Aedui Celt who had become a citizen of Rome invoked the rule of Hospitium. The Aedui vouched that Turk was a friend, and that he would supply Turk's needs and see to his protection while he was in Rome. This act of kindness on the part of a Roman citizen prevented the city watch from imprisoning the Mayri trader, much to the displeasure of the Julian family. Vopiscus Julian, believing that hiding the Celt behind Hospitium insulted his family name, began to make plans to have Turk and the Aedui assassinated.

The Aedui, after long years of exile, knew well the workings of the Roman mind. "I have spent the better part of my youth learning about these people. Our lives are in jeopardy. Therefore, we are in no position to rescue your friend. Is there anyone you can contact who might assist us?"

"I have a number of warriors waiting where the Boii territory ends. We can count on them to give assistance." Under cover of darkness, Turk and the Aedui set out for the meeting-place where Roith and his warriors camped.

Po Valley
After surviving a perilous journey over the slushy Alpine trails, Mick and his small party were surprised at the cool welcome they received when they finally staggered, bone weary into the Insubres' oppidum. None of the tribal leaders were present, and the young people appeared to be fashioning weapons for a major encounter. No one would explain to Mick's satisfaction the purpose of the war preparation. The exhausted party spent two nights among the Insubres before they journeyed on without benefit of an escort. However, the time was not entirely wasted. Hugh and Katlyn

conversed with the tribal Druids, while Danous entertained and listened, a trait he learned well while traveling with Ragenos. "There is something afoot, and it concerns your sister. Of that I am certain," Danous declared to the two anxious brothers upon returning from his surveillance mission.

Katlyn told a similar, more detailed story. "I was drinking with a young Druidess, when I learned that Una was hurt while crossing the Alps. She recovered at a Druid settlement a short distance from here. Following her recovery, the Druids released her to the protection of the tribe. That much I've learned, but I know not where she is now. Oh! There is one more point. The leaders of the Insubres are conferring with the Boii about going to war."

Upon hearing that news, Mick immediately set plans to depart, while Hugh counseled that they should visit the hut where Una was last seen. Hugh's logic prevailed, and the party investigated the scene of Una's capture. It took the better part of a day, asking questions of the suspicious inhabitants, before Danous obtained information about Una's last known whereabouts.

"Since so many horsemen had visited the scene, it's useless to sort out who went where," Mick declared.

Having no other plan of action, the brothers and their companions rode toward the home of the Boii. Mick was very unhappy about the delay, and he let his brother know at every opportunity. "I told you that visiting the hut was a waste of time."

Rome
Suffering from a blistered back, Conel lay on his stomach and tried to eat the meager meal set on the wooden trencher before him. His fellow slaves offered no comfort, since one of their favorites lost his life in order that Conel could join the household. Nor could Conel enjoy the conversation of his fellow captives because most spoke a tongue with which he was unfamiliar. Day after day as his back healed, his body weakened because of the sparse diet.

Boii Oppidum
Just as Mick and his party arrived at the gates of the Boii oppidum, they met a large raiding party returning with scores of prisoners from the land of the Etruscans. After the guards would not provide any information, the brothers burst into a Boii council meeting, demanding to know what happened to their sister. The impetuous Mick, acting with the arrogance of a warrior chief's son, could not contain his anger and swore fierce retribution if anyone withheld

information. His case was made more emphatic by the backing of a massive Druid whose anger was the equal of his brother's.

Only the quick wit of the bard, arriving seconds later, prevented a massive shedding of blood as the seated Boii did not take kindly to being called liars. Danous began strumming on his lyre and singing in a low voice. The music and soft voice compelled all to pause and listen:

> Forgive my companions who feel bound to yell, their hearts are nigh breaking at this tale I tell.
> The Druid's vision, his sister is in danger. Her life depends on the will of a stranger.
> Would you deny them the honor of saving her life, just to bloody your sword and to handle your knife?
> Will you forgo the famous hospitality of the Boii, to fight the sons of Conel, Chief of the Mayri?

Upon hearing the satire by the bard, all anger dissipated. No longer willing to withhold the sad tale of the capture of Una, Dhulack, the Boii chief, filled in the gaps in the intelligence that the brothers had gathered. "The Insubres council met with me to share their grief. The families of the guilty have been imprisoned and await their execution by fire because of their kinship. We have combined our forces and are raiding the lands of the Etruscans, trying to gather information as to the whereabouts of your sister. When we have what we need, we will assemble the entire force of Celts, this side of the mountains, and attack."

Mick agreed wholeheartedly with the plans to do battle, only again to be interrupted by his brother. "What have they learned from the prisoners they have interrogated?" he asked.

"They claim to have no knowledge of any kidnapped maid. That is what I expected them to say," answered a son of Dhulack.

"Then let me have a try before they are executed," Hugh requested.

Dressed in Druid white, he met individually with each of the Etruscans. All swore that they did not partake in any kidnapping, nor would any admit they had any knowledge of such an event. The Boii chief and Una's older brother both tried their favorite methods to extract information, and did no better than Hugh. Returning to the council hall, neither Dhulack nor Mick could offer any additional facts on the whereabouts of Una. The fates of those interrogated were left in the hands of their captors.

"I suggest a two pronged approach," Hugh said to Dhulack. "Provide us with a person knowledgeable with the geography of the Etruscan countryside, and we will continue our search while you continue yours."

"How do you propose we obtain information when hundreds of Celtic warriors cannot?" an angry and disturbed Mick asked.

"We will make use of the talents we possess. Danous is a bard, who when wearing his blue cloak, can easily penetrate the defenses of a city; whereas, ten thousand warriors could lay siege for months without a clue as to Una's whereabouts. Then think back as to why you argued so passionately to allow me to accompany you. I can detect her whereabouts if I get close enough. Finally, we have Katlyn who can also enter a town as a priestess and obtain information. My brother, sometimes it pays to think small." Mick swiftly agreed to the sage advice. The Mayri party remained for the night to rest and obtain supplies. Dhulack provided them with his finest tracker, fresh horses and his promise to follow them with a armed force.

Etruria

Mounted on fresh horses, Mick led the group at an unrelenting pace. He allowed rest stops only to prevent the animals from becoming overly tired while ignoring the fatigue of his companions. Only when the darkness made travel unsafe would he reluctantly agree to set up camp. The weary riders quickly consumed hot meals before they turned in for a few hours sleep. To save time, they ate a cold breakfast as the sun appeared each dawn, mounted and left using the early morning's light to see the path. The sound of pounding hoofs alerted the few travelers sharing the trail, who moved aside and allowed the small, armed party to pass unchallenged. The tracker easily found Roith's camp, where they learned that Conel had departed with Turk to return the girl and had not as yet returned.

Mick ordered the tracker to return to the Boii' oppidum and inform Dhulack that their father went on to Rome. "Tell him not to do anything until he hears from Conel!" Then turning to Roith, he said, "Wait here for my father. Inform him of Una's danger and follow any instructions that he gives you. We will continue on and try to find some trace of her."

"Perhaps I could be of further assistance if I went with you," Roith argued. "I know a little of their dialect. Believe me, the Etruscans can be very difficult to understand, and if it comes to fighting, another sword would be useful."

Mick and Hugh both agreed with the young Boii's common sense and included him in their plans. They left the four Mayri warriors behind with Roith's men. Refusing any additional armed warriors, who would delay them and call unnecessary attention to them, the small group set off in their search.

North of Rome

In their haste to find help, Turk and the Aedui missed the turn in the narrow trail leading to the encampment where Roith was waiting. They spent several days trying to correct their mistake. Signs of large parties of horsemen, engaging in skirmishes, only added to their confusion and their frustration.

"We cannot keep wandering around like a couple of minstrels or Conel will surely die," Turk said as they briefly rested. He decided to continue on to reach the oppidum of the Boii, and asked the Aedui to sneak back into Rome to spy for him. Although knowing that certain death might await, the Celt reluctantly agreed to the task.

"My thanks and those of my kindred are with you, my friend," said the parting Turk in all sincerity. "I need you in the city to obtain information and to keep an eye on my friend as best as you can. When I return, I promise you will be amply rewarded." Turning his horse northward, Turk mounted and began his lonely journey.

The Alps

'No sense having both Conel and I held captive,' determined the travel-wise trader as he avoided the settlements of the Etruscans on his weeklong journey. 'The next decision will be, do I stop at the oppidum of the Boii, or do I continue?' Turk decided it was more important to get the message of Conel's imprisonment to Meva than to enlist the support of the Boii. 'The Boii have neither the strength nor the military intelligence to carry off Conel's rescue.'

To avoid traveling through the more populous portion of Etruria and risk getting captured or delayed, a mounted Turk and his packhorse climbed the Apennines to the east. Because he started out well provisioned, the early portion of the journey went relatively smoothly. The mountain passes were lower, and the climb less arduous than what he would face when crossing the Alps. Even the weather cooperated with sunny days and balmy nights making the extremely wearisome trip enjoyable for the seasoned traveler. Things turned for the worse when Turk tried to cross the Alps using a mountain pass east of those with which he was familiar. He traveled by day through slushy terrain that increased in altitude the further he went. Since he journeyed alone, Turk avoided linking up with the few wagon trains that were moving in the same direction because he feared either unnecessary delay or robbery.

Several times, his packhorse failed to negotiate a narrow stretch of trail and slid down the slope until it was finally able to come to a halt. Following these incidents, the animal became naturally skittish, and Turk had to remove most of the supplies or risk losing them. He tethered the packhorse to his mount, and prayed to every Celtic god, with whom he was familiar, to grant them safe passage. Gods, as Turk soon discovered, had strange senses of humor. The packhorse not only stumbled yet another time, but this time it pulled Turk and his mount down as well.

Turk labored the better part of the day to pull himself free of the horse, which landed on top of him, pinning one of his legs to the ground. He became aware that some rib bones were broken because he had difficulty breathing, and every breath resulted in great pain. Using his foot and leaning against the squirming body of the mule, he pushed the horse away to free his leg

Both animals suffered severe injury and had to be slain because neither could make it back to the path. It took considerable time and many trips to carry the salvageable supplies up the slushy mountainside to the ridge. The strain on the injured Turk was beyond compare. With the transfer finished, he sorted through the supplies and selected those that were vital. Wet and exhausted, he strapped as much of the provisions as he could manage to his back, and began the remainder of his journey on foot. Before long his feet became numb from the wet leather, causing him to stop several times to gather grass and straw to stuff his boots. Between his prayers to the gods, he chastised himself often for not stopping at the Boii oppidum. Realizing that he had to keep moving at night using the light of the moon or he would freeze as the temperatures dropped, he plodded along, challenging the elements. After a time, his legs gave out, and he surrendered to the wind and the chill. Turk, even while collapsing, tried to inch forward in his iron determination to reach his destination.

Perhaps the gods had listened to his pleading because a party of Druids came across the prostrate wanderer in time to prevent hypothermia and early death. "Why would a traveler attempt to make such a dangerous trip alone?" one Druid asked of another.

"He is a very foolish person," another said. "His mission, however, must have been sufficiently important for him to risk his life."

The hot liquid being poured down his throat revived Turk sufficiently to make him aware that he was in the hands of others. The sun reflecting off the snow had damaged his corneas to the point that he could not distinguish night from day. Knowing his last reserves were being depleted, even as he lay in the warmth of their blankets, he begged through parched lips for his rescuers to assist him in accomplishing his mission.

The Druids were reluctant to entertain any notion of delaying their own purpose to aid an almost dead traveler. When he explained in a whisper that his friend and chieftain Conel was captured while on an assignment at the bequest of the now dead Druid Master, Munli of the Helvetii Tribe; however, the Druids relented, and assigned two of their party to see him safely home.

"Maybe, we were destined to travel this route rather than the easier one to the east. The Master Druid may have called upon us from his grave to assist this man in his quest," one remarked.

Etruria
Hugh's party encountered little trouble because he convinced Mick that it would be safer if only Danous and Katlyn entered populated areas. "We will camp in a concealed location a short distance away and be prepared to intervene if they don't return in a timely fashion," the warrior brother declared.

Using what little Etruscan he picked up during his spying mission, Danous strummed his lyre and mumbled a few words familiar to the audience who lay feasting before him. His musical talent enabled him to roam without interference throughout the city and come and go through the arched gates as often as he desired. He was amply provided with food and with small round pieces of gold decorated with the heads of demons. He found he could exchange this coin for other goods. Each night, he would describe his daily adventures to his companions.

One night, as he shared the food he concealed underneath his cloak, Katlyn arrived from her mission and interrupted his storytelling. "I've seen her!" she declared. Then, she realized her unfortunate choice of words when Mick rose quickly from his outstretched position and darted across the short distance separating them.

"Where is she? What was she doing?" the overjoyed brother asked.

"I didn't actually see her, but I saw a likeness of her. It might be a sculpture of her," Katlyn hastily said, trying to calm Mick down.

"What do you mean you saw a likeness of her?" Mick, demanded halting in his stride and forgetting his original intent to kiss Hugh's friend.

"Just that!" she said. "I saw what might be a likeness of her."

At that moment, Hugh put his massive arms around Katlyn and forced her to sit beside him. Then, he said, "Now, slowly explain what you saw and where you saw it."

Taking a moment to catch her breath, Katlyn told her tale. "While I wandered in the town's marketplace, deciding on my plan of action, I encountered two female acolytes on their way to the temple. From their conversation, I was able to understand that this town is called Tarquinii, and it contains the holiest temple of the Etruscans. I tagged along behind them, picking up scraps of conversation though most of what they said I could not understand. After a time, we came upon a large open area in the center of the city. The two acolytes continued across the open space toward a large building elaborately decorated, with its roof supported by round columns of stone resembling trees. The two walked toward a crowd admiring a sculpture consisting of flying horses."

"Horses don't fly!" Mick interrupted.

"These horses had wings growing out of their backs. Besides, they were not real horses. They were made of stone!" Katlyn exclaimed.

"Let's settle down and hear the rest of the story," Hugh said.

Katlyn continued. "There were two of these winged creatures, which were being watered by a life-sized maiden carved from stone. This maiden looked like the beautiful sister that Hugh has so often described. In fact, she resembled a female Mick."

"That would be just like Una to get some foreigner to sculpt her," Danous said.

Hugh, smiling at the bard's wit, agreed with his assessment of their sister. Then in a more serious tone, he continued. "We need to make certain that Una modeled for this display." At that point, he took command of the conversation. "More than one of us has to get into the city and see the carving. Let me think! Danous and Katlyn seem to have easy access, but I doubt that they would let the others walk about in their city. And we are the ones who would recognize her."

"They would if they thought you were slaves," Danous stated.

"And whose slaves are we going to be?" Mick asked.

"Why, mine, of course," Danous answered. "I just have to obtain a couple of leather slave collars, have you conceal your weapons, and we are all set. There are many slaves in the town. A few more won't attract much attention."

The group spent the next several hours refining their plan. They decided that Roith should be one of the slaves because he understood the Etruscan language better than any of them. If Una were held captive in the city, Hugh, with his ability to detect his sister, would be invaluable. Katlyn was needed to lead them to the temple, leaving a very disgruntled Mick to remain and guard the horses and supplies.

They entered the city without incident. Katlyn traveled as a single priestess on a pilgrimage. Hugh and Roith wore the slave collars that Danous obtained that morning. The two Celts pretended to have had their tongues cut to prevent their talking. Danous covered for them by remarking to passersby as they entered the city. "What storyteller would want a slave who could repeat his lines?" He recited the words Roith taught him in a singsong fashion, receiving smiles from all who listened, including the guards on duty. The group reassembled once they were safely beyond the gates and wandered the lanes of the unfamiliar city. Katlyn, after several failed attempts, was able to lead them to the spot where she saw the three-dimensional likeness.

"It is Una all right," Hugh said with certainty. "The artist even copied the engraving of the Goddess Sulis from her neck torque. From the expression on her face she seems content, even happy," he mused. "In fact, the artist was so kind as to leave his mark. See the letters VULCAN."

"Now that we are certain the likeness is really that of Una, how do we find her?" Katlyn asked.

"That's easy. We inquire as to the whereabouts of the artist," the experienced traveler, Danous, answered.

The first few inquiries led only to curious looks. No one understood them, or did not know the work of Vulcan. Finally, a Roman slave told the seekers, in her native tongue, that Vulcan hailed from the city of Clusium. Using the slave as an interpreter, they found out the location of that city, which lay off in a northeasterly direction. The searchers quickly took leave of Tarquinii and returned to inform Mick.

    Because it was getting dark by the time they arrived back at the camp, they delayed for the night before departing. After they had eaten, Hugh formed a circle and had each cut his or her hand and take a blood oath. "Press your cut against the cuts of the others then repeat after me. I swear that I am willing to shed my life to rescue Una." Drawing his sword, Mick spit on it and swore a second oath to take terrible restitution on this Vulcan who had enslaved her.

Chapter 20
Blood for Blood

The Alps circa 388 BC

Turk struggled to move his arms pinned beneath the blanket that kept him strapped onto the rickety stretcher pulled by the young Druid acolytes. Every jolt drove unbearable pain throughout his body. The agony shot up both his arms and legs, causing him to lapse into unconsciousness. Then the need to urinate overtook him, and Turk screamed in a vain effort to regain his dignity. "Release me! I have to attend to myself."

    "We must tell him that he suffered frostbite, that his skin was blackened, and we could do little else but amputate," emphasized the young servant of the oak. "He must be made to understand that the frost congealed his life's blood, or he would be dead already."

    "The telling may kill him."

    "Then I will do the telling for I believe he has the willpower to complete his mission despite the loss of his limbs."

    Kneeling beside Turk, the young Druid whispered in his ear, "I pray you can bear the suffering that I am causing you without too much distress. There are only two of us, and we cannot carry you and survive this journey over the pass. Already the night wind kicks up as we near the summit. Should we fail to clear the high point, I am afraid we all will perish. I pray also that you find forgiveness for my fellow acolyte. He has only traveled this way once and is terrified of both the height and the cold."

    "I can fend for myself if only you will loosen the knots that bind me," an almost delusional Turk whispered.

As gently as he could, the attendant described Turk's present state, "The healer had to remove both of your hands, one foot, and an ear. They were black from the frost and would have brought a quick death if we had left them alone. I am studying to become a healer, which is why I have been chosen to accompany you.'

"I have one foot!" Turk screamed in horror as he tried to rise. "If I have no hands then I am no longer a man!" he said in terror while he struggled to escape the security of the robes. A feeling of desolation finally set in and his will to live began to fade.

"We carry you back to your people because you have a need to deliver a message about your chieftain being held captive. Our healer thinks that is the only thing keeping you alive," the student said as he tried to minister to his patient.

Upon hearing these words Turk found new resolve to honor his pledge to his friend Conel. "Carry on," he cried in pain. "I will bear up as well as I can."

"In a short while, we will crest the highest peak. The journey will become swifter as we descend. When we reach the point where the melt from the snow feeds the lakes, we will turn you over to one of the boatmen who ply their trade among the many tribes that have settled along the water. The boat ride will be smoother, and I pray that your strength will hold out until you reach your destination. I can do no more for you, except pray for your spirit," the acolyte said as he worked with his companion to pull the burden over the ice-crested snow. Before the healer finished his short declaration, Turk lapsed into unconsciousness.

Etruria
Refusing to listen to reasons for further delay, Mick insisted that they take the wide level road that runs parallel to the river, rather than once again cross into the forest. "I know the slower way may be safer, but I will cut my way through any Etruscan that opposes me," he declared.

Not even Hugh felt up to the challenge to take on his headstrong brother any longer, so they fell in behind his lead. The road, although less wearisome that the forest trail, forced the group to follow a tributary of the Tiber and circumvent a large lake. Their slowness taxed Mick's patience, and he demanded that everyone maintain his pace. "The longer we delay," he complained, "the more likely the one who used Una as a model will no longer require her services."

Hugh tried to reason with his brother. "I can't keep up with you. Besides, the statue was completed some time ago. Therefore if her owner decided he no longer needed her, he made this decision some time ago as well. Let us set a reasonable pace before you kill the only horse capable of carrying my weight."

"Do not ever again call the depraved one who captured my sister her owner, or your mount will not need to carry you much further," Mick shouted, threatening his brother. "Nor will I hear any talk that my sister is dead!"

"I didn't say she was dead," Hugh replied angrily. "I would know if that were the case. I'm only saying that she is either still with the person, or she has been sold. In that event we will need all our energy and resolve to continue on our quest."

Katlyn stepped into the heated exchange between the two brothers before it flamed into a physical confrontation. Realizing that Mick needed activity to compensate for their lack of progress, she suggested a plan, "Why don't you and Roith go on ahead and scout out the land while Danous and I accompany Hugh? By the time we arrive, you can have an adequate camp prepared."

The now separated travelers moved in a northeasterly direction across the Etruscan countryside. Even squads of Etruscan troops decided that two large, and well armed Celts shouldn't be disturbed, especially when they were moving on.

The party consisting of the bard and two Druids attracted significantly greater attention, mostly from inquisitive traders and ordinary citizens who frequented the byway. At night, their campsite was surrounded by their fellow travelers seeking entertainment to relieve their trip's drudgery. Danous was delighted to oblige, even if only a few of the listeners understood the strange words to his sagas. The crowd that traveled with the three Celts proved to be an advantage. They protected Hugh's party from the attention of Etruscan military and highwaymen, either of whom would prey upon minimally armed wayfarers.

Clusium
By the time Hugh's party arrived in the vicinity of Clusium, Mick and Roith had already setup a primitive camp and had scouted the city walls to discover any secret entrances. Finding none, the two warriors settled down to a daily routine while awaiting the arrival of their companions. Mick would ride around the city while Roith sat near the gates and listened in on conversations of those entering. He also kept an eye out for his companions. That's how he spotted

the three stragglers long before they saw him resting by the side of the road, obscured by the brush and trees. "Well, you three don't look any worse for the long journey," he said as he greeted them.

"I'm exhausted," exclaimed Hugh. "Guide me to a bed."

The others laughed when Danous commented, "Thank the Gods you did not have to chase Ragenos across half of Celtdom. Where is the worthy nephew of the warrior of whom I speak?" he asked.

"If you mean Mick," the Boii replied, "he is circling the city trying to find a safe way in. To date he has not been successful, even though he has made the same circle so often he has worn a rut in the dirt surrounding the walls."

"My brother is so obstinate he doesn't know when to stop," Hugh responded as he dismounted. "I don't care how far I have to go. I'm walking."

Mayri Oppidum

Guards came to Meva with word that a fisherman arrived with an injured Turk. "He is too weak to be brought to the oppidum, but he insists on talking with you. I have sent for a Druid healer."

Leaping onto a nearby horse, Meva raced down to the lakefront. The sight of the once strong Turk almost turned her stomach. "What happened to him?" she asked the boatman.

"I don't know. He was in that state, when another boatman passed him on to me. I was told to bring him here as swiftly as I could. I rowed through the night to get here before he perished."

Bending over the trader, Meva listened anxiously to what he would reveal. "I did the best that I could, but the Romans have taken Conel captive," he whispered through dry chapped lips. "Contact Seanos of the Adequi tribe in Rome for he can lead you to Conel. Hurry, it has been several months since I last laid eyes on him." After asking Meva to make an offering in his name to the Goddess Sulis, Turk closed his eyes and died.

For the first time in her life, Meva was so truly frightened that her body trembled, and she could not hold back the tears. For the next hour, she knelt by the corpse of her husband's companion and confidant of many years and prayed for the well-being of the one she loved. The training by her father took control before the mother and wife allowed herself to become despondent. Steeling herself, as only she could do, she returned to the oppidum. Once at home, she began to make plans. 'First I need Rochlos. He will help me.'

Screaming at a slave to fetch Rochlos, she sent for her brother-in-law.

"The Romans have captured Conel!" Meva exclaimed as Rochlos entered her household an hour later. "Una is in some kind of danger. What am I to do? I told him; nay I begged him not to go, but he wouldn't listen." Then for the second time in her life, Meva broke down and sobbed.

Rochlos, as steady as his brother, helped himself to some wine and poured a goblet for the totally unnerved Meva before answering. "We must assemble a force and seek revenge for any harm done," he said while pausing to sip the alcoholic beverage. "I will leave my son, Roanlos, with you to protect the hillfort and take several dozen warriors."

"That will not be sufficient," Meva said. "I will extract revenge of a type that will push the ambitions of those arrogant people back a hundred years. I will deplete the treasury if I have to! Where is Ragenos?" she demanded.

"I doubt that the council of elders will allow you to deplete the treasury," Rochlos replied as quietly as he could in an effort to calm her. "We do, however, need Ragenos' council. I will send the news to him immediately. He is traveling somewhere near the border of the Germans." Then as if in afterthought, Rochlos continued, "We can use the funeral of Turk to infuriate the clan elders and draw them to our cause."

A combination of the wine and the calming effect of her in-law brought Meva back to her senses. "Thank you for your wise counsel. I will attend to the funeral arrangements, while you prepare for a foray into the land of the Roman."

As Rochlos had predicted, the elders of the clan objected. "The old ones have become tranquil with age. They no longer have the stomach to fight. I am ashamed," he said.

It took all of Meva's nerve to keep her head, "I will find a way to win them over even if I have to challenge each one to a duel. We can obtain the support of other clans and yet our own won't prepare to save their chief. Either the council will bend to my wishes, or I'll personally kill them all!"

Turk's funeral began to assume a life of its own. Meva decided to give their faithful friend a burial suited for a clan chieftain. Knowing that all Celts love a celebration, she invited the nobles from the entire Helvetii nation to participate. When questioned by the elders about the extravagance of such a funeral for a mere trader, Meva answered. "Turk brought more wealth and glory to this clan than anyone. Therefore, he deserves such an honor." She knew that Turk had touched the lives of many people.

The Mayri erected tents on the great plain that surrounded the oppidum, dug pits to roast the pigs, lambs, cattle and erected the hundreds of caldrons to cook vegetables to feed the arriving multitudes. Women baked thousands of loaves of bread, while men rolled vats of beer and ale from storage.

While Meva attended to the food, the Druids prepared for the funeral ritual. They commissioned a deep shaft to be dug on the wide, grassy plain facing Lake Lucerne. The diameter of the fifteen meter deep shaft measured five meters across. Alongside the pit, they assembled the ritualistic hollow tree trunk and a wagon with spoke wheels to carry the trader on his rounds in the next life. The life of a slave was spared when the Druids from the Helvetii capital arrived with a criminal, who had already been sentenced to death to accompany Turk on his journey to the otherworld.

Goods that Turk traded were laid alongside the cart; including amber from the North Sea, Etruscan and Greek wine amphorae, salt from Naking, tin from Cornwall and animal furs from the great forest. Meva even included jewelry from her personal possessions as a sign of her affection.

A Mayri artist crafted wooden hands and a foot to be buried with Turk, so that he would enter the otherworld with all his extremities. Records, written on pieces of leather, describing his trades over the decades would also accompany Turk to aid him when he returned to this world. As part of the rite, the Druids delayed the payment of all debts owed to and by Turk, until he returned to this life. In addition to the funeral preparations, each day, Meva climbed to the rampart and looked for her brother.

Clusium

Hugh, after tossing and turning in an attempt to get comfortable, finally fell in to fitful sleep. In a dream, he found himself sitting beneath the great stone arch of the Clusium gates. People and carts passed on both sides without disturbing him, or moving to get out of his way. What bothered Hugh most was his embarrassment over sitting in such a public place without any clothes. Though no one seemed to notice that he was naked, Hugh's ability to move from this public area was restricted by the fact that any movement would call attention to his dilemma. As he remained frozen in his predicament, Munli, the old Master Druid, who was also naked, settled beside him. "It is my custom to wander this world without clothes, so all that I meet must be in the same condition," he said to ease the triplet's discomfort.

"I have come to aid you in your search for your sister. In the city there lives a businessman named Arruns, whose wife was seduced by a rival. Arruns seeks revenge and is looking for some fierce supporters to avenge his dishonor. Wait beside these very gates and his attendant will approach you." Then the shadow of Munli disappeared and Hugh fell into a deep sleep. Unlike most dreams, which are forgotten with the coming of dawn, this particular one lingered and disturbed Hugh mightily.

The next morning just as the sun cast a shadow from the great arches across the ground, a small, black man wearing the leather collar of a slave approached Hugh, who rested with his back to the stone wall. "Are you one of those who war against the Etruscans?" the slave asked in Latin.

The dark color of the person's skin disturbed Hugh as much as the dream of the previous night. But he tried not to let his discomfort show. "My people have warred against the Etruscans, but presently we are at peace. Perhaps you seek a Latin or a Roman. They seem to be at war," Hugh answered.

"Are you a companion of the large warrior that circles the city looking for a way to enter unobserved?" the slave asked, brushing aside the comment about the Romans.

"I may know about the person of whom you seek, but why should I answer you?"

"Are your people ferocious and brave?" the slave continued.

"We are only afraid of the sky falling on our heads and of nothing else that exists in this land," Hugh boasted.

"Then my master is seeking you, and I am to take you to him."

Hugh clumsily arose from his seated position and followed the slave through the gates of the city to the door of a dwelling housing three floors. The Druid was taken to the rear of the building into an open area where a man in a toga lay on a sofa drinking wine and eating fresh grapes. Hugh was motioned to join the man and be served in a like manner. After some initial skirmishing over which language to speak, they chose Greek to conduct their business, partially to conceal the discussion from the slaves who attended them.

Mayri Oppidum

Druids, Celts, and Romans

Large chunks of ice from the mountains preserved Turk's corpse, while Meva planned the funeral to the final detail. She selected her finest dress and her most precious gems to decorate her still attractive figure. After strapping a jewel-covered scabbard with a similarly decorated sword around her waist, she deemed herself worthy to bury her husband's friend.

The bearers carrying Turk's body walked thrice around the oppidum toward the sun when they processed around the walls of the oppidum before heading for the burial site. In excess of a dozen Druids led the assembly, chanting the Celtic death song as they slowly made their way across the meadow. Meva led the nobles, townspeople, farmers, hunters, herders and their families.

When all had assembled in a circle surrounding the grave, the hollowed tree of life was lowered by rope to the bottom of the pit. The criminal was choked, stabbed and bashed on the head to claim his life before they dropped his body into the gaping hole. This sacrificial ritual cleansed the felon of his crimes and released his spirit to accompany that of Turk. Next, the wagon was lowered over the edge, followed by all the trade goods Meva collected. As each item was ceremoniously thrown on top of the wagon and victim, Meva called aloud for all to hear the connection of Turk to the item. Finally, the bearers lowered the body of the trader to join the burial items. With his legs stretched out, and lying on his side facing east, the remains of Turk joined the worldly possessions intended to assist him in his next life.

Then each in attendance selected a large stone from a pile near the mouth of the grave and tossed it into the opening. Because of the large turnout, the stones almost filled the entire gap. As Meva led the assembly to the funeral celebration, slaves finished the chore of filling up the hole by shoveling dirt on top of the stones.

Following the burial, Meva sat among the women gazing down at the great hall where the men enjoyed the funeral festivities. Her hand clenched and re-clenched the handle of her sword as her mind grasped the magnitude of the moment. 'I must convince the elders, or my Conel will perish.' Her mood equally divided between periods of uncontrollable anger and periods of deep-rooted fear. Only prayers to the Goddess Sulis enabled her to maintain her focus.

While Meva fretted impatiently, the bards sang of Turk's heroics far into the night. Preserving for the annals of his people, the story of the one returned almost dead to tell of his master's fate. As dawn broke across the hillside, sensing that the appropriate moment drew near, Meva climbed down the ladder. Striding to the head of the long table, she stared momentarily at those assembled then began to speak. Although uncommon, it was not unknown for a woman to address a funeral feast. Many awarded Meva the same respect they would have given Conel and put down their joints of meat and mugs of ale to hear what she had to say. She directed her words to the council of elders, assembled near the middle of the table, who sat frozen in humiliation. Without preamble, she spoke in stern, harsh tones, forcing her anger to dominate her fear:

> Warriors of Helvetii, why do we argue about who to blame?
> Are we behaving like frightened children cowering in shame?
> Conel set forth on an honorable mission that brought our nation pride.
> Now we stand and dispute his actions. Behind needless debate, we hide.
>
> On this day, we buried Turk whose valor we all know well,
> an example to children of one that defied the face of hell.
> Turk sacrificed his life to tell of our chieftain's lonely pain,
> Captured by the unworthy Roman and held by them in chain.
>
> To the south lives our enemy, who will destroy our Celtic way,
> if we fail in our duty to challenge and hold this opponent at bay.
> Old age comes to those whose courage falters before the evil foe.
> Rather death should take us quickly before others strike the blow.
>
> Are you warriors? Or are you rabbits, who hide when duty calls?
> Do you squirrel away your fortune behind your fortress' walls?
> Show the world you have courage to lend credence to the fight.
> Join me! Free your chieftain from the bondage of Roman might.
>
> For many eons, we bragged of our valor, and told of stories grand.
> Now is the test for us to know, unequivocally, where we stand.
> For the honor of the Helvetii Nation for the glory of our race,

stand shoulder to shoulder. Let each among us, take his rightful place."

Meva's anger penetrated the alcohol-sodden brains of the diners who roared in approval at her challenge to the council. Then, while holding her arms aloft to gain silence, she faced down the mighty warriors who sat enjoying the feast. When a semblance of silence returned, an assistant cut the golden warrior's torque from Meva's neck.

"This torque symbolizes the wealth I offer to the worthy who will join with the Mayri warriors to regain Celtic honor stolen by the Roman." she said as she placed the torque on the table and began to strip other jewels and golden bracelets from her arms and neck to be added to the pile. Her final contribution consisted of a jeweled scabbard and sword, a possession that the mighty in the land would prize. "My father, Ragelnos, gave me this sword on the day that I became a warrior. It serves a far better purpose if it helps bring my husband, and your chieftain, home."

The symbolic gesture of a woman giving up her prized possessions to regain the honor for her tribe, gripped the hearts of all those gathered. As though on cue, Rochlos and his son arose and added gems to the Meva's pile. Others of the Mayri followed suit until all those in the audience pushed forward to add their wealth. When all resumed their positions on the floor, Meva walked to the middle of the great room and stood directly in front of the small group of elders. She announced that she will, alone if need be, undertake a pilgrimage to free Conel. Then she let fear linger in their hearts, when she described the vengeance that her brother, Ragenos, would extract should she perish on the journey. Pounding on the table Meva strove to win their allegiance.

"Surely you do not expect to accept my husband's captivity and not answer my challenge. I will delight in taking a sword against one and all who sit on this council. I expect that in time I will grow weary, and one of you will emerge the victor. But no matter, I know within my heart that my brother, Ragenos, and my son, Mick, will extract great retribution. If you fail to act like men, then you will die like cowards and traitors. Your souls will roam this earth for eternity. You have my promise on this." Drawing a knife, Meva cut her hand to seal her blood oath.

A weary and dejected council met all that day and far into the next night before Meva finally gained her way and the elders capitulated. They opened the Mayri's treasury to recruit mercenaries from all across the Celtic Empire to join one great army and invade the land of the Romans.

To the amazement of all, the treasury of the Mayri seemed as though it was stored in a bottomless cauldron. No one had realized the extent of their clan's worth until this climactic time in their lives. Only then did they appreciate the contribution that Turk's trading made to the clan.

Ragenos, after receiving word that he was needed, rode through the night, constantly changed horses, allowing little time for rest and arrived the day following the decision to invade. "How could this have happened?" he asked his sister as he embraced her.

"Perhaps we angered the gods?" she answered. "I am heartsick with the thought of losing my husband and daughter all because of a slave. Help me, Ragenos. Help me save them, and if they were harmed, help me avenge them."

"You know that I will collect the revenge due you."

The war council led by Rochlos and supported by the clan elders quickly elected Ragenos as brennos, 'the one who leads.'

"If we are going to cross the Alps and invade a fortified city, we need far more warriors than the Mayri clan can provide, nay even the Helvetii nation can provide," Ragenos said as he met with Rochlos to plan the incursion. "We have to provide weapons and supplies to a fair sized army. Can the Mayri craftsmen accomplish such a task?"

"We can use the store of weapons that were produced and retrieved from the last time the Germans invaded in force. And we can augment those weapons," Rochlos answered. "What is the size of the force you anticipate to be successful?"

"I don't know. I will enlist as many as I can as quickly as I can," Ragenos answered.

Blacksmiths and bronzesmiths began to fire up their shops. Carpenters sent assistants into the vast forest to cut saplings for spears while older cattle were slaughtered for their leather. Provisions for a long journey were stockpiled and knitting looms spun in every home. The clan was going to war.

As brennos, Ragenos gathered a force of messengers to recruit across all the land that he had roamed from Iberia to Belgae. During the following weeks, the tempo in the oppidum reached a fever pitch.

Druids, Celts, and Romans

Enrolling the bards currently in the Helvetii countryside, Ragenos charged them to bring as many warriors to his command as they could. Young Druids were sent out as well to persuasively aid the call to arms.

Helvetii youth looking for adventure showed up within weeks of the summons. These first arrivals from the Helvetii were sent to the northeast to recruit other Celts from among the Tigurini, Boii and Volcae. The bards that traveled east along the Danube River as far as the borders of Thrace attracted warriors from the Tauirisci, Eracisci and Scordisci. Those that traveled west returned with soldiers from the Allobroges, Aedui, Arvenii and Biturigies.

When hearing that Ragenos sent out a call for assistance, warriors poured in from the Belgae federation that included the Belgae, Atebates, Nervii and a mixed Celtic-Germanic tribe, the Treveri. Soldiers from the Parisii, and their neighbors the Carnutes from Northwest Gaul, answered the call. Entire tribes, whose land could no longer support them, came with all their wives, children, and household belongings. These included the Senones, Ambarri, Auleric, Elitavios, Cenomani, Libu and Salluvi.

As the months passed, the recruits in the tens of thousands were housed in and around every oppidum in Helvetia. Keeping peace among the soldiers became a full time job for Rochlos and the Helvetii soldiers. The elders of the Mayri and the chiefs of the Helvetii, concerned with the strain such a large army placed on their diminishing resources, demanded that action be taken. To prevent further denuding of their land and the slaughtering of their livestock, Ragenos decided to have some of the army begin the long march south, when the most surprising group of all arrived at the Mayri stronghold.

The Gaestae famous for fighting fight naked came looking for plunder. Their appearance sealed the decision to move out in a hurry. No tribe desired to have the most feared mercenaries in all of Celtdom settle on their land for any reason.

Meva, much to her disgust, remained behind to host mercenaries that would follow. She also assumed the duty of training children to be members of the home guard.

The Alps

When all was deemed ready, the Brennos led an army of over twenty-five thousand over the Alpine passes. Rochlos continued in the role of supply master and gathered tons of grain and salt pork to supplement the foodstuffs the army carried until they reached the fertile grounds of the Po Valley.

Chapter 21
A Slave in Rome

Rome circa 387 BC
In his weakened condition, there was little Conel could do when the household manservant cut off his trousers, and he was given a white woolen toga. The garment made for a shorter person reached only to the knees of the tall Celt, so the servant did not need a girdle to cinch the garment. The first days of captivity seemed like an eternity to Conel who always had the freedom to do what he chose and to go where he pleased. The only light in the shed came from a small window with iron bars. Initially, he thought of prying the bars loose, but he would not fit through the window in any event. After giving up on the idea of escaping through the window, he used his fingernails to loosen the material holding the blocks of stone. After several hours of scratching, his fingers bled and the stone remained in tact. Overpowering a guard seemed to be his only remaining option. Unfortunately, he had no opportunity since the attendants shoved his water and food through a small slot in the door. Conel retained his sanity by thinking of his family and praying to his gods. Although he tried to maintain his strength, the confines of his prison limited his movements. As time passed, the half-ration diet began to take its toll and Conel lost weight, strength and the desire to escape.

After the first month of confinement, the Celt was given liberty to walk around the atrium for an hour each day under the watchful eyes of the city guard. This small act of kindness provided a glimmer of hope to the despondent chieftain. Soon, Conel noted a change in his station when the Romans began to serve him solid food instead of the liquid swill that barely nourished his broad frame. Initially, the meals had consisted of grain pounded by slaves and mixed with water into a mortar. 'The fact they are trying to fatten me up means they have found a use for me. I will have to bide my time and await my fate,' he pondered as he eagerly consumed the meal that was placed in front of him.

"On your feet, slave," the attendant ordered. Conel arose anticipating a walk around the atrium when the attendant surprised him. "Today, you will meet with our master. I must make you presentable. If you try to resist or make trouble, I have permission to whip you. Do you understand?" The Celt nodded, indicating that he understood.

Conel dry shaved and washed using sand to remove the prison grime. Thankfully, he was allowed to retain his moustache. When the manservant thought that Conel looked tolerable, he took him to Lucius Julius. The hunger-weakened Celtic chieftain decided it was in his best interest to play the dumb slave. Consequently, he pretended he could not understand nor could he speak Latin very well. In keeping with his ruse of being slowwitted, he decided to act as though he was clumsy. While waiting, Conel sat on the floor under instructions to rise when Lucius entered the room. He made getting up from the floor a greater effort than his weakened condition called for.

"Your isolation was meant to teach you that I am your master. Anything that I order, you will do! Do you understand me?" Lucius Julius demanded.

"I understand," Conel answered in a restrained voice, slurring the Latin as he spoke.

His granddaughter had been pestering him to have the Celt work the farm. Lucius Julius, who knew that the Celts were horse masters, hesitated to grant Julia her wish. The Julian house had floundered in the past several races. Lucius, who purchased only the finest horses, decided his driver was at fault and sought a replacement.

"I am told that your kind make excellent chariot drivers. If this is so, I will allow you to remain with my household only if you bring glory to my name. If you are not an expert horseman, then you will work on one of my farms till the day you die. Do you understand?"

"I understand."

"Tomorrow, you will take your horses and chariot down to the Circus Maximus, and we shall see if you live up to your people's reputation."

Turning to his manservant, Lucius Julius ordered that Conel be taken to his mounts. For the first time since his capture, he lapsed into melancholy. The horses reminded him of the home and freedom he might never again attain. With that thought in mind, he decided he would kill himself rather than be subject to life-long servitude, should he be sent to farm the land. Conel realized that his only hope for Turk to rescue him depended on his remaining in Rome. 'As long as I am allowed to be around my animals, I shall preserve my spirit.' The visit to the stables helped Conel learn a little about the layout of this large city with its multitude of narrow winding streets. He studied the city much the same way a hunter studied the forest by trying to fix positions and directions in his mind. Each time he turned a corner, he memorized where he had been associating the various land marks and buildings with the length of time he walked.

Upon arriving at the stables, he examined the animals first to make certain that they were healthy. Ignoring the stares of the other slaves and onlookers, he spent the next several hours cleaning their hooves and brushing down their chests, backs and flanks. Next, he examined the leather bridle and reins to insure they were still in working order. He noticed that the free-moving rings of the snaffle bits, which held the reins and harness, had become dislodged. After asking the manservant about getting the bit repaired, a metalsmith was called over.

"I have made a temporary fix. I will, however, need to take this to my shop in order to repair it correctly," the metalsmith said to Lucius Julius' manservant. "Perhaps it would be useful if he came along while I am doing work to make certain it is done correctly," the metalsmith said after pointing to Conel. "These Celtic snaffle bits are constructed differently than the curb bits used by the other charioteers."

Lucius' manservant agreed that it made sense for Conel to be present while the smith did the work. He failed to detect the slight Celtic accent the metalsmith placed on certain words.

Conel picked up the slur immediately and wondered whether the metalsmith intentionally mispronounced the Latin, but held his own counsel. After the metalsmith departed and after he had examined the animals, Conel turned his attention to the chariot's wheels and spokes. Conel fixed the bent yoke, attached the beasts to the chariot and led the team onto the field called the circus. The circus lay in a valley between two hills adjacent to the bridge that Conel and Turk used to enter the city. He memorized that knowledge. The circus included a u-shaped arena with seats provided for spectators. The chariots entered at the open end of the u and ran counter clockwise, southeast to northwest, around the track.

The manservant implied that Conel was to try out his team on the muddy oval track that ran alongside the spectator seats. As he drove around, several other chariots yelled at him while passing. Conel, aware that he was being challenged, wanted to test the composition of the riding surface. So he refused to take the bait, knowing that in his weakened condition it would be foolish.

On the second time around, he observed that the track was not level and slanted toward the grass where it rounded the infield. He concluded that on dry days there would be an advantage in hugging the inner grass when rounding the sharp turn. On wet days as indicated by the muddy puddles at the turn, he realized that this was an area he should avoid.

On his third rotation, he watched the other drivers as they roared passed and noticed that neither had full control of their vehicles. This, too, he stored away for future use. Finally, he indicated to the manservant that he was satisfied to the disgust of the onlookers, who waited to see how well the large barbarian could race. "He doesn't stand a chance," one yelled to the manservant. "He is too big and clumsy. My master's driver will win easily!" Not certain as to why he did it, Lucius Julius' manservant made a wager with the one who spoke. The other driver chastised him. "You are foolish for making that bet. Can't you see your rider is too weak to control his horses."

When he returned to his master's quarters, the manservant wondered whether he had been wise or if he had acted too rashly. Vowing to himself that Conel would feel the sting of the whip if he embarrassed the Julian household, the servant was uncertain if he looked forward more to winning the bet or to whipping the slave. Then he recalled the remark made by the second driver and thought, 'I must feed the Celt to strengthen him if I am to win my wager.' "You will have to prove yourself worthy before the master will allow you to wear the green of the Julian racing team."

On their return to the residence, Conel, in halting Latin, questioned the servant about the race, "How many times does a chariot have to circle the grassy plain?"

"Both the two horse and four horse chariots go around the track seven times," he answered.

"Is it like a battle? Do the drivers carry weapons?"

"It is a race, not a war," the manservant replied, wondering about the slave's mental capacity.

"Do the drivers of the chariots foul each other? Do they try to prevent their opponents from winning?"

"Of course, they do! Some even join with other teams and work together to prevent another house from winning. This is not child's play, and I am afraid that you may never be qualified to wear my master's colors," the manservant said, beginning to regret making the hasty gamble.

"Master, I know not horses," a very frightened manservant said to Lucius Julius. "I noticed, however, that the other charioteers, who were practicing, kept their distance. Their actions must count for something." He did not tell his master that he wagered on the next race.

From that night on, Conel bunked with the other slaves on a hard pallet set in a room some distance from the open court. The room, though lacking both light and ventilation, proved to be an improvement over his initial quarters. His meals improved as well with bread and olive oil being added. During special holidays, he was rewarded with olives, cheese and honey.

At the formal midday meal, the master of the household paid reverence to his family's ancestors, who Romans believed resided in spirit form. Before the family ate, the paterfamilias of the Julian family lit the incense burner and then laid out the meager offering of food and drink for the souls of the Julian ancestors that hovered around the premises. As a patrician family, their food was cut into in mouth-sized chunks and served by slaves under the supervision of Julia's mother who, since the death of her mother-in-law, served as the materfamilias for the household. Julia's mother acted as though she was afraid to be present in the same room with her daughter, who ignored her completely.

Even while enjoying such splendor, Julia would glare at Conel, whom she blamed for all her ills. Conel felt the presence of Julia whenever she was near. The young girl sneered at her former captor with a malice that would frighten a lesser person. He disregarded her expressed hatred, but wondered about its source. He could not have known that the mere enslaving of Julia cost her the opportunity to become a Vestal Virgin and bring honor to her family. Now the Roman female had only marriage to a minor family to anticipate, since none of the patrician families would consider having their lineage tainted by a former slave. Furthermore, Conel was surprised that neither Lucius nor Vopiscus seemed concerned with the lack of respect that the daughter showed her mother.

In Roman households, females were forbidden to drink wine, and a wife could be divorced if her husband smelled wine on her breath. Suspicious husbands would often kiss their spouse upon entering the home to establish grounds for divorce. Vopiscus Julius was considering kissing his wife because of the listless attitude she brought to her household duties ever since Julia returned. Her daughter had been performing more and more of the materfamilias' duties, a situation that alarmed him.

Circus Maximus

Elico, the metalsmith, who left that morning in good-humor, returned a worried man to his small shop near the bridge of Sublicius, the very bridge where Horatius Cocles delayed the Etruscan army from entering Rome. Elico had been taken captive many years before by an Etruscan raiding party and was subsequently sold to the Romans, who soon learned to value his skill as a blacksmith. During the intervening years his Latin improved to the point where he was allowed to become a citizen of this city-state. Now, that status was in peril. He had made a promise to a Roman citizen from the Aedui tribe to do what he could to free Conel; however, he had never expected to actually meet him. Now that he had, his Celtic loyalty bound him to keep his word. Even his slurring of the Latin speech to indicate his kinship to Conel could have cost him his position and perhaps his life.

Within the week, Conel accompanied by one of the lesser slaves of the Julian household arrived with the broken bit. Elico was both gratified and terrified to be in the presence of a Celtic chieftain. The slave that accompanied Conel was ordered to sit in front of the door to insure that no one entered, and that Conel did not try to escape. Convinced that he couldn't be overheard, Elico hugged his countryman then spoke in his native tongue. "Welcome to my simple workshop. I have met with your friend from the Aedui tribe, and I understand your situation."

"I can't express my joy," Conel answered, a little puzzled as to who the person from the Aedui tribe might be. 'Perhaps he is an acquaintance of Turk. Since I have not heard from him, Turk must be in hiding.' Conel kept these thoughts to himself. "I was afraid I would never hear the Celtic tongue again."

"I have given my word that I would help you escape, and I mean to keep that promise." Elico did not mention that a threat was made on his life, should he fail. "There is an upcoming celebration for General Marcus Furius Camillus who several years back triumphed over the Etruscans. The Romans always celebrate by having the victorious general parade through the streets while displaying all the war spoils he gained and the prisoners he captured. Perhaps that occasion will give us an opportunity to make good your escape."

"The Goddess Sulis will smile on you," a grateful Conel said.

"A word of caution, the Romans expect a slave to be servile in all things. To gain their trust which we need to succeed, you must master two things. First of all become proficient in the Roman tongue. Study how they pronounce words and structure sentences. They admire only those who speak fluent Latin. This is a throwback to the days when the Etruscans ruled. The Etruscans were too proud to learn Latin properly and were despised because of that slight."

"I can speak fluent Latin. I have been disguising my ability so that they might think less of me and perhaps provide me with more freedom. I will follow your advice, I will change my strategy."

"Secondly, be the most submissive of all the slaves in the household, even if you are beaten. This will lower their guard and perhaps provide you an opportunity to escape."

"You are a wise man, Elico, and I will forever hold you in my debt. Furthermore, I bind my people to this personal obligation."

Julia used every opportunity to make Conel's life miserable. The young woman took advantage of Conel's strength by requesting that he be one of the litter bearers every time that she ventured out. Often the litter descended Palatine Hill to the Forum for a shopping expedition, only to have Julia discover she had forgotten something, and she would then make the bearers retrace their steps.

On her less sadistic days, she would show off the wonders of Rome. The litter would stop at temples to Diana, Janus, Vesta and the triad temple dedicated to Jupiter, Juno and Minerva. Her comments would always downgrade the architecture of the Celts. One time while stopping at a stone wall that surrounded a cherry tree, Julia related the history of the tree. "Romulus himself planted this tree. While demonstrating his strength, he threw a dart from Aventine Hill all the way to this spot. It landed so deep that no one was strong enough to pluck it from the ground. After a time, the shaft from the Coneal Tree sprouted branches. Should anyone ever see the tree begin to wither, that person, under penalty of death, must call all the neighbors to bring buckets of water."

Sites of horror were among her favorite sightseeing spots. "When I am through using you as my personal slave, the army will torture you in the underground chamber of the Tullianum, before I have them toss your worthless body off Tarpenian Rock. As you know by now, all villains are thrown from the rock. I look forward to the day when your body is flung out into space." When Julia would finish making her declaration, she sneered and then laughed.

Conel did his best to ignore Julia and concentrated on learning about the layout of the city. He counted the number of times the chair turned toward his sword hand and the number of times it turned toward his shield hand. He memorized the number of street openings they avoided during their travels, and looked at every building, trying to imprint its shape on his mind. His resolve to escape was never far from his thoughts.

Julia did not have the opportunity to take the full measure of revenge on Conel that she had dreamed about, during her years of captivity. One day, following the conclusion of the midday meal, Lucius Julius announced. "I have reached an agreement with the Tillius family to obtain their warehouse on Aventine Hill. They bargained hard and would settle only for a connection with our family. Therefore, I agreed to the betrothal of Julia to their second oldest, Gauss Tillius."

The blood drained from the young girl's face. "The Tillius family is nothing but beggars. I'll not stand for it!" a bitterly disappointed Julia screamed at her grandfather. Then she used her small fists to beat against his chest.

The Senator was appalled at such behavior from a female child. He coldly looked at Julia's mother as though she was at fault for such unbecoming behavior. "The child will do as I say or both you and she will suffer the consequences. The decision has been made!"

Without rising from her seat at the table, Julia's mother backhanded her daughter across the face with all the anger she could summon. She did not intend to endanger her position in the Julian household because of any willful child. "You will obey!" her mother demanded.

When even the servants ignored her, Julia sulked in pain and misery. She could argue no more, lest her paterfamilias sell her into slavery for daring to disgrace the family. The hatred that she employed to endure during her long exile with the Celts began to flame anew, as she stared at the woman who bore her.

Po Valley
On orders from Ragenos, Rochlos led a party of Celtic warriors over the pass. The party consisted of contingents of Insubres and

Boii who could relate to their brother tribes already settled in the valley. The vanguard of the Senones and other small Celtic tribes, who desired to relocate south of the land of the Boii, provided the bulk of the warrior guard.

    Druids and bards of various tribes also accompanied the warrior chief. They would go forth, as messengers to the Celtic tribes already settled in the valley. They were authorized by Meva to explain the mission and to invite their tribe to join and share in the booty once Rome was destroyed. In addition, Rochlos set up intermediate camps along the way to aid the army that followed.

Rome

Within a week of his first race, during Conel's visit to pick up the mended snaffle bit, he and Elico connived to make the repair temporary. With a quick twist of his wrists, Conel could easily snap the bit, providing him with the opportunity to insist on seeing it immediately repaired. This ruse would give them a chance to continue meeting.

    "Tell any who inquire that a Celtic horse with its unique teeth structure needs a special bit that can only be adjusted by a master metalsmith. Even then, I can temporarily repair it at best. I will tell the same story should I be questioned," the metalsmith advised the chieftain, so that neither would be trapped into revealing their subterfuge.

    The morning of Camillus' triumphal parade proved to the most festive that Conel had encountered since he entered Rome. The weather was warm even by Roman standards, and the dust from the crowd walking on the dry field of the forum, adjacent to the circus, choked all who breathed deeply. Lucius Julius, one of the three pontifices, had planned well to avoid an unlucky day. He had the augurs of the temple release a flock of pigeons to observe the direction of their flight. In addition, a ram was led around the perimeter of the forum before being taken and sacrificed to the God Mars. The crowd stood hushed as the animal was sprinkled with sacred salt cake and undiluted wine. Then the priests stunned the beast with a blow to its head, following which they plunged a sacrificial knife into its heart. The blood was captured in a golden cup and poured over the altar, allowing the runoff to saturate the ground below. Next, the entrails were cooked over an open flame and shared among the pontifices, priests and augurs. Only when these rituals were observed did the pontifices stroll to the Bridge of Sublicius to invite the victorious army to enter the city.

The crowd noise grew ever louder in their excitement, and even Julia laid aside her hatred to join in on the celebration. The slaves were given time off from their duties to mix with the masses as they assembled at the forum. Conel, wearing the charioteer's green of the Julian family because he was to race for the first time in the circus later that week, followed submissively behind the other slaves of the Julian household. He used this opportunity to study the egress to the city for future reference. His height and garb allowed him access that the smaller, white-tunic slaves were denied, standing as they were at the rear of the immense crowd. When he, along with his fellow slaves, was finally brought to a standstill, Conel boldly made his way to a slight rise in the ground to get a better view. Those who already were stationed there grumbled only slightly as they stared in awe at the colors he wore.

Patricians and plebeians mingled with lower classes as they moved in one body to greet the victorious general. Wearing only rings as jewelry, the male patricians distinguished themselves by their white togas. Patrician women wore ornate necklaces and their finest earrings, along with pins and brooches to decorate their gowns. Many dyed their hair a golden-red for the occasion. On this day, women were allowed to drink wine and not fear that their husband would detect its aroma with a kiss. It was a day of fun and freedom for all the inhabitants of Rome, and the noble ladies in particular meant to take full advantage.

A tumultuous shout went up from the crowd, when the army war trumpets announced the arrival of the parade. Chained wild animals from foreign lands were led and at times dragged down the avenue. Animals that Conel had only heard about, and whose existence he doubted, were now paraded before his eyes. The children in the front of the crowd, who were allowed to pet the monkeys, surged forward only to retreat quickly at the approach of more vicious beasts. Elephants meekly followed their handlers while lions roared their indignation at being caged.

A large cadre of trumpeters followed the animals, announcing that the mighty legions who defeated the Etruscans were on the move. Conel stood entranced watching soldier after soldier parade past in a coordinated manner. The squadrons of marching men, led by standard bearers, were separated by mounted soldiers of the Roman cavalry.

From his vantage point, Conel could see Lucius Julius, sitting on a raised platform. A slave sat beside Lucius to remind him of the name of everyone of importance and to whisper the person's name when he processed past. Conel noted that none of the wives of the nobles were among those seated in places of honor.

As he stood among the spectators, there came a scene that sickened Conel. Thousands of Etruscans followed the wagons full of loot. Men with chains around their necks stumbled along. Legionaries cracked whips over their heads and onto the backs of those who did not move at a brisk pace, often driving the prisoner to the ground. No one, not their fellow prisoners nor those watching, stopped to aid the fallen. Upon entering the city, the captives passed under a wooden yoke to symbolize they were no longer men but beasts of burden.

"There must be over twenty thousand," exclaimed one onlooker. "They must have emptied the entire city!"

"This is a greater victory than the one over the Sabines," his companion answered.

"This victory far outshines the defeat of the Faliscans," cried the first on-looker; although, neither he nor his companion was alive at the time of the earlier victories.

"The slave markets will be busy for months to come," yelled yet another as he testified to the life that awaited the captives.

As evening approached, a second cadre of trumpeters announced the arrival of Marcus Furius Camillus, the victorious general in the siege of Veii. A mass of senators and magistrates, led by twenty-four priests of the Salii Order, walked in front of the general. The two dozen followers of the God Mars, dressed in military armor, halted at various places to entertain the crowd with their ancient hymns and ritual dances. These armed priests with their precision twirling and leaping mesmerized even the Celtic chieftain. They marched in formation until they arrived at a predestined spot where they halted their forward progress and began to parade in a crisscross fashion. The space between the marchers allowed little chance of a misstep. The priests in their short purple frocks clashed their daggers against their shields and shouted in unison. Then each would reverse direction and cross between others moving opposite them. Soon their step quickened, and the march became a leaping dance where each individual would swing a short sword above his head when he reached the climax of his leap. As quickly as they appeared, the Salii priests moved on.

Conel was surprised to see Marcus Furius riding in a gilded chariot. He had only seen these vehicles ridden by charioteers at the circus. The general dressed in bronze body armor wore a helmet adorned with feathers of an eagle. He carried a short sword on his right side encased in an elaborately decorated, silver inlaid scabbard. The cloak attached to his neck fluttered with the wind while the chariot moved forward at a steady pace, stopping only to salute the three pontifices.

The crowd surged forward, joining the parade marching behind the general's chariot that continued on to the plaza in front of the Temple. Here the general descended from his chariot, grasped the chains binding two prisoners, and flung them in front of the three pontifices, who had left their platform of honor and approached Marcus Furius.

"I, Marcus Furius Canillus, present the leaders of the villains, who opposed the authority of Rome."

Before the Pontifices could reply, the crowd took up the chant. "Execute them, execute them!"

Fearing the wrath of the multitude, the pontifices had little alternative but to submit to their wishes. The public did not witness the execution. Instead, the selected victims were taken to an underground chamber below Capitoline Hill. Later a monument would be built, signifying they were sacrificed to honor the great victory. Marcus Furius Canillus was awarded the highest honor, the corona obsidionalis, or siege crown, for his meritorious action. The crown was made from grass taken from the now destroyed city of Veii. The next highest honor, a gold corona muralis, was awarded posthumously to the soldier who forced the fracture in the wall of Veii. Hundreds of others proudly wore oak leaves to signify they took part in the campaign. Necklaces, armlets and coins stamped for the occasion were awarded as well. Units of the army received flags, indicating they took part in the campaign.

Following the ceremony, the crowd spread throughout the city to consume the free food and wine provided for the victorious occasion, and they celebrated until the daylight. Conel, on the other hand, made his way back to the Julian household. Remembering his earlier vision of the Roman General, Julius Caesar, he was sickened by the sight of thousands of slaves uprooted from their homes merely because they tried to defend them.

The day of the races dawned before Conel recovered from his distaste of Rome's brutal treatment of her victims. The household awoke amid a flurry of activity. Picnic lunches were prepared for the outing while the noble ladies complimented each other on their attire. The slaves were of good humor because they were allowed to wear ribbons of the household green. Thus honored, they were expected to root for the chariots of the Julian household. Even Lucius' manservant treated Conel with deference on this day. He remembered the bet he had foolishly made on a chariot driver who had never raced before. The other two drivers for the Julian household talked silently and strategized together, ignoring the tall Celt. Conel knew he would not get any help from that corner since all drivers were rivals for the attention of their master. One of the other Julian drivers had accepted a price to hinder the Celt.

The day was dry and the oval track seemed to be fast to Conel, when he exercised his horses. 'I'll keep to the inner portion when I turn the curves,' he decided while he watched the other drivers take wide turns when they shied away from the more dangerous tight maneuver.

The crowd hushed as the dozen chariots jockeyed for the first position. One of Lucius Julius' fellow pontifices dropped a white cloth, and the chariots took off on the first of the seven laps around the track. The track was sufficiently wide to allow four chariots to ride alongside each other. Conel intentionally lingered behind at the start of the race. Before he even crossed the starting line, he felt the whip from one of the Julian drivers. The leather struck his face just below eye level and broke his nose. He had no time to react and momentarily dropped the reins to wipe away the blood hindering his vision. Before he fully recovered, two opponents moved their chariots into his oncoming horses almost causing the chariot to overturn. Dust from the charging vehicles flew into his face, further interfering with his sight and breathing. Conel frantically grabbed and yanked on the reins to avoid a collision. Fear of failure plagued him as he wildly fought for his life. When instinct finally took over enabling him to get untangled and regain control of his horses, he lagged well behind the other eleven competitors. The closest chariot, carrying a driver wearing the blue colors of the Flavian household, was the only one distinguishable from Conel's vantage point. He knew that if he was ever to gain his freedom, he had to win this race. Ignoring the pain and swelling, Conel used his reins as whips, urging the most from his horses.

The first turn assisted Conel in gaining position as he passed two racers on the inside. Saying a prayer to Cernunnos, the Celtic horse god, for the act of desecration he was about to commit, Conel lashed his whip across the forehead of the nearest horse he passed on the curve, blinding the animal. Luckily, the crazed horse cut to the right in an effort to avoid the source of the pain, thereby crashing into the paired horse of the team. This change in direction caught those on the opposite side in a pincer movement between the chariot that was veering from the left side and the onlookers on the vehicle's right. Carts careened off the rails, crashing into the unprotected multitude aligning the track. The screams and moans of the injured and dying were ignored by those standing nearby, still mesmerized by the race and unheard by Conel, who had already rounded the curve.

He swept past the next tier of competitors only because his chariot was built for warfare and not for the pleasure of racing. Trying to knock the now hard-charging Celt from the track, the red driver used the a wheel of his chariot to lock up with Conel's rig. The sturdier built Celtic wheel easily sheared off the wheel of the offender, sending the opponent veering across the track into the crowd causing bedlam and severely injuring dozens.

Halfway down the straightaway, Conel passed the starting line, signifying that he had completed the first lap. The second curve gained Conel additional ground when he took this one on the inner edge as well. The hot-blooded crowd risked their lives leaning out onto the track to observe the competition. Several barely avoided the chariot of the Celt as he narrowed the ground needed to take the curve safely. The earlier wreckage slowed several of the competitors still in the race sufficiently to make them veer out of Conel's path as he charged passed. Steadily, Conel surged on and passed all but two of the competitors.

By the time he entered the fifth lap, Conel drew a bead on the leaders. One wore red, the other the green of the Julian house. Realizing that his freedom, even his very life, was in jeopardy, he took desperate measures. The turn near the finish proved to be all the more dangerous because of a downward slope that caused both his rivals to reduce their speed. Relying on an old trick remembered from his boyhood days, Conel leaped over the front of the chariot onto the link separating his two horses and walked the yoke until he stood at the heads the two beasts. Grabbing the stallions by their flying manes he screamed encouragement and urged them onward.

The other Julian driver, still in the race, was dumbfounded as a seemingly riderless chariot shot past on his left. This loss of focus cost him an opportunity to prevent the Celt from winning, a momentary lapse that would cost him dearly when those that bet on him came to retrieve their money. The remaining contender was too absorbed in controlling his own horses to realize that a driver stationed between two horses was riding his left shoulder. He was so absorbed, in fact, that he was unaware of the whip cracking toward his neck until the arm-strength of the Celt yanked him off his chariot. When Conel crossed the finish line and stopped his horses, the ecstatic manservant, who just won a year's wages, placed the standard of the Julian household into Conel's hands and told him to take a victory lap at a slow pace.

Instead of joining in the celebration after the race, Conel took his re-broken bit over to Elico's shop for additional work. At this meeting, they decided to wait until the Etruscan captives were moved out of the city before attempting an escape. At the appropriate time, Conel would be smuggled among the prisoners. Elico would follow several days later and free him once outside the city limits.

The days following the victorious race were busy ones for the Julian household staff. The long anticipated wedding of Julia and Gaius quickly approached. Lucius Julius made every effort to insure that the rituals for a valid marriage were adhered to in Julia's case, although, he remained highly insulted that his granddaughter had resisted his decision that she should marry. He had been heard saying to his manservant. "If that snip of a girl defies me, I will sell her to the Sabines. They know how to handle an obstinate slave."

Lucius Julius consulted the haruspices, as well as the augures, to interpret the will of the gods by reading the entails taken from sacrificed animals. The color and markings of the examined livers and gall bladders foretold that the wedding would be welcomed. Not being content with the readings, he also employed a fulgurator to interpret lightning during a thunderstorm as to its intensity and frequency. This too, was well received.

To further insure the wedding fell on a lucky day, Lucius Julius reviewed the sacred scriptures. The first day of every month and the day following were considered unlucky as was the ninth day before the ides as well as each monthly ides. Lucius knew some people considered the seven days preceding the ides to be unlucky as well, but he considered such judgment just superstition. The entire third month and the first half of the fourth were also avoided as were the days when the entrance to the underworld was open. Because of potential conflicts, the great holidays also had to be avoided, because a great many of the invited guests would be unable to attend. After exhaustive research and much reflection, Lucius Julius finally selected a date.

On the day before the wedding at the family's midday meal, Julia asked permission to address Conel the slave. Because of the upcoming rituals, she was granted permission for this unusual request. "You, slave, have destroyed my future. I have considered leaping to my death from the Tarpenian Rock because I betrayed my family by being taken as a slave and coming back to disgrace them. If you had any honor, you would have killed me.. Even if I had to die in disgrace, you would not endure pain from such an act. I mean to live so that you may still suffer for bringing me home." Julia handed Conel a thin sheet of lead with his name inscribed. Not knowing what to do, Conel thanked her.

"You ignorant barbarian, I have just given you a curse tablet and for that you thanked me. I asked the gods to damn you and your entire race, and I pray that one of my descendants will deliver the killing blow."

As she awaited the groom's arrival, Julia knelt before the shrine to her ancestors, and dedicated the bulla that she had worn since childhood in their honor. She then meekly allowed her mother and the attendants to dress her in a gown that flowed down and covered her feet. This gown was tied around the waist with a woolen band and secured with the knot of Hercules, the guardian of wedded life. Only her new husband could untie such a knot. To remind her of the ancient custom of acquiring brides by the rite of capture, a spear was used to divide her hair into six locks that were tied by ribbons. She then gathered a wreath of flowers from the family courtyard and awaited her groom. The atrium was decorated in flowers through which the wedding guests had entered an hour before sunrise. Julia and Gaius clasped hands and consented to be married before the assembled guests. Julia, by the words of her marriage vow, acquiesced to be taken into the family of the groom and to be owned by him as though she were chattel. Then she and her new husband sat on sheep pelts provided by animals killed especially for the ceremony.

The wedding feast was attended by all who lived in the household, with the exception of one slave. Conel hid in the shadows as Gaius pretended to capture Julia and drag her off, surrounded by a procession of his friends. The Celt would never see the vengeful Julia again, but the memory of her curse would remain with him for the rest of his life.

Chapter 22
Etruscan Encounter

Clusium circa 387 BC
Una sat partially clothed for most of the morning as Vulcan destroyed mold after mold trying to capture her image. She could tell he was disturbed and not focusing on his work. She was certain that the running argument that he had with his spouse for the past several months caused his unrest. Furthermore, she was convinced that she was central to that argument which bode her little good.

In a different part of Clusium, forewarned by his dream-talk with Munli, Hugh waited patiently for the Etruscan to begin the conversation.

The dainty Arruns sat idly sipping his wine and munching from the tray of grapes and cheese while taking the measure of Hugh, who faced him from the opposite couch. Arruns wondered how much he could trust the barbarian. When he decided, he would then know how much he would tell him. Furthermore, he was curious about why a small party would camp outside the city. For the past week, slaves from Arruns' household spied on the Celts, following them wherever they went. 'What do they hope to learn?'

'Either I have a simpleton or a very cagey negotiator sitting before me.' Arruns could not decide which one of those two extremes Hugh represented. Being a prudent businessman, he decided that a discussion regarding trade would be his safest course of action. Then if the Celt could not assist him militarily, he could pretend it was a case of mistaken identity and dismiss the barbarian without showing his hand. "I own a vast grape orchard west of the city, and I produce the finest wines in this entire district. A situation has arisen, the Latins have cut off the southern trade routes, forcing me to pay too much money to ship by sea. Therefore, I'd like to establish friendly trade relations with the Celtic people to our north," he said in his most formal business tone, trying to intimidate the giant without letting the Celt know that he was completely afraid of him. 'It never pays to disclose too much.'

To the discomfort of the Etruscan, Hugh sat quietly for a few moments. 'This is not the conversation that I anticipated,' he thought. 'Perhaps, I should play along for a while to see what develops. I can always become a bully, and if need be to extract what I need to know.' With this in mind, he assumed the demeanor of a trader. "My people reside north of the Alps. As you may be aware, we can't grow grapes equal to the quality cultivated on your land." Hugh wasn't sure of this fact, but it made sense.

"If I were to make an agreement with you to redirect my trade northward, what could you offer me in return?" Arruns asked, also puzzled by the direction the conversation was taking.

"Our people, great artists and metalsmiths, could easily match the value of your amphorae of wine with items of equal worth. In my travels, I observed that your city has few iron ore mines within its territory. We could fill this need as well." Hugh noted the businessman's excited reaction when he considered the implication of iron weapons.

"How could I be assured that my merchandise would reach your people north of this mountain chain of which you speak?" Arruns let his greed take over, 'What if I could break the monopoly that the city of Populonia has over the iron trade? I would be a very, very rich man.'

Watching Arruns' eyes, Hugh immediately realized that he had gained a tremendous advantage and replied, "To consummate such a bargain there is one favor that I need from you."

"What can I offer to seal our friendship?"

"I need to know the whereabouts of a tall, red haired, Celtic maiden, whom I know is held captive in this city," Hugh said.

"I believe I know of whom you speak. I can help you, if you could assist me in avenging my honor," Arruns answered, omitting that he recently forced himself on Vulcan's red haired slave.
"Tell me, what can we do to help avenge your honor?" Hugh asked. The two representatives of significantly different cultures spent the remainder of the day discussing their objectives.

The moon had already arisen before Hugh returned to his camp. The Celts listened quietly to what Hugh told them. When he hesitated a moment, Mick interrupted. "Let me get this straight," he said, "That Etruscan will aid us in releasing our sister only if we gather an army to invade some city and defeat some rival of his?"

"In essence, that is the offer on the table. He is, however, also interested in a trade agreement," Hugh added, knowing that last statement would excite his hot tempered brother.

Danous, who normally remained mute when the warriors argued, took this opportunity to speak his piece. "I suggest that Roith return to his oppidum and gather the strongest force he can muster. Mick and Hugh should remain at the camp, in case Arruns tries to make contact. Meanwhile, Katlyn and I will enter the city disguised as traveling musicians. We will attempt to locate the house where Una is kept and free her if we can. If not, we'll stay in the vicinity to lend our help if we get the opportunity."

"When you find the house where Una is detained, I want to know immediately!" Mick demanded. Danous yielded to Mick's demand. All nodded agreement to the plan the bard devised. Without hesitation, Roith set out for the home of his people.

Po Valley
Ragenos was delighted to have the cold, rainy mountain pass behind him. He wondered aloud about conditions in the dead of winter, since the rivers were frigid even at the height of summer. The Celtic general led the final force of the army Meva ordered assembled, including the legendary Gaesatae. Ragenos smiled to himself when he noticed that the Gaesatae did not shed their clothing to meet the frigid weather of the mountain passes. He and Tomas tried to keep the lesser known mercenaries from challenging them. Defeating one of these fearsome warriors would be worth the possibility of death; however, to entertain the troops, he allowed a few of challenges to be met in single hand combat, which in every case the Gaesatae won.

In the two confrontations that Ragenos personally participated in to gain control of this unruly bunch, he decided to forgo the verbal posturing and take on the opponent directly. One time, the Gaesatae backed down, claming he did not want to kill the Brennos, of the army. The other time Ragenos had to slay his adversary. He passed the knowledge of avoiding the verbal posturing onto Tomas, who also put it to good use in his efforts to maintain order.

Delighted as he was to have the treacherous passes behind him, Ragenos was even more delighted with Rochlos' organization. At the end of each day's march, messengers led them into fully stocked, fortified campsites. When they were several days travel from the mountains, he encountered the massive camp of the Senones, a tribe forced to relocate due to overcrowding and one that intended to remain after their mission has been completed. Furthermore, the number of tribes from south of the Alps, that sent warriors to join his army, dumbfounded Ragenos. Each day, many warriors of the Insubres left their oppida to follow their northern brethren in search of plunder.

"You will marshal over thirty thousand warriors when the Boii send their commitment," Rochlos told him when the two finally met. "The Boii have also pledged to send guides, who will take us through the forest to Rome where Conel is held captive."

"How many more days will it take before we join with the Boii?" Ragenos asked.

"It would only take two days if you and I traveled alone. With this herd, however, it will take several weeks," Rochlos answered with a weary smile on his lips, which Ragenos noticed did not reach his eyes.

Boii Oppidum

Roith was surprised at the activity he found when he entered the fields surrounding his home. Farmers were harvesting grain much earlier than normal while hundreds of warriors were staging mock combat drills. "What is going on?" he asked the first group of soldiers he came upon.

"Roith, it is good that you have returned. Haven't you heard? We are going to invade the south to free some northern chieftain who got himself captured. He must be important because every warrior in the tribe is going."

"What is the name of the chieftain?"

"I don't know. You will have to ask your father."

Roith was flabbergasted when Dhulack told him that the Romans betrayed Conel. "We heard that Una was captured by renegade Insubres, and we sent scouts to follow their trail. The Mayri trader, Turk, made it back across the mountains and told the Mayri about Conel's capture."

The news that Roith had for Dhulack about Una's enslavement was even more intriguing. "We saw her likeness carved from stone, and her brothers immediately set out for the city where she is held captive."

"What a catastrophe. The Mayri send two messengers to our land and both of them get captured," Dhulack said, almost to himself. "I had better get the troops ready to move out as soon as the others get here."

"What others?"

"Conel's brother, Rochlos, came to recruit our fighters. Someone is leading an army from across the Alps. Because of our association with the Mayri, I promised him that we would assist them. I'm glad you are here. You can serve as one of the guides."

"Since Una is being held captive between here and Rome, we should probably free her first. We have little time to lose. Lead your men toward the Etruscan City of Clusium. Una' brother is camped outside the walls, and he might do something foolish if we don't hurry," Roith announced. "In the meantime, I will ride north and meet up with this so-called army and guide them on a shorter route." After eating and changing horses, Roith turned his mount to leave the oppidum, but not before a finale admonishment to his chieftain. "Father, don't forget. Our objective is to free the prisoners. You don't have to fight every Etruscan you meet on the way." Dhulack laughed as he waved off his second-oldest son, knowing he had no intention of following the young man's advice.

Clusium
Fortune shone upon Danous and Katlyn for they joined up with a group of Etruscan minstrels who traveled from city to city. They came to Clusium to entertain at a funeral attended by many of the city nobility. The crowd laughed and clapped every time the young Celtic bard fumbled with the Etruscan tongue. Even as they sang and strummed their lyres, Danous and Katlyn searched the faces of the crowd for any sign of Una. At the end of each performance, they asked about the sculptor who created that marvelous work of art displayed on the temple at Tarquinii. Most knew of the master sculptor, but no one had seen him for some time. "Perhaps he is at some other city displaying his work," the people would say.

One or the other would leave the city daily and report to the two brothers whose tempers were growing shorter as the time passed. "We can't just sit here and wait," Mick said. Finally, he wore Hugh down to the point that he agreed to act if Roith was not back within the next seven nights. Danous, who was the messenger that day, hurried back to the city to redouble their efforts to find the missing girl before Hugh could no longer restrain Mick.

Rome
Meanwhile, fortune had smiled on Conel. After he had captured the honors with his fourth win in a row, he was given free rein to wander the city without a companion. His original intent to quickly escape was replaced with a growing desire to get even with those

who held him captive. He climbed the seven hills that made up the swarming city and wandered the narrow alleys and streets, looking for any and all weaknesses. The green embroidery around his slave's tunic made him recognizable anywhere he wandered. Young children stopped him and begged him to teach them to drive a chariot. "My father will pay you lots of coin and even grant you your freedom if you drive for our family," Conel was often told during his wanderings. The thought of freedom was inviting, but the desire for revenge grew stronger.

During the few times they met, Elico begged the chieftain to forget retribution until both of them could safely escape. Only the pleas of the metalsmith prevented Conel from immediately slaughtering the entire Julian household. "Our time will come. I promise," Elico entreated.

Po Valley

As he peered down into the vale, Roith had never seen such commotion in his entire life. Thousands of people, wagons and animals made their way in long, dusty lines across the landscape. Turning his horse in the direction of the centermost line, Roith headed into the dust storm. After stopping sporadically to ask for the brennos, he was finally given an escort to a group of riders deep in conversation. He gave an arm salute to the largest of these men, hoping he had identified the headman. Ragenos, looking up at the young horseman who had interrupted, indicated that he should take a place at the back of the line. A second look at the man's clothing told him that he was from the Boii. "Are we nearing your oppidum?" Ragenos asked, hoping for an affirmative answer.

"I have come to lead you directly to the Etruscan town of Clusium. Can we pull over to where there is some quiet so that I may inform you about what has occurred?"

"There is no place where we can speak quietly," an amused Ragenos answered. "Speak your piece loudly so all may hear. That will save me from repeating what message you bring."

Roith introduced himself to the leaders of the Celtic army and began to tell his story.

Rome

The invasion of Etruria by a Celtic army numbering in the tens of thousands could not go unnoticed. The word spread to the city, where the Senate led by Lucius Julius was in session. He, along with the others, listened intently to what the courier had to relate. "They have departed the land of the barbarians, bypassed the city-state of Arezzo, and are headed down the valley of the Tiber in the direction of Perusia."

"When you say there are tens of thousands of these barbarians, surely you jest?" Lucius Julius asked, demanding an answer by the tone of his angry question.

"No, my Lord, I only wish I did. I disbelieved those who told me, and delayed my report until I could confirm the information personally. There are thousands armed to the teeth. They do not come in peace."

Turning to his fellow senators, Lucius said sternly, "Let us retire to some privacy where we can discuss this fully. Such an army invading the land to our north is a direct concern to the Senate. Then he thanked the courier for his report, and informed the weary traveler he would reward him for his perseverance.

"We cannot let the populace know that disaster may be on the horizon. My priests have informed me that a voice was heard announcing that the Gauls were approaching, and they would sack Rome," the Chief Priest of Rome announced to the members of the Senate who gathered around Lucius Julius. "I recommend that we erect an altar to the God Aius Locutius in gratitude for this most timely warning."

"We do not know if this army is the Gauls that the gods warn us about. I agree, however, to build such an altar," Lucius Julius said to the high priest. Then he turned to another messenger and ordered him to deliver a message to Marcius Furius Canillus and have the general come to the Julian household.

Clusium

The grace period of a week ended without any word from Roith, nor any sign of help from the north. "I say we find a way to enter the city. Once inside we will easily find our lost sister. I can assure you," Mick insisted as he oiled his sword.

"Let us wait until nightfall, and discuss the situation with either Danous or Katlyn, whoever comes," Hugh said.

"I'll give you one more day. Then I will act on my own."

Meanwhile, the word of an advancing force of Celts reached Arruns, who, upon hearing of their location and direction, had the messenger killed in order to insure his silence. He then sent his envoy to Hugh's camp with a wax-sealed letter asking him to follow

Druids, Celts, and Romans

the servant to his house. The servant returned before nightfall with the news that the camp was deserted.

Through pure chance Danous, while performing on stage, noticed a tall person, whose face was covered with a cloak, move clandestinely from pillar to pillar in an entryway across the square. 'Could that be Mick?' he wondered since neither of the brothers was at the camp the previous evening. Turning ever so slightly, he looked for Hugh, but he could not distinguish anyone fitting his stature. The tall person was now moving out of his sight, and he knew he had to act quickly. Pretending he had fainted, Danous dropped his lyre and fell face forward toward the ground, grabbing the nearby Katlyn for support as he fell. "Are you ill?" his concerned companion asked.

"We have to get out of here. I think I spotted Mick across the square. He must have made it past the guards at the gate. We need to find him or he will surely get himself killed."

"Friends," Katlyn announced in a loud voice, "my bard had taken ill and we must recess for an interval."

A cry of "continue, continue" went up from the crowd.

"We will return shortly," she promised as she assisted the now prone Danous to his feet, and quickly carried the small bard across the square.

"Where did he go? Do you see him?" Danous asked as he looked around even as Katlyn was carrying him.

"What was he wearing?" asked his companion.

"A white cloak with a purple border, wherever did he get it?" After they had moved a safe distance from their audience, the two decided to split up. Danous went through the entrance of the building where he had seen the fugitive, while Katlyn took the street to the left. She had not gone a far before she noticed the tall person to whom Danous referred. 'That is not Mick. He isn't broad enough.' Then she realized the person's identity and uttered aloud, "May the Goddess Sulis preserve us," while she hurried toward the stealthy creature, the figure turned, bearing a knife. Looking at the streaming clump of red hair, Katlyn exclaimed. "Are you Una?"

Quickly recovering from nearly stabbing the speaker, the dazed escapee could not believe how wonderful the Celtic accent sounded and asked, "You know me?"

"We have been looking for you for months. I am with your brothers, Hugh and Mick," Katlyn responded.

"Take me to them as quickly as you can. I am being followed even as we speak."

"I don't know where they are. But Danous is with me now, and we will get you to safety." As she spoke, the bard rounded the corner of the building and rushed to join the two.

Using a stolen donkey cart, the couple smuggled Una out of Clusium to the relative safety of their camp. Katlyn and Una both hid beneath the refuse in the cart to make the guards at the gate believe that only one person, a male, left the city. Upon arriving at their campsite, they chose sufficient supplies to last for several days, leaving the remainder, and then made a new camp within sight of the old. Danous explained that Arruns, an Etruscan merchant, was already aware of the camp's location. "I'm leaving some of the supplies as a cover, in case the Etruscans connect your disappearance with our visit. Nonetheless, we must remain within eyesight to spot Mick and Hugh when they return."

Rome

The Senate sat in session while the envoys selected from the eight ruling families were assembled to receive their final instructions. The envoys from the house of Julius were being sent to the Etruscan City of Vetulonia, located between the Ligurian and the Tyrrhenian Seas. Others went to different cities with the Fabii family assigned to the city of Clusium.

Three brothers led by Quintus, eldest son of Ambustus Fabius, were chosen last, following a great debate among the many senators. Lucius Julius an arch-enemy of the Fabii gen, thought them to be too hot headed to serve as ambassadors. Others believed their temperament would panic the uneducated barbarians from the north and send them scurrying back to their homeland. "The barbarians will wilt when representatives from Rome appear," these supporters claimed. As a consequence, the Fabii brothers were given vastly differing instructions about their mission.

Lucius Julius was of a different persuasion. "I have a Celtic slave in my household. Although uneducated, he is not afraid to fight. Look at his ability to handle horses. He does not shrink when other drivers challenge him. No, I think it would be foolhardy to encourage the hotheaded Quintus Fabius to negotiate with such people. Order him to simply observe and report back to the Senate if his party is the one to encounter the barbarians."

The Fabii saw their mission as an opportunity for their family to gain glory. Quintus Fabius, in particular, had no intention of missing such an opportunity.

Clusium

The farmer was none too pleased to provide transportation for the two massive Celtic bandits as his wagon rolled toward the gates of the Etruscan city. He maintained his silence on account of the life of his oldest son, who lay covered by the same vegetables as the Celts, was at stake. Once within the city gates, the two quickly departed with a warning to the very frightened peasant, and began their search for Una. Hugh could not persuade Mick to be patient. His brother grabbed the nearest well-dressed male and demanded under threat of death that he lead them to Vulcan's residence. Fortunately for the terrified native, he knew the whereabouts of the sculptor and brought the savages to the vicinity of the house. After pointing out the location, he fled.

The door slave lost his life when he tried to give an alarm. Mick dragged his body into the entryway in order not to call undue attention to their break-in. Unknown to the brothers, even before the two burst into the atrium, the household was already in a panic over Una's flight. At that very moment, a manservant was reporting to Vulcan that he had apprised the city guard of her escape, and they turned their entire force out to join in the search. "Where is my sister? Where is Una?" Mick demanded in the Celtic language after he and Hugh gathered the household occupants into the eating area.

"Who are you? What do you want?" insisted Vulcan, speaking in Etruscan.

If it weren't for the seriousness of the matter and his concern over the whereabouts of his sister, Hugh would have burst into laughter. He allowed the two angry males to shout at each other in languages that neither understood. After several outbursts from each, he finally stepped in and took charge of the situation.

"Do you, or does anyone here speak Greek?" Hugh asked in that language.

"Of course, I speak Greek. Do you think that I'm a barbarian?" Vulcan answered.

"You will be dead unless you show some respect and answer my question!" Mick shouted as he joined the Greek conversation. "Where is my sister? Where is Una?"

Finally, Vulcan realized why the tranquility of his home was disrupted. "Your sister is no longer here. We do not know where she went."

"What do you mean she is no longer here?" Mick shouted.

At this point Hugh again interrupted and asked in a lower tone of voice. "When did she leave?"

"She escaped just this morning," Vulcan replied. "She went to the market and failed to return. We are beginning the search to find her." Desiring to get these two angry young men out of his home as quickly as he could, he told them she headed toward the city gates. Without looking back, Mick raced out of the house with Hugh reluctantly in pursuit. The Druid tried to contain his brother until they could develop some type of plan, but Mick was determined. The two charged down the hill with their swords drawn and ran through the narrow streets in the direction of the city gates. Meanwhile, Vulcan ordered his manservant to alert the city guard that two wild and armed Celts were loose in their domain. He then had the other servants unlock the chains securing the dead door slave and haul his body to the city dump.

As he turned onto the open space between the last building and the city wall, Mick skidded to a stop with Hugh almost plowing into him a few moments later. "We just can't charge across this open area. And besides, we don't even know if she has left the city," Mick announced as though Hugh were the deficient one. "Why couldn't she just stay put until we got here?" he muttered as much to himself as to Hugh. The two brothers ducked into the entryway of a building to give them time to consider their options. From their vantage point, they could observe the guards at the gate searching every wagon that departed. "They apparently have already been warned that we are in the city," Mick said.

"Not likely, since we can outrun any servant in the sculptor's household and no horses passed us. We'll first search the city before we try to get past the guards," Hugh decided. "Let us stay near the gate, so we can see either Danous or Katlyn enter."

"If we are unable to find her within a few days, we will steal some horses and fight our way out," Mick announced.

Outside Clusium's gates

The party bearing the Fabii brothers arrived with great pomp and demanded to be brought to the king for they bore instructions from the Senate of Rome. The guards, who were on alert because of a escaped slave and two wild men loose somewhere in the city, refused to pay attention to the envoys. News of an approaching army had already reached their ears, and the residents were growing frightened. The appearance of Roman ambassadors added to the panic. Rumors spread that the Latins were on their way to lay siege to Clusium. With the recent defeat of Veii on their minds, the unrest of the citizens verged on hysteria.

The Fabii were ordered to remain outside the gates until the city council met with the king. The council ordered that preparations for a long siege be put into effect while they kept the Romans waiting. Messengers were sent out to the countryside to call for the farmers to harvest what they could and destroy what remained. The standing army was put on alert and auxiliaries were called up. Families residing outside the city began to seek the safety of the walls, further adding to an already frightening situation. Among the citizens, only Arruns kept his composure, believing that the army consisted of Celtic forces coming to do his bidding. In the midst of all this confusion, the two Celtic brothers were spotted hiding within the holy place. The city guard, supplemented by a squad of regular army, surrounded the temple, but did not enter because they were afraid to violate the sacred grounds. Mick sized up the situation, took several of the priests as hostages and sent a young acolyte out to bargain for their safety. The city council was as apprehensive of the situation as the city guard. They had never expected to face such a situation when they agreed to serve their terms in office. Romans were outside the gates demanding to be allowed entry, wild men were holding hostages, and an army, or maybe two, was rumored to be approaching. Concern for the loss of the slave, Una, had long since vanished from their minds.

For several days, the bard and the females awaited the return of the brothers. When the pair failed to show up, they agreed that the two were trapped within the city or perhaps even imprisoned. Una took over as leader, and insisted they relocate to a position nearer the city where they could observe its daily life. While spying on the city from the vantage point of their new camp, they spotted the Roman delegation and saw that they were denied entrance. "The guards seemed to have tightened security," Katlyn noticed. "Perhaps you are a greater celebrity that you imagined," she said to Una with some amusement.

"More likely, they have discovered my brothers and are afraid that we may try to rescue them. Notice how carefully they check each wagon and how they plunge their spears into the contents.

They are looking for someone trying to sneak into the city," Una declared.

"They have other concerns as well," Danous interjected. "Have you observed that the crowds wanting to get into the city are much more numerous? Just yesterday the line reached to that group of trees, now it stretches over the hill and out of sight."

"Many enter but few leave," Una said. "Something of a greater threat than my escape is bothering them."

"I wonder if their concern has to do with that group that arrived several days ago and are camped within spear-lengths of the gate?" Danous questioned.

"Maybe," Katlyn answered. "Or perhaps Roith is coming with a band of his warriors."

"No, it is more than that," Una replied. "The people wouldn't desert their homes and gather in the city for safety if only a band of warriors were coming. I think it has something to do with the group over there."

"Let me sneak up close to them and see if I can hear anything of value," Katlyn suggested.

Meanwhile, Arruns volunteered to enter the temple and converse with the Celts, a suggestion the council quickly accepted. "What, are you crazy?" he asked upon arriving. "You were supposed to await an army and invade the city of my rival. What are you doing here?"

"We entered the city to rescue our sister," Hugh answered as Mick watched over the cowed priests. "Only to find out she has vanished. Do you know where she is?"

"I only know that she is still missing, and Vulcan is furious at losing two slaves. The escaped slave is not the problem. You and the army that approaches have that distinction."

"Roith," both brothers exclaimed at once.

"Who?" asked Arruns.

"Another of our party rode north to gather some troops to help rescue Una. He must be near," replied Hugh.

"For the love of Jupiter," Arruns cried. "What are we going to do now?" He thought for a few moments then exclaimed, "I know! Remain here and do not harm any of the priests. I will try to secure your safe passage out of the city." With that admonishment, Arruns took his leave.

Even though Katlyn did not understand Latin, she understood that this party spoke that language. Upon determining this fact, Katlyn returned to their hiding place. Una, who was fluent in the

Druids, Celts, and Romans

Latin language from her tutoring by Julia, took Katlyn's place as night fell. She returned after dark with news. "It seems that the Etruscans are preparing for an invasion. The delegation from Rome wishes to advise the Etruscans on how to handle the army when it arrives. They claim it is just a rag-tag bunch of barbarians. That means Roith is coming, and we must be prepared to present ourselves to him."

After Quintus Fabius waited for a week, he was finally allowed to present his petition. In the arrogant fashion of the Fabii family, Quntius took charge; the instant, he was presented to the King and the council. "I am an official ambassador from Rome. How dare you treat me as though I were a commoner? I should have been invited in and given a reception worthy of my rank. We have shown our strength when we plundered the city of Veii, and we know how to deal with barbarians. Either follow my lead or perish." Quintus, knowing that the army descending on the city consisted of Celts, further admonished the council for allowing two of the enemy to hide within the city. "You should storm the temple, behead those northerners, and hang their headless bodies from your city gates. This action will so terrify the invading barbarians that they will turn on their heels and flee." Exclaiming the superiority of the Roman, he cowed the terrified council, with the sole exception of Arruns.

Arruns believed he had knowledge of the Celts' intention, whereas Quintus had none. He pleaded with the council to save the lives of those trapped within the temple. "We can use them as bargaining chips for this force that is descending upon our city to kill them will only infuriate the invaders. I am convinced that I can redirect their encroachment to the city where Lucomo lives. Rather they lay siege to his city than to ours." He convinced the council to delay any decision until the invaders actually arrived, without giving the slightest hint that his quarrel with Lucomo might well be the cause of their invasion.

Late that day, a greatly relieved Arruns reappeared at the temple to tell the brothers that he arranged for a reprieve. "We will await the arrival of your friends before any decision is made."

Quintus Fabius, on the other hand, was furious with the decision. He plotted with his brothers on ways to encourage the Etruscans to war against the barbarians. "If they destroy this city, it will be Rome's for the taking."

North of Clusium

As the Fabii brothers plotted, Una and Katlyn left Danous to keep watch at the gate, and set out to learn the reason for Roith's delay. They sighted the vanguard of the army before they were more than a few hours from their starting point. Like Roith before them, Una and Katlyn were amazed at the sight they beheld. Expecting several hundred mounted troops, the females were overwhelmed at the lines of the march that stretched northward for leagues. Without waiting for her companion, Una, mounted on Mick's horse, galloped toward her countrymen. Roith, who was leading the advance guard, sighted the two riders charging toward them. Expecting to find an angry Mick, he was astonished to see the beautiful Una sitting astride her brother's mount. "We were on our way to rescue you," he shouted over the noise of the advancing column. Leaping from his horse, he hugged Una, who dismounted first. Then he hugged Katlyn in turn.

"Where did you find all these people?" Una asked after being introduced to Roith. "You have brought half the Celtic nation."

"We are about to camp for the night. Come, your Uncle Ragenos is the brennos for this campaign."

"My Uncle Ragenos, what is he doing here?"

At the campfire, niece and uncle exchanged stories. "Before we rescue Father, we have to find out what happened to Mick and Hugh," she insisted.

The orders were given that no camp would be set that night. They would only rest. "We will be at that city's walls before the sun comes over the horizon," the brennos said to his captains. "I want to look this enemy eye-to-eye before I destroy him and his city." Then, he sat with Una and Katlyn to learn about the lay of the land and the deployment of the enemy troops.

"The enemy has concentrated his forces within the walls of the city, which will be difficult to breach. Their defenses are made of a material that will not burn. The wall is over three spear lengths thick and over three spear lengths high," Katlyn related

"Furthermore, they have been preparing for this attack for several weeks. Farmers have been bringing wagonload after wagonload of food every day. I agree with Katlyn. It will not be an easy place to attack. We can count on a long siege, which will delay our rescuing Father," A downhearted Una spoke from her heart, wondering whether her comments just condemned her brothers or her father to die in chains.

"When the foe looks out over his ramparts and sees the size of the force that opposes him, I believe he will be in a mood to parley," an angry Ragenos said.

Clusium

The Brennos split his force in two with each line flowing as a stream passing a rock until they had the city surrounded. Ragenos decided to set up his camp on the land side to prevent those trapped within the walls from attempting to escape. Aware that the Celtic temperament could not endure an extended siege, he ordered the Gaesatae to assemble in front of the army and terrify the inhabitants. Ragenos knew the sight of thousands of blue dyed, naked warriors, astride their mounts and screaming about their accomplishments would soon bring the populace to the bargaining table.

The next morning, the guards sounded the alarm that their city was surrounded. Thousands of horn blowing, wild looking men, with bleached hair, beat their swords against their shields and screamed in a language that the terrified guards could not understand.

Chapter 23
Roman Army Defeated

Clusium circa 387 BC
Rumors led the city council to anticipate an attack by the northern barbarians for weeks. Unfortunately, the magnitude of the force surrounding their city froze them in fear, making them unable to act cohesively. The ability of an enemy to move so quickly without detection surely spelled doom to those trapped inside Clusium. Furthermore, the city guard had failed in several armed attempts to dislodge two of these barbarians who held Etruscan priests captive in the temple, and now rabble surrounded the city. The noise of the howling invaders screaming in a foreign tongue demoralized everyone in the hallowed halls of the palace as the terrified council members tried to gather their wits. If the invaders were not enough, the square in front of the palace was packed with thousands of panicky citizens, none of whom had any sleep, demanding that the council do something to protect them. Adding

to the confusion, the army leaders quarreled among themselves in front of the council about the best course of action.

One group felt that they should settle in for a long siege. "We have supplies enough to last us for months. There is nothing left in the fields for hundreds of kilometers. A force that large will either starve or move on in quick order."

Another clique thought that a quick attack by the cavalry could burst through the Celtic mob and escape to their sister cities. "Let the first squad leave through the south gate to summon aid from Volsinii. With an army at their backs despite their numbers, these ragtag invaders will disperse quickly enough."

Still others pleaded for negotiations. One of the council members was widely quoted as having said, "Have you all taken leave of your senses? They outnumber our forces ten to one. After the cream of our fighting men has been slaughtered, do you plan to man the ramparts with women and children or perhaps old people like myself? I have campaigned in the Po Valley against these warriors. Let me assure you that they are the most vicious fighting men, we will ever encounter. I say bargain fairly and pray that they will move on." Few listened to the last petitioners since none wished to throw themselves at the mercy of such barbarian riffraff.

Only Arruns and the Fabii brothers acted with determination, and each of these parties opposed the advice of the other, leaving the council more befuddled than before. Quintus Fabius arrogantly ignored the invaders at the city gates and demanded that the council declare war and run the rabble back to their homeland. "In my role as a representative of Rome, I will parley with this ignorant bunch of foreigners and describe what they will face should Rome enter the fray." Quintus rationalized that it would be to Rome's advantage for the Etruscans to do battle first, leaving the Romans with the simpler task of dealing with the survivors. The possibility of being made governor of this city after Rome intervened had also crossed his mind.

Arruns, fearing that his plot to overcome his rival Lucomo was quickly unraveling, hotly argued that he should be the one to meet and negotiate with the enemy. "These Romans are babbling nonsense. Have you looked over the city walls and seen the tens of thousands of savages who are encamped on our land? They will not leave with mere threats by these three diplomats," he told the terrified council. "I have met with the two Celts who hold our priests captive. I know how to deal with these people."

"How are you going to approach their leader? They will have your head before you take ten steps," Quintus Fabius retorted.

"I will take the two trapped in the temple as my escort. Surely, they will not attack their own kind. I assure you that I can tame the wild nature of those who surround our city," Arruns replied to the council, ignoring the Roman's interference.

After wasting the better part of that day and the several days that followed, the council decided that Arruns would be sent out to talk with the leader of the barbarians. They reasoned that all their other options would still be viable even if Arruns failed. Furthermore, the two Celts would be gone, leaving them with one less problem.

Under a flag of truce, alone and unarmed the businessman, dressed in his finest tunic, went to talk with the Celts in the temple. Hugh met him at the great bronze door and listened to his request. After conferring with his brother, the two agreed to accompany Arruns only if a group of the priests now held captive walked with them to the city gates. "After all," said Mick, "You enslaved our sister. How can we trust you?"

Their demand was agreed upon and shortly thereafter, Arruns and the two Celts, along with a half dozen robed priests, set out for the gates. The priests were freed as soon as Mick and Hugh passed from the city. Arruns courage left him, and he hid behind the brothers the instant the massive gates closed behind him. At that very moment, he saw a blue faced, naked warrior on horseback galloping toward him, screaming in a foreign tongue and waving a massive sword. He cowered before the charging savage. Because of the late hour with the sun directly in his eyes, the lonely Etruscan negotiator was further blinded by the dust storm created by the swirling horses of the Celtic mercenaries. Arruns leaned against the bronze gates to support himself, and fearfully prayed to any god he could recall before he worked up his courage to leave the relative safety of the walls. Charging horsemen drove their steeds to within spear-lengths of the threesome before turning around and racing back toward their lines. Unlike the timid Arruns, the two brothers howled back at the horsemen in the Celtic tongue. Looking into the sun, the Etruscan did not see some Celts approach on foot until they were within arms reach. Already at his wit's end, the Etruscan businessman jumped when the first one, recognizing Mick and Hugh, shouted with joy. The three were quickly escorted to Ragenos' tent.

"Etruscan, we honor your flag of truce. We are not savages," Ragenos spoke in Greek with his guttural, northern accent. "Quickly state the purpose of your business, and we will allow you to return safely before we destroy your city."

"I represent the city council of Clusium. We do not want war with your people. I am the person who sent for you to attack the city of my enemy, Lucomo," he stuttered in imperfect Greek, hoping the Celt would be able to understand.

"No one sends for a Celt," came the curt reply. "We answer only to our own needs and come at our own pleasure." With this comment the inquisitors, led by Ragenos, left the tent leaving Arruns unattended, as the uncle embraced his nephews. "I was afraid we would have to lay siege to get you two out."

The two brothers were taken to their sister, and the triplets hugged in joy. For the remainder of the day, the family ate and drank while Danous entertained them with his lute and stories of their journey.

Ragenos had in hand the report from Rochlos, stating that only an extended siege could overcome the sturdy stone ramparts of this fortress. As brennos of the Army, he was torn between allowing the Celts to avenge the capture of Una and his duty to rescue his brother-in-law from the Romans. Hugh's quick mind came to the general's rescue. "Uncle, if it is plunder you want, you should listen to what this man suggests," Hugh proposed. "Since our sister has been returned unharmed, his city should pay damages for her imprisonment, and we can then proceed to rescue our father."

After much discussion, they decided that Dhulack, chief of the Boii clan, would negotiate for the Celtic army. He was the most fluent in the Etruscan language. Arruns walked alone back to the city, even as the horsemen roared past him to continue their harassment of the city guards. He was given the responsibility of setting up the arrangements for the two sides to parley.

Quintus had his way with the council when he insisted the negotiations take place within the city walls on the open square in the shadow the temple. "The grandeur of the city buildings, the nearness of the gods and facing Roman negotiators will quickly drain the nerve of their representatives. Furthermore, we will allow only three of them within the walls. When they find themselves surrounded by the armored troops of the city, they will quickly come to terms." The Roman did not let on that he intended to antagonize the enemy until they had no choice but to attack the city. Ragenos saw the number three, a charmed number, as a good omen and agreed to the terms offered.

Rome

The moment had come for Conel's escape from Rome. "Conel, it's time for you to disguise yourself as an Etruscan prisoner," Elico said as he described the Roman preparation to move thousands of prisoners from the city. "An alien army is rumored to be at the gates of an Etruscan city. The Senate's afraid that they may attack Rome and ordered the army to position itself near Allia, a tributary of the Tiber. The call for volunteers has already gone out and many citizens have responded. With all the confusion, you will find it easy to leave."

Elico provided Conel with a ragged tunic reminiscent of the clothes the Veii prisoners wore. He tucked the tunic under his outer garment to smuggle it into the Julian household. Late that night, he arose silently and made his way to the front door. Although the slave chained to the door was asleep, Conel quietly snapped his neck, lest he should awaken when the door was opened. Next, Conel broke into the iron box that held the family's wealth to retrieve his gold neck torque and armband. Then, he made his way to the corral at the Circus Maximus where the prisoners were detained. Here he changed into the prisoners' tunic. He made his way past both guards and sleeping slaves by crawling on his belly until he found himself well within the prisoners' protective mass. Then, he drew his knees to his chest while lying on his side and tried to get some sleep.

Lucius was furious when the alarm sounded, soon after finding the body of the door slave. A search of the neighborhood and questioning of the guards at the city gate did little good. Only the paterfamilias of the Julian household saw the danger of an escaped Celtic chieftain, knowledgeable about Rome's defenses, linking up with the invading army. Daily, Lucius commanded his household slaves to comb the city looking for the escapee. Few outside the Lucius household were in a mood to look for a runaway slave amid all the commotion of forming an army to meet the menace of the barbarians, who at this very moment were rumored to be attacking the Etruscan City of Clusium. Even Vopiscus Julius was uninterested in searching for Conel. The Senate recently named Aulus Quintus Sulpicius to head the army and Vopiscus looked forward to acquiring honor and glory. Quintus Sulpicius put

Vopiscus Julius in charge of training the inexperienced citizens on how to march in formation, making the finding of Conel even less of a concern.

Quintus Sulpicius placed Rome on wartime alert and began to assemble a forty thousand man army to defeat the Celts should they turn their attention toward Rome. Messengers were sent throughout the expanding empire, from Veii in the north to Cumae in the south, demanding that more and more men along with their mules to transport supplies be sent to fill the ranks. The army victories at Veii, and earlier at Aequi as well as Volsci, had depleted the Roman cavalry. Because few citizens owned horses and could afford to equip them, the counselor decided to employ the phalanx, a tactic used by the Greek Hoplites. Long rows of infantry armed with spears and shields fought in close formation. The soldiers overlapped their small round shields to provide protection while they thrust their spears at the charging enemy. When those in front were injured or killed, the soldiers immediately to their rear stepped up to take their place. This tactical maneuver depended less on cavalry, but it called for a larger army of foot soldiers.

Clusium
The more the Etruscans attempted to satisfy the Celtic negotiators, the more belligerent Quintus Fabius became. Shrieking at the Etruscan nobles, he demanded that they reduce their offer, "Are you weaklings? These scum do not deserve a penny of reparation. Order them to withdraw immediately. If they fail to leave, tell them Rome will come to your aid."

After listening to the wrangling among the Romans, Dhulack finally lost his patience and started to storm out of the city. To the astonishment of all, Quintus drew a knife from beneath his tunic and stabbed the Boii chieftain in the back of his neck, killing him instantly. The nervous city guard surrounded and slaughtered the two Celts attending Dhulack before they could escape and warn their compatriots. The swift act of the Roman froze the terrified city council in a permanent state of inaction.

Arruns, afraid that his opportunity for revenge against Lucomo was quickly vanishing, spoke up first. "Let us kill the Romans and offer their bodies to the horde at our gates. This represents our only possible salvation."

Quintus Fabius, showing no remorse for the slaying, argued that he and his party could bring a large Roman army to attack and defeat the barbarians, "My brothers and I will return within the week with an army that will dwarf those surrounding your city. You just have to hold out for that short time."

The council quickly chose sides and a bitter quarrel over who to blame for the killing took place. After many debates, Quintus convinced the council that the damage could not be undone and no amount of retribution would satisfy the bloodthirsty savages who surrounded the city. "Your only hope is to permit us to go to Rome and return with an army." After winning over the council, the Fabii brothers were allowed to take their leave from the city over Arruns' strenuous objections.

"How do you plan to get past their lines?" Arruns asked.

"Simple my antagonistic friend, you will accompany us to prove that we are associated with the treaty. Since you are so friendly with the savages, you will explain to them that we are going to Rome to get additional gold and silver to meet their demands," Quintus said as he pointed to Arruns.

Ragenos interviewed the party of four carrying a white flag, and agreed to let them pass only after Arruns assured him that they would return within four days. The ploy worked and the Fabii brothers left with Arruns in the lead. That night at their first campsite, Arruns finally drifted into a troubled sleep. Satisfied that he no longer needed the Etruscan businessman, Quintus slit Arruns' throat before he could put up a struggle. If anyone bothered to look, he would have found the body of an Etruscan businessman within one day's walk of Clusium.

After failing to hear from the Roman delegation for five days, Ragenos ordered his army to circle the walls of the city and begin to sound the battle cry on the great horns. This deafening noise, along with menacing Celts surrounding the city, forced the city council to make one last effort to placate them. In the best interests of their city, they decided the battle should take place closer to Rome. Mules manned by slaves and loaded with treasure were sent out from the city gates. The Greek slave leading the parade was instructed to inform the Celtic leadership of the death of the Celtic negotiators, and that those responsible had sneaked off to Rome where they intend to defy the might of the Celtic army. Therefore, the Celts should look to that city for revenge. Because of the candid advice offered by this slave, Ragenos spared his life and gave him his freedom. While this took place, the citizens of Clusium hid behind their fortified city walls.

The Celts argued long and fiercely with the Boii pitting themselves against the remainder of the army. The Mayri and their supporters wanted to depart immediately for Rome while the Boii wanted revenge for the death of their chief. Tempers flew to such a degree that the two sides unsheathed their swords.

While the warriors argued, Hugh took Una to one side, and they had a serious discussion. As the two groups stood facing each other ready to do battle, Hugh, dressed in his Druid regalia strode between the two warring factions. His presence brought calm to both sides. When he had finally silenced thousands, he spoke, "We could settle this disagreement in the traditional Celtic manner with one champion from each side meeting in single combat. But before we allow this single combat, I request that Roith, the second son of the murdered Dhulack, meet with my sister, Una, who was most demeaned by her Etruscan enslavement." Hugh suspected that he could use their mutual attraction to his advantage. "If they fail to reach an agreement, then the champions should fight."

Roith faced a dilemma. On one hand, he was obliged to extract vengeance for the death of his father, and on the other, he admired, and perhaps even loved, the beautiful daughter of the Celtic Chieftain. Furthermore, he knew that the Boii's champion would surely lose to his northern counterpart. With sorrow in his heart, he agreed to the Druid's terms.

The two sat in the field between the forces and began their debate. "My father was killed in a cowardly fashion, and I have a right to restitution. Every person hiding behind those walls must answer for their failure to abide by international law."

Una, in turn, stated an argument crafted by Hugh. "I have spent a year in captivity. During that time, I came to know them and admire them as a civilized people. A cancer appeared among them, which caused the death of your beloved father. This malignancy, the Romans, holds my beloved father in captivity. Much of this army traveled over the Alps to win the release of the great chieftain of the Mayri. For this objective, your father gave his life. I do not know whether or not my father still lives. I do know that his life is now in jeopardy because the Romans were allowed free passage through our lines. Our duties to avenge your father and to save the life of my father have not changed. We owe it to the ties between our tribes as well as to each other to unite in brotherhood and continue on our mission. To save the fate of the entire Celtic nation, we need to destroy Rome." Then in her own way, Una won the heart of Roith by telling him of Munli's prophecy.

As a further incentive, she promised the Boii would receive a full half of the treasure surrendered by the Etruscan City of Clusium. Roith, too smitten to refuse the beautiful maiden, settled the dispute by cutting his wrist and taking a blood oath of loyalty to the brennos.

Rome

Arriving shortly thereafter, a mission of a dozen Celts demanded that the Roman Senate abide by the accepted behavior of nations and surrender the Fabii brothers. The appearance of these barbarians, dressed in multi-colored garments, arguing a point of law to the Senate, dumbfounded even the most learned of the noble Romans.

The Fabrii brothers had delayed their entry into the city in order to converse with Quintus Sulpicius, and tell him how pleased they were as they passed the lines of marching legionnaires. This joy was short lived when, upon entering Rome, they were called in front of the Senate to report on their behavior and to answer the charges of the Celtic delegation. Speaking for himself and his brothers, Quintus Fabius defended the action that he took against the barbarians surrounding the city of Clusium. "My fellow citizens dressed in the purple of the Senate, I'm here to describe the disaster that is certain to occur. Clusium stands as the first line of defense between the barbarians and our civilization. The Etruscans are good fighters, and, if properly motivated, will cause great harm to the horde that now faces them. I saw it as my duty to make certain the Etruscans could not allow foreigners free passage to attack our city. The ramparts of Clusium are stronger than the walls that protect Rome; therefore, it's the logical place for an encounter with the northern invaders. My action guaranteed that the Etruscans would have to engage and defeat the barbarians, thereby, weakening their own defenses and allowing our forces free access to their city."

Lucius Julius agreed with the Quintus logic, but he could not allow a rival to best him. "Your instructions were to spy on the size of the force and report back to the Senate. Instead you provoked them in such a manner that they can do nothing else but attack us. You are a fool sent on a fool's errand, and you made a mess of it. Now we must face the wrath of these mighty warriors. Did not these savages, as you call them, displace the Etruscans in the valleys north of the Po River? I tell you that they did. Because of your irresponsible actions, you have brought them to our very gates. The hundreds of Roman citizens who will be endangered at the river near Allia will be on your head. I appeal to the good sense of our Senate to turn you and your families over to these Celtic envoys to preserve Rome."

After much posturing, the Senate voted to deprive the Fabii family of their possessions and turn them over to the Gauls. While he saw it as cold comfort, Lucius took pride in his ability to persuade his fellow senators.

Lucius Julius' triumph in the Roman Senate faded, as the crafty Ambustus Fabius, Quintus' father, left the Senate, turned to the people and asked for their protection for his sons. "Plebeians of Rome, today the patricians who rule the Senate have voted to cast out my sons and their families. The Fabii family has served this great city for generations. Our fathers struck at the establishment, and won the plebes rights when they forced the patricians to agree to the Conflict of Orders, which granted you political freedom. I implore you to invoke your rights under this agreement, and force the Senate to revoke their judgment against my family."

The anger was evident on the face of Lucius Julius, and it increased when he heard the roar of approval from the common people resounding across the curia. "Listen as the rabble displays their hatred of the ruling class. We will rue the day that we allowed the commoners to overturn this vote."

In an angry mood, Lucius sent for Vopiscus and explained to him the actions of the Senate. "I have raised you to follow in my footsteps and bring glory to our family name. Today by their actions, the Fabii family has overtaken our role as leaders of Rome. You must redeem our family's name. Show no mercy to anyone who disobeys your authority and make the invaders severely pay for having the affront to attack Rome. Make certain the troops know that you will enforce the ancient punishment of decimation. The Fabii family made a grave mistake by their action. They so enraged the enemy that they will attack without restraint. Be certain that you lead the reinforcements. Let the troops under Sulpicius and the Fabii take the brunt of the attack, then move in and attack the Celts from the rear. Bless you my son. Listen to my words and you will come home a hero."

Clusium
Riding their horses until they dropped from exhaustion, the ambassadors, sent to Rome by Ragenos, sped back to their

comrades with the news. "The Romans turned down our request to be awarded the murderers. They violated the Law of Nations. Not only did they let the murderers walk free, the Romans even rewarded them for their treachery by promoting them to positions of honor. This calls for war! Furthermore, we heard discussions of a vast army being assembled at a place called Allia."

With this announcement, the rancor that had developed between the Boii and their allies evaporated. With a hand wave from Ragenos, the trumpeters sounded the signal to break camp and prepare to move out. Banners were pulled from the earth and the massive movement turned away from the besieged Clusium.

Roman Camp at Allia

Each day, the army under Quintus Sulpicius grew in number as they positioned along the Allia. He assembled the eighteen hundred cavalrymen into a cohesive unit, instead of assigning them to the various squads. In determining strategy with Quintus, Vopiscus decided to use the cavalry as a probe to soften up the barbarian forces before he committed his ground forces. Meanwhile, he trained the newcomers in the intricacies of the phalanx. Various leaders of Rome's allies saw the new formation as an attempt to minimize their authority over their subjects. Vopiscus, who in military matters deferred to the advice of his father, put several of the ringleaders to death, quelling the possibility of revolt.

The army, subsisting on a diet of wheat bread, cheese and sour wine, dug ditches and built protective mud walls around their camp whenever they were not training. Vopiscus Julius and Quintus Sulpicius stood on a windswept hillside and gazed in contentment at the unified movement. "When the barbarians see this cohesive army, the rout will already be started," Vopiscus said.

Vopiscus had his trumpeters order the troops to fall into formation in front of their commanders. "Soldiers of Rome," he shouted from his vantage point, "in the near future we will face a vast array of savages who mean to invade our great city. Each of us must resolve to stand steadfast and prevent even a single barbarian from setting foot on our soil. Those that fail to perform will be dealt with severely. Should you flee in the face of the enemy, you will be hunted down and slain. Should you lose your armor during the battle, your unit will face the ancient punishment of decimation. Each unit will be divided into tens, and one of the ten will be selected by lot to die for the loss of weapons. Do I make myself clear?" The roar of response warmed even the cold heart of the representative of the Julian household.

Rome
When those assigned to watch the enemy forces sent word of the advancing Celtic army, the Senate considered evacuating the city's Etruscan slaves. "We cannot afford to have several thousand potential enemies linger within the walls of our city should the Celts get past our army," Lucius Julius argued against those who could not even conceive of such a circumstance. As usual, Lucius proved to be more persuasive. He won the debate, and the order was given for the prisoners to be moved to a secure location south of the city.

Conel, who was more physically fit than the starving prisoners surrounding him, managed to keep a low profile and walked bent from the waist to conceal his great height. Staying in the middle of the pack, he avoided detection as the guards freely used whips to move the crowd through the streets and across the Tiber before they headed south.

The first night, three guards forfeited their lives as Conel made good his escape. The third guard also lost his armor and food supply. The death of their comrades left the ranks of the guards even more depleted, so Conel was free to flee eastward without interference. Because of their months of subsistence on starvation rations, none of the Etruscans who saw the tall Celt make his escape attempted to follow. The guards drove the remaining thousands without mercy, leaving hundreds dead along the way.

Celtic Camp at Allia
The advance scouts informed the brennos that the enemy had gathered less than a day's march ahead in a small valley between two hillsides with a river to their back. Furthermore, he was told of how the massive lines of marching men swung as a unit to face the direction of an attack. "What size is their mounted force?" he asked.

"It is small as best we can determine," the head scout answered. "There are less than two thousand, and none have reserve mounts. Our cavalry will easily rout them. Furthermore, we did not see any archers, nor did they practice tossing the javelin. It seems that they are trained to fight a defensive battle only."

"Brennos, to honor the death of my father, I demand that the Boii be given the honor position at the center of the attack," Roith said to Ragenos.

"Because you brought your troops back into our fold, I will grant your request. Furthermore, I will station my own Mayri clan on your right. May your charge bring us victory." Forming a fist, which he slapped against his chest, Roith acknowledged with a slight bow, the honor that was bestowed upon him.

A pleased Ragenos then informed Rochlos of the battle formation that he desired and issued orders revealing where each of the tribes and clans should position themselves in line. "The Boii will be given the honor position with our Mayri at their right. The cavalry will form on the left and outflank the enemies' right side. When the command to attack is given, they will engage and destroy the opposing mounted force as quickly as possible.

"Before engaging in combat, we will first determine if they choose a personal confrontation between champions. If they reject this option, we will break their will with a display of war chariots. We will show these impudent southerners how real warriors fight." The charioteers immediately took their horses and drivers through their paces after so long a period without training.

Later that day, he appointed Mick the captain of the Mayri clan and acknowledged Hugh as the chief Druid for the battle. Una, standing beside Roith, smiled with pleasure as her brothers were given such high honors for men so young.

They established camp early because Ragenos wanted an advanced force in position before the Romans were prepared to fight. Such a strategy usually contributed to the enemies' fear, and Ragenos understood that the Celts used fear as part of their arsenal. Setting an early camp in no way helped the Celtic force get rested for the battle. Bands of fighters spent the night moving from one campfire to another bragging about what they would do when they heard the battle cry. Beer and ale flowed freely as the Celts sharpened their swords and polished the armor that would embellish and protect them.

Una sat between her brothers and Roith, who had wandered over from the site of the Boii. "I foresee great honors and glory for all," she said, glancing from the brothers that she loved to the enchanted Boii warrior.

"I will bring you the head of their general to carry on your saddle," Roith announced.

"Not very likely," Mick said. "I claim the honor of decapitating the leader of those who stand between my father and freedom. My dear sister, just so you won't miss out on the prize, I intend to give it to you."

"What do you think I'll be doing while you two search for the leader? I fully expect to claim that prize for myself," she answered with a laugh. Then she dipped into the lime pot to lighten her hair and create the illusion of spikes to terrify an opponent. Even as Una prepared herself for battle, the Gaestae were dyeing themselves blue to identify each other in the midst of the fight and to strike fear into the hearts of their opponents. At the height of darkness, word came from the brennos that the families accompanying the warriors should continue the din and maintain the fires of the partying while the soldiers would quietly leave the camp and form up into their units at the appointed spots.

Roman Camp at Allia
The wild noise in the Celtic camp did not go unnoticed by the Roman scouts, who quickly sent word that their opponents would be in no shape to fight the following day. Vopiscus carried this word to Quintus Sulpicius. "My scouts tell me that the barbarians are spending this night drinking and singing aloud. I suggest that we send a force into their camp to slaughter them as they sleep off this excess."

"Vopiscus, my friend, you are too quick to want a battle. If the barbarians have consumed too much fermented grape, I would prefer to face them under the scorching sun than while the alcohol runs hot in their blood. Furthermore, the priests haven't given us their omen as to whether or not today will be a good day to engage the enemy. I refuse to blow the battle trumpets without a good omen. I suggest that you go to their tent and see if they are ready to share their forecast."

Vopiscus, a very superstitious man, was leery of obeying the order to visit the domain of the priests. He was also afraid of being tagged as a coward and thus dishonors the family name. The scene he encountered when he approached the sacred tents both frightened and appalled him. Dozens of headless chickens were scurrying through the compound, spraying blood on all that stood in their way. Some of the Augures watched with growing interest the eating habits of the chickens that retained their heads. More frightening than the chickens were the arguments between various factions of the assembled priests as they debated the meaning of the length of time the poultry took to die. Meanwhile, the Haruspices sat disemboweling lambs to study their livers while they discussed the meaning of the quivering organs' shape, color and markings. The Fulgurators sat by themselves and moaned over the lack of lightning requires to interpret the future. Other forecasters argued over the omens foretold by the flight of birds.

'Have I wandered into the den of madmen?' Vopiscus asked himself as he tried to make sense of the commotion. He stood in amazement, until he was noticed and ordered to leave the presence of the holy ones. He reported that priests were not enough of one mind to furnish a prediction. This lack of a good omen bothered the commander as he took to his tent for the night.

The Battle of Allia circa 387 BC

Vopiscus' visit to obtain information on god's will as to when to start the battle went for naught. The Celtic horde determined the day and time of the encounter. Before the breakfast signal could be sounded, the enemy appeared across the narrow valley on the opposite hills. To be awakened by the sound of war trumpets, the clashing of swords against bronze shields, the singing of wild songs and the horrible war cry of the blond giants was more than most of the citizen soldiers could stomach. Breakfast was not enjoyable for the Roman army on this morning.

Quintius' battle plan was simple and certain to succeed. The army would make a sudden flank attack, and when the battle reached its climax, the cavalry would mop up the retreating Gauls. Satisfied with the arrangements, he smugly waited among the veterans for events to unfold.

On the leeward side of the hill, Vopiscus tarried to order the reserves into battle when the time was right. He stationed the reserves on a slight rise to the right of the veterans. From his vantage point at the crest of the hill, he began to feel a knot of fear grip his stomach. The Gauls' large curved swords when compared to the short swords used by his men concerned the Roman field leader. While the veterans wore breast armor of beaten bronze, the sun shone off the chain mail of his opponents. Even from this distance, the Gauls' metal shields seemed far superior to the small, leather-covered shields used by his forces. Although some of the regulars were outfitted with long, curved, oval body shields; their position at the rear of the line minimized their usefulness. 'It's unfortunate that we can't trust the soldiers. So our best and most experienced men must be at the rear to prevent others from deserting. I wonder if my opponent has the same concern?'

As he attached his helmet to its padded inner lining, Vopiscus stationed the final element in the Roman arsenal, the stone slingers accompanied by their small contingent of archers, who were to be used in the event that the foe came within range.

The fact that the foe was better armed and armored than the mighty Roman army disturbed Vopiscus, but it frightened the foot soldiers at the front of the Roman line and terrified the reserves stationed at the rear. As he readied himself to observe the combat, Vopiscus noticed minor movement among the Gauls on the opposite hill as the screaming warriors parted. He also saw the Fetiales, who were responsible for the rituals of war, align themselves in front of the Roman army to await their moment of glory.

Hugh, adorned in his white cloak with gold trim, passed through the screaming Celts and made his way down the hillside toward the Roman ranks. He was accompanied by a half-dozen, similarly dressed Druids making their way across the divide between the armies to determine if the Romans would rather a fight to the death by a champion from each side.

Unaccustomed to the rituals of his adversary, Hugh did not notice that one of the Fetiales advancing toward them was armed with a spear. Nor did he know that according to Roman customs, a Fetiale declared war by tossing a spear into a space occupied by an enemy. Before the two delegations of priests reached shouting distance, the Fetiale let the spear fly, landing harmlessly at the feet of the advancing Druids. Hugh and his companions, believing the spear was an unwarranted provocation, turned swiftly and fled back to their own ranks. The Fetiales did likewise. On this ignominious note, the battle of Allia began.

Ragenos grew furious when he observed the Roman's ignorance of international behavior. Even before the Druids cleared the field of combat, he ordered the chariots, which until now were hidden behind the line of screaming warriors, to begin the attack. Roith, as the captain of the center, was given the honor of being the first charioteer to take the field. Mick followed less than a split second behind and quickly passed the less skilled Boii. Charging down the hill's incline, the hundreds of two-man chariots roared toward the line of Roman regulars standing to the left of the battle zone. While the front line Roman foot soldiers watched in horror, the onslaught of horses, traveling at excessive speeds, bore down on them. Some instinctively backed into the men behind them, causing the entire line to buckle inwardly. Others stared in amazement, as the athletic Celts stood on the yoke between their two moving horses and hurled five foot long javelins into the lines of the waiting Romans. The flimsy leather shields proved no match for the heavy spear of the charioteer. Often the javelins pinned the shields to the body of the bearer. Pulling out a jagged point designed to rip the flesh did more damage than the initial penetration. Because the soldiers were so densely packed, the javelins that missed the upheld shields often pierced and pegged feet to the earth.

The screams of the wounded and the weight of the dead caused the first lines to collapse, resulting in further confusion and disorder. The veterans, charged with keeping order by killing deserters, were busy slaughtering the men who ran from the mighty Celtic war machine. Horns used by the captains to maintain order were totally useless for even those nearby could not hear over the din created by the enemy. Chaos reigned supreme, as Mick's charge drove fear into the heart of even the bravest defender. The wave of chariots, led by the Mayri triplet, ignored the disorganized and terrified foot soldiers and turned in the direction of the cavalry on their left. The Roman horses reacted to the rain of javelins. Rearing on their hind legs, they pawed at the approaching danger and bucked off their owners, who were trampled under the hooves of the terrified animals.

To add to their agony, the disorganized Roman horse soldiers were overwhelmed by the cavalry charge led by Roanlos. Slashing with his long curved sword, the Mayri decapitated all within range. The agonized cries of the dying, along with the crush of the fleeing reserves, further demoralized the remnants of a once orderly defensive line.

After he gave the command for the Celtic cavalry to advance, Ragenos complained to Rochlos who stood by his side. "I gave Roith the lead, and Mick outran him. Worse yet, Mick attempts to take on the entire battle front by himself."

"If you look closely, my dear friend, you'll see that he is succeeding," Rochlos answered with a laugh, all the while hoping he would be given the opportunity to bloody his sword.

A cry from the ground troops, led by the ferocious blue-dyed Gaesatae, notified Ragenos that his army had lost patience and did not wait for his signal to advance. Looking at his lifelong friend,

Ragenos mounted his horse. "No sense letting everyone else have all the fun," he yelled, turning the animal's head in the direction of the slaughter and taking off on a gallop. Rochlos was quick to follow.

Without even trying to take advantage of an army unfamiliar with chariot warfare, Mick led the hundreds of charioteers in a broad turn to the right, circling back to where they originally entered the valley. To the amazement of the Roman leadership, he led a charge up the hillside directly toward Vopiscus Julian and his untried reserves. Despite all his maneuvering, Mick could not shake Roith who clung to his left side, less than a horse length behind. These two drivers were several lengths ahead of those who charged after them with the Boii and the Mayri intermingled, as the chariots of other clans brought up the rear.

Vopiscus, astonished at the charge of the thundering chariots, failed to react to the oncoming Mick and was cut to pieces under the hooves and wheels of the Mayri. The Roman reserves deserted their post, fleeing into the regulars on their left. The blindsided charge by their own troops proved to be too much even for the front line soldiers, who broke formation and fled in terror, running over the veterans stationed at their rear to prevent such a rout.

Confusion ruled the day. After using the vehicles to destroy any semblance of a defensive line, Mick turned the reins over to the handler, unsheathed his sword and leapt over the bodies of the dead Romans. The chariot handler turned the horses to face the Celtic line then awaited his leader's return. Each charioteer mimicked the move of Mick and followed him as he swung his massive sword into the backs of the retreating reserves. Among the reservists who died was a young expectant father, Gaius Tillius, Julia's spouse.

The final terror, one that would remain in the minds of Romans for generations to come, was the screaming charge of the naked, blue-colored blond giants beating on their shields with their swords even as they ran. The victorious Celts butchered the retreating Romans on a significant scale. Drowning in the river, however, caused the most Roman deaths. Those who survived the battle discarded their weapons on the riverbank before taking the plunge. Those who survived the crossing took off for the safety of Rome or ran in the opposite direction toward the remnants of Veii's fortifications. Many soldiers ripped their clothing in a vain attempt to prove that they had fought courageously. A single Roman company had the courage to rescue Quintus Sulpicius and hurry him toward of one of the few boats available for safe passage down the Allia into the nearby Tiber.

Chapter 24
The Invasion of Rome

Outskirts of Rome circa 387 BC

Conel thought the noise coming from the road was another search party looking for him until he heard children crying while being dragged along by their parents. Peering between bushes, he was amazed to see the long line of civilians making their way out of the city. Most carried their possessions on their backs; although, a fortunate few towed carts piled with goods. On the other hand, the wealthier refugees rode in carriages with guards to clear the way. Unbeknownst to Conel, several of the carriages contained the Fabii brothers and their families who were escaping to their country estates. As he watched, many of the older refugees collapsed along the roadside. Those helped by other family members continued the journey. The remainder died where they fell. During the daylight hours, he gathered information by listening to the various conversations within hearing distance of his hiding place. The exhausted civilians did not bother to set out guards when they stopped for the night, making it easy for Conel to steal food and water.

Each night, he worked his way further north, making certain that he gave the city a wide berth. Slowly, he pieced together enough information to realize that some foreign army, probably Etruscan seeking revenge for the siege of Veii, was in the process of attacking Rome. Not wishing to find himself in more difficult circumstances than those he had escaped, and with the turmoil created by so many people fleeing the invaders, he did not attempt to rendezvous with Elico. He also decided to travel east, cross the Apennines and make his way toward the Boii oppidum.

Camps of stragglers, mostly former slaves, were springing up all along the path of those fleeing the city, surviving by robbing and murdering those in flight. Conel decided to join one such group for his own self-preservation, rationalizing that they were merely preying on the enemies who had enslaved him. The leader of this band owned a horse, the one item that Conel needed to escape. Daily he observed this bully, a former slave from across the sea to the east, who stood as large and as broad as Conel himself. As though sensing a threat, Tazha, the Scythian, gave Conel a friendly nod whenever the two came near each other. Despite the fact that the Celt was less well armed, Tazha remained wary.

Rome

Lucius Julius, seizing the role of chief pontiff from the ineffectual Marcus Papyrius, assumed control of the government from the Senate. In addition, he took over the remains of the army from the military tribunes by issuing daily-orders in an effort to create discipline out of a chaotic situation.

Slaves strengthened the eastern rampart, the earthwork defense that protected that approach. Like all previous rulers, Lucius depended on the Tiber River to provide protection from the west, which meant the Bridge of Sublicius would again have to be destroyed. He had already assigned men to stem the flow of the homeless from the outskirts. Since the threat most likely would come from the north, he ignored the defense of the southern approaches and ordered the engineers to erect fortifications around the upper part of Capitoline Hill. Next, he proposed that the patrician families be relocated to Capitoline, a low-lying hill in the center of the city, which could be most easily defended.

The defense preparation enabled Lucius to shrug off the death of his son. When he announced the demise of Vopiscus Julius and Gaius Tillius to his family, he was unaware of the glee that filled Julia's heart. He was just as unaware of the dread that consumed Julia's mother, who gazed in horror at her daughter.

Lucius' first action intended to rebuild morale in the army, instead it replaced morale with fear. He appointed Marcus Manlius to assume the command of the Roman forces and carry out the ancient punishment of decimation. Lucius Julius conducted the ceremony to dishonor the former consul Quintus Sulpicius. "Soldiers of Rome," Lucius shouted, while standing on Tarpeian Rock accompanied by Quintus Sulpicius. "Your commander fled the field of battle before an enemy of Rome. For shaming the legions that he led, he must face the most dishonorable death we can devise."

Shaken by the charges, Quintus tried to interrupt, but Lucius continued, "You, Quintus Sulpicius have earned my disdain." With these words Lucius Julius pushed Sulpicius in the back, causing him to lose his balance. To serve as an example to all deserters, the ill-fated commander was thrown to his death from the Tarpeian

Rock. Quintus screamed until his body crashed into the rocky ground below the cliff. Thus Quintus Sulpicius, commander of the defeated army, became the first of those defeated at Allia to meet his fate. Other officers followed him in death.

Manlius, the commander of Rome, ordered the remaining survivors of Allia to count and form into groups of ten. He walked through the thousands that stood in small circles and randomly placed his sword on one in each circle. The soldier so designated was subsequently hacked to death by his companions. The survivors were assigned to the defense of Capitoline Hill.

Later that same day, Lucius dispatched Cominius Pontius with orders that Marcus Furius Canillus, the captor of the city of Veii, should return from exile. Furthermore, Marcus Furius was commanded to reassemble the army that fled to that city and attack the Celts from the rear. The fear of the Roman populace mounted daily as stragglers from the battle of Allia made their way to the safety of the capital. The Circus Maximus, once occupied by thousands of Etruscan prisoners of war, now served as the temporary settlement for thousands of Roman citizens who fled the countryside. The conditions were primitive, and diseases, which once killed their enemy prisoners, were now claiming the lives of their own citizens.

Sensing that merely closing the gates would not deter people from taking refuge in Rome, Lucius ordered the army to go door-to-door and force the inhabitants to leave. The rabble who had settled on the Circus Maximus were finally driven away by soldiers swinging whips. Only the families of the patricians found shelter within the city's defenses. Lucius announced to the nobles that these measures were necessary to allow the original bloodlines to survive, "We have neither the food nor the patience to handle such a disorderly crowd. Nor can we deplete our stores to feed those less worthy."

In desperation, Lucius Julius ordered the sacred idols from the temples to be buried in a secret place. Vestal Virgins, who guarded the eternal flame, fled to the Etruscan City of Caere. The image of the Greek Goddess, Pallas Athena, brought to Rome after the fall of Troy, was smuggled out of the city. Panic spread as the very symbols that protected Rome were removed. What began as an orderly evacuation turned into a riot as brother fought brother over family heirlooms.

Then Lucius Julius assembled the heads of the original patrician families and announced, "There is little chance to properly defend our city, and I, for one, will not wait to see it destroyed. I intend to release my door slave and sit in front of my residence. I am too old to fight. If I fail to dissuade these barbarians from destroying our city, I will go willingly to my death."

The patrician paterfamilias took an oath to follow the lead of Lucius Julius. After their families had been safely ensconced within the defensive ring on Capitoline Hill, each settled in an ivory chair before the door of his residence and awaited the invader.

Allia

As he knew they would, Hugh watched in amusement while the victorious Celts scoured the battlefield searching for the bodies of the fallen Roman commanders. Ignoring the efforts of the marauders, vultures and other animals of prey feasted as the fields along the Allia lay stained red. Hugh knew the Romans fertilized their fields with blood, and the farmers would view the slaughter as a good omen. It promised excellent harvests for decades to come.

Una, the first to discover the body of Vopiscus Julius, could tell by his armor that he was one of the leaders. Removing his helmet and pulling his hair to stretch his neck, with one clean swipe she cut off his head. "Mick, judging by the insignia on his shield, this must be the leader for whom you are searching," she told her warrior brother. Then swinging the head by its hair, she tossed it to him.

Mick, elbow deep in blood and gore looking for something salvageable, was embarrassed by his sister's find. "That was to be my present to you, my dear sister," he said while looking around to see if Roith was paying attention.

While Mick tied the severed head of the son of the Julian family's paterfamilias to his saddle, others were mounting heads to poles to form a great circle at the crown of the hill where the Roman defenders had made their stand. The line of priests walked around the spiked heads three times before they entered the center. Hugh forced an opening near the spot where Mick's chariot first penetrated the Roman line. Then he led the procession of Druids within the circle. Bodies of those who lost their lives were carried by their comrades and piled alongside a large pit dug within the improvised compound. The priests placed torches along the inside of the wall and began to chant, so the souls of the dead would have easy transport to the otherworld. Hugh, as chief Druid,

Druids, Celts, and Romans

made certain that the appropriate rituals were observed to insure their successful journey.

As the moon rose over the battlefield, Hugh gave permission for those who dug the ditch to begin filling it in. He then turned to the leaders of the army, and congratulated them on their victory while reminding them that the Mayri chieftain was still a captive. Only when this service was performed did Celtic tradition deem the battle to be over. Now the army could turn its attention to conquering Rome.

Northeast of Rome
What started out to be easy pickings from unarmed civilians, fleeing the war, turned ugly for those who preyed. As more and more slaves and fugitives fled the city, fights for territorial rights developed frequently between the raiding factions.

With the moon centered high in the sky, Conel rolled over in his stolen blanket, alerted by silent shadows creeping across the ground where his comrades lay. The killers stifled the death cry of those they slew. Not wanting to call undue attention until he could properly defend himself, Conel kept silent. His opportunity came when one intruder crawled toward him while looking backward at a mountain of a man who was just getting to his feet. The sound of Conel snapping the intruder's neck was muffled, as an aroused Tazha shouted the first cry of warning. Swinging two swords, the Scythian rose to meet the attack on his band of thieves. He was surprised to find an armed Celt defending his back. The cry to action came too late for most of the band, who were slaughtered as they woke. Sensing the desperation of their situation, the two giants fought their way toward the temporary corral, mounted the few motley horses and made a dash for freedom.

Later the next night, Tazha, speaking in a mix of Latin and Greek, said, "Of all those who followed me, I pictured you the most likely to kill me for my horse."

"Your instincts were not far wrong. Only fate saved your life, for I no longer need your mount."

"What are your intentions? I don't have the stomach to assemble another crew."

"And I no longer have the stomach to rob unarmed people. I intend to head north to the land of the Boii, and there assemble a force to revenge my enslavement," the Mayri leader answered.

"What makes you think that the Boii will welcome you?"

"My people have been trading with them for centuries."

"Will they assist your comrade, should he aid you during your travels?"

"You have my word as the Chieftain of the Mayri. As a sign of my pledge, I give you my gold armband that I retrieved from the Romans. Any Celt seeing the design of the Goddess Sulis etched on this band will come to your aid."

"Then you have the word of Tazha the Scythian." Reaching into his shirt Tazha retrieved a chain from his neck from which hung a small gold symbol. "This is the totem of our Deer Goddess."

Placing the symbol of the Scythians around his neck, Conel said: "My family, and all those who come after, will hold the totem of your people in the highest honor.

Outskirts of Rome
Because of the celebrating among the various combatants, it took several days before Ragenos could regain sufficient control to build the formation of an army. Only on the third day, when Hugh threatened to have them shunned if they refused to obey the orders of their leaders, did the massive force begin to put on its war face and assemble into units.

As the Celts descended upon the city, they encountered lines of ragged refuges making their way to safety. Many refugees tried to discourage the northern warriors from taking their possessions, and those unfortunates paid for such interference with their lives. Small towns and farms along the way were also visited by plunderers, who took what they wished and destroyed the rest, often setting fire to the deserted buildings. Smoke from these blazes could be seen as far away as Veii in the north to Palestrina south of Rome. The defenders at the citadel on Capitoline Hill could easily gage the uninterrupted approach of the invader.

The flush of victory dissipated along the march. The Celts, a people that were easily satisfied once they finished the first rush of fighting, settled into a melancholy mood as they advanced along the dusty road. Their depression grew when they arrived at their destination, only to be shocked because it was undefended. More incredible was the fact that the Colline gate was not even closed. "What evil lurks within?" those in the lead asked each other only to be met by eerie silence from the seemingly deserted ramparts.

After the delay of an hour, one courageous soul walked up to the gates and screamed in defiance at the silence that greeted him. He banged his sword against his shield to challenge any and all to come and meet him in hand-to-hand combat, but no one came. He ridiculed the ancestors that could produce such cowards, but no one answered. Then, he tossed away his weapons and offered to take on his adversaries bare handed, but no one accepted. Finally, he returned to his position at the front of the line, refusing to advance against the evil that resides inside.

The triplets, the first of the commanders to enter the city, took the lead. Mick and Una with Roith at her right side rode boldly past the city gates. Meanwhile, Hugh sprinkled water from the Spring of Sulis to bless their passage.

After they halted to listen for any screams of anguish, the superstitious Celtic warriors followed the Mayri triplets into the doomed city. Their anxiety, which had so quickly developed upon seeing the unprotected ramparts, was reinforced as they encountered the deserted streets and open doors. Fearing the unknown, the army assembled at the open marketplace and ventured in small groups down the narrow winding streets. Many within a city's walls for the first time looked in wonderment at the thousands of structures, while mentally comparing such wonder to their simple oppida. The fear of the unknown gripped every combatant as they avoided the buildings whose doors were ajar and entered only those that had to be forced. After a rudimentary search, the superstitious, long-limbed fighters quickly departed the dwelling and with companions who waited in the street rejoined the thousands swarming into the forum. Often, those returning would brag about how they heroically faced down the demons. Mick assembled parties of mounted combatants and ordered them to investigate the entire city and report back with information within an hour. Many returned with strange tales. Some described life sized statues of old men sitting in white chairs outside some of the structures.

Ragenos received a message from his nephew telling him the only inhabitants were assembled in a defensive position on top of one of the hills. Mick did not mention the fear, which gripped the Celts scattered within the city. Determined to see for himself these statues of gods described by the returning patrols, he set out for one of the hills reported to contain such lifelike images. "What have we here?" Mick said aloud in Latin as he approached the household of the Julian family.

Thinking that he was being addressed, Lucius Julius replied, "I am a Roman Senator, and I demand that you and your force leave our city."

As Mick stood his ground, Hugh approached and asked. "Do you have a name, old man?"

Lucius, surprised to hear a barbarian speak Latin so clearly, answered, "I am Lucius Julius, a member of the Senate, one of the three pontifices of Rome and the paterfamilias of the Julian household. I am sitting here to defend my home."

"That is a strange way to defend one's city," a now amused Hugh replied.

After he regained his composure, Mick joined in. "I am Mick of the Mayri, and I have come to claim my father or to avenge him."

Only after hearing the name of the Celtic clan did the leader of Rome realize his role in the death and destruction that had ravaged his beloved home and city. The old man's shock intensified when he gazed on the head of his son hanging from the bridle of the barbarian. Retrieving a small knife he had hidden in his belt, Lucius Julius slit his wrists. Mick and his party shrugged their shoulders at the suicide of the Julian paterfamilias then made their way into his house.

Lucius was only the first to lose his life that day. Marcus Papyrius, upon having his beard pulled by a curious Celt, took his ivory scepter, and struck the offender across the head. The startled warrior instinctively used his unsheathed sword to strike down the Roman. The Celts, realizing these were men and not gods, soon slaughtered all the others.

Word was quickly sent to Ragenos, who moved his headquarters from a tent on the outskirts to a manor house inside the city walls. The other leaders of the clans did the same with the triplets selecting the residence of Julia, their former slave.

After viewing the situation first hand, Ragenos ordered random buildings to be set a flame to discourage those on the hill while he negotiated to learn the whereabouts of his brother-in-law. In explaining his actions, Ragenos said to his commanders: "These people have stayed to defend their city. If they see it being destroyed before their very eyes, they will have less spirit to resist. Because of their strategic and heavily defended position, we are at a disadvantage. We cannot make use of either our horses or our chariots. Nor can we rely on our numerical strength because the entry ways to the occupied part of the hill appear to be narrow and well defended."

"Rochlos, how do their provisions compare to ours?" Ragenos asked.

"They are in the better position. Though the ground we stand on seems to be dry, it was at one time a swamp. Look at the large channels needed to drain off the excess water. When the rains come, we will be camped in swampland. Furthermore, the grain fields have all been harvested. The herds were driven away as our army advanced, and what could not be carried was destroyed. I have already assigned men to forage far and wide to feed the thirty to forty thousand warriors and camp followers that surround this city."

Hugh spoke before his brother could get the next word. "Uncle Ragenos, that's all the more reason to attack and destroy them quickly. One thing that Uncle Rochlos did not mention is the possibility that our force will quickly tire of waiting for their plunder and may begin attacking each other."

"When the enemy awakens tomorrow, they will find Celts at their fortifications," the brennos announced. "Mick and Roith assemble your troops and begin to climb after dark."

Although the Celts fought bravely, they could not overcome the natural advantage the Roman defenders enjoyed. Wave after wave of screaming Celtic foot soldiers met their destruction trying to clear the deep pit and scale the stone wall that Roman engineers erected. Though the naked blue-skinned Gaesatae terrified those crouched beyond the walls, even they couldn't force entry into the entrenched garrison. Celtic javelins flew over those protected by the walls without causing any harm. Meanwhile, the Romans retrieved and tossed the missiles back at the tightly packed attackers, wounding many and frustrating their leaders. After a time, Mick directing the frontal attack and Roith commanding the rear ordered the tossing of javelins to cease. "If you can't see the face of the enemy, hold your spear," they commanded.

While dozens of Romans met their deaths, the Celts lost hundreds. That night, after the attackers withdrew, the Roman reserves climbed over the ramparts and tossed the bodies of their comrades and those of the Gauls down the hillside to the consternation of those below. Marcus Manlius, experienced in siege warfare, knew that dead bodies brought disease.

During the first weeks of fighting, the Celts left the Roman corpses lie where they were thrown and buried only their own dead. Soon the stench of rotting corpses overcame any psychological advantage of seeing the dead enemy, and Rochlos ordered the cremation of the dead within sight of the defenders. The flaming pyres ignited wooden shacks that comprised most of the city's housing and resulted in devastating damage.

The odor of the dead, rising in the clouds of ashes, drained any enthusiasm for war from both sides; although, the stalemate continued for months. The lack of fulfillment of the Celts was far more injurious to their cause than to that of the defenders. Clan after clan demanded a share of the spoils, so they could return to their oppida. The first to leave were the mercenary Gaesatae whose temperament and impatience could not tolerate siege warfare. The daily burning of the corpses slowed but did not prevent the spreading of dysentery and other diseases. Rome had long since been stripped bare of any supplies, and hunger became as much a problem as disease. With their early rage long since spent, the majority of the army had its fill of waiting for a victory that was slow to come. The leaders' tempers, already on short leashes, grew shorter when watchers reported that an enemy was seen making his way up a gully.

Capitoline Hill
After being missing for several months, Cominius Pontius finally reported back to Manlius. "We have located Marcus Furius Canillus. He had been exiled to the Etruscan City of Volsinii. He is now with our forces in Veii and has given his word that as soon as he has the army in fit condition, he will relieve Rome."

"I gave orders for immediate relief. We cannot hold out until he has the army fit to fight. If the Gauls feel the pressure at their backs, they will soon disperse."

Furius Canillus, either unable or unwilling to march to the relief of the entrapped defenders, spent the remainder of the campaign attacking the parties that Rochlos sent out to gather food from the countryside.

Celtic Camp
After learning of the concealed gully, a sense of confidence returned to Mick. "I can lead a party of attackers and catch the Romans napping," he declared.

That night, with a hand picked company of warriors, Mick ascended the gully where Pontius was observed. Each attacker left his spear and sheath behind, lest the noise of the clinking would arouse the sleeping Romans. The party also covered themselves with wet mud to prevent the moon from shining off their white skin. "I want no noise. Do you understand me?" Mick commanded. Convinced of their agreement to remain silent, he led his small company two by two up the steep slope. Trees and bushes obscured most of the trail, which at its widest could accommodate two people. Using the occasional rock for support, Mick and his companion pulled themselves up by grabbing the bushes and tree limbs that protruded across the narrow track. There was not even a sneeze from those who climbed in the dust of those who climbed ahead. Finally, Mick arrived at the pit that surrounded the earth and stone walls of the defensive fort.

"I'll go first," his companion volunteered. He lay on the top of the rampart and was placing one leg across the boundary when nearby geese began to cackle, awakening the sleeping guards. The fight was fierce, but all too short for the liking of the Celts, who were out-manned at the point of entry by a dozen to one. Several lost their lives. Even Mick was wounded before he began the humiliating climb down the dusty draw, dragging the dead along with him.

While the struggle to outlast each other continued, the scarcity of fresh vegetables and meat took its toll. At the same time contaminated water, collecting in the forum as a result of the mass of people and animals, raised the sickness suffered by the besieging army to epidemic levels. Daily, the death toll mounted. Hundreds of the invading force departed the territory each week to return to their homelands, carrying with them plunder from the empty homes and farmhouses along the route.

Unlike those who gave up the fight, the triplets and their companions were amazed at the luxury of the Julian house. Visitors came often and sometimes stayed for weeks at a time. Roith of the Boii, for example, became a permanent tenant. "Why doesn't that Boii live with his mates?" Mick asked Hugh.

"Your lack of romance continues to astound me. The Boii is madly in love with Una."

"I though that Danous was madly in love with her?"

"He is," Hugh answered. "Both of them are, which will make life interesting around here."

"How do you know all this?" Mick asked.

"I watch and listen. Haven't you noticed that every time Roith enters the room Una instinctively brushes back her hair while she takes little notice of the bard? Ignoring a bard is not a good thing"

"In her heart, Una knows that she could never marry a bard," Mick said. "So why doesn't she simply tell him?"

"She is young, and having the affections of several handsome males striving for her attention is a very heady thing. I pray that she does not frighten off the young Boii because the future of our bloodline depends on her marrying a warrior."

Una usually paid little attention when other members of the household conversed. Her ears, however, perked up when she overheard her brothers talking about her. The thoughts of having two handsome males pursue her both thrilled her. She spent the remainder of the afternoon thinking about being married to either of the two competitors. She knew from the first moment that Danous was infatuated. He always followed her around. Whenever she pretended not to notice him, he would strum his lyre or sing to the children just to attract her attention. On the other hand, the handsome warrior had characteristics of the two people she loved the most. He was almost as skilled with a horse and sword as Mick, and in addition he was as clever and funny as Hugh. 'Before I let either of them know my feelings, I think I will enjoy the attention that I get.'

Ragenos had initially used the talents of the bards that accompanied the troops to keep their spirits up while awaiting an opportunity to fight. But as time dragged on, volunteering to forage the nearby countryside for food, an activity that offered the slim possibility of encountering an enemy patrol from Veii, provided the only other diversion. The skirmishes between the Celts and the Romans stationed at Veii were becoming more and more infrequent. The Celtic warriors were getting restless and starting to take their anger out on one another.

Northeast of Rome
After two skirmishes with armed bandits, Conel and Tazha decided to head east across the narrow range of the Apennine to escape the pursuit of the Roman and Etruscan soldiers.

The relative safety on other side of the mountains brought its own set of difficulties. Although army regulars did not hunt them and the region wasn't bustling with other bands of desperate men, they still faced considerable danger. The desolate land hardened its Sabine rulers, who were farmers, shepherds, woodsmen and most of all, fighters. Furthermore, they knew the land and all its dangers.

After fighting their way through the territory of the Umbri, Conel and Tazha led their now depleted band back across the Tiber into the hill country of the Etruscans near the city of Arezzo. Whenever possible, they avoided contact with armed parties and raided only small farms or unprotected hamlets. One morning when they arrived on the banks of the Ario River, Conel hugged his friend and told him that the land of the Celt was just days away.

Rome

Hugh, sitting in the atrium of the Julian house, pondered on the wisdom of a drawn out siege in a foreign clime. Then, he turned to his brother and resumed an argument the two had been waging for the past several weeks. "We are unaccustomed to the heat and dry air of this climate. Our people are dropping like dead flies from some type of sickness that neither I nor any of the Druids can heal. We must give up the siege and go home!"

"They have captured our father and for that they must pay!" Mick stubbornly replied.

Knowing that he could not change his brother's mind, Hugh turned to his sister and pleaded with her. Una, who normally took Hugh's side in arguments, would not budge on this issue either. "You have never been enslaved. You have never had to endure the humiliation and loss of dignity that comes when someone else has control over your body. Father would never forgive us if we leave him in slavery."

"Would you be more inclined to relent if we find out what happened to Father?" Hugh asked.

"If Father is no longer alive, and we repay those who enslaved him, perhaps, and only perhaps, I will relent." Una replied.

Later that afternoon, Hugh approached his two uncles on the subject. "If we find that Conel is already dead and we can get fair compensation from those entrapped above, Una and I agree to calling off the siege."

"What does Mick have to say on the subject?" Ragenos asked.

"Uncle, you know my brother. He will never relent until every enemy is laid sprawled out with the ravens eating their remains."

Capitoline Hill

"We have less than a twenty-day supply of dried food remaining. We cannot last until the gardens that we planted last fall bear fruit," one of the Roman defenders stated. "Can we fight our way out and make it to Furius' army at Veii?"

"Do not mention that traitor's name in my presence," Marcus Manlius answered. "Even with hunger, pestilence and desertions depleting the Gaulish army, he hesitates to attack. No, we are too weak both in numerical and physical strength to try to break out. I am in constant conversation with the priests of the temple waiting for a good omen to sue for peace. I'm sorry to say we have fought bravely but in the end, we have lost. Only a miracle can save us now!"

Boii Territory

As these conversations were taking place, a small, travel-weary band of warriors found themselves surrounded. As Conel contemplated what his future might hold, he realized that those mounted men coming forward with swords drawn spoke Celtic. When he heard his own language, he wept. "Put aside your weapons men. These are my brothers," Conel shouted in Greek and Roman. Then calling out in his native tongue, he welcomed the adversaries. "I am Conel, Chieftain of the Mayri Clan of the Helvetii Tribe. Who might you be?"

"Welcome, Conel. I am Elvanios, acting chief of the Boii, and brother of Roith, who led the party that escorted you on your way south."

"What happened to Dhulack?" Conel asked. "He was chief when I was here last year."

"It is a long and sad tale. Come, let us retire to our oppidum, and I will tell you a story of treachery that will no doubt match your own."

"I request safe passage for those who fought with me and aided me in reaching the safety of your realm," Conel said authoritatively.

"All who fought with Conel are friends of the Boii. Come join us in celebration." That night the stragglers, who survived the land of the Roman, feasted. The next morning a messenger went south with the good tidings that Conel was safe. After resting for a fortnight, the Celtic chieftain and Tazha the Scythian hugged as they parted, each destined to take different passages home.

"If you are ever in our land, I will teach you how to ride properly," Tazha shouted as he bear-hugged his friend. "A Celt from your tribe is always welcome among our people."

"And any from your tribe is welcome with ours," Conel replied as he turned his horse north toward his beloved Meva.

Rome

The messenger from the Boii was the most welcome news that reached the weary triplets since they left home. "Father is safe!" shouted Una, the first to return from the camp's headquarters with the news.

Along with their friends and other clansman, the Celtics from the Mayri tribe celebrated for the better part of three days. Only Hugh survived without experiencing a gigantic hangover. "Uncle Ragenos, I think it is time we call off this siege and return to our homeland," he announced. "Furthermore, I've been thinking. They should be as weary of this fighting as we are. Perhaps they will pay us to leave."

"You mean that we could collect ransom?"

"Well, wouldn't you be willing to pay a fee to get thousands of enemy troops out of your city? Let's ask them for a thousand pounds of gold and see what they reply. I'll take them the offer under the protection of a white banner."

Dressed in the white robe of a Druid, Hugh hiked up the hillside to the main entrance to of the Capitoline Hill defenses. After much discussion, Cominius Pontius, now a tribune, was sent to parley with the Celtic holy man.

"I come in peace with an offer to end the hostilities," Hugh announced, as the Roman climbed over the barricade and made his way partway down the hillside toward Hugh.

"What is your offer?"

"We will leave your territory if you are willing to pay a fair price."

The suspicious Pontius asked Hugh about the reason for the decision to withdraw. "We came to free Conel, the Chieftain of the Mayri clan. Word has just reached us that he is safely within the domain of the Boii tribe. Therefore, our business here is concluded. We, however, expect to be compensated for the Fabii brothers' breech of International Law that brought our forces into your city."

"What amount of compensation are you requesting?"

"We ask for the minor sum of one thousand pounds of gold."

"That is not a minor sum. You have destroyed our city, plundered our wealth, killed and maimed our people. For months, you have kept us trapped on this hill. And now you want to be compensated?" the Roman asked sarcastically.

"The dishonor belongs to the Romans," Hugh countered. "First, the House of Julian unlawfully took Conel as a slave when he merely wanted to return their child Julia, who was never harmed by the Celts while she enjoyed their hospitality. Secondly, don't forget the interference of the Fabii family to which I earlier referred. The offer is fair. You had more than ample time to either bury most of your treasure or haul it up the hillside to your fortified position. We are a stubborn people and will remain in place until we are fairly compensated."

"What about the spoils that you have already taken from the homes you destroyed?" the clever Pontius asked.

"Those spoils were justly taken, since you refused to tell us the whereabouts of Conel, the Mayri Chieftain. Do you accept our fair offer, or do we continue our stalemate?"

"I must take your offer to the leaders of my people. I will return at this time tomorrow with their reply."

Capitoline Hill
The arguments among the Romans, over who dishonored whom, continued till early light. Julia begged her supporters not to give in to the barbarians. But the dwindling food supply combined with the lack of rescue by Marcus Furius sealed the bargain. The Roman command voted to capitulate and rid their city of its northern invaders.

Roman Forum
A scale was placed into the ground of the forum with two pans of equal weight. The Celts placed fifty-pound weights on one pan, and the Romans filled the other with objects of gold until the pans balanced. The gold was then removed, dumped into a pile and the procedure was repeated. The gold brought by the Romans proved to be insufficient. Instead of offering more, Pontius complained about the Celt's faulty counter balancing weights. An argument ensued, and Ragenos was called to intervene. Upon hearing what had happened, he removed his sword and added it to the weights used by the Celts, saying as he did so, "Vae victis!" Then he translated into Celtic, "Woe to the conquered!"

Seeing they would not change the Celtic general's mind, the Romans contributed additional gold. After collecting their full ransom, the Celts broke camp and started for their homelands.

Chapter 25

The Aftermath
Rome circa 386 BC

After waiting for a day and night to make certain that the invader was not delaying until the barricades were dismantled before returning, the Romans felt sufficiently safe to leave their citadel. Finding their city in ruins, most of them decided to join the survivors of their army who waited out the siege in the safety of Veii. Of the leaders, only Marcus Manlius and Julia held to the belief that Rome should be rebuilt. Standing before the Colline gate, Manlius pleaded with his fellow citizens. "The barbarians have left and won't be returning. Stay and help me rebuild Rome."

The plea fell on deaf ears. Afraid to see the humiliation in each other's eyes, the survivors departed. Never before had their people been so degraded that they had to ransom their freedom. As the defender of the city pleaded his case, Marcus Furius Camillus marched into the city at the head of the remnants of the once glorious army. He immediately saw an opportunity to make up for his failure to attack the Gauls. Being a harsh overseer and a bright organizer, he took command from the flabbergasted Manlius. None dared challenge him, though many remembered his cowardice for not coming to the defense of Rome. "My fellow Romans, did hundreds die in order that you could abandon Rome? Will the spirits of our ancestors be abandoned as well? Will the Temple of Diana be left empty? Have you no pride?" the general asked. "I challenge you to stand with me and rebuild that which the barbarian destroyed. I challenge you to rebuild the walls of Rome in a manner that will enable it to stand against invaders for a thousand years."

Those about to depart felt shame, as the commander of the Veii force condemned them for their weakness. Because the temples were all destroyed, the people had no gods to comfort them. As their first task, citizens located every sacred relic that they could find. Julia, while sifting through the ashes of the destroyed Temple of Mars, discovered the Lituus, a crooked staff belonging to Romulus. The staff he used to divide the heavens into quarters to observe the flight of birds. Using her cunning, she deemed her good fortune to be a sign from the gods to claim her rightful place as the head of the Julian family. While holding the staff, which all recognized, she stood before the surviving members of the Senate and claimed, "I am the last of the Julian family, one of the original founding families of Rome. I carry within me the great-grandson of

Lucius Julius, who gave his life for the safety of all here. On behalf my child, I claim the right to be paterfamilias of the Julian family until he becomes of age. If any oppose me, I shall destroy this staff and with it the future of the city."

The Senate was incensed that a female should enter their chambers; let alone address them. "Who does that woman think she is?" some asked.

"We should behead her," others demanded.

"Do you really believe she will destroy the Augural Staff of Romulus?" a more timid member asked.

"She is a descendant of Lucius Julius. Therefore, I believe she will do as she threatens," Marcus Furius answered. "Since she is merely a vessel carrying the child, we should compromise and allow her to take the seat of her grandfather until the child is born. If it is a boy, she can remain until he becomes of age. If it is a girl, then we can execute her at Tarpeian Rock." The Senate reluctantly voted for Julia to remain and declared her paterfamilias of the Julian household until the boy child came of age.

The old woman became both annoyed and afraid when she rang for the third time to get some attention. No one answered. After hours elapsed, a slave appeared with a message that brought dread. "Your presence is requested in the office of the paterfamilias," the vassal said. Julia's mother followed the servant to Lucius Julius' office and cringed when she saw her daughter in the dead senator's place. Julia lounged on the couch and scratched a cat, in a pose reminiscent of her grandfather, taking her time to study the fear on her mother's face before she spoke, "I see by your expression that you have not heard the Senate's order making me the Julian family paterfamilias."

The old woman's face went ashen as she tried to comprehend the appalling news coming from the mouth of her daughter. "That can't be! You are a female."

"It can be because it is," Julia replied. "When you return to your quarters, you will find a vial on the dresser. If you fail to drink it, I will be forced to call in the slavers."

"Who would pay to buy one as old as myself?"

"You don't understand. I will pay them to take you!" Even the slaves who endured Julia's mistreatment did not believe the hate in her eyes when her mother retreated from the room. The daughter never saw the relief that flooded her mother's face, as she gladly returned to her room and sought the vial of poison. After dealing with her longstanding enemy, Julia could afford to be magnanimous. She opened the Julian home to all patrician families who had lost their quarters during the Celtic invasion; thereby, saving many from the cold winds of February. With this gesture, she reclaimed the leadership role so effectively played by her grandfather, and began to plot her revenge against the Gauls. More importantly, her actions insured that the Julian name would survive as one of the powers of Rome, and her son would have allies among the patricians when his time came.

Mayri Oppidum

Meva stood on the rampart and looked toward the lake at the boat that approached. Word had reached her weeks before that her beloved Conel was safely within the oppidum of the Boii and would soon depart for home. Daily, she offered prayers of thanksgiving to the Goddess Sulis for his safe return, and just as often, she mounted the walls of the oppidum to look in the direction her Conel would come. 'How has he changed?' she wondered. This and other concerns bothered her ever since she heard from him. But she never doubted that his love for her enabled him to survive whatever he had to endure.

The commotion coming from those on the shore told her all she needed to know. Her mare was haltered and awaiting her in the stables. She had the horse galloping toward the shoreline before she had both legs in position. She raced over very familiar territory because she had dreamed of this gallop daily while she imagined the joy Conel would feel when he saw her coming toward him, and Conel didn't disappoint her. If he could swim, he would have long since left the docking vessel. He too had imagined this meeting, running up the path toward a galloping horse where he would catch the lady as she jumped off. Not waiting for the boat to cover the final spear length, the Celtic chieftain stood on the railing and leapt toward the dock. Those on the pier grabbed their chief, saving him from landing in the water.

Rather than staging the celebration that the clan assumed to be their due, Conel and Meva chose to spend their first few nights alone in their home. On the third day, the oppidum dwellers saw their heroic chieftain walking around the rampart of the oppidum for the first time in over a year. The stroll that had been so much a part of his daily habit gladdened their hearts. Observing Meva argue with the wine merchant over the vintage or the price brought him joy once again. Conel was home at last. He then looked toward the meadow, expecting to see the triplets at play, and melancholy overcame him. He suddenly became aware that his children were grown and leading lives of their own. He knew they were safe because stories of their exploits had been told nightly over the campfires at the oppidum of the Boii. Lost in his thoughts and feelings, he felt the loving arms of his spouse as Meva embraced him.

"I didn't hear you come. I was daydreaming about the children. I will always remember when you and I stood at this very spot and watched them depart on their first day of Druid school. I can't wait to see them again, and at the same time, I will be sad to see how they have matured. "

"You needn't explain yourself to me. I have been afraid to daydream for so long that I have lost the ability. I wake each morning and reach over to make certain that you really returned. While we are on the subject, the townspeople are asking about a celebration in your honor."

"What did you tell them?"

"I told them to be patient. I want you to myself for a while. I did, however, say it would be wise for them to start planning the celebration of a lifetime when our warriors return."

"And how did they accept your advice?"

"They slyly let me they had already begun to plan."

North of Rome

The Celts took several routes when they left Rome. The Senones, settled in the vicinity south of Rome. The Gaesatae wandered the peninsula, selling their services to any city with the means to pay them. Those of the Boii and the Insubres that fought for the brennos returned to their homeland in the Po Valley. Ragenos took the remainder of the army, which now numbered less than eight thousand, back across the Alps.

"I must return to my oppidum, and I beg with all my heart that you will accompany me," Roith asked Una one night as they sat around a campfire.

"My father has trained me to become the chieftain when he retires, I must honor that trust," Una answered.

"Your stay need not be long. My older brother, who wishes to assume the leadership of the tribe, needs my support. The tribal elders oppose him." Then Roith became more serious than he had ever been in his life. "Una, I love you with all my spirit. I want to spend my life with you and have my children by you. I beg you, stay with me for a while, and I will accompany you wherever you wish to live."

A very confused Una heard the sincere words and felt the warmth of his body as he embraced her. After hesitating for several moments, she accepted his offer. Some obstacles, however, could impede a happy marriage if they weren't cleared up immediately. At that moment, she decided to make herself totally vulnerable, by telling Roith about her life as a slave. "Roith, I can judge you because I have two brothers to measure you against, and I trust you. I believe that I understand what type of husband you will become. But I am different than any maiden you have ever met. I honor your proposal because for the sake of our people, I must raise children that are intelligent and strong. I know you have the ability to father such children because you are a cross between my brothers. For that, I love you." She then paused to take a breath before deciding how to continue this conversation.

At that point, Roith intervened. "You do not need to outline your faults. I am the son of a tribal chief, and I have learned from my own mother how female warriors are raised."

"Roith, please let me finish. This will be difficult enough. Then if you still want me to visit your oppidum, I will." The young Celtic warrior nodded his head, indicating that he would listen without interrupting.

"Two things make me different than any female you have encountered. First, I am a triplet and secondly, I have been a slave. These two things have shaped my life. Whether for good or evil I cannot say, but each has made a profound effect on me as a person."

Again after hesitating for a moment, Una cleared her throat and continued in a quiet voice telling the tale of Munli. "I, the female of the trio, was born to ensure that the secret oath of my father is passed down through my children. I cannot tell even my husband the substance. If we fail, the ramifications will be disastrous for the entire Celtic people. On this point, there can be no compromise. I must marry a man who will honor my oath, one who will not question me about it. I have sworn to tell only my female children its contents and to ensure that they take the oath as well."

"I cannot understand the seriousness of such an oath," Roith replied. "But if it is Druid business, I do not want to involve myself in it. I am a simple warrior. Still, I cannot live my life without you. Therefore, I will give you my oath in blood." Without hesitation,

Roith drew his dagger and ran the sharp blade over his thumb, leaving the trickle of blood drip onto the soil. "I, Roith of the Boii, swear to you, my beautiful Una of the Mayri, that I will honor your oath wherever it may lead."

Una shivered as she realized the depth of his love. She then took the dagger from his hand and slit her own thumb. Upon doing so, she pressed the wound against her beloved's thumb. "I, Una of the Mayri, accept your oath, and I swear that as your wife, I will provide you with children who will make you proud." The couple kissed fervently before retiring to the nearest tent. The thought of describing her life as a slave disappeared entirely from Una's thoughts and never entered her mind again.

Mayri Oppidum

Danous was heartbroken when he learned that Una decided to remain behind with Roith, while he was honor bound to follow Ragenos back to the land of the Mayri. On the long trip home, his mood darkened until he contemplated taking his own life. Only the love and understanding of his brother, Tomas, could relieve the bard's dark depression.

Watchers spotted the long lines of returning victors once they crossed the summit of the Alpine pass, and the word of their coming reached Conel within days. He met with Meva to plan the celebration for the returning heroes. So great was her desire to welcome her children, brother and brother-in-law, that Meva encouraged the wine merchant to offer his private stock to any who desired. "Let no one say that the Mayri clan cannot welcome their kinfolk in proper style," she said to her beloved as she oversaw planning of the festivities.

Leaders from the Helvetii nation and its clans were beginning to settle around the oppidum to await the return of the victors. The celebration began long before the first veteran of the Roman war set foot on the land. Meva wept tears of joy as she hugged Ragenos after hugging Mick. Then she looked around for Una and became deeply concerned. "Where is your sister?" she asked Mick. "I don't see her. She did come back didn't she?"

"I hoped Hugh would be the one to tell you," Mick answered. "Una met a warrior from the Boii tribe and returned with him to his oppidum. But don't worry," he said putting up his hands as if to defend himself. "She promised to come here right after his brother is elected chief."

Meva, relieved that Una was safe, felt a longing for her daughter. She wanted to be the one to select Una's husband. While the others celebrated, she collared Hugh and over his strenuous objections made him accompany her to Sulis' grotto. There she and her Druid trained son prayed that Roith was the right selection for Una's mate. Hugh assured her that Roith would be a proper husband, "Mother, please believe me. I would not have let the romance blossom if I did not believe that he was the one for Una." Hugh's testimony relieved Meva of some of her fears, but did not satisfy the mother's desire to determine her son-in-law.

Boii Oppidum
Una felt as though she were a queen as the Boii celebrated the return of their warriors. Being the only stranger among the tribesmen, she was stared at and even adored. The younger children followed this maiden with striking red hair, day and night, leaving her little quiet time with Roith. The first days and weeks were exhilarating as she gloried in all the attention, but as time passed the lack of activity began to grate on her.

Roith divided his time between attending to his betrothed, celebrating with his buddies and campaigning for his brother with Una receiving the least attention. Being ignored in this manner did not sit well with a young female warrior who was accustomed to being involved in every activity that occurred. "I am not like other maidens who can sit content and await visitations from their males," Una said. "Nor do I have children by the gross to keep me occupied," she complained vigorously one night. "When are we going home!"

"The vote for the new council will be coming within a fortnight. Then I will be free to go north. Can you remain content until my brother is installed as the newly elected chief? I cannot leave until I am assured that my tribe will be well governed. In the meantime, why don't you begin to make preparations for our journey? I don't think we will be the only ones leaving. Many of the young warriors who fought against the Romans are looking for new adventures."

As Roith returned to men's affairs, Una began to make plans of her own. She was aware of the young men who wanted to seek action, and those who would be willing to become mercenaries. Using the idle time, and her gift of obtaining her own way, Una began to seek out those most likely to become soldiers of fortune.

"I am certain that my brother, Mick, will be looking for combatants. Given his nature, he cannot be long without warfare." She said to everyone she approached. Most agreed to join her party when she and Roith headed north.

Mayri Oppidum
Hugh, even though subordinate to most of the Druids, assumed authority as though he were born to it. To remember the many souls adrift above Rome, he insisted that proper rituals be given precedence before staging any of the planned horse races. Upon his request, Druids arrived from the nearby clans in sufficient number to oversee the rituals required to satisfy the gods. Though he was a minor Druid, the role he played in the conquest of the Roman gave him status among both his peers and superiors. Blowing on a great war-horn to get their attention, he announced, "The ceremony of the dead will be observed before any tournament takes place." Although many individuals both within the Druid community and without grumbled, no one dared to deny him the privilege of taking charge. "We have to honor those who rest in shallow graves in foreign soil. Furthermore, we must do what we can to retrieve the souls that have been denied proper burial, those whose ashes may yet be wandering this earth seeking a way to enter the otherworld. The owners of these souls died bravely and deserve a warriors' ritual."

A chant began at the rear of the enclosure to signify the beginning of the three-day service to appease the lost souls. Druids laid relics of the dead around a fire that consumed the thick boughs of an oak tree cut from the woods sheltering the shrine of Sulis. The fire sputtered and then flared as the flame consumed the sap from the branches. Every hour acolytes walked counter clockwise and sprinkled the fire with precious herbs to send white smoke skyward to invite the wandering souls of those departed to join the ritual. As Hugh read the names of the dead, a relative or close friend would arise and announce the courageous deeds the fighter performed. Special accolades were pronounced for all who could claim to have killed an enemy, or to have saved a brother Celt. Mothers and wives wailed loudly when their son or husband received his glory. Then they would depart the ceremony and take their place with a growing number of women who keened over the dead. The women's lamenting grew louder and louder as the names were read. This moaning for the dearly departed continued for the full length of the three-day service. Those who didn't have

Druids, Celts, and Romans

the strength required to continue the shrieking collapsed where they knelt, and were left to remain in this position until the ceremony ended.

A procession of white-cloaked Druids, carrying lanterns through the nearby woods, added a surreal movement in the late night hours. As they passed through the undergrowth of trees, the lights flickered, creating an illusion of thousands of fireflies. Daylight hours brought a different twist to the sacramental service. Mounted knights rode in a moving figure eight to reflect the ever-evolving transfer of spirits to and from the otherworld. Whenever the heat of the day and or the lack of water felled a rider, thus breaking the circle, the body was pulled away and left by the side as another took the warrior's place.

As night fell on the third day, the families and friends threw the relics of their dead into the flames, fueling a gigantic fire. The Druids took up a chant to unite the souls to their bodies in the otherworld. When the chant drew to a close, as a final tribute, all assembled honored the dead by maintaining an hour of silence.

After the three days to honor the dead, Mick took over as master of the activities. He was astounded that his father not only entered the chariot race but that he defeated Mick and his nephew Roanlos, both known to be excellent horsemen. "When did you ever become such an expert in driving a team of horses?" he asked as he ran over to congratulate him. "I never expected to be beaten by an old man," Mick laughed as he hugged his father.

"Do you think I spent my time in slavery doing household chores?" Conel grinned as he accepted his son's hug. Then becoming serious for a moment, he said, "When Una returns, I need to tell you three all that I learned during my captivity. I believe the trouble with Rome has only begun!"

"I wanted to continue the siege and then defeat the army camped in Veii, but few agreed. Most were tired of living in that hot climate and wanted to return to their homes," Mick answered in agreement.

"We may live to regret that decision."

Boii Oppidum

The election for the council of the Boii turned out to be the most vigorously contested in decades. It pitted the older tribe members against those who joined the Mayri in their quest. The veterans wished to strengthen the oppidum to withstand an attack by the

Romans. The older members desired to live in peace with the southerners. Many observers attributed the victory of the younger generation to the influences of Una who persuaded the mercenaries to wait until after the election before leaving to seek their fortunes. "There is merit to my claim that a new enemy will arise in the south. Remember my father, who was captured by the deceitful Romans when he was on a mission of honor. He makes such a claim. Please keep that in mind when you decide." Una repeated these words often in the weeks leading up to the election.

Another event occurred that helped insure the victory for the younger set. Elico, the Helvetii metalsmith and long a resident of Rome, made his way north to the friendly confines of the Boii. He described the arrogance of Roman citizens. "Romans are unforgiving. They laid siege to the town of Veii for ten years before they subdued the inhabitants," Elico explained. "Then they killed the warriors and enslaved all the elderly, the women and the children. When I fled the city, my family and I had to hide to avoid being captured. We witnessed the deaths of many who were left along the roadside after falling from lack of food and water. Romans will avenge the invasion, and you need to be prepared for the day when they consolidate their position in the south. Then they will look north for conquest. Elect your finest warriors for only they can save you."

Una was delighted to meet her fellow Helvetian, and she spent hours talking to him about the deeds of her father while he was held captive. "Because of your devotion to Conel," she announced one evening, "I make you an honorary member of the Mayri clan. When my father leaves office as our chief, I offer you a position with Leemn, our clan's metalsmith, whose work is known throughout the Celtic world. I hope you will make the trek north with us."

"I am honored to accept your offer. For I have been away many years, and I do not know what reception that the Helvetii will give me."

Within a fortnight following the election, a small war party, led by Roith, left the oppidum of the Boii to deliver Una safely to her people. Elico, as expected, accompanied them. While he hoped for employment with the Mayri, the warriors of the party looked for adventure along the way and the opportunity to join Mick as mercenaries.

Tears of happiness ran down Una's face when the mist cleared, and she looked across Lake Lucerne at her beloved oppidum.

Roith, standing beside her, wondered what type of reception he would receive from her parents.

Mayri Oppidum

The welcoming of Una and Roith was not as dramatic as that which greeted the return of Conel, but it was every bit as warm. Through watery eyes, Meva looked over the tall Celt who dismounted first before helping Una. Then she ran over to hug and kiss her daughter who returned her welcome just as lovingly. Meva directed Conel to get Roith settled in while she and Una walked over to the grassy knoll where they talked on the day before the daughter departed for the south. The conversation began slowly as though they were two strangers meeting for the first time, but it quickly returned to the intimacy shown by a loving mother and her loving daughter. "Is he the one?" Meva asked looking for any facial expression that could provide more information than mere words.

"Yes Mother, he's the one," Una answered, her face all aglow. Meva never again felt the need to measure Roith's suitability as a mate for Una.

The beauty and maturity of Una overwhelmed Danous while the evident passion between her and Roith tore at his heart.

"I don't know the customs of your people," Roith said solemnly to Conel and Meva, "but in my world, we always ask the parents for permission to marry their daughters. I'm asking you for that permission."

Of the two parents, only the father was caught speechless. The instant the two rode into the oppidum, Meva knew Roith would soon propose. She smiled to herself as she looked at the expression on her husband's face. Turning toward her daughter, she glanced at the lovesick face of the bard, and her heart almost crumbled. But the look of radiance on Una's face told her all she needed to know. "You have my blessing," she said, taking the hands offered by Roith. "And you will have the blessing of my husband as soon as he recovers from the shock of losing his daughter to another."

Hugh seldom slept on the nights before the wedding. He found himself as nervous as the bride. The Druid reviewed the simple ritual for the hundredth time. He would first present his sister to her parents, who had to give their blessings. Next he would place her hand in the hand of her intended. The two would then follow him, walking in a procession behind two young maids tossing flowers until they reached the mistletoe-covered oak. The couple actually married themselves. He was simply a witness in case any issue came up later. Perhaps the severing of the tight bond the triplets felt since childhood made him apprehensive.

    As Una walked down the aisle, a strumming lyre caused a great silence to descend over the vast throng. After playing a few bars, Danous lifted his voice and sang lyrics of such clarity that no one dared breathe. Una could feel the pain the bard carried within him and allowed tears, caused by the loss of a loved one, to run down her face. She would miss his company, his mirth and his music. But on this the happiest day of her life, she felt the loss of a friend. She had presumed that he had long since departed. Perhaps true love really refers to the willingness to remain faithful when the one you desire is lost. She stood peacefully and listened to the crooning of Danous' song:

My body was dead like a soul without light.
When along came a blue bird, a vision in flight.
Like an actress born to a part where she starred,
Born with a smile that melted the heart of a bard.

The wind carries her laughter over the strand,
this loveliest of fairies to dwell in our land.
As a smitten suitor, I can do nothing but stare
at the first rays of morning brushing her hair.

I had little to offer when she captured my heart,
so I've tried to snare her splendor with art.
My music couldn't touch the lure of her charm,
but I would give my life to keep her from harm.

I have dwelt in her shadow, asking only a share
of the joy, she dispenses to all who dwell there.
Does she consider me one of many that abound,
or does she derive pleasure, having me around?

This day, she has chosen another to share her life.
A creature I envy, who claims her for his wife.
A warrior of renown, who war has made hard.
a fellow human, who broke the heart of a bard.

I vow where I wander throughout this vast land.

My memory of her will make my heart expand.
Should ever she need me, I will come with speed,
even if the journey will cost the life of my steed.

Those who may harm her will soon face my wrath.
I will satire them forever no matter their path.
Their very souls will suffer as none has known.
The heart of a bard will always atone.

When he finished his wedding gift to the beautiful Una, Danous flung his lyre upon his back and left the compound to assume the lonely life of a traveling poet.

The two young Druids, Hugh and Katlyn, were the next to leave, as they returned to finish their studies. "I may not be the next to wed, but as soon as the Master Druid gives permission, I intend to take Katlyn for my wife," Hugh announced as he mounted his horse.

Mick's parting tore at the heart of his mother, because she felt that he would never return. "Mother, I love you and I love my people, but I must follow the call for which I was born. We have been offered much gold to fight for a king who rules a Greek city-state in Sicily far to the south of Rome. I believe this to be a wise decision. I don't want to become a rogue mercenary in the pay of another Celtic tribe. The latter choice would likely pit me someday against my Uncle Ragenos, and I could never allow that. I love you and Father as much I love my brother and sister. This is my vow. I will return when I feel in my bones I am needed."

Conel hugged his warrior son and wished him well, as Mick mounted to lead his small band of mercenaries to gain fame and fortune. "My son, you likely will find yourself fighting the enemy that you defeated on the banks of the Allia. In my days of traveling with the Greek and during my stay in captivity, I have learned that Romans neither forgive, nor forget. Furthermore, they continually strive to improve to avoid repeating past mistakes. Defeated as they were, I fear the Romans will gain more from our victory than we."

"I'll add your wisdom to that which I carry in my heart," Mick said with a wave. Then he rode off, never to look back.

Author Bio

A grandfather and self-made Irish-American History Authority, Philadelphia-born James Francis Smith, a LaSalle University graduate with an MBA from Pacific Lutheran, now living in the Pacific Northwest, opened a Financial Planning practice after retiring from a Fortune 500 company, His first book, the highly acclaimed, now out-of-print, *Path to a Successful* Retirement, sparked a desire to write. Jim, second generation Irish, married Betty McGinty, whose parents emigrated from Donegal and Cork. Irish to the core, he craved to preserve the Irish accomplishments and contributions to America from this desire came, *The Irish-American Story.*

Smith's Blog: www.the-irishamericanstory.com

This popular blog, featuring over 30-articles in eight categories, celebrated its six-month anniversary with thousands of visitors from 52-countries.

Smith's Books:

The first book of this narrative-history series begins with the origin of the Celtic race; others carry through the times of America's major wars, the Kennedy era, and beyond. Several of these tales originate in Ireland.

The following books are available from Kindle and Nook. *Druids, Celts, and Romans* is the first in print version, the others will soon follow:

Druids, Celts, and Romans – Europe circa 400BCE
Irish in the Revolution – USA 1755-1783 (soon to be published)
The Civil War's Valiant Irish – USA 1859-1865
The Last of the Fenians – Ireland 1913-1923 (includes WWI
The O'Donnells of Philadelphia – USA 1918-1945 (Includes WWII)
Rory O'Donnell and the Kennedys – USA 1946-1968 (includes Korea, Vietnam, and JFK's assassination)
Unholy Conspiracies – USA 1990-2010 (A political novel)
Irish-American Chronicle. A collection of short stories which spans the timeframe of the other books.

www.ingramcontent.com/pod-product-compliance
Lightning Source LLC
Chambersburg PA
CBHW070847290526
45795CB00001B/13